· LE CORDON BLEU ·

complete cook

HOME COLLECTION

THUNDER BAY
P·R·E·S·S

Contents

History of Le Cordon Bleu School

The name Le Cordon Bleu (meaning the blue ribbon) is rich in history and heritage. The title originated with the 16th century French order of knights, L'Ordre du Saint Esprit (the order of the Holy Spirit). The members, royalty included, were called Cordon-Bleus after the broad ribbons on which they wore the cross of the Holy Spirit. The sumptuous banquets that accompanied their award ceremonies became legendary and the term Cordon Bleu was from then on associated with culinary excellence.

The school was founded in 1895 by journalist Marthe Distel, who wrote a weekly journal called "La Cuisinière Cordon Bleu." She invited some of the greatest chefs in Paris to teach and gave her first demonstration in January 1896 in the Paris Palais Royal, where guests were given a glimpse of the latest culinary technology—the electric stove.

Le Cordon Bleu grew and flourished in the following decades. Originally a purely Parisian institution, the school quickly gained international acclaim and an enviable reputation, attracting students from around the world. By 1905 students were coming from as far away as Japan to learn about classical French cuisine. Britain's Daily Mail wrote in 1927: "It is not unusual to find up to eight different nationalities in a classroom."

One of France's most famous chefs, author of "L'Art Culinaire Moderne" (translated into five languages) and "La Cuisine Familiale Pratique," Henri Paul Pellaprat, disciple and friend of Auguste Escoffier, taught at the school for over 40 years.

In 1933, one of Chef Pellaprat's students, Rosemary Hume, established "L' Ecole du Petit Cordon Bleu" in London. In 1942, during the war, Dione Lucas, a London Cordon Bleu teacher, opened a School and a Restaurant in New York. The success of the London school was confirmed in 1951 by its participation in catering for the Coronation of Queen Elizabeth II. The famous recipe for Coronation Chicken was created for this event.

After the Second World War, Le Cordon Bleu, Paris continued to prosper and grow under the direction of Madame Elizabeth Brassart. She welcomed two generations of cooks to Le Cordon Bleu, revised the curriculum and saw the school gain official recognition.

Renowned celebrity chef and food writer Julia Child began studying at Le Cordon Bleu, Paris in 1948. She was awarded the Grand Diplôme du Cordon Bleu and proceeded to facilitate the teaching of French cuisine in the United States.

By the 1950s, Le Cordon Bleu represented not only the highest level of culinary training but had become a symbol of Paris itself. The famous film "Sabrina" was set in Paris, with a young Audrey Hepburn taking a class at the Paris School where she was taught to make a classic French omelet.

For over a century Le Cordon Bleu has grown to become a leading authority on culinary techniques, training and development. In 1984 André J. Cointreau, a descendant of the founders of the Rémy Martin and Cointreau liqueur companies, became President of Le Cordon Bleu. He strengthened the curriculum, recruited the finest chefs of France and relocated the Paris school. The London school became fully part of the Le Cordon Bleu group in 1990.

Expansion continues around the globe, not only with respect to the number of colleges (20 in 10 countries) but also in the scope of programs offered. Bachelor of Business degrees in Restaurant and International Hotel and Resort Management; Master of Arts in Gastronomy; and various Master of Business Administration degrees now complement Le Cordon Bleu Cuisine and Patisserie programs.

Consulting partnerships in the culinary and hospitality industries have been established, as well as an extensive culinary product line and a wide range of publications for culinary professionals and enthusiasts. Le Cordon Bleu International is dedicated to promoting the advancement of education, training and the appreciation of gastronomy worldwide. Because of this mission the name evokes images of quality, tradition and a commitment to excellence at every level.

Foreword

Le Cordon Bleu is proud to present the Le Cordon Bleu Complete Cook. This very special book contains a selection of over 500 of the best recipes from our 26-book series "Home Collection" (which has sold over five million copies worldwide in less than four years).

Founded in Paris in 1895, Le Cordon Bleu has over 100 years' experience in culinary education training with schools situated in France, Great Britain, Japan, Korea, Australia, Canada, USA, Brazil, Peru and Mexico. A corporate office in New York ensures that Le Cordon Bleu and its 20 schools are at the heart of many different markets.

Le Cordon Bleu has a global team of over 80 Master Chefs who come from Michelin-starred restaurants and prestigious hotels. They share their knowledge of classic French techniques—the fundamentals of world cuisine and pâtisserie—with students from over 50 countries, inspiring them to appreciate and develop their skills, potential and creativity. Le Cordon Bleu maintains close links with the evolving culinary industry by attending over 30 international events each year.

Throughout the world, Le Cordon Bleu also serves as a technical consultant to several companies in the gourmet and hospitality industries. This includes our newly formed partnership with Radisson Seven Seas Cruises. Le Cordon Bleu Master Chefs direct Signatures, the first gourmet restaurant at sea, as well as providing passengers with the option to create dishes at the Le Cordon Bleu Classe Culinaire de Croisières, the first-ever culinary workshop on board a cruise ship.

Enjoy our compilation of the best recipes from the Home Collection Series in one large volume, to inspire you with delicious and mouth-watering recipes to impress your friends and family.

How to use this book

BEFORE YOU START

The golden rule of cooking is to always read a recipe from start to finish before you begin preparing, or even shopping, in case there is work that needs to be done ahead of time. For example, puff pastry takes about a day to make, beans and legumes sometimes have to be soaked overnight and ice-cream maker bowls need to be fully frozen in advance. There may also be fruit and vegetable preparation such as peeling peppers or tomatoes, or salting eggplants, which should usually be done before the recipe is started. And you should always check that you have the required equipment, such as a food processor or electric mixer and the correct size containers for baking. Organizing and preparing a recipe, weighing out ingredients beforehand and getting all the equipment ready on the work counter will ensure that once you start to cook there should be no unpleasant surprises. Remember also to check that your oven or broiler is preheated when it needs to be. Preparation is known as *mise-en-place*.

CHEF'S TECHNIQUES

Reading through the recipe before you start will also allow you to look up any techniques and ingredients that might be cross-referenced in Chef's techniques. These pages are at the back of the recipe section (pages 518–57) and give very detailed instructions, with step-by-step photographs, for commonly used techniques, such as making stock or mayonnaise, peeling peppers and shrimp, deep-frying or kneading bread dough. Following these should give you all the instruction that you need for any more tricky techniques, in more detail and with fuller illustrations than if we were to put them in the recipe method. This section also includes basic recipes for different types of pastry with step-by-step photographs. You may find that within the recipe the ingredient list will simply state "1 quantity puff pastry, see page 542." It is up to you whether you make your own, following the recipe, or use the same weight of bought pastry. Similarly, the recipe method might state "prepare the crab following the method in the Chef's techniques on page 523" so that you can follow the photography and in-depth method.

EQUIPMENT PAGES

For those setting up a kitchen or buying new cookery equipment, the following pages give advice as to the most useful, hard-wearing and appropriate equipment to choose with explanations as to their use and whether there is an alternative available. These are set out by common group, e.g. bakeware, knives.

MENU PLANNERS

We have compiled a selection of menu planners, themed by event, such as Cocktail Party or Summer Lunch, to give you an idea of how to compile a selection of dishes for a special occasion meal. The number of people each menu serves is stated and the quantities of each dish adjusted accordingly. Even if you don't follow the exact list of dishes, the quantities should give you an idea of how to feed larger numbers of people. In the introduction to this section we also give advice about how to choose recipes for feeding larger numbers of guests, how to present dishes and quantities to serve.

GLOSSARY

A glossary of ingredients, technical and kitchen terms (pages 558–64) allows you to look up any unknown or unfamiliar ingredients or techniques. Some French and Italian terms are also included along with examples of "kitchen French." This glossary is also useful for reading menus.

Equipment

KNIVES AND CUTTING IMPLEMENTS

KITCHEN KNIVES

Buy the best you can afford. Make sure they are comfortable to hold and that the handle and blade are well balanced. You will need a large knife for chopping, a medium knife and a small serrated knife for fruit with tough skins and tomatoes—the serrations easily pierce the skins, thus helping keep the flesh intact. For slicing bread loaves, a serrated bread knife is best, otherwise the loaf is squashed rather than cut. Store knives in a wooden block to keep them sharp—if they clash against things in a drawer they will quickly become blunt. A cleaver is useful for cutting through bones. Use a hand-held steel to keep knife edges keen, and sharpen before every use. For baking, buy a flexible bladed knife for spreading.

SPECIALTY KNIVES

These are required if you plan to be more adventurous with your cooking. For opening oysters, you will need an oyster knife—it has a short, flat blade with two cutting edges that slides easily between shells. A metal guard on the handle protects your hand. For basic meat preparation, a boning knife with a very strong, thin blade will help. The width of the blade means you can make narrow cuts, even when the whole length of the blade is pushed into the meat. A fish knife with a long, flexible blade makes boning and filleting fish less of a challenge. Small paring knives with curved blades make preparing vegetables easier. A ham knife with a long, narrow, fluted blade makes slicing cold meats and smoked salmon simpler.

SPECIALTY CUTTING TOOLS

A mezzaluna is a double-handled knife with one or two curved blades, which are rocked from side to side to chop herbs. Some come with a special board with a dip for holding the ingredient. Citrus zesters and canelle knives easily peel zest off citrus fruit in thin or thick shreds using a row of small holes or a deeper V-shaped cutting edge. Kitchen scissors should have tough blades, preferably with a serrated edge. The lower handle should be large enough to grip with three fingers. Poultry shears have a cutting point near the pivot for gripping bones as you cut them. A mandolin will help you cut wafer thin slices of anything. Buy one with a moveable blade to vary the thickness. The rippled blade can be used for crinkle cutting or matchsticks.

GRATERS, PEELERS AND GRINDERS

Graters vary in shape, but the important part is the cutting edge, which should be very sharp. A box grater does not slip easily and is good for grating large quantities. A Microplane® grater has very sharp blades and works well for smaller quantities as it can be held over a bowl or a dish of food. Good vegetable peelers shave off only a thin skin. Grinding and crushing can be done in a bowl (mortar) with a slightly rough surface, using a crushing stick (pestle) that fits the curve of the bowl and provides the second grinding surface. Pepper mills with a steel grinding mechanism are best for efficiency and for an adjustable grind. Salt should only be ground in a salt mill with a noncorrosive nylon grinder.

Equipment

SAUCEPANS, FRYING PANS AND CASSEROLES

SAUCEPANS

Buy saucepans that are a good quality and the most expensive you can afford. Stainless steel saucepans with a sandwiched bottom containing a metal such as copper, which conducts heat well, are a good choice for even heat distribution. Copper saucepans with stainless steel lining are excellent but expensive. Stainless steel is nonreactive so it will not be affected by the use of an acid. Choose saucepans with comfortable handles, bearing in mind that you don't want the handle to heat up. Lids must have a tight seal. You will need one large saucepan and a couple of smaller ones for everyday use. Saucepans bought as a set will often give you a good range of sizes. A nonstick saucepan is essential if you often make scrambled eggs.

FRYING PANS

Like saucepans, frying pans should be of good quality. Cast iron ones are heavy but last a very long time. Test their weight before you buy to make sure they are right for you. Nonstick frying pans have to be used with wooden or plastic implements but are easy to clean. Buy good-quality ones and treat them carefully. A frying pan with a flameproof handle is useful for making anything that needs to be finished in the oven or under a grill, such as a frittata or tarte Tatin. An omelet pan is a useful size for both omelets and pancakes and nonstick versions are the most useful. Tiny cast iron or nonstick pans are available for making blinis and also for perfectly shaped fried eggs. A ridged or flat griddle pan is good for cooking over a high heat.

CASSEROLES AND FLAMEPROOF DISHES

These should be of good quality and suitable for use on the stove top as well as in the oven. Casseroles should be heavy enough to absorb and retain heat and, need tight-fitting lids that prevent moisture from escaping. Cast iron or enameled dishes are generally the best as they conduct heat well. You will need several sizes as it is important that the recipe fits the casserole—a small amount of stew will dry out in a large casserole. Baking and gratin dishes should be fully flameproof and able to withstand high heat. For these, enamel, cast-iron and stoneware are good options as they are attractive for serving. Soufflé dishes and ramekins are made from ceramic, porcelain or glass (all are interchangeable) and are presentable for the table.

SPECIALTY PANS

These are pans that you may not use every day but which are useful to have. A pasta boiler with a fitted drainer is useful, not only for cooking pasta, but also potatoes and other vegetables. A sauté pan is useful both for frying and for making risotto. It has sloping sides and is slightly deeper than a frying pan. If you heat up a lot of milk or soups, you may want a milk pan, which has a pouring lip. If you plan on making stock you will need a stockpot: a deep saucepan that will hold several quarts of liquid. A stainless steel one will last a long time. For making jam, you need a jam pan with sloping sides and a pouring lip on one side. Steamer sets have one or two steamer compartments and a saucepan that they fit neatly onto.

Equipment

BAKEWARE

ROASTING PANS AND BAKING SHEETS

Roasting pans should be made from stainless steel or anodised aluminum so that they can be used over direct heat without buckling. You will need several sizes if you do a lot of roasting. One pan needs to be big enough for a turkey or large cut of meat. Racks that sit in the pan for holding poultry or meat are useful for keeping the food above the fat and also collecting the fat and juices underneath. Baking sheets should be heavy-duty with a lip at one end. The open sides mean that you can easily slide things on and off without having to lift and risk damaging them. They need to be heavy-duty and preferably steel, so that they conduct heat well and don't buckle in a very hot oven.

CAKE PANS

Cake pans are designed to respond to all-round heat. They act as both container and mold for their contents. Black, nonstick surfaces will brown baked goods faster than shiny, metal ones that reflect heat, so for dark tins you may need to reduce the oven by 50°F. You will need a size appropriate to your recipe. Loose-bottomed versions are easy to unmold but make sure that the bottoms fit tightly or they will leak. A springform pan can be used for cheesecakes, cakes and gateaux. The spring clip means the side can be gently eased away from delicate textures. Jelly roll pans are baking sheets with four sides. Muffin pans are available in different sizes and nonstick versions work well. Fluted madeleine molds are available as a pan.

TART PANS, TART RINGS AND PIE PLATES

For quiches and tarts, buy a metal, fluted tart pan with a loose bottom so you can easily remove the tart. Recipes call for all sorts of sizes, but an 8-inch (serves 6) or 10-inch (serves 8) tin should fit most recipes. Tart rings can also be used: these are placed on a baking sheet and the ring lifted off when the tart is cooked. Individual tartlet pans are good for attractive presentation if you enjoy entertaining. These come in many different sizes from single serve tarts to petits fours. A pie plate should have a good lip so you can stick the pastry down well, otherwise the pastry will slide down into the pie as it cooks. Oval (for savory fillings) or round dishes (for sweet fillings) are available in ceramic, glass or porcelain.

SPECIALTY PANS AND MOLDS

For loaves of bread, pound cakes or terrines, you will need a loaf pan. Buy one with welded, nonleaking seams. Most recipes for breads and cakes will fit in an average 9 x 5 x 3 inch pan, despite the measurements given in the recipe. Fancy-shaped pans like brioche (a deep, fluted tin with sloping sides), angel food cake (a round, deep pan with sloping sides and a funnel down the center) and kugelhopf molds (fluted pans with a rounded bottom and a funnel down the center) are also available. Use these as specified in the recipe. Charlotte pans have sloping sides and small, flat handles at the top. Smaller molds such as dariole molds and tiny metal pudding molds are used for both baking and cold desserts.

Equipment

KITCHEN UTENSILS

SPOONS AND SPATULAS

Spoons are useful for stirring, mixing and beating. Wooden spoons are good because they don't conduct heat, don't scratch and are nonreactive. Some spoons have a flat edge and corner to help you get into the side of a saucepan. Metal spoons are used for folding ingredients as their sharp edges cut easily through the mixture without squashing out air. A perforated spoon is useful for draining. Ladles are made for serving liquids. Rubber spatulas scrape a bowl completely clean and are particularly useful for removing food from food processors and blenders. Wooden spatulas are useful for nonstick frying pans. Fish lifters need to have enough flexibility to slide under things and a large enough surface area to pick things up.

STRAINERS AND COLANDERS

Strainers come in a range of sizes. Larger colanders are best for draining. Make sure they have a pattern of holes which will drain easily. Round-bottomed stainless steel strainers have a coarse mesh suitable for sifting and puréeing (they don't react with the acid in fruit) that comes in different grades of fineness. Nylon mesh strainers are for fine sifting and puréeing fruit and are also nonreactive. A chinoise is a conical strainer that is useful for puréeing. The cone shape directs the liquid out in a narrow flow. Food mills are rotary strainers that purée fruit and vegetables by forcing them through a flat metal strainer, removing any lumps or hard bits that can then be discarded. They have a range of plates to purée to fine, medium or coarse.

CUTTING BOARDS

A good cutting board is an essential piece of equipment. There is endless debate as to whether wooden or polyethylene boards are more hygienic and views change on a daily basis. Whichever you choose, your board should be kept spotlessly clean. All boards should be large enough to cope with large amounts of chopping. A small indent around the edge is useful for catching juices if you are using the board for carving. A set of colored polyethylene boards is useful if you want to keep separate boards for meat, fish, garlic etc. A piece of marble, though not suitable for cutting as it will blunt knives, is an excellent cool surface for making pastry.

WHISKS AND BEATERS

Whisks beat air into mixtures or beat lumps out. Hand whisks consist of loops of stainless steel joined by a handle. They range from large for egg whites, through to small for sauces and dressings. Buy flexible whisks that are not too stiff or they will not whip well. Rotary beaters must be good quality to work efficiently and they give slightly less volume than hand whisks. Flat whisks, which consist of a wire coiled around a loop, are useful for using in saucepans or containers with flat bottoms or on flat plates. An electric mixer is invaluable for cake-making and for beating large amounts of egg whites. Some are hand-held, some come with stands and others are single large whisk attachments for free-standing appliances.

Equipment

KITCHEN UTENSILS

BOWLS

You can never have too many bowls in a kitchen. Glass, heatproof bowls or stainless steel bowls are useful both for whisking egg whites and melting chocolate, as well as mixing. A very large mixing bowl is invaluable for large quantities, especially for bread-making. Plastic bowls are a good nonbreakable option. However, they are not good for whisking egg whites as they hold grease and prevent the whites aerating. A set of small, stacking bowls is useful for holding ingredients that are measured out prior to starting a recipe (*mise-en-place*). As the ingredients are used, the bowls can be stacked out of the way. A deep, round bowl is good with an electric mixer as the ingredients are contained and don't fly out.

PASTRY-MAKING EQUIPMENT

Pastry brushes are made with either nylon or natural bristles and can be flat or round. Be careful when using nylon bristles with hot liquids as they may melt. Cooling racks are raised wire racks used for cooling cakes and pastries so the air can circulate under them easily. Choose a large wire rack that can comfortably hold a large item or several small ones. Rolling pins should be long enough to roll out a full sheet of pastry in one go as this will ensure a smooth surface. They can be of any thickness, but thinner ones are often easier to handle. Blowtorches are used to caramelize sugar on the top of brulées and small ones can be found in cookware shops or hardware stores.

MASHERS AND GRINDERS, PROCESSORS AND BLENDERS

Potato mashers work on all cooked vegetables. Old-style mashers with a cut grid often work better than those made with a wire coil. They may be made of strong plastic or stainless steel. Ricers are used for mashing and puréeing. They look like giant garlic presses and will hold a couple of potatoes at a time. Grinders need to be heavy-duty. They are clamped to a table edge to hold them in place while meat is forced through the hopper and onto the grinding plate. They are very useful for making good-quality ground meat from steaks, etc. Food processors and blenders are good for chopping ingredients together. Blenders make a smoother purée but need more liquid to work efficiently. Mini processors are good for small amounts.

JUICE EXTRACTORS AND SQUEEZERS

Citrus fruit squeezers are available in glass, ceramic, plastic, stainless steel and wood. The squeezers with a strainer around the edge, which collects the seeds, and a container underneath for collecting the juice are the most useful. Juicers should have a large enough reamer to fit snugly into the fruit without splitting it. If you make lots of fresh orange juice then find one that fits oranges well or buy a citrus press with a squeezing mechanism and keep it solely for that. For squeezing out just a few drops of juice, there is a spouted reamer that plugs into the fruit. Electric juicers are useful for large quantities and for juicing fruit and vegetables such as apples and carrots. Buy a good-quality one that will last well and is easy to clean.

Equipment

KITCHEN UTENSILS

MEASURING EQUIPMENT

You only need one set of scales. A balance scale holds the weights on one side and the ingredients on the other. It can weigh very small amounts. An electronic scale has a digital display but is often less accurate for small weights under 1 oz. Spring weight scales have a scale pan on top of a calibrated scale and they have an adjustable tension screw. Wet/dry measuring cups should be plastic or glass so you can read them easily. Choose one with the calibrations visible on both the inside and outside. Measuring cups and spoons are used for dry and liquid measures. They are available in metal or plastic and in fractions and multiples of cup and spoon measures. Dry measurements should be leveled off with a knife for accuracy.

THERMOMETERS

Thermometers are essential for accurate and safe measurements in the kitchen. A kitchen thermometer is used for measuring oil temperatures when deep-frying, and for measuring sugar temperatures when making sugar syrup or jam. Before using glass thermometers, warm them in water as they can crack if added to a hot liquid when they are very cold. An oven thermometer is used to ensure that the thermostat is registering accurately in your oven. They hang from the oven shelf. A meat thermometer is pushed into a joint of meat to tell how done it is, or into whole poultry to check that the internal temperature is hot enough for the bird to be cooked through. Poultry should be at least 165°F inside to kill any bacteria.

CUTTERS AND SLICERS

Cutters for cookies and pastry come in different shapes and sizes. They can be bought in graded sets, both plain and fluted. Store in their tins and dry thoroughly to prevent them from rusting. Tiny, decorative cutters and decorative pastry cutters can be used for all manner of sweet and savory decorations. They work on doughs and frostings and are good for cutting vegetable shapes from slices of carrot, etc. A cheese slicer cuts thin slices much more effectively than a knife and it works well on harder cheeses. A cheese wire is essential if you buy large pieces of hard cheese as the wire cuts through easily in a straight line without making crumbs. An egg slicer is used to cut a whole, peeled egg into neat slices with a frame of wires.

MISCELLANEOUS KITCHEN EQUIPMENT

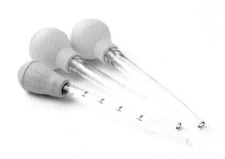

It is worth buying good-quality pieces of kitchen equipment whether they are used every day or less often. There is nothing more irritating than something that does not work properly. It is worth buying a good-quality can opener that grips properly and cuts efficiently. A cherry pitter/olive pitter is useful if you want to make cherry jam. It should have a decent spring action so you don't crush the cherries. Bulb basters are useful both for basting and for removing the fat from the surface of liquids. Buy a plastic one as the glass ones break easily. Larding and trussing needles are useful standbys that you may need occasionally. Buy them as you need them. Storage boxes are also useful. Buy ones you can use in both the fridge and freezer.

How to plan a menu and present food

When planning a menu, whatever the occasion, it is best to follow a few simple rules. First decide on a food theme. This can be as simple as choosing comfort food in winter and salads or light dishes in summer, or it might be based around a seasonal ingredient such as bay scallops or the Thanksgiving turkey. You could even base your theme around a particular cuisine, perhaps French, Italian or Greek.

Don't forget to plan your menu around food that is in season and so at its best. If you have planned to serve asparagus with hollandaise sauce and then discover asparagus is not in season, prepare something else instead. If you are in any doubt, ask your greengrocer, fishmonger and butcher what is best.

Next, do a little research into your guests' eating preferences to find out if any of them have food allergies or are vegetarians. If so, you will have to plan your meal around these demands or provide an alternative dish or two. Most people find the easiest way to do this is to serve a vegetarian appetizer for everyone: that way you only need to make one separate main course.

If you are having two or three courses, you need to think about whether the dishes complement each other without being repetitive or clashing in style and flavors. For example, if you serve a seafood or fish appetizer then you will probably not want fish as a main course. Likewise, you should not serve more than one course containing pastry. You probably wouldn't want to serve a creamy pasta dish to start, followed by a rich buttery main course. For balance, try to alternate heavy and light dishes across the range of appetizer, main course and dessert.

QUANTITIES

One of the aspects of entertaining that people often find the most difficult is judging the quantities of food needed for a large group of people. There are a few simple things to bear in mind.

For sit-down meals involving fewer people you can serve food which is already portioned, eg whole fish, steaks or chicken breasts. Allow one each.

For large groups of people, offer a choice of easily portioned dishes such as a whole ham or boeuf bourgignon. The more choices of dish that you offer, the smaller a portion each person will need. And the larger the number of people eating, the smaller the amount of food they will consume per person. So, for 40 people you would not need to make 10 quantities of a recipe that serves four. Eight or nine quantities should be quite sufficient.

It is always a good idea to serve bread and butter. This takes the edge off appetites and makes sure the more hungry people have something to fill up with. There is a vast array of breads available today, so choose something to suit your theme.

PRESENTING A BUFFET

Buffets should offer a wide range of dishes for people to choose from, with main courses that should ideally feature both meat and seafood alternatives.

Unlike a sit-down meal, where the dishes appear one by one and are rarely seen all assembled on the table together, a buffet, laid out en masse, should look eye-catching and delicious.

Choose simply styled dinnerware to show off your food to its best advantage. Keep your decorations and garnishes simple, especially if you have a lot of dishes on the table. Choose a theme for a garnish, such as small bundles of herbs, and use it for everything appropriate. Large dishes often benefit from a small garnish but smaller dishes may look fussy. Be careful about decorations that look unattractive once half the dish has disappeared, such as slices of tomato or lemon wedges around the edge of a large platter. Keep colors simple and use appropriately colored garnishes.

Keep the dish piled high in the center; this shows off the food better than when it lies flat. But do not put too much on a plate or it will be hard to serve and quickly look messy.

Meat can be sliced in advance but make sure the serving platter has been warmed or the meat will grow cold quickly. Warm plates in the oven, by immersing in hot water for a few minutes, or by heating in the microwave for 30 seconds in a stack with a small amount of water between each plate. Work out beforehand how you will keep food hot or cold.

Arrange petits fours and canapés in contrasting rows. Diagonal rows look better than horizontal or vertical ones.

There is nothing as unappetizing as wilted or tired-looking food—make sure that everything is absolutely fresh.

Menu Planner

SUNDAY BUFFET BRUNCH
for 12 people

Croissants

Stewed rhubarb with ginger · 424 ◆◆

Salmon kedgeree · 142 ◆◆

Eggs Benedict · 101 ◆◆

Frittata · 102 ◆◆

Blueberry muffins · 488 ◆◆

Bagels · 470   or
Croissants · 429

Danish pastries · 485

SPRING LUNCH
for 4 people

Ratatouille

FIRST COURSE
Smoked trout pâté · 3o

MAIN COURSE
Rack of lamb with
herb crust · 255

Ratatouille · 338

Sautéed potatoes · 323

DESSERT
Crêpes Suzette · 379

AFTERNOON TEA
for 6 people

Viennese fingers

Cheese and herb muffins · 113

Leek tartlets · 43

Crumpets · 481 or
English muffins · 480

Viennese fingers · 493

Gingersnaps · 494

Black Forest torte · 500

Dundee cake · 502

◆◀ Multiply the recipe by 1¹/₂   ◆◆ Double the recipe   ◆◆◆ Triple the recipe

Menu Planner

WEDDING BREAKFAST
for 24 people

Creamed Roquefort (top) and Crostini

FIRST COURSE
Creamed Roquefort and walnuts · 47

*Crostini of roasted peppers
and basil · 47* ♦♦

MAIN COURSE
*Whole baked salmon with
watercress mayonnaise · 163* ♦♦

Mustard seed potato salad · 122 ♦♦♦

*Artichoke, spinach and
pine nut salad · 130* ♦♦♦

Tabbouleh · 124 ♦♦♦

DESSERT
Iced raspberry soufflé · 405 ♦♦♦

Cherry brandy snap baskets · 406 ♦♦♦

CHRISTMAS LUNCH
for 8 people

Roast turkey

FIRST COURSE
Celery root and Stilton soup · 75 ♦♦

MAIN COURSE
*Roast turkey with bread sauce
and gravy · 207*

Roast potatoes · 316 ♦♦

*Roasted parsnips with honey
and ginger · 336*
Green beans with bacon · 321

DESSERT
Traditional Christmas pudding · 399

Whiskey sauce · 371

Brandy butter · 371

Mincemeat pies · 511

NEW YEAR'S EVE DINNER
for 6 people

Chocolate rum truffles

APPETIZER
Mini blinis with caviar · 24

FIRST COURSE
Lobster bisque · 71 ♦◄

MAIN COURSE
*Breast of duck with
winter vegetables · 208* ♦◄

Gratin dauphinois · 339 ♦◄

DESSERT
Orange blossom crème caramel · 420

Langues-de-chat · 514

Chocolate rum truffles · 457

♦◄ Multiply the recipe by 1½   ♦♦ Double the recipe   ♦♦♦ Triple the recipe

Menu Planner

SUMMER BUFFET
for 30 people

Sherry trifle

Bruschetta with prosciutto
and Gorgonzola · 26 ◆◆◆

Spiced shrimp balls · 38

Minted pea and cilantro triangles · 54

Colcannon and smoked
chicken canapés · 59

Leek and Brie flamiche · 110 ◆◆

Chèvre and watercress quiche · 112 ◆◆

Coulibiac · 180 ◆◆

Coronation chicken · 192 ◆◆◆

Barbecued marinated vegetables · 331 ◆◆◆

Fattoush · 128 ◆◆◆

Caprese · 126 ◆◆◆

Waldorf salad · 119 ◆◆◆

DESSERT
Millefeuille · 441 ◆◆◆

Sherry trifle · 400 ◆◆◆

Chocolate and chestnut terrine · 418 ◆◆

ITALIAN WINTER LUNCH
for 4 people

Garlic shrimp

FIRST COURSE
Garlic shrimp · 154

MAIN COURSE
Osso buco · 251

Green beans with bacon · 321

DESSERT
Zabaglione with lady fingers · 410

HOLIDAY DINNER
for 6 people

Roast potatoes

FIRST COURSE
Cream of cauliflower soup · 68 ◆◀

MAIN COURSE
Roast beef and Yorkshire
puddings · 239

Roast potatoes · 316 ◆◀

Braised Belgian endive · 337

Vichy carrots · 326

Broccoli purée with blue cheese · 328

Thickened pan gravy · 346

DESSERT
Treacle tart · 512

Crème anglaise · 365

◆◀ Multiply the recipe by 1½   ◆◆ Double the recipe   ◆◆◆ Triple the recipe

Menu Planner

COCKTAIL PARTY
for 30 people

Salsa oysters

Roquefort in Belgian endive leaves · 25

Onion tartlets · 27

Crab fritters with a lime and yogurt mayonnaise · 44

Spinach and feta packages · 36

Smoked salmon pancake rolls · 37

Mini brochettes · 49
Beef and horseradish canapés · 35

Blue cheese and tomato canapés · 35

Creamy oysters and salsa oysters · 148

Chocolate dipped fruits . 454 ◆◆◆

LIGHT SUPPER
for 8 people

Summer shrimp and cucumber soup

FIRST COURSE
Summer shrimp and cucumber soup · 97

MAIN COURSE
Goat cheese with a watercress and mâche salad · 127 ◆◆

DESSERT
Molded fruit terrine · 414

CELEBRATION SUPPER
for 25 people

Honey-glazed spiced ham

FIRST COURSE
Gravlax · 143 ◆◆

Spinach and crab roulade · 145 ◆◆

Quiche Lorraine · 107 ◆◆

Caesar salad · 120 ◆◆◆

MAIN COURSE
Honey-glazed spiced ham · 272

Boeuf bourguignon · 237 ◆◆◆

Chicken with mushrooms and onions · 216 ◆◆◆

Sautéed potatoes · 323 ◆◆◆

Mixed glazed vegetables · 315 ◆◆◆

Green beans with bacon · 321 ◆◆◆

DESSERT
Pecan tart · 448 ◆◆

Baked apple and fruit charlotte · 395 ◆◆

Chocolate profiteroles · 408 ◆◆◆

◆◄ Multiply the recipe by 1½   ◆◆ Double the recipe   ◆◆◆ Triple the recipe

Menu Planner

SUMMER DINNER
for 6 people

Veal with lemon and capers

FIRST COURSE
*Smoked salmon soup with
lime chantilly cream · 94*

MAIN COURSE
Veal with lemon and capers · 253 ♦◄

Barbecued marinated vegetables · 331

Sautéed potatoes · 323 ♦◄

DESSERT
Pavlovas with fragrant fruit · 402

AUTUMN DINNER
for 4 people

Mixed glazed vegetables

APPETIZER
Gougères · 115

FIRST COURSE
Chicken liver pâté · 188

MAIN COURSE
Sole meunière · 173

Mixed glazed vegetables · 315

DESSERT
Lemon tart · 444

VEGETARIAN DINNER
for 4 people

Gratin of summer berries

FIRST COURSE
*Warm fennel and cherry
tomato salad · 138*

MAIN COURSE
*Herb tagliatelle with mushrooms
and olive oil · 297*

Country sourdough · 465

DESSERT
Gratin of summer berries · 381

♦◄ Multiply the recipe by 1¹/2   ♦♦ Double the recipe   ♦♦♦ Triple the recipe

hors d'oeuvres

Mini blinis with caviar

Brightly colored and extremely appetizing, these small pancakes topped with sour cream and caviar or roe are bound to disappear very quickly.

*Preparation time 45 minutes
+ 30 minutes resting
Total cooking time 35 minutes
Makes 40–45*

*1/4 oz. fresh yeast or 1/8 oz. active
dry yeast
2/3 cup lukewarm milk
2 teaspoons sugar
1/2 cup all-purpose flour
1/2 cup buckwheat flour
2 eggs, separated
3 tablespoons butter, melted
but cooled
sour cream, to garnish
caviar or lumpfish roe, to garnish
sprigs of fresh dill or chervil,
to garnish*

One Dissolve the yeast in the lukewarm milk, then mix in the sugar, flours, egg yolks and a large pinch of salt. Cover and allow to rest for 30 minutes in a warm place. After resting, the batter should be foamy and thick. Mix in the melted butter.

Two Beat the egg whites with a pinch of salt until soft peaks form. Gently fold into the batter.

Three Over medium heat, melt a little butter in a nonstick skillet. Using a small spoon, place dollops of the batter in the pan, trying to make them as uniform as possible and being careful not to crowd the pan. Once the batter begins to set around the edges and the surface is bubbly, carefully flip the blinis over. Cook for another 2–3 minutes, or until brown. Transfer to a wire rack to cool (you can overlap them, but do not stack). Repeat until all the batter has been used.

Four If necessary, use a small round cutter to trim the blinis to the same size. Arrange on a serving platter, place a spoonful of sour cream in the center of each and top with caviar or roe. Finish with a sprig of dill or chervil.

CHEF'S TIPS *If you have any fresh yeast left over, it can be stored in the refrigerator, lightly wrapped in waxed paper, for up to 2 weeks.*

Other types of caviar appropriate for this recipe include salmon or red caviar.

Roquefort in Belgian endive leaves

*The butter used in this recipe helps to soften both the texture
and the distinctive salty taste of the Roquefort, a blue-vein
sheep's milk cheese from southern France.*

Preparation time 20 minutes
Total cooking time None
Makes 40–45

8 oz. Roquefort or other strong
blue cheese
1/2 cup unsalted butter,
at room temperature
1 tablespoon port or Madeira
4 heads Belgian endive
2 tablespoons chopped walnuts
sprigs of fresh parsley,
to garnish

One Place the cheese, butter and port in a food processor and process until smooth. Season to taste with freshly ground black pepper and more port if desired. Transfer to a bowl and set aside.

Two Remove any damaged outer leaves from the endives and discard. Cut about 1/4 inch from the bottom and carefully remove all the loose leaves. Repeat until all the leaves are loose.

Three Put the cheese mixture in a pastry bag fitted with a medium star tip and pipe a small rosette of cheese at the bottom of each endive leaf. Sprinkle each rosette with some chopped walnuts, then arrange the endive leaves on a round platter with the tips of the leaves pointing outward like the petals of a flower. Form the parsley into a small bouquet and place it in the center. Serve immediately.

CHEF'S TIP *The cheese filling may be prepared ahead of time and stored, covered with plastic wrap, in the refrigerator; but once the endive is cut, it tends to discolor, so prepare the leaves just before serving.*

Bruschetta with prosciutto and Gorgonzola

*Italians are great bread-eaters. Bruschetta are
thin slices of bread, broiled and rubbed with a clove
of cut garlic—the original garlic bread.*

Preparation time *10 minutes*
Total cooking time *5 minutes*
Makes 8

*1 loaf Italian bread
2 cloves garlic, halved
¼ cup extra virgin olive oil
8 sun-dried tomatoes in olive oil
6 oz. Gorgonzola cheese
4 slices prosciutto, cut in half*

One To prepare the bruschetta, cut the
bread into thin slices and broil or toast
to golden brown. Rub one side of each
bruschetta with the cut surface of the
garlic. Drizzle with the olive oil and
sprinkle with salt and freshly ground
black pepper.

Two Drain the sun-dried tomatoes,
scrape off any seeds and cut into thin
strips. Press or spread the cheese onto
the bruschetta, lay the prosciutto on top
and garnish with strips of tomato.
Season with a few grindings of freshly
ground black pepper and serve.

CHEF'S TIPS *If Gorgonzola is too
strong for your taste, use a creamier,
milder cheese like Dolcelatte instead.*

*As a variation, marinate diced fresh
tomatoes, garlic, and chopped fresh basil
leaves in enough balsamic vinegar to
moisten well. Drain the excess juice and
place a spoonful on top of the warm
slice of bruschetta.*

LE CORDON BLEU ✠ COMPLETE COOK

Onion tartlets

*These delectable golden onion tartlets must be served warm. The onion
filling can be replaced with a mushroom filling, as described in the
chef's tip below. If short of time, you could use sheets of frozen puff pastry.*

Preparation time *45 minutes*
+35 minutes chilling
Total cooking time *45 minutes*
Makes 24

PASTRY
1²/₃ cups all-purpose flour
¹/₄ teaspoon salt
3 tablespoons unsalted butter,
cut into pieces and chilled
2 egg yolks
4–5 tablespoons water

ONION FILLING
2 tablespoons unsalted butter
2 onions, finely chopped
1 small bay leaf
2 sprigs of fresh thyme

²/₃ cup whipping cream
4 eggs
4 egg yolks
pinch of ground nutmeg

One Grease 24 individual mini-tartlet pans or 24 mini-muffin cups.

Two To make the pastry, sift the flour and salt into a large bowl. Using your fingertips, rub the butter into the flour until the mixture resembles fine bread crumbs. Make a well in the center and add the egg yolks and water. Work the mixture together with a flexible bladed knife until it forms a rough ball. Turn out onto a lightly floured surface, form into a ball and cover with plastic wrap. Chill in the refrigerator for 20 minutes.

Three To make the onion filling, melt the butter in a skillet over medium heat. Add the onions, bay leaf and thyme with a pinch of salt. Cover and cook slowly for 15 minutes, then remove the lid and cook for 15 minutes, or until the onions are dark golden. Remove the bay leaf and thyme and allow to cool.

Four Roll out the dough to a thickness of ¹/₈ inch, then refrigerate for 5 minutes. Preheat the oven to 350°F. Remove the dough from the refrigerator and, using a biscuit cutter slightly larger than the tartlet pans, cut out 24 rounds of pastry. Place the rounds in the pans, pressing down on the bottom so the dough extends slightly above the tops of the pans. Place in the refrigerator to chill for 10 minutes.

Five Whisk together the cream, eggs, egg yolks, nutmeg and salt and pepper.

Six Divide the onion filling among the tartlet shells, then cover with the egg mixture. Bake for 12–15 minutes, or until the tops of the tartlets are lightly browned. Remove the tartlets from the pans while they are still warm and serve them immediately.

CHEF'S TIP *If you want to replace the onion with a mushroom filling, melt 2 tablespoons butter in a saucepan over medium heat, add 3 finely chopped shallots and cook for 3 minutes. Toss 2¹/₂ cups finely chopped mushrooms in 1 tablespoon lemon juice, add to the shallots and cook for another 10 minutes, or until dry. Set the filling aside to cool.*

Chicken liver pâté

*This simply made pâté dip (pictured top right) has
lots of flavor. If you want a stronger taste,
try making it with duck livers.*

Preparation time *15 minutes
+ 15 minutes cooling*
Total cooking time *10 minutes*
Serves 4 *as an appetizer*

*½ cup unsalted butter, at room
temperature
2 shallots, finely chopped
2 cloves garlic, finely chopped
8 oz. chicken livers, trimmed
sprig of fresh thyme
bay leaf
large pinch each of ground nutmeg,
cloves and cinnamon
1 tablespoon brandy or port
2 tablespoons whipping cream or
crème fraîche*

One Place 2 tablespoons of the butter in a skillet and add the shallots and garlic. Cook over a gentle heat until they soften and turn transparent.

Two Over medium heat, add the livers, thyme, bay leaf, spices and some salt and pepper to the shallot mixture. Fry for 3 minutes. The livers should be barely pink in the center. Set aside to cool for 15 minutes.

Three Remove the thyme and bay leaf from the mixture and process in a food processor until smooth, then push through a sieve if you prefer an even smoother texture. Beat in the remaining butter with a wooden spoon, then add the brandy or port. Carefully fold in the cream or crème fraîche and season to taste with salt and freshly ground black pepper. Spoon the pâté into a serving bowl and serve with slices of Melba toast or toasted bread fingers.

CHEF'S TIP *You can prepare the pâté in advance and refrigerate for up to 3 days. You might find it too firm to be eaten as a dip straight from the refrigerator—the flavor and texture is better if it is allowed to soften for 30 minutes at room temperature before serving.*

Salmon rillettes

*This modern version of the classic French
meat rillettes—similar to pâté—uses both fresh
and smoked salmon (pictured bottom right).*

Preparation time *10 minutes + 1 hour
chilling*
Total cooking time *10 minutes*
Serves 4 *as an appetizer*

*4 oz. salmon fillet, skin and bones
removed
2 oz. smoked salmon slices,
finely chopped
⅓ cup unsalted butter,
at room temperature
¼ cup plain yogurt
1 teaspoon lemon juice
2 tablespoons chopped fresh chives*

One Steam the fresh salmon for about 10 minutes, or until cooked through. Cool on a clean kitchen towel or several pieces of paper towel.

Two Using a whisk or fork, mix the smoked salmon with the butter until as smooth as possible. Add the yogurt, lemon juice and chives. Mix until well combined, season to taste and set aside.

Three Gently crush the fresh salmon to make large flakes and add to the smoked salmon mixture. Mix until completely incorporated. Transfer to a small serving bowl or terrine and refrigerate for 1 hour, or until set. Serve with Melba toast or French bread.

CHEF'S TIP *You can also make a mackerel rillette by replacing the fresh salmon with 4 oz. fresh mackerel fillets, skin and bones removed. Replace the smoked salmon with the same quantity of smoked mackerel and substitute lime juice for the lemon juice.*

Smoked trout pâté

*A stylish but easy-to-make pâté, with a combination
of fresh and smoked trout. For a variation, you could
use smoked and fresh salmon or mackerel.*

Preparation time 30 minutes + cooling
+ 1 hour refrigeration
Total cooking time 5 minutes
Serves 6

1 tablespoon white wine vinegar
1 bay leaf
4 white peppercorns
¼ lb. fresh trout fillet,
skin on
¾ lb. smoked trout fillet,
skin removed
¾ cup cream cheese
⅓ cup unsalted butter, softened
1 tablespoon fresh lemon juice
4 sprigs of fresh parsley, chervil or
dill, to garnish

One Put the wine vinegar, bay leaf, white peppercorns and ½ cup water in a shallow saucepan and bring slowly to a simmer. Put the fresh trout fillet skin side down in this poaching liquid, cover and gently cook the trout for 3–4 minutes, or until cooked through. Allow to cool in the liquid. Using a fish turner or spatula, transfer the trout carefully onto a plate and remove and discard the skin and any bones.

Two Put the fresh trout and smoked trout fillets in a food processor and process until they form a smooth purée. Add the cream cheese, butter, lemon juice and some salt and black pepper and process until all the ingredients are thoroughly combined.

Three Divide the pâté among six 1-cup ramekins, 3 inches in diameter, and place them in the refrigerator for 1 hour. To serve, garnish with a parsley, chervil or dill sprig and accompany with Melba toast.

CHEF'S TIP *This makes an excellent cocktail dip if served soft at cool room temperature. Alternatively, put the mixture into a pastry bag and pipe it onto small rounds of toast as a canapé. Garnish with a dill or chervil sprig.*

 LE CORDON BLEU COMPLETE COOK

Crudités

*A colorful selection of crunchy fresh vegetables served
with a choice of dipping sauces is an ideal summer
lunch or light appetizer.*

Preparation time *35 minutes
+ 1 hour chilling*
Total cooking time *None*
Serves *8–10*

SOUR CREAM DIP
*1 cup sour cream
2 tablespoons mayonnaise
1/4 cup grated Parmesan cheese
1 teaspoon lime or lemon juice
1/2 teaspoon Worcestershire sauce
1 teaspoon prepared horseradish
1/2 teaspoon Dijon mustard
1/4 teaspoon celery salt*

*1 English cucumber
2 stalks celery
1 red bell pepper
1 yellow bell pepper
1 small head broccoli
12 fresh or 13 oz. canned
baby corn
1 cup snow peas
12 baby carrots
20 cherry tomatoes*

HERB DIP
*2 tablespoons Dijon mustard
1/3 cup red wine vinegar
1 cup olive oil
1/2 tablespoon each of chopped fresh
chives, basil, parsley and tarragon*

One To prepare the sour cream dip,
combine all the ingredients in a bowl
and mix well. Chill for at least 1 hour
before serving.

Two With a fork, scrape down the length
of the cucumber to create a ridged
pattern, then cut into 1/4-inch slices. Cut
the celery and peppers into 2–3-inch-
long sticks. Blanch the broccoli, corn,
snow peas and carrots in boiling water

for 1 minute. Drain, refresh in cold
water and drain. Cut off and discard the
broccoli stem. Cut the broccoli florets
into bite-size pieces. Arrange all the
vegetables on a serving platter. Cover
with damp paper towels, wrap in plastic
wrap and refrigerate until ready to serve.

Three To prepare the herb dip, place the
mustard in a bowl and whisk in the
vinegar. Gradually whisk in the oil
before adding the herbs, then season
with salt and freshly ground black
pepper. Serve the vegetables with the
dips on the side.

Eggplant caviar

*The name of this dish comes from the rather
grainy appearance of the eggplant. Delicious served
with crisp Melba toast or warmed pita bread.*

Preparation time 10 minutes
+ 1 hour refrigeration
Total cooking time 30 minutes
Serves 6

1 1/2 lb. eggplant
1/3 cup chopped pitted black olives
1 clove garlic, crushed
1/3 cup finely chopped fresh chives
2/3 cup olive oil, plus extra
for brushing
1/2 teaspoon sweet paprika

One Preheat the oven to 350°F. Cut the
eggplant in half lengthwise. Brush the
cut sides with a little olive oil and
sprinkle with salt and pepper. Place the
halves cut side down in a baking dish or
roasting pan.

Two Bake for 25–30 minutes, or until the
flesh is very soft. Drain the eggplant to
remove any liquid. Scrape out the flesh
with a spoon, chop the flesh and put in
a bowl.

Three Add the black olives, garlic and
half the chives. Mix everything together
using a fork, pressing the eggplant flesh
against the sides of the bowl to break it
down. Add the olive oil very slowly,
stirring it into the mixture with the fork.
Add the paprika and season to taste with
salt and pepper. Refrigerate for 1 hour.

Four Spoon into a chilled bowl, sprinkle
the top with the remaining chives and
serve with Melba toast.

CHEF'S TIP *For a particularly special
presentation, use two spoons to shape
the mixture into small oval quenelles
and arrange on individual plates.
Sprinkle with chopped chives.*

Shrimp gougères

Traditionally, a gougère is a round or ring-shaped cheese pastry.
This variation uses plain cream puff pastry to make small puffs that
are filled with a cold shrimp and mayonnaise mixture.

***Preparation time** 40 minutes*
***Total cooking time** 25 minutes*
Makes about 20

CREAM PUFF PASTRY
2/3 cup all-purpose flour
1/2 cup water
3 tablespoons unsalted butter,
cut into small pieces
2 eggs, lightly beaten
pinch of ground nutmeg

1 beaten egg, for glazing
8 oz. cooked shrimp, shells removed
(see Chef's tip)
1/2 cup mayonnaise
1 tablespoon finely chopped
fresh chives

One Preheat the oven to 350°F and lightly butter two baking sheets.

Two Make the pastry following the method in the Chef's techniques on page 545 and adding the pinch of nutmeg to the pan with the butter.

Three Spoon the pastry into a pastry bag fitted with a small plain tip. Pipe out small balls of dough the size of walnuts onto the prepared baking sheets, leaving a space of 1¼ inches between each ball. Lightly brush the top of each ball with the beaten egg, being careful not to let any excess egg drip down onto the baking sheets, as this may prevent the balls from rising evenly. Bake in the oven for 30 minutes, or until the balls have puffed up and are golden brown. Remove from the oven and transfer to a wire rack to cool.

Four Coarsely chop the shrimp and place in a bowl, then add the mayonnaise and

chopped chives and mix together. Season to taste with salt and freshly ground black pepper. Refrigerate the shrimp mixture until ready to use.

Five Once cooled, cut the pastry balls in half and remove any soft dough from

inside them. Fill each ball with a small spoonful of the shrimp mixture. Replace the tops, arrange on a platter and serve.

CHEF'S TIP *If you are purchasing unshelled shrimp, you will need to buy about 1¼ lb.*

Blue cheese and tomato canapés

*Serve warm while the cheese is still melting and
these canapés (pictured far left) will disappear in an instant.*

Preparation time *15 minutes*
Total cooking time *20 minutes*
Makes 60

*15 thin slices day-old white or
wheat bread*
2½ tablespoons tomato paste
*6½ oz. firm blue cheese, such as
Stilton, crumbled*
*1½ tablespoons chopped fresh basil
or oregano*

One Preheat the oven to 375°F. Using a 1½-inch biscuit cutter, cut out 4 rounds from each slice of bread, discarding the trimmings. Place the rounds on two baking sheets and bake for 15 minutes, turning them halfway through cooking.

Two Spread the rounds with the tomato paste and put them back on the baking sheets. Cover each one with blue cheese and sprinkle with half the basil or oregano. Return them to the oven for 2 minutes, or until the cheese just starts to melt, but is not so liquid that it runs off the canapés. Season with black pepper, sprinkle with the remaining herbs and serve immediately.

CHEF'S TIPS *For a variation, other blue cheeses such as Roquefort can be used, but this will give a much stronger salty taste.*

To prepare ahead of time, cool the bread rounds after baking. Just before serving, spread with the tomato paste and top with cheese and herbs. Either bake in the oven or under a preheated broiler at the highest setting to melt the cheese and heat the canapés through.

Beef and horseradish canapés

*A bite-size classic combination of
roast beef and horseradish sauce (pictured left).*

Preparation time *15 minutes*
Total cooking time *5 minutes*
Makes 32

*8 thin slices day-old white or
wheat bread*
5 oz. rare roast beef, finely chopped
*2 tablespoons fresh horseradish,
finely grated, or 2 teaspoons
prepared horseradish*
*4 tablespoons whipping cream, lightly
whipped, or sour cream*
sprigs of fresh chervil, to garnish

One Preheat the broiler. Using a 1½-inch biscuit cutter, cut out 4 rounds from each slice of bread and discard the trimmings. Toast the circles on each side under the broiler and remove to a cooling rack.

Two Place the chopped beef in a bowl and mix in the horseradish and the cream. Season with salt and black pepper, bearing in mind how hot the horseradish is.

Three Using a teaspoon, mound the beef mixture neatly onto the cooled rounds of bread and garnish with a chervil sprig.

CHEF'S TIP *For a variation, use the same ingredients, but do not chop the beef. Mix the horseradish, lightly whipped cream and salt and black pepper in a bowl. Pipe or spoon onto the toast, then place thinly sliced rounds of beef on top. Dust half the canapés with paprika and place thin slices of gherkin on the other half.*

Spinach and feta packages

*These delicious small packages, resembling beggars' purses,
have a lovely crisp exterior and a soft creamy center.*

Preparation time 30 minutes
+ 15 minutes cooling
Total cooking time 20 minutes
Makes about 45

¹/₃ *cup unsalted butter, melted*
1 tablespoon olive oil
*6¹/₄ cups spinach, washed, trimmed
and torn*
³/₄ cup crumbled feta cheese
*¹/₄ cup ricotta or small-curd
cottage cheese*
1 egg, beaten
1 tablespoon chopped fresh parsley
1 tablespoon chopped fresh basil
6 sheets phyllo pastry

One Brush 2 baking sheets with a little
melted butter.

Two Heat the oil in a skillet. Add the
spinach and cook for 2 minutes, stirring
constantly. Stir in the feta and ricotta
until they become soft and coat the
spinach. Season to taste with salt and
freshly ground black pepper. Remove the
pan from the heat, allow the mixture to
cool slightly, then stir in the egg, parsley
and basil. Set aside for 15 minutes to
cool completely.

Three Preheat the oven to 375°F.
Following the method in the Chef's
techniques on page 549, lay the sheets of
phyllo pastry to produce three stacks,
each with two layers of phyllo pastry.

Four Cut each stack into 3-inch squares,
discarding any leftover pastry. Put
1 teaspoon of filling in the center of
each phyllo square, then gather up the
corners over the filling. Gently pinch the
pastry, just above the filling, to seal
without splitting.

Five Place the packages on the baking
sheets and drizzle with some of the
remaining melted butter. Bake for
15 minutes, or until crisp and golden.

CHEF'S TIP *If you are using cottage
cheese instead of ricotta it will not be as*
*smooth, so drain the cottage cheese
thoroughly and press through a strainer
before using.*

LE CORDON BLEU ❋ COMPLETE COOK

Smoked salmon pancake rolls

One of the attractive features of this recipe, which successfully combines the flavors of smoked salmon and horseradish, is that the pancakes may be prepared in advance and frozen.

Preparation time 1 hour + 15 minutes resting + 1 hour refrigeration
Total cooking time 10 minutes
Makes 30–35

CHINESE PANCAKES
1 cup all-purpose flour
2 teaspoons sesame oil

5 oz. cream cheese, at room temperature
1 tablespoon prepared horseradish
1/2 teaspoon lemon juice
6 oz. smoked salmon slices
chopped fresh chives or herbs, to garnish

One To make the Chinese pancakes, bring 1/3 cup water to a boil and then follow the method in the Chef's techniques on page 537.

Two Stack the pancakes on a plate and keep them wrapped in a slightly damp cloth to prevent them from drying out.

Three Soften the cream cheese in a small bowl and mix with the horseradish and lemon juice until smooth.

Four Place a pancake on a work surface and trim off the upper third of the circle. Spread with a thin layer of the cheese mixture, then cover with a layer of salmon. Roll up as tightly as possible. Wrap in plastic wrap to keep it from unrolling and set aside. Repeat with the remaining pancakes. Refrigerate for at least 1 hour.

Five Just before serving, trim the ends of each roll, then slice into 5/8-inch pieces and pierce with a cocktail pick. Scatter a few chives or fresh herbs in the center of each roll, arrange on a platter and serve.

CHEF'S TIP *The pancakes can be prepared in advance and frozen. Briefly steam to soften before using.*

Spiced shrimp balls

*The fried sesame seeds enclosing the tasty shrimp mixture
will give a strong, distinctive flavor and a lovely golden
brown color to these delicious savory snacks.*

Preparation time 15 minutes
+ 20 minutes chilling
Total cooking time 15 minutes
Makes 24

1½ lb. large uncooked shrimp
1 tablespoon oil
2 cloves garlic, crushed
½-inch piece fresh ginger,
finely chopped
¼ teaspoon salt
2 teaspoons sugar
1 teaspoon chopped fresh cilantro
1 teaspoon cornstarch
½ egg white
⅔ cup sesame seeds
oil, for deep-frying

One Remove the shells from the shrimp and devein following the method in the Chef's techniques on page 522. Pat dry with paper towels.

Two Put the shrimp in a food processor and process to a coarse purée. Transfer to a bowl and add the oil, garlic, ginger, salt, sugar, cilantro and cornstarch and mix well to combine.

Three Lightly whisk the egg white until it just forms soft peaks, then add just enough of the egg white to the spiced shrimp mixture to obtain a smooth, stiff mixture that will hold a shape.

Four Divide the mixture into 24 even-size balls. Roll in the sesame seeds to coat, set them on a baking sheet and chill in the refrigerator for 20 minutes.

Five Heat the oil in a deep-fat fryer or deep saucepan (see Chef's techniques, page 537). Deep-fry the balls in three batches, for 4–5 minutes, or until they are golden brown and crispy on the outside and cooked through. Drain on crumpled paper towels. Arrange them on a serving plate and serve hot.

LE CORDON BLEU ❦ COMPLETE COOK

Satay beef sticks

Widely cooked throughout Southeast Asia, a satay consists of marinated meat, fish or poultry, threaded onto bamboo or wooden skewers, broiled or barbecued, and served with a sauce.

*Preparation time 35 minutes
+ 2–3 hours marinating*
Total cooking time 15 minutes
Makes 20

¼ teaspoon ground anise
¼ teaspoon ground cumin
1 teaspoon ground turmeric
1 teaspoon ground coriander
1 shallot, chopped
1 clove garlic, finely chopped
½-inch piece fresh ginger, finely chopped
1 stalk lemongrass, white part only, finely chopped
1 tablespoon brown sugar
2 tablespoons peanut oil
1 teaspoon soy sauce
6 oz. beef tenderloin, cut into 20 thin strips

SATAY SAUCE
1 clove garlic
⅓ cup smooth peanut butter
3 tablespoons coconut milk
few drops Tabasco sauce, or to taste
2 teaspoons honey
2 teaspoons lemon juice
2 teaspoons light soy sauce

One Soak 20 short wooden skewers in water for 1 hour to prevent them from burning under the broiler. To make the marinade, add the ground anise, cumin, turmeric and coriander to the shallot, garlic, ginger, lemongrass and brown sugar in a medium bowl. Mix well and add the oil and soy sauce.

Two Thread a strip of beef onto each wooden skewer, weaving the skewers throught the meat, and place the satay sticks in a shallow dish. Thoroughly coat in the marinade and leave in the refrigerator for 2–3 hours.

Three To make the satay sauce, put the garlic into a small saucepan and cover with cold water. Bring to a boil and simmer for 3 minutes, refresh under cold water, then drain and finely chop. Combine the garlic with the peanut butter, coconut milk and ¼ cup water in a medium saucepan. Stir over medium heat for 1–2 minutes, or until smooth and thick, then add the Tabasco, honey, lemon juice and soy sauce. Stir until the sauce is warm and thoroughly blended. If the mixture starts to separate, stir in 1–2 teaspoons water. Cover with plastic wrap and place in the refrigerator until ready to use.

Four Preheat a broiler or barbecue until hot. Cook the satay sticks for 1–2 minutes on each side, turning three or four times during cooking. Once they are cooked, arrange on a plate and serve with the satay sauce.

Marinated fish and tapenade on toast

Tapenade, a simple spread from Provence in France,
is made by puréeing black olives, anchovies,
capers, olive oil and lemon juice (pictured bottom right).

Preparation time 10 minutes
+ 15 minutes marinating
Total cooking time 10 minutes
Makes 16

2 fillets (6 oz. total) sea bass, or
other firm, lean white fish, skin and
bones removed
1 clove garlic
2 tablespoons olive oil
4 slices bread, crusts removed
1/3 cup tapenade
16 pink peppercorns
16 sprigs of fresh dill
small wedges of lemon, to garnish

One Preheat the oven to 425°F. Cut each fish fillet into eight pieces. Place the garlic clove in the olive oil, toss into the fish and allow to marinate for 15 minutes.

Two Toast the bread and spread with a thin layer of tapenade. Cut each slice diagonally into four triangles and arrange on a baking sheet. Place the marinated fish on the prepared toasts and, just before serving, place in the oven for 2–3 minutes, or until the fish is just cooked (it will flake when lightly pressed with a fork).

Three Remove from the oven and transfer to a serving tray. Place a small dot of the tapenade on the top, then a pink peppercorn in the center. Decorate each one with a sprig of dill and a lemon wedge.

CHEF'S TIPS *As well as sea bass, red mullet goes particularly well with this recipe, but can be difficult to obtain. Check with your local fish merchant for availability.*

Tapenade is available at gourmet delicatessens or you can use the quick and simple recipe on page 52.

Parma ham and melon fingers

An extremely refreshing all-time favorite
that is best made with paper-thin slices of
Parma ham or prosciutto (pictured top right).

Preparation time 10 minutes
Total cooking time None
Makes 32

1 small cantaloupe
11 slices Parma ham or prosciutto

One Cut the melon in half lengthwise and, using a spoon, remove the seeds and gently scrape clean. Slice each half into eight wedges.

Two With a sharp knife, starting at one end of a melon wedge, slice between the flesh and the thick rind of the melon. Cut each piece of peeled melon in half.

Three Cut each slice of Parma ham or prosciutto into three long strips.

Four Wrap a strip of Parma ham or prosciutto around each wedge of melon and secure with a cocktail pick.

Shrimp bouchées

*Bouchées are small round shells of puff pastry with a tasty filling.
These were fashionable at the French court of Louis XV and
his wife, who was renowned for her hearty appetite.*

Preparation time 15 minutes
+ 35 minutes chilling
Total cooking time 20 minutes
Makes 8

1/2 *quantity puff pastry (see page 542)*
1 *egg, beaten*

FILLING
2 *tablespoons unsalted butter*
1/4 *cup all-purpose flour*
1 *cup fish or shellfish stock,*
or milk
1/2 *lb. cooked shrimp, shells removed*
(see page 522)
2 *tablespoons chopped mixed*
fresh herbs

One Brush a large baking sheet with butter, and refrigerate until needed. Roll out the pastry on a lightly floured surface to a 1/4-inch thickness. Brush off any excess flour from the surface and cut out eight rounds with a 2 3/4-inch fluted biscuit cutter. Sprinkle the prepared sheet with a little cold water, turn the rounds over and place on the sheet. Brush with the egg, chill for 5 minutes, then brush again. Using a floured 2-inch plain biscuit cutter, press into the pastry three-quarters of the way through to mark an inner circle. Chill for 30 minutes.

Two Preheat the oven to 425°F. Brush the top of each pastry round again with beaten egg. Bake on the middle shelf of the oven for 10–12 minutes, or until the pastry rounds are well risen, crisp and golden. Remove from the oven and cut around the center circle to remove the lid while still warm. Scrape out the excess soft pastry from inside the little shells. If you wish, return to the oven for 30 seconds to dry. (You can turn off the oven and use the residual heat to do this.)

Three To make the filling, melt the butter in a saucepan, add the flour and cook over low heat for 1 minute. Remove from the heat and pour in the stock or milk, blend thoroughly with a wooden spoon and return to the stove. Stir constantly over low heat until the sauce is free of lumps. Increase the heat and stir until the mixture boils, then simmer for 2–3 minutes. Just before serving, stir in the shrimp to warm through. Finally add the herbs and season to taste with salt and freshly ground black pepper.

Four Spoon the filling into the pastry shells while both are still warm. If you wish, garnish with chopped herbs or extra shrimp. You may replace the lid or not.

CHEF'S TIPS *If using frozen cooked shrimp, they must be well thawed and drained before use. Do not wash them, or thaw in cold water, as they will lose a lot of flavor.*

After cutting out the pastry rounds, they are turned over on the baking sheet to help them rise with straight sides.

If the cooked shells are left to cool, reheat in a 350°F oven for 5 minutes before serving and then fill with the hot filling.

LE CORDON BLEU COMPLETE COOK

Leek tartlets

*These small tartlets filled with leek and cumin are ideal
served warm with drinks. Alternatively, they could be
made as larger tarts and served as a first course.*

*Preparation time 45 minutes
+ 15 minutes chilling
Total cooking time 40 minutes
Makes 30*

FILLING
*3 tablespoons unsalted butter
1 large leek, white part only,
thinly sliced
1 bay leaf
pinch of dried thyme
pinch of salt
1/4 teaspoon ground cumin
2/3 cup whipping cream
1 egg
1 egg yolk*

*1 quantity short pastry (see
page 544)*

One To make the filling, melt the butter
in a saucepan over low heat. Add the
leek, bay leaf, thyme and salt. Cover and
cook slowly for 5 minutes, then uncover
and continue cooking for 5–10 minutes,
or until the mixture is dry. Remove the
bay leaf. Add the cumin, mix well and
set aside to cool.

Two Grease 30 mini-muffin cups. Roll
out the short pastry on a lightly floured
surface to a thickness of 1/8 inch and
refrigerate for 5 minutes. Preheat the
oven to 325°F.

Three Using a 2³/4-inch biscuit cutter, cut
out 30 rounds from the pastry. Press the
rounds into the prepared muffin cups,
pressing down on the bottoms so the
dough extends slightly above the edge of

the cups. Refrigerate the lined cups for
10 minutes.

Four Whisk together the cream, egg and
egg yolk, and season with salt and
freshly ground black pepper. Fill each
pastry shell with 1/2 teaspoon of the leek
mixture, then carefully pour in the
cream mixture. Bake for 10–15 minutes,
or until the filling is set. Remove the
tartlets from the cups while they are
still warm. If they stick, loosen the
tartlets carefully with the tip of a small,
sharp knife.

Crab fritters with a lime and yogurt mayonnaise

*Warm crab and herb fritters are served here with a light
tangy dipping sauce. The yogurt and lime in the sauce provide
a refreshing contrast to the richness of the mayonnaise.*

Preparation time *20 minutes*
Total cooking *15 minutes*
Makes about 30

LIME AND YOGURT MAYONNAISE
2 teaspoons grated lime zest
1/2 cup plain yogurt
1/2 cup mayonnaise
fresh lime juice, to taste

CRAB FRITTERS
*8 oz. white fish fillets, such as cod
or halibut, skin and bones removed*
1 egg white
1/4 cup whipping cream
8 oz. cooked white crabmeat
*2 tablespoons chopped mixed fresh
herbs, such as dill, chives, parsley
and tarragon*
3 cups fresh bread crumbs

oil, for deep-frying

One To make the lime and yogurt mayonnaise, stir the lime zest into the yogurt. Mix in the mayonnaise and lime juice, then season with salt and pepper. Cover with plastic wrap and refrigerate.

Two To make the crab fritters, purée the fish fillets in a food processor. Add the egg white, season well and process again until well blended. Using the pulse button on the processor, carefully add the cream. Do not overwork or the cream will separate. Transfer the mixture to a large bowl and set inside a larger bowl of ice. Using a large metal spoon or rubber spatula, fold in the crabmeat and mixed herbs. Using two teaspoons, shape the mixture into small ovals, or roll by hand into balls, about 1 1/4 inches in diameter. Sprinkle the bread crumbs onto a sheet of waxed paper and roll the balls in them to coat each one, using the paper to help press on the crumbs without handling the soft mixture too much.

Three Following the method in the Chef's techniques on page 537, deep-fry the fritters for 4–6 minutes. Season with salt and serve warm with the lime and yogurt mayonnaise on the side.

CHEF'S TIP *Once shaped and coated, the crab fritters can be covered with plastic wrap and refrigerated for up to 24 hours before frying.*

Cranberry chicken cups

*These delicate, creamy little mouthfuls are quick to
prepare and guaranteed to impress.*

Preparation time 20 minutes
Total cooking time 10 minutes
Makes 26

6 sheets phyllo pastry
²/₃ cup unsalted butter, melted
3 skinned, boneless chicken breasts,
cooked and cut into ¹/₂-inch cubes
1 tablespoon cranberry sauce
¹/₄ cup whipping cream or
crème fraîche
2 scallions, finely chopped
¹/₂ teaspoon finely grated lemon zest
fresh cilantro leaves,
to garnish
zest of 1 lemon cut into julienne strips,
to garnish

One Preheat the oven to 400°F. Following the method for layering phyllo pastry in the Chef's techniques on page 549, lay a sheet of phyllo pastry out on a work surface and lightly brush with the butter. Place a second sheet on top and brush with butter, then repeat to make two stacks, each with three layers of phyllo pastry. Do the same with the remaining phyllo.

Two Using a 3-inch plain biscuit cutter, cut 26 rounds from the phyllo pastry and, buttered side down, press gently into individual fluted tartlet pans that are about 2 inches across the tops and ³/₄-inch deep.

Three Place small rounds of waxed paper into the pastry shells and fill with pie weights or rice. Bake the pastry shells for 10 minutes, or until golden. Remove the weights or rice and paper and cool the pastry in the pans.

Four Mix together the cooked chicken, cranberry sauce, cream or crème fraîche, scallions, lemon zest and some salt and pepper. Spoon into the tartlet shells and garnish each with a cilantro leaf and some julienne strips of lemon zest.

CHEF'S TIP *The chicken can be replaced with cooked turkey, duck or flaked smoked trout.*

Creamed Roquefort and walnuts

These delicious easy-to-make toasts (pictured top left)
are best served within 30 minutes of being made,
so that they keep their crisp texture.

Preparation time 15 minutes
Total cooking time 10 minutes
Makes 40

¼ cup coarsely chopped walnuts
10 slices whole grain bread,
¼ inch thick
2 oz. Roquefort or other strong
blue cheese
2 oz. cream cheese
chopped fresh parsley, to garnish

One Spread the walnuts on a baking sheet and toast them under a preheated broiler for 3–5 minutes, shaking the sheet frequently to ensure that they are evenly browned and do not burn. Alternatively, toast the walnuts in the oven at 350°F for 7–10 minutes. Set aside to cool.

Two Cut the bread slices into 1½-inch rounds with a biscuit cutter. Toast lightly on both sides under the broiler and then set aside.

Three Break up the Roquefort with a fork, add the cream cheese and mix well. Stir in half the chopped walnuts, then spread the mixture onto each round of toast. Sprinkle with the remaining chopped walnuts and a little parsley and serve the toasts immediately.

Crostini of roasted peppers and basil

The name crostini comes from the Italian word crosta, meaning "crust."
Crostini are small rounds of toasted bread with toppings such as pâté,
cheese or, as in this case, roasted vegetables (pictured bottom left).

Preparation time 25 minutes
Total cooking time 10 minutes
Makes 12

½ small red bell pepper, halved
½ small green bell pepper, halved
2 tablespoons shredded fresh basil
¼ cup olive oil
½ day-old French baguette
1 clove garlic
shavings of Parmesan cheese,
to garnish

One Preheat the oven to 400°F. Roast the peppers, following the method in the Chef's techniques on page 535.

Two Cut the peppers into thin strips and put them into a bowl with the basil and 1 tablespoon of the olive oil, or just enough to bind the mixture. Season with salt and freshly ground black pepper

Three Cut the baguette into slices about ⁵/8 inch thick. Toast the slices on both sides under a preheated broiler or in a toaster, then brush them with the remaining oil. Rub the garlic clove over the crostini and spoon some of the roasted pepper mixture onto each one. Top with the Parmesan shavings and serve immediately.

Melting morsels

As the name suggests, these rich cheese pastries melt in the mouth.
They can be prepared up to a week in advance as they keep well
if stored in an airtight container in a cool place.

***Preparation time** 35 minutes*
+ 50 minutes chilling
***Total cooking time** 10 minutes per*
baking sheet
Makes 64

melted butter, for brushing
3/4 cup all-purpose flour
pinch of celery salt
1/3 cup unsalted butter, cut into cubes
and chilled
2/3 cup grated Cheddar cheese
2 tablespoons grated Parmesan cheese
1 egg yolk
1 egg, beaten
1 tablespoon finely grated Parmesan
cheese, for the topping

One Preheat the oven to 375°F. Brush two baking sheets with melted butter and refrigerate.

Two Sift the flour, celery salt and a pinch of salt and freshly ground black pepper together into a medium bowl. Add the butter cubes and, using a pastry cutter, cut the mixture from the center to the edges of the bowl with a quick action.

Three When the flour has almost disappeared into the butter, add the Cheddar and Parmesan and continue cutting until the mixture is blended and coming together in rough lumps. Make a well in the center and cut in the egg yolk until combined. Gather together by hand to form a ball.

Four Wrap the dough loosely in plastic wrap and flatten slightly. Chill for about 20 minutes until firm.

Five Place the dough on a lightly floured work surface. Cut in half and roll out each half to an 8-inch square, 1/4 inch thick. Cut each square into 16 small squares, then cut each square in half to form triangles. Using a flexible metal spatula, carefully place enough triangles to comfortably fill the two baking sheets, and chill for 30 minutes.

Six Brush each triangle with beaten egg and sprinkle with a pinch of the extra Parmesan. Bake for 10 minutes, or until golden brown. Cool on a wire rack. Repeat with the remaining mixture, preparing the baking sheets as instructed in step 1.

CHEF'S TIP *If you want, vary the topping by sprinkling with finely chopped nuts and sea salt or some grated Parmesan mixed with a pinch of cayenne.*

LE CORDON BLEU ❖ COMPLETE COOK

Mini brochettes

It is important to marinate the ingredients as this will bring more flavor to the brochettes and make sure that the meat is deliciously tender.

*Preparation time 25 minutes
+ 1 hour marinating
Total cooking time 15 minutes
Makes 20*

*3/4 cup veal or chicken stock
2 cloves garlic, crushed
2 teaspoons chopped fresh
ginger
2 tablespoons dark soy sauce
2 teaspoons sesame oil
1 skinned, boneless chicken breast
half, cut into 1/2-inch cubes
1/2 red bell pepper, cut into
1/2-inch cubes
1/2 yellow bell pepper, cut into
1/2-inch cubes
2 scallions, sliced diagonally
1 teaspoon cornstarch*

One Simmer the stock in a saucepan until it is syrupy and reduced by a third.

Two Mix the reduced stock with the garlic, ginger, soy sauce and sesame oil to make the marinade. Allow to cool.

Three Thread the chicken, pepper and scallion onto the skewers. Place the brochettes in a flat dish and season well. Pour half the cooled marinade over the brochettes. Cover with plastic wrap and refrigerate for at least 1 hour.

Four To make the dipping sauce, heat the remaining marinade in a small saucepan, then mix the cornstarch with a little water and stir in until the sauce boils and thickens. Set aside and keep warm.

Five Preheat the broiler or barbecue. Drain the brochettes and cook for 3 minutes, turning, until the meat is cooked. Serve with the dipping sauce.

Spring rolls with pork stuffing

*These rolls are deep-fried, however, if you do not have a deep-fat fryer,
it is possible to use a heavy-bottomed saucepan. The results will be just
as good, but extreme care should be taken with the hot oil.*

Preparation time *40 minutes*
+ 30 minutes chilling
Total cooking time *40 minutes*
Makes about 40

2 tablespoons oil
8 oz. lean ground pork
1/2 Chinese cabbage, finely shredded
2 scallions, sliced
1 teaspoon grated fresh ginger
2 tablespoons finely chopped
bamboo shoots
3 button mushrooms, thinly sliced
1/2 teaspoon dried sage
1 teaspoon soy sauce
2 teaspoons cornstarch
20 spring roll wrappers, about
8 inches square
soy sauce, to serve

One Heat the oil in a large skillet over
high heat, add the pork and cook,
stirring, for about 3 minutes. Transfer to
a bowl to cool. Add the Chinese
cabbage, scallions, ginger, bamboo
shoots, mushrooms, dried sage, soy
sauce and 1 teaspoon of the cornstarch.
Stir well, then season to taste.

Two Add a little water to the remaining
teaspoon of cornstarch to make a paste.
Roll up the spring rolls by following the
method in the Chef's techniques on page
537. Place in the refrigerator to chill for
at least 30 minutes before cooking.

Three Heat the oil in a deep-fat fryer or
deep saucepan (see Chef's techniques,
page 537). Deep-fry the rolls in batches
of four or five for 3–5 minutes, or until
cooked and golden brown. The spring
rolls will float to the surface of the oil
when cooked. Drain on crumpled paper
towels and serve hot with the soy sauce.

CHEF'S TIP *These could also be made
using phyllo pastry. Brush sheets of
phyllo with melted butter (as directed on
page 549), wrap around the filling, then
bake in a 400°F oven for 10 minutes, or
until golden and crisp.*

LE CORDON BLEU ✣ COMPLETE COOK

Smoked salmon and trout roulade on pumpernickel

Pumpernickel, a coarse, dark bread made using a high proportion of rye flour, has a slightly sour taste, which complements the rich creaminess of the smoked fish topping.

***Preparation time** 25 minutes*
+ 30 minutes chilling
***Total cooking time** None*
Makes 20

4 oz. smoked trout fillet
4 oz. cream cheese
1 tablespoon lemon juice
6 oz. smoked salmon slices
20 slices pumpernickel
sprigs of fresh chervil or parsley,
to garnish

One Remove any skin or bones from the trout and place into a food processor with 3 oz. of the cream cheese. Process until blended and smooth, then season with salt and pepper. Add the lemon juice and process once more to combine.

Two Lay the smoked salmon slices onto a piece of plastic wrap in a 8- x 6-inch rectangular shape, with the edges of the slices overlapping. Spread an even layer of the smoked trout mixture onto the salmon, then roll the slices up from the widest side, like a jelly roll, using the plastic wrap to help lift as you roll. Wrap the salmon and trout roulade in

plastic wrap and place it in the freezer for 30 minutes, or until set and firm enough to slice.

Three Using a 2-inch biscuit cutter, cut out 20 rounds from the pumpernickel. Spread the remaining cream cheese onto the pumpernickel rounds. Remove the salmon roulade from the freezer, discard the plastic wrap and cut across the roulade, using a very sharp knife, to make about 20 slices. Top each piece of pumpernickel with a roulade slice and decorate with a sprig of chervil or parsley. Cover with plastic wrap and keep chilled until ready to serve.

Prosciutto, smoked ham and mustard roulade

Simple to prepare, yet full of flavor, these
are ideal for serving with cocktails
or wine (pictured bottom right).

***Preparation time** 15 minutes*
+ 10 minutes chilling
***Total cooking time** 5 minutes*
Makes about 35

4 oz. smoked ham pieces
1/2 cup mayonnaise
1 tablespoon Dijon mustard
4 oz. prosciutto slices
3 day-old petits pains (small French rolls)
fresh chervil sprigs, to garnish

One To make the filling, purée the ham pieces in a food processor, add the mayonnaise and mustard and process to bind. Season with salt and pepper.

Two Lay the slices of prosciutto, slightly overlapping, on a sheet of plastic wrap and spread the filling mixture over the prosciutto with the back of a spoon. Roll up the prosciutto lengthwise like a jelly roll and put in the freezer for 10 minutes to firm.

Three Thinly slice the petits pains and toast until golden brown. Cut the prosciutto roll into thin slices and place a slice on each piece of toasted bread. Garnish with the fresh chervil.

Crostini with tapenade

Crostini are Italian canapés, ideal with soups or as an accompaniment to vegetable
dishes and salads. Here they are served with a tapenade (pictured top right),
which is very intense in flavor and should be spread thinly.

***Preparation time** 15 minutes*
***Total cooking time** 25 minutes*
Makes about 60

1 day-old French baguette
olive oil, for cooking
1/2 cup pitted black olives
1 small clove garlic
8 anchovy fillets

One Preheat the oven to 350°F. Cut the baguette into very thin slices. Pour enough of the oil into a large skillet to lightly coat the bottom and heat gently. Lightly fry the bread in batches on both sides, then transfer to a baking sheet. Bake in the oven until both sides are golden. Remove the crostini and cool to room temperature.

Two To make the tapenade, place the olives, garlic and anchovy fillets in a food processor and pureé to a thick paste with a spreadable consistency, adding a little olive oil if it is too dry. Season with freshly ground black pepper, but avoid salt—the saltiness of the anchovies will be enough. Spread sparingly over the crostini.

Minted pea and cilantro triangles

Despite being a little time-consuming to prepare, the advantage of these tasty savories is that they can be made in advance and baked in the oven as required. Baking time is only 15 minutes.

*Preparation time 55 minutes
+ 20 minutes cooling
Total cooking time 30 minutes
Makes 30*

sprig of fresh mint
1¼ cups fresh peas, shelled
1 tablespoon vegetable oil
1 onion, cut into cubes the same size
as the peas
5 oz. potatoes, cooked and mashed
2 teaspoons ground coriander
1 tablespoon chopped fresh cilantro
1 tablespoon finely chopped
fresh mint
1 tablespoon lemon juice,
to taste
¼ cup unsalted butter,
melted
6 sheets phyllo pastry

One Place the sprig of mint into a saucepan of salted water and bring to a boil. When boiling, add the peas and cook for 2 minutes. Pour into a colander to drain, then remove and discard the sprig of mint.

Two Heat the oil in a skillet over low heat, add the onion and cook for 7 minutes, or until the onion is soft and translucent. Increase the heat to medium, add the peas and potato and stir to combine. Transfer the vegetables to a small bowl and allow to cool for 20 minutes.

Three When cool, stir in the ground coriander, cilantro, chopped mint and lemon juice, then season to taste with salt and freshly ground black pepper. Preheat the oven to 375°F. Brush two baking sheets with some melted butter and set aside.

Four Lay the phyllo on a work surface and brush each sheet with melted butter (see Chef's techniques on page 549). Cut across each sheet to form five strips, about 3 inches wide. Put 2 teaspoons of the filling on the corner of one end of each strip. Fold the pastry over diagonally to form a triangle at the end. Then keep on folding diagonally up the strip until you have reached the other end.

Five Place the filled triangles onto the prepared baking sheets, brush the tops with a little melted butter and bake for 15 minutes, or until the pastry is crisp and golden brown.

CHEF'S TIP *These triangles can be prepared a day in advance and refrigerated before baking. Serve them straight from the oven.*

Cheese palm leaves

These small pastry savories are delicious served with cocktails or soups. They can either be shaped as palm leaves or as the twisted sticks known as cheese straws. If you don't have time to make your own puff pastry, use 1 sheet of frozen puff pastry, thawed.

Preparation time 30 minutes
+ 45 minutes refrigeration
Total cooking time 10 minutes
Makes 40

2 egg yolks
1 egg
1/4 teaspoon sugar
melted butter, for brushing
3/4 cup grated Parmesan cheese
1/2 teaspoon paprika
1 quantity puff pastry (see page 542)

One Beat together the egg yolks, egg, sugar and about 1/4 teaspoon salt and strain into a clean bowl.

Two Brush two baking sheets with melted butter and place them in the refrigerator. In a bowl, combine the Parmesan, paprika, 1/2 teaspoon salt and some freshly ground black pepper.

Three On a lightly floured surface, roll out the puff pastry and trim to a 12-inch square. Cut the square in half, brush both halves lightly with the egg mixture and sprinkle with the Parmesan mixture.

Using the rolling pin, press the cheese mixture into the pastry. Carefully slide the pastry sheets onto the two baking sheets and refrigerate for 15 minutes.

Four Transfer the pastry sheets to a lightly floured surface and trim back to 12- x 6-inch rectangles. With the back of a knife, lightly mark each pastry into 2-inch-wide strips, parallel to the short ends. Sprinkle with a little water.

Five Fold the two outer strips of each sheet inwards over the next strip. Their non cheese undersides will now be on the top. Brush with a little water and fold over onto the next marked strips, brush with water again and fold into a neat stack. Transfer to a baking sheet and chill for 15 minutes. Cut the stacks crosswise into 1/4-inch slices and place them cut side down and well apart on the prepared baking sheets. Press to lightly flatten, then turn over and chill for 15 minutes.

Six Preheat the oven to 400°F. Bake the palm leaves for 8 minutes, or until golden and crisp. Transfer to a wire rack to cool.

CHEF'S TIPS *To make cheese straws, use the same ingredients and follow the method for steps 1–3. Cut the puff pastry sheets into 1/2-inch-wide strips and twist each several times to form a long, loose ringlet. Lay on the baking sheets and press both ends down firmly. Chill for about 15 minutes, then bake at 400°F for 12–15 minutes, or until golden. Immediately cut each straw into 4-inch pieces and transfer to a wire rack to cool.*

Cornish pasties

In the eighteenth and nineteenth centuries, Cornish pasties were eaten by miners as a complete meal. There was meat at one end and apple or jam at the other, with scrolled initials in the pastry to indicate the difference. This recipe is for smaller savory pasties that can be served as finger food.

Preparation time *35 minutes*
+ 30 minutes chilling
Total cooking time *30 minutes*
Makes 48

PASTRY
4 cups all-purpose flour
pinch of salt
³/4 cup unsalted butter, cut into cubes
and chilled
¹/4 cup lard, cut into cubes
and chilled
8 tablespoons water

FILLING
3 oz. potato, coarsely chopped
3 oz. rutabaga, coarsely chopped
1 tablespoon unsalted butter
¹/2 onion, finely chopped
4 oz. lean ground beef
2 oz. beef kidney, finely chopped,
optional

melted butter, for brushing
milk, for brushing

One To make the pastry, sift the flour and salt into a large bowl and add the butter and lard. Using fingertips, rub the butter and lard into the flour until the mixture resembles fine bread crumbs. Make a well, add 1 tablespoon of the water and mix with a pastry blender until small lumps form. Continue to add the tablespoons of water, making a different well for each one and only using the last tablespoon if necessary. When the mixture is in large lumps, pick up and lightly press together. Knead the pastry on a lightly floured surface until just smooth. Wrap in plastic wrap and chill in the refrigerator for 20 minutes. Brush two baking sheets with melted butter and set aside.

Two To make the filling, put the potato and rutabaga into a food processor and, using the pulse button, finely chop but do not purée. Melt the butter in a skillet, add the onion and cook gently for 4 minutes. Add the potato and rutabaga, increase the heat to medium and cook for 2 minutes, stirring occasionally, until just tender. Add the beef and kidney, increase the heat to high and fry, stirring constantly, for 5 minutes. Drain off the excess fat, season well with salt and pepper and allow to cool.

Three On a lightly floured surface, cut the pastry in half and roll out each half to ¹/8 inch thick. With a 2¹/2-inch biscuit cutter cut out about 24 rounds from each half of pastry, and place 1 teaspoon of the filling on one side, ¹/4 inch from the edge. Moisten the edge of the pastry with water and fold the unfilled side over to form a semicircle, pressing the edges together well to seal. Using a fork, press down on the edge of the pastries to form a decorative pattern. With the point of a knife, twist to make a small steam vent on top of each pastry and then lay them on the prepared baking sheets. Place in the refrigerator to chill for 10 minutes.

Four Preheat the oven to 400°F. Using a pastry brush, brush the top of the pasties with a little milk and bake in the oven for 15 minutes, or until the pasties are golden brown.

Corn and chicken fritters

Golden kernels of juicy sweet corn with the distinctive flavor of cilantro and soy sauce make these fritters irresistible.

Preparation time 20 minutes
+ refrigeration
Total cooking time 45 minutes
Makes about 65

2 eggs, lightly beaten
2 x 14 oz. cans corn kernels,
well drained
¼ cup cornstarch
12 oz. skinned, boneless chicken
breast halves, finely chopped
2 tablespoons chopped·
fresh cilantro
1 tablespoon sugar
1 tablespoon soy sauce
oil, for frying

One In a large bowl, combine the eggs, corn kernels, cornstarch, chicken, cilantro, sugar and soy sauce and mix well. Cover and allow to chill in the refrigerator for at least 1 hour, or overnight if possible.

Two In a large skillet, heat ⅛ inch of oil. Using a tablespoon, drop in enough corn mixture to make 1¼-inch rounds, taking care not to crowd the pan. Fry the fritters for 3 minutes, or until they are golden, then turn over to brown the other side. Remove and drain on crumpled paper towels.

Three Repeat with the remaining mixture, adding more oil to the pan when necessary. Serve the fritters warm.

CHEF'S TIPS *Make the first fritter a small one, taste to check the seasoning and, if necessary, add salt and pepper to the mixture before cooking the rest.*

These fritters are delicious topped with some plain yogurt and a drizzle of sweet chile sauce.

Colcannon and smoked chicken canapés

These delicious appetizers of smoked chicken and cranberry chutney have an Irish twist with a filling of buttery potatoes and cabbage.

Preparation time 35 minutes
+ 30 minutes refrigeration
Total cooking time 45 minutes
Makes 24

PASTRY
1²/₃ cups all-purpose flour
¹/₄ teaspoon salt
2²/₃ tablespoons unsalted butter, cut
into cubes and chilled
2 egg yolks
3 tablespoons water

COLCANNON
1 medium or 2 small baking potatoes
³/₄ cup cabbage
1 tablespoon oil
¹/₂ small onion, finely chopped
¹/₃ cup smoked chicken,
finely chopped

CRANBERRY CHUTNEY
¹/₃ cup cranberries, fresh or frozen
2 teaspoons light brown sugar
2 teaspoons white wine vinegar

One Brush 24 mini-muffin cups or mini-tart pans, 1¹/₄ inches across and ⁵/₈ inch deep, with some melted butter.

Two To make the pastry, sift together the flour and salt into a large bowl. Using your fingertips, rub the butter into the flour until the mixture resembles fine bread crumbs. Make a well in the center and add the egg yolks and water. Work the mixture together with a flexible bladed knife until it forms a rough ball. Turn out onto a lightly floured work surface, form into a ball and cover with plastic wrap. Chill in the refrigerator for 20 minutes.

Three Preheat the oven to 325°F. Roll out the dough between 2 sheets of waxed paper to a thickness of ¹/₈ inch. Using a biscuit cutter slightly larger than the muffin cups, cut out 24 rounds. Place a round in each cup, pressing down on the bottom so that the dough extends slightly above the edge of the cups. Place in the refrigerator to chill for about 10 minutes. Lightly prick the bottom of the pastry and bake for 12–15 minutes, or until lightly browned, then cool completely before use.

Four To make the colcannon, place the potatoes in a saucepan of salted, cold water, cover and bring to a boil. Reduce the heat and simmer for 15–20 minutes, or until the potatoes are fork tender. Drain, return to the saucepan and shake over low heat for 1–2 minutes to remove excess moisture. Mash or push through a fine strainer into a bowl and season with salt and black pepper.

Five Place the cabbage in a saucepan of salted, cold water and bring to a boil. Blanch for 1 minute, then remove the cabbage and finely chop. Heat the oil in a frying pan, add the onions and cook for 1 minute over high heat, stirring occasionally. Add the potatoes and cabbage and stir to combine with the onions. Cook over medium heat for 10 minutes, or until the mixture has a caramelized appearance, then add the chicken, season with salt and black pepper and keep warm.

Six To make the cranberry chutney, place the cranberries, sugar, vinegar and 1 tablespoon water in a small saucepan. Bring slowly to a boil, stirring to dissolve the sugar, then raise the heat to medium and simmer for 5–10 minutes, or until the mixture is almost dry and is thick and reduced. Remove from the heat and set aside.

Seven Fill the cooled tart shells with a teaspoon of the colcannon and top with a small amount of the chutney. Arrange on a platter and serve warm or cold.

Puff pastry with asparagus and mushrooms

Ideal for serving with drinks or as a brunch dish, these crisp pastries are filled with subtle flavors that come together harmoniously in a creamy sauce. If you don't have time to make your own puff pastry, use 2 sheets of frozen puff pastry, thawed.

Preparation time *30 minutes*
+ 20 minutes chilling
Total cooking time *25 minutes*
Makes 6

15 asparagus spears, trimmed
1 quantity puff pastry (see page 542)
1 egg, beaten
3 tablespoons unsalted butter
1/4 cup all-purpose flour
1 cup milk
1/4 cup crème fraîche or
whipping cream
2³/4 cups thickly sliced button or
oyster mushrooms
melted butter, for brushing

One Bring a saucepan of salted water to a boil. Tie the asparagus into a bundle and cook for 4 minutes, or until tender, following the method in the Chef's techniques on page 535. Refresh, drain well and set aside.

Two Roll out the pastry on a lightly floured surface to make a rectangle about 12 x 8 inches. With a large sharp knife, trim to straighten the two long sides and cut into two long strips. Now cut each strip into three diamonds or squares. Place them slightly apart on a damp baking sheet and chill for 20 minutes.

Three Meanwhile, preheat the oven to 400°F. Brush the top surface of the pastry with the beaten egg. Do not brush the edges of the pastry because the egg will set and prevent the pastry from rising. Lightly score the tops of the pastry shapes in a crisscross pattern with a thin knife. Bake for about 10 minutes, or until well risen, crisp and golden. Split in half horizontally with a sharp knife. Scrape out and discard any soft dough.

Four Melt 2 tablespoons of the butter in a saucepan, add the flour and cook for 1 minute over low heat. Remove from the heat, pour in the milk and blend thoroughly with a wooden spoon or whisk. Return to low-medium heat, stir briskly until boiling and simmer for 2 minutes, stirring constantly. Add the crème fraîche or cream and stir over the heat for another minute. Remove from the stove and cover with foil. In a skillet, melt the remaining butter and toss the mushrooms over medium heat for 2 minutes, or until cooked. Trim the asparagus tips to 2½-inch pieces and reserve. Cut the remainder of the tender spears into ³/4-inch lengths. Add the mushrooms and small pieces of asparagus to the sauce and mix briefly.

Five To assemble the pastries, spoon the warm sauce onto the six pastry bottoms and place the asparagus tips on top. Brush them with a little melted butter and replace the pastry lids. Warm through in the oven at 325°F for 5 minutes before serving.

CHEF'S TIPS *The pastry can be baked, split and scraped out the day before. Reheat in a 300°F oven before adding the filling.*

Note that you may have a little of the mushroom mixture left over after filling the pastries, depending on the size of asparagus you use. This is delicious eaten on toast as a snack.

Potato and smoked fish croquettes

*These deliciously crisp, golden brown potato croquettes are
flavored with smoked fish and garlic. They can be served
with tomato sauce, garlic mayonnaise or salsa.*

Preparation time 30 minutes
+ 15 minutes chilling
Total cooking time 45 minutes
Makes 40

1 lb. baking potatoes, such as
Idaho or russet
1 tablespoon unsalted butter
1 egg yolk
pinch of ground nutmeg
1 tablespoon olive oil
2 cloves garlic, crushed
1/3 cup whipping cream
5 oz. smoked haddock, trout or
salmon, bones removed, crumbled or
thinly sliced
1/2 cup all-purpose flour
3 eggs, beaten
1 tablespoon peanut oil
2 cups fresh bread crumbs
oil, for deep-frying

One Cut the peeled potatoes into uniform pieces for even cooking. Place them in a medium saucepan, cover with cold water and add a large pinch of salt. Bring to a boil, lower the heat and simmer for at least 20 minutes, or until they are quite tender.

Two Drain the potatoes and dry them by shaking them in their pan over a low heat. Press them through a sieve or finely mash and add the butter, egg yolk, nutmeg and some salt and pepper. Place the mixture into a large bowl to cool.

Three Heat the olive oil in a saucepan, add the garlic and cook for 1 minute to soften. Stir in the cream and simmer until reduced by half. Add the fish to the potato mixture with the reduced cream. Season with salt and pepper and mix to combine well.

Four Season the flour with salt and pepper and place in a shallow dish. Place the beaten eggs and peanut oil into a shallow bowl and the bread crumbs onto a large piece of waxed paper. Shape the potato mixture into ovals about 1 1/2 x 3/4 inches in size and roll each one carefully in the flour, patting off the excess. Dip them in the egg mixture, then drain off the excess and roll them in the bread crumbs, lifting the edges of the paper to help the bread crumbs fully coat the croquettes. Sometimes it is necessary to coat the croquettes twice in the egg and bread crumbs, especially if your mixture is a little too soft to hold its shape well. Chill in the refrigerator for 15 minutes.

Five Heat the oil in a deep-fat fryer or deep saucepan (see Chef's techniques, page 537). Deep-fry, in batches, for 3–4 minutes, or until golden brown. Lift out, draining off excess oil, and drain on crumpled paper towels. Serve the croquettes with a sauce and lime wedges.

CHEF'S TIP *The potato must not be too wet or the moisture will cause the croquettes to split and absorb the oil. Using bread crumbs on a large piece of paper enables you to coat the croquettes without too much mess. Always shake off or press on excess bread crumbs or they will fall into the oil when frying, burn and then cling to the croquettes as unsightly specks.*

Blue cheese puffs

Any type of blue cheese, such as Stilton or the creamy Italian Dolcelatte, can be used to make these puffs. However, if you use the strong salty Roquefort cheese, omit the salt in the recipe.

Preparation time 10 minutes
Total cooking time 25 minutes
Makes about 55

CREAM PUFF PASTRY
⅓ cup unsalted butter
¾ cup bread or all-purpose flour
2 eggs, beaten

3 oz. blue cheese, crumbled or mashed
pinch of dry mustard, optional
oil, for deep-frying
fresh chives, finely chopped, to garnish

One To make the cream puff pastry, melt the butter and ¾ cup water in a large saucepan over low heat, then add the flour and eggs, following the method in the Chef's techniques on page 545. Stir in the blue cheese and season to taste with salt, freshly ground black pepper and the dry mustard if desired.

Two Heat the oil in a deep-fat fryer or deep saucepan (see Chef's techniques, page 537). Using two lightly oiled teaspoons, scoop out a small amount of the mixture with one and push off with the other spoon to carefully lower into the hot oil. Cook the mixture in batches until puffed, golden brown and crisp, turning with a long-handled metal spoon to ensure even coloring. Drain on crumpled paper towels.

Three Sprinkle the warm puffs lightly with the chives and serve immediately.

CHEF'S TIPS *The puff mixture can be prepared in advance, covered with plastic wrap and refrigerated for a few hours before deep-frying.*

Dolcelatte is sometimes known as Gorgonzola dolce.

soups

Vichyssoise

*This creamy chilled leek and potato soup is an American
"down-home" favorite developed from the classic
French version. It can also be served hot.*

Preparation time *25 minutes
+ 2 hours chilling*
Total cooking time *40 minutes*
Serves 4

*2 tablespoons unsalted butter
3 large leeks, white part only, thinly
sliced
1 stalk celery, thinly sliced
2 small potatoes, cut into small cubes
1 quart chicken stock (see page 519)
¾ cup whipping cream
1 tablespoon chopped fresh chives*

One Place the butter in a large saucepan
and melt over low heat. Add the leeks
and celery and cover with buttered
parchment paper. Cook the vegetables,
without allowing to color and stirring
occasionally, for 15 minutes, or until
they are soft.

Two Add the potatoes and stock and
season to taste with salt and freshly
ground black pepper.

Three Bring the soup to a boil, then
reduce heat and simmer for 15 minutes,
or until the potatoes become very soft.

Purée the soup in batches in a food
processor or blender, pour into a bowl,
stir in ½ cup of the whipping cream and
season with salt and pepper. Cover with
plastic wrap and allow to cool before
placing in the refrigerator to chill for at
least 2 hours.

Four Serve the soup in chilled bowls.
Softly whip the remaining ¼ cup of
cream and spoon onto the center of the
soup. Sprinkle with chives to garnish.

CHEF'S TIP *Instead of leeks, you can
use mild Bermuda or Spanish onions.*

LE CORDON BLEU ✠ COMPLETE COOK

French onion soup

Known in France as Soupe à l'oignon gratinée, *this onion soup has always been a very popular first course on cold winter's evenings in Paris.*

Preparation time 20 minutes
Total cooking time 1 hour 5 minutes
Serves 6

3 tablespoons unsalted butter
1 small red onion,
thinly sliced
3 white onions,
thinly sliced
1 clove garlic, finely chopped
3 tablespoons all-purpose flour
3/4 cup white wine
6 cups brown stock (see page 518)
or water
1 bouquet garni (see page 520)
1 tablespoon sherry

CROUTES
12 slices French baguette
1 1/2 cups finely grated
Gruyère cheese

One Melt the butter in a large heavy-bottomed saucepan over medium heat. Add the onions and cook for about 20 minutes, stirring often, until caramelized and dark golden brown. This step is very important as the color of the onions at this stage will determine the color of the final soup. Stir in the garlic and the flour and cook, stirring constantly, for 1–2 minutes.

Two Add the white wine and stir the mixture until the flour has blended in smoothly. Bring to a boil slowly, stirring constantly. Whisk or briskly stir in the stock or water, add the bouquet garni and season to taste with salt and freshly ground black pepper. Simmer gently for 30 minutes, then skim the surface of any excess fat if necessary. Add the sherry to the soup and adjust the seasoning to taste.

Three To make the croûtes, toast the bread slices under the broiler until dry and golden on both sides.

Four Ladle the soup into warm flame-proof bowls and float a few croûtes on top of each. Sprinkle the top of each soup with Gruyère cheese and place the bowls under a preheated broiler until the cheese melts and becomes golden brown. Serve the soup immediately.

CHEF'S TIP *The flour can be omitted if a lighter soup texture is desired.*

Cream of cauliflower soup

In France, this soup is known as Potage du Barry. *It is named
after a mistress of Louis XV of France, Comtesse du Barry, whose
name is mysteriously given to a number of dishes that contain cauliflower.*

***Preparation time** 25 minutes*
***Total cooking time** 35 minutes*
***Serves** 4*

1/2 small cauliflower, chopped
1 tablespoon unsalted butter
1 small onion, finely chopped
*1 small leek, white part only,
thinly sliced*
1 tablespoon all-purpose flour
3 cups milk

GARNISH
3/4 cup small cauliflower florets
*1/3 cup clarified butter
(see page 520) or oil*
4 slices bread, cut into cubes
1/4 cup whipping cream
chopped fresh chervil, to garnish

One Put the cauliflower in a large saucepan with 1/2 cup water. If the cauliflower is not completely covered by the water, add milk to cover. Bring to a boil, reduce the heat and simmer for 7 minutes, or until soft. Purée the cauliflower and cooking liquid together in a blender or food processor until smooth.

Two In a medium saucepan, melt the butter over low heat. Add the onion and leek, cover with a buttered piece of parchment paper or a lid and cook the vegetables for 5 minutes, or until they are soft but not colored. Add the flour and cook for at least 1 minute, stirring constantly, until pale blond in color. Remove from the heat, add the milk, stirring until the mixture is smooth, then return to the heat and bring to a boil, stirring constantly. Add the purée of cauliflower to the saucepan and season. Remove from the heat, cover and keep to one side.

Three To make the garnish, bring a small saucepan of salted water to a boil and cook the cauliflower florets for about 2 minutes, then refresh in cold water. Drain well in a colander or strainer and set aside.

Four Heat a skillet with the clarified butter or oil over high heat. Add the bread cubes and fry, stirring gently, until golden brown. Remove, drain on crumpled paper towels and sprinkle with salt while warm to keep them crisp.

Five Reheat the soup, season with salt and freshly ground black pepper and pour into warmed serving bowls. Use the cream to thin the soup if the texture is too thick. Alternatively, lightly whip the cream and then stir into the soup so that the swirls show as streaks through it. Sprinkle with the cauliflower florets, chervil and croutons to serve.

Cream of tomato soup

This soup is best made with fresh tomatoes that are in season and very ripe. The result is a soup with a beautifully sweet tomato flavor.

Preparation time 15 minutes
Total cooking time 35 minutes
Serves 6

2 tablespoons olive oil
1 onion, sliced
2 cloves garlic, chopped
3 large stems of fresh basil
1 sprig of fresh thyme
1 bay leaf
2½ tablespoons tomato paste
2 lb. very ripe tomatoes, quartered
pinch of sugar
1 cup chicken stock (see page 519)
⅓ cup whipping cream
fresh basil leaves, cut into thin strips,
to garnish

One Heat the oil in a large saucepan and gently cook the onion for 3 minutes, or until it is soft and translucent.

Two Add the garlic, basil stems, thyme, bay leaf, tomato paste and the fresh tomatoes. Season with the sugar, salt and black pepper. Pour in the chicken stock and bring to a boil, reduce the heat, cover and simmer for 15 minutes. Discard the bay leaf.

Three Purée in a blender or food processor and strain through a fine strainer. Return to the saucepan, stir in the cream and reheat gently without boiling. Check the seasoning.

Four Serve the soup in bowls or one large soup dish, garnishing the top with strips of basil.

CHEF'S TIP *If tomatoes are out of season and lack flavor, two 16-oz. cans of tomatoes can be used and will also give excellent results.*

Mussel soup

This is a delicious and delicate mussel velouté soup, lightly flavored with saffron and cooked in a sauce of white wine and fish stock.

Preparation time 35 minutes
+ 10 minutes soaking
Total cooking time 30 minutes
Serves 4

2¹/₂ lb. mussels in shells
3 tablespoons unsalted butter
1 stalk celery, finely chopped
4 shallots, thinly sliced
¹/₂ cup chopped fresh parsley
1¹/₄ cups dry white wine
1¹/₄ cups fish stock (see page 519)
1¹/₂ cups whipping cream
2 large pinches of saffron threads
1¹/₂ tablespoons all-purpose flour
3 tablespoons unsalted butter, cut into cubes and chilled
2 egg yolks
fresh chervil leaves,
to garnish

One Scrub the mussels well (see page 523). Using a blunt knife, scrape off any barnacles and trim away the hairy beard on the straight side. Discard any mussels that remain open when tapped gently on a work surface.

Two Melt 2 tablespoons of butter in a large saucepan and gently cook the celery and shallots until soft but not brown. Add the mussels, parsley and wine. Cover and simmer for 4 minutes, or until the mussels have opened. Take the mussels out of the saucepan and reserve the cooking liquid. Throw away any mussels that have not opened and remove the mussels from the shells of those that have opened.

Three Strain the reserved liquid and simmer to reduce by half. Add the fish stock and 1¹/₄ cups of the cream and simmer. Add the saffron and black pepper to taste. Combine the remaining 1 tablespoon of butter and the flour together in a bowl and whisk into the soup. Simmer the soup to cook the flour and then add the chilled butter, shaking the saucepan until it has blended in.

Four Mix the egg yolks and the rest of the cream together in a bowl, pour in a little hot soup and then add to the saucepan. Do not allow it to boil, simply warm the soup or the yolks will become small scrambled pieces.

Five Add the mussels to the soup to heat them through. Serve garnished with some fresh chervil leaves.

CHEF'S TIP *The mussels must be alive when cooked. They deteriorate quickly and if, before cooking, they remain open even when they are tapped on the work bench, they are not alive and should not be used.*

Lobster bisque

Smooth, creamy bisques are thought to have their origins in Spain. In the province of Biscay they were originally made with pigeons or quail before shellfish took over as the main ingredient in the seventeenth century.

Preparation time 30 minutes
Total cooking time 30 minutes
Serves 4

1 large or 2 small uncooked lobsters,
1¹/2 lb. total
2 tablespoons olive oil
¹/2 carrot, cut into cubes
¹/2 onion, cut into cubes
¹/2 small celery stalk,
cut into cubes
2¹/2 tablespoons brandy
²/3 cup dry white wine
4 large tomatoes, peeled, seeded
and quartered (see page 534)
1 bouquet garni (see page 520)
6 cups fish stock (see page 519)
¹/2 cup rice flour
2 egg yolks
1 tablespoon whipping cream
1 teaspoon finely chopped fresh
tarragon

One If you have bought live lobsters, kill them according to the method in the Chef's techniques on page 524. If you prefer not to do this, ask your fish merchant to do it for you.

Two Prepare the lobster following the method in the Chef's techniques on page 525. Heat the oil in a large saucepan, add the lobster pieces in their shell and stir for 2 minutes over high heat. Add the carrot, onion and celery, reduce the heat and cook for 2 minutes.

Three Add the brandy and immediately ignite at arm's length, then allow the flames to subside or cover with a lid. Pour in the wine and stir to blend in any sticky juices from the saucepan bottom. Add the tomatoes, bouquet garni and stock and bring to a boil.

Four Using a slotted spoon, remove the lobster pieces from the stock, roughly break into small pieces with a knife and return to the saucepan with the rice flour. Stir to combine, bring to a boil and simmer for 10 minutes.

Five Pass the soup through a fine strainer, pressing the solids with the back of a spoon to extract the juices, then discard the contents of the strainer, pour the liquid into a clean saucepan and season with salt and pepper. The bisque should just coat the back of a spoon. If not, bring to a boil and simmer to reduce.

Six Mix the egg yolks and cream together in a bowl, stir in about ¹/2 cup of the hot bisque, then pour back into the saucepan. Check the seasoning and then reheat for 5 minutes, stirring continuously, without boiling. Sprinkle with the tarragon and serve in warm bowls or a soup tureen.

Scotch broth

*This warming Scottish soup is sometimes served as two courses,
the unstrained broth followed by the tender meat. Traditionally made
with mutton, it is now more often made with lamb.*

Preparation time *30 minutes*
+ 1–2 hours soaking
Total cooking time *1 hour 30 minutes*
Serves 4

2 tablespoons medium pearl barley
12 oz. boneless lamb shoulder
2 tablespoons unsalted butter
1 small carrot, finely diced
1/2 small turnip, finely diced
1 small leek, finely diced
1/2 small onion, finely diced
1/3 cup frozen green peas
1/2 cup chopped fresh parsley,
to garnish

One Place the barley in a bowl, cover well with cold water and allow to soak for 1–2 hours. Drain the barley and rinse under cold running water. Bring a saucepan of water to a boil, add the barley and cook for 15 minutes, or until tender. Drain the barley and set aside.

Two Trim any excess fat from the meat, then cut the meat into small cubes. Half-fill a medium saucepan with salted water and bring to a boil. Add the lamb and cook for 2 minutes, then drain and plunge the lamb into a bowl of cold water. This process will give clarity to the soup and further remove traces of fat. Rinse the pan, half-fill with salted water once more and bring to a boil. Add the meat, reduce the heat and simmer for 30–40 minutes, or until the meat is tender. Strain, reserving the meat, and measure the cooking liquid to 1 quart, adding extra water if necessary.

Three Place the butter in a large saucepan and melt over medium heat. Add the diced vegetables to the saucepan and cook, stirring often, until tender but not colored. Drain the vegetables and wipe out the saucepan with paper towels. Replace the vegetables, then mix in the lamb, barley and peas. Add the measured stock and bring to a boil. Reduce the heat and simmer for 30 minutes, while frequently skimming the surface to remove excess fat and impurities. Season to taste. Serve with a sprinkling of parsley.

Chicken consommé

A consommé is a classic clear soup made from meat, chicken or fish stock.
The name comes from the French word consommer, *meaning to finish or use up*
and is so called because all the goodness of the meat goes into the soup.

Preparation time *45 minutes*
Total cooking time *3 hours 15 minutes*
Serves 4

2¹/₂ lb. chicken drumsticks
8 oz. lean ground beef
1 teaspoon oil
1 small carrot, coarsely chopped
1 small leek, coarsely chopped
1 small stalk celery, coarsely chopped
1 small onion, halved
2 whole cloves, stuck into the onion
1 bouquet garni (see page 520)
1 teaspoon salt
6 peppercorns
2 egg whites

TO SERVE
1 tablespoon unsalted butter
¹/₂ small leek, white part only, cut
into julienne strips (see Chef's tips)
¹/₂ small carrot, cut into
julienne strips
¹/₂ stalk celery, cut into
julienne strips

One Preheat the oven to 400°F. Remove the skin from the drumsticks and discard. Scrape the meat from the bones, following the method in the Chef's techniques on page 530, place in a food processor and process until finely ground. Place the ground chicken and the beef in a bowl in the refrigerator. Coarsely chop the chicken bones, place in a roasting pan and bake for 30–40 minutes, or until well browned.

Two Heat the oil in a large stockpot, add the carrot, leek and celery and cook until lightly colored. Set aside. Heat a cast-iron or stainless steel skillet and add the onion, cut side down. Cook over medium heat until the onion has blackened.

Three Place the bones, carrot, leek, celery, onion, bouquet garni, salt and peppercorns in a large stockpot and cover with 2 quarts cold water. Add the egg whites to the ground meat and mix with a wooden spoon, then add 2 cups water and mix well. Add to the stockpot and mix well. Place the stockpot over medium heat and bring slowly to a boil, stirring every 2 minutes. Reduce the heat and allow to gently simmer for 2 hours. Line a fine strainer with cheesecloth and place over a clean saucepan. Gently ladle the consommé into the strainer and strain into the saucepan.

Four To serve, melt the butter in a small skillet. Add the julienned vegetables along with a pinch of salt and cook, covered, over low heat about 10 minutes,

or until the vegetables are cooked but still firm. Strain and pat dry to remove the excess butter, then place in four soup bowls and pour in the hot consommé.

CHEF'S TIPS *Julienne strips are even-size strips of vegetables the size and shape of matchsticks. They cook quickly, are simple to prepare and make attractive decorations for any dish. The strips may be cut into whatever length is desired.*

To remove the maximum amount of fat from the soup, the consommé is best made a day in advance and kept refrigerated overnight, or until the excess fat solidifies on the surface. Simply skim off the fat before reheating the consommé over a saucepan of gently simmering water.

Borscht

This vegetarian version is based on a recipe from the Ukraine, where Borscht is the national soup. It is characterized by its thickness and the deep red color of its main ingredient—beets.

Preparation time 40 minutes
Total cooking time 45 minutes
Serves 6

1 tablespoon tomato paste
1 lb. fresh beets, cut into julienne
strips (see Chef's tip)
1 carrot, cut into julienne strips
2 small parsnips, cut into
julienne strips
4 stalks celery, cut into julienne strips
1 onion, finely chopped
2 cloves garlic
4½ cups coarsely shredded green
cabbage
6 ripe tomatoes, peeled, seeded and
coarsely chopped (see page 534)
½ cup finely chopped fresh parsley
½ cup all-purpose flour
½ cup sour cream
sugar, optional

One Bring 3 quarts of water to a boil in a large saucepan and season with salt and pepper. Add the tomato paste, beets, carrot, parsnips and celery, stir well and simmer for 15 minutes. Add the onion, garlic and shredded cabbage and simmer for an additional 15 minutes.

Two Check the soup for seasoning. Add the tomatoes, simmer for 5 minutes and stir in the parsley. Thicken the soup by mixing the flour and sour cream, then stirring into the soup over low heat until well combined. Do not allow to boil.

Three Borscht should be slightly piquant, but not sweet—add salt and sugar if necessary. This is best made a day in advance and reheated just before serving.

CHEF'S TIP *Julienne strips are vegetables cut to the size and shape of matchsticks.*

Celery root and Stilton soup

*Celery root tastes like a sweeter and more nutty version
of celery and is partnered here with Stilton.*

Preparation time *5 minutes*
Total cooking time *40 minutes*
Serves 4

2 tablespoons oil or unsalted butter
1 onion, sliced
*1/2 small celery root, peeled and
thinly sliced*
3 oz. Stilton cheese, crumbled
fresh watercress, to garnish

One In a large saucepan, heat the oil or
butter and add the onion. Cover the
saucepan and cook over low heat until
the onion is translucent. Add the celery
root and 1 quart water, cover and bring
to a boil. Reduce the heat and simmer
for 30 minutes, or until the celery root is
very soft.

Two Add 2 oz. of the Stilton and purée
the mixture in a blender or food
processor. Return the soup to a clean

saucepan and reheat gently. Season with
salt and pepper to taste, bearing in mind
that Stilton can be very salty.

Three Serve with the remaining cheese
crumbled over the surface. Garnish with
watercress and black pepper.

CHEF'S TIP *Celery root discolors when
it is peeled, so if preparing in advance,
place in a bowl, cover with water and
add a tablespoon of lemon juice.*

Bouillabaisse

Fishermen in Marseilles made this fragrant soup using fish that were difficult to sell. These were tossed into a simmering pot, hence the name bouillabaisse, from bouillir *(to boil) and* abaisser *(to reduce). You can use any combination of the fish below in the soup and increase the amount of one fish if another is not available.*

Preparation time 3 hours
Total cooking time 1 hour 10 minutes
Serves 4–6

1 lb. John Dory or turbot, bones
removed and reserved (see page 526)
1 lb. sole, bones removed and reserved
1 lb. monkfish, bones removed and
reserved
1 lb. halibut, bones removed and
reserved
1 lb. conger eel, cut into pieces,
or 12 littleneck clams, well-washed,
or 12 sea scallops
⅓ cup olive oil
2 cloves garlic, finely chopped
pinch of saffron threads
1 each carrot, bulb fennel and leek
(white part only), cut into
julienne strips (see Chef's tip)
24 thin slices French baguette, for
croûtes
3 cloves garlic, halved, for croûtes
chopped fresh basil, to garnish

SOUP
1 small leek, onion and bulb fennel,
thinly sliced
1 stalk celery, thinly sliced
2 cloves garlic
2 tablespoons tomato paste
2 cups white wine
pinch of saffron threads
2 sprigs of fresh thyme
1 bay leaf
4 sprigs of fresh parsley

ROUILLE SAUCE
1 egg yolk
1 tablespoon tomato paste
3 cloves garlic, crushed into a paste
pinch of saffron threads
1 cup olive oil
½ lb. baked potato

One Season the seafood with salt and black pepper and toss with half the oil, the garlic, saffron, carrot, fennel and leek. Cover and refrigerate until needed.

Two To make the soup, heat the remaining oil in a stockpot over high heat, add the reserved bones and cook for 3 minutes. Stir in the leek, onion, fennel, celery and garlic and cook for 2 minutes, then mix in the tomato paste and cook for 2 minutes. Pour in the white wine and simmer for 5 minutes. Finally, add 4 cups water, the saffron and herbs and simmer for 20 minutes.

Three Ladle the stock in batches into a strainer over a bowl. Gently press the solids with the ladle to extract all the liquid, then discard the solids. Put the soup in a saucepan and simmer for 15 minutes until slightly thickened, skimming off any scum on the surface.

Four To make the rouille, whisk the egg yolk in a small bowl with the tomato paste, garlic, saffron and some salt and

black pepper. Continue to whisk while slowly pouring the oil into the mixture. Press the flesh of the potato through a sieve and whisk into the sauce.

Five Lightly toast the baguette slices under a preheated broiler, cool, then rub both sides with the cut sides of the half cloves of garlic to make garlic croûtes.

Six Cut each fish fillet into 6 pieces and add to a large pot with the eel, clams or scallops and julienned vegetables. Pour the hot soup over and simmer for 7 minutes, or until the fish is cooked. Remove the fish and vegetables and place them in a large earthenware or metal dish.

Seven Whisk 3 tablespoons of the rouille into the soup to thicken it a bit, then pour the soup over the fish and sprinkle with the basil. Serve with the garlic croûtes and the remaining rouille.

CHEF'S TIP *Julienne strips are vegetables cut to the size and shape of matchsticks.*

about saffron...

Threads of saffron, the world's most expensive spice, are the red stigmas of a type of crocus. The use of saffron is traditional in bouillabaisse—it adds both color and an earthy fragrance to the broth. The best quality saffron comes from either Spain, Iran or Kashmir. It is always expensive and is usually packaged in small boxes or jars.

Cream of asparagus soup

*Asparagus is one of the most delicious of the spring vegetables.
In this simple soup, which can be served hot or cold,
the flavor of the asparagus comes to the fore.*

Preparation time *15 minutes*
Total cooking time *20 minutes*
Serves 4

*1½–1¾ lb. green or
white asparagus
2 cups chicken stock (see page 519)
1 cup plus 4 teaspoons
whipping cream
pinch of sugar
4 teaspoons cornstarch
1–2 tablespoons water or milk
2 tablespoons chopped fresh chervil,
to garnish*

One Peel and discard the tough skin from the bottom of the asparagus and trim the thick ends. Wash and drain. Cut off the tips 1¼ inches down the asparagus and set aside. Slice the spears into thin rounds. Bring a saucepan of salted water to a boil, add the asparagus tips and simmer briefly for 2 minutes. Drain and place in a bowl of iced water to stop them from cooking further.

Two Add the chicken stock and 1 cup of the whipping cream to a large saucepan with the sugar and some salt and pepper and bring to a boil. Add the sliced asparagus to the saucepan and cook gently for 10 minutes.

Three Purée in a food processor or blender, then pass through a fine strainer. Return the mixture to a clean saucepan and heat again. In a small bowl, mix the cornstarch with the water or milk until it forms a smooth paste. Pour a little hot asparagus mixture into the paste. Blend, return to the saucepan, and bring to a boil, stirring constantly. This procedure ensures a lump-free result when using a dry, starchy powder

to thicken a hot liquid. Season to taste with salt and black pepper.

Four Pour the soup into a dish or individual bowls. Swirl 1 teaspoon of cream in the center of each, arrange some asparagus tips on top and sprinkle with the chervil.

Cream of vegetable soup

You can use different vegetables for this soup depending on the season. This is a thick, winter version, but a spring vegetable soup is also delicious.

Preparation time *15 minutes*
Total cooking time *1 hour*
Serves 6

⅓ cup unsalted butter
2 potatoes, cut into cubes
1 carrot, cut into cubes
½ onion, cut into cubes
2 small leeks, white part only, thinly sliced
1 stalk celery, thinly sliced
1 bouquet garni (see page 520)
¾ cup whipping cream
chopped fresh chervil or parsley, to garnish

One Heat the butter in a saucepan, add the vegetables, cover, and cook over low heat until soft. Add the bouquet garni. Pour on 6 cups water, boil, reduce the heat and simmer for 30 minutes. Remove and discard the bouquet garni.

Two Purée the soup, in batches, in a blender or food processor, then strain into a clean saucepan and cook over low heat for 10 minutes.

Three Add the whipping cream and season with salt and pepper. Serve very hot, sprinkled with the chervil or parsley and accompanied by crusty bread.

New England clam chowder

Clams are very popular on the east coast, where they are caught in the coastal waters and eaten raw or cooked the same day. Make sure the clams you use for this chowder are very fresh.

***Preparation time** 40 minutes*
+ 30 minutes soaking
***Total cooking time** 1 hour 15 minutes*
Serves 4

2 lb. quahog or large clams
1 tablespoon unsalted butter
3 tablespoons all-purpose flour
2 cups white wine
1 bay leaf
2 sprigs of fresh thyme
1 tablespoon oil
3 oz. slab bacon, rind removed and cut into cubes
1 onion, chopped
2 stalks celery, sliced
1 small potato, cut into small cubes
3/4 cup whipping cream
1 teaspoon shredded fresh flat-leaf parsley

One Rinse the clams under running water two or three times to remove as much grit as possible. Drain.

Two Melt the butter in a large saucepan over low heat. Add the flour and mix with a whisk or a wooden spoon and cook for 3 minutes. Remove from the heat and allow to cool.

Three Add the white wine, bay leaf and thyme to a large stockpot, bring to a boil and cook for 5 minutes over medium heat. Add the washed clams, cover and simmer for 5–7 minutes, or until the clams have opened. Strain the clams over a bowl, keeping the cooking liquid for later, and discard any clams that did not open. Set the remaining clams aside to cool. Once cooled, remove the clam meat from their shells, chop up and set aside.

Four Strain the cooking liquid again through a fine strainer into the pan with the butter and flour mixture. Whisk together, place over medium heat and simmer for 10 minutes, skimming the surface twice, and then set aside.

Five In a large stockpot, heat the oil over medium heat and cook the bacon for 5 minutes, or until nicely colored. Reduce the heat, add the onion, cover and cook, without allowing the onion to color, for 3 minutes. Add the celery and cook, covered, for 6 minutes, then add the potato and cook, covered, for 3 minutes. Pour in the thickened clam liquid, cover and simmer for 15–20 minutes, or until the potatoes are tender. Add the chopped clams and the cream and simmer for 5 minutes. Serve the soup sprinkled with the shredded parsley.

CHEF'S TIP *Shellfish can contain lots of sand and grit. Always rinse several times, using lots of running water.*

Shrimp bisque

*The original bisque was a crayfish purée, thickened with bread.
Today, all kinds of shellfish are used and the soup is usually finished
with fresh cream. The result is a rich and elegant soup.*

Preparation time *35 minutes*
Total cooking time *1 hour*
Serves 6

1¼ lb. small cooked shrimp, shells on
2 tablespoons unsalted butter
1 small carrot, chopped
½ small onion, chopped
1 stalk celery, chopped
½ leek, chopped
1 tablespoon brandy
1 tablespoon tomato paste
2 ripe tomatoes, cut into quarters
3 sprigs of fresh tarragon
1 bouquet garni (see page 520)
⅔ cup white wine
1½ cups fish stock
(see page 519)
1¼ cups whipping cream
small pinch of cayenne pepper
3 tablespoons unsalted butter, cut into
cubes and chilled
1 teaspoon cornstarch (optional)
fresh chopped dill,
to garnish

One Reserve 18 whole shrimp for decoration. Coarsely chop the remainder with the shells.

Two Heat the butter in a large saucepan and add the carrot, onion, celery and leek. Cover and cook over low heat until the vegetables are soft, but not colored. Add the chopped shrimp and their shells and cook gently for 5 minutes. Add the brandy and boil, scraping the bottom of the saucepan to pick up any sticky juices, then allow the liquid to evaporate. Add the tomato paste, tomatoes and tarragon and cook for 30 seconds, stirring constantly, then add the bouquet garni. Pour in the white wine and allow it to evaporate to a syrup before adding the fish stock and the cream. Bring to a boil, reduce the heat, cover and allow to simmer gently for 15–18 minutes.

Three Mix vigorously, then strain the mixture through a fine strainer. Check the seasoning, adding salt and cayenne pepper as desired. Mix in the chilled butter, shaking the saucepan until it has blended in. The soup will thicken as the liquid takes in the butter to form an emulsion.

Four If the bisque is not thick enough, mix the cornstarch with a little cold water and then gradually whisk this mixture into the hot bisque until the desired consistency has been achieved. If it is too thick, dilute with a little more fish stock.

Five Divide the reserved whole shrimp among six bowls, placing three in each bowl. Pour the soup over them and just before serving garnish with a little chopped dill.

Minestrone

Although there are many variations of this hearty soup, according to the region of origin and the season, it will always consist of vegetables and broth with the addition of pasta or rice.

Preparation time *45 minutes*
+ overnight soaking
Total cooking time *2 hours 20 minutes*
Serves 6–8

8 oz. dried beans, such as kidney beans or navy beans
5 oz. salt pork or belly bacon, diced
2 tablespoons olive oil
1 large onion, chopped
2 carrots, diced
2 potatoes, diced
1 stalk celery, diced
2 cloves garlic, chopped
1 tablespoon tomato paste
12 cups brown stock (see page 518) or water
1 bouquet garni (see page 520)
¼ head cabbage, finely sliced
1 cup dried macaroni or any small pasta
grated Parmesan cheese, to serve

One Cover the beans with cold water and allow to soak for 8 hours or overnight. Drain the beans and then place in a large saucepan with 8 cups water and simmer for 1½ hours, or until they are tender.

Two Meanwhile, place the salt pork or bacon in another saucepan and cover with cold water. Bring to a boil, strain and refresh in cold water. Spread on paper towels to dry.

Three In a large heavy-bottomed saucepan, heat the olive oil and lightly brown the salt pork or bacon over medium heat for 3 minutes. Add the onion, carrots, potatoes, celery and garlic, reduce the heat and cook for 5 minutes without coloring.

Four Add the tomato paste and cook for 3 minutes. Add the brown stock or water and simmer for 10 minutes, skimming any fat from the surface. Add the bouquet garni and cabbage and simmer for 5 minutes. Remove from the heat and set aside.

Five Drain the beans and add to the soup mixture. Return to the heat and simmer for 10 minutes. Add the pasta and cook for 15 minutes, or until the pasta is soft. Check the seasoning and remove the bouquet garni. Sprinkle the grated Parmesan over the top to serve.

Minted green pea soup with croutons

*Mint and green peas are a classic culinary partnership,
here they are puréed together into a deliciously fragrant
soup with a fairly light consistency.*

Preparation time *25 minutes*
Total cooking time *40 minutes*
Serves 4

*1 small butterhead lettuce, such as
Boston or Bibb, coarsely sliced
12 scallions or 1 small onion, sliced
3 cups frozen baby peas, thawed
1–2 sprigs of fresh mint
5 cups chicken stock (see page 519)
4 slices bread
oil, for cooking
2 tablespoons unsalted butter
¼ cup all-purpose flour
⅔ cup whipping cream*

One Put the lettuce, scallions or onion,
peas, mint and stock in a large saucepan.
Bring to a boil, then reduce the heat and
simmer for 25 minutes. Purée in batches
in a blender or food processor, then push
the liquid through a fine sieve.

Two Remove the crusts from the bread
and cut into small cubes. Heat the oil
and fry the cubes until lightly browned,
stirring to color evenly. Drain on
crumpled paper towels and salt lightly
while hot to keep them crisp.

Three Melt the butter in a large saucepan
over medium heat, stir in the flour and
cook for 1 minute without browning.
Remove from the heat, add the puréed
soup and mix well. Return to low to
medium heat and bring slowly to a boil,
stirring constantly. Add the cream and
season with salt and pepper. To serve,
put the croutons in bowl and pour the
soup over the top.

CHEF'S TIP *To vary the garnish, cook
¼ cup more baby peas and use them to
replace the croutons.*

Pumpkin soup

*The golden color and firm texture of pumpkins
makes them perfect in soups; and the citrus fruits
give a tangy taste to cut their sweet flavor.*

Preparation time *30 minutes*
Total cooking time *45 minutes*
Serves 6

1½–2 lb. pumpkin (see Chef's tip)
3 large potatoes, chopped
3 large tomatoes, halved and seeded
2–3 strips orange or lemon zest
5 cups chicken stock (see page 519),
vegetable stock or water
2 tablespoons long-grain rice
pinch of nutmeg
1 tablespoon unsalted butter, optional
¼ cup whipping cream

One Cut a wide circle around the pumpkin stem with a small, sharp, pointed knife, and remove the top. Using a large metal spoon, scrape out the seeds from the pumpkin and discard, then either scrape as much flesh as possible from the pumpkin with the spoon or cut the pumpkin into wedges. Slice just inside the skin to release the flesh and chop it roughly.

Two Place the pumpkin, potatoes, tomatoes and orange or lemon zest into a large saucepan with the stock or water. Season to taste. Bring to a boil, reduce the heat and simmer for 25–30 minutes, or until the potatoes are soft. Remove the orange or lemon zest and discard.

Three While the soup is simmering, add the rice to a saucepan of boiling salted water and bring to a boil. Cook for 12 minutes, or until tender. Drain the rice in a strainer and rinse in cold water. Set aside and allow to drain well.

Four Transfer the soup to a blender or food processor and purée until smooth. Return to a clean saucepan, add the nutmeg and adjust the seasoning. The soup should be thick, but drinkable from a spoon. If too thick, add a little milk. Stir in the rice, butter and cream, then heat through. Garnish with freshly ground black pepper and some herbs.

CHEF'S TIP *Pumpkin is a member of the gourd family, which also includes squash. If they are available, you can use other types of winter squash for this recipe such as buttercup, butternut or hubbard.*

LE CORDON BLEU ✣ COMPLETE COOK

Garlic and zucchini soup

*Two whole heads of garlic may seem a powerfully
large amount, but you will find it takes on
a mellow creaminess when cooked.*

Preparation time 35 minutes
Total cooking time 1 hour 15 minutes
Serves 4–6

olive oil, for cooking
1 onion, finely chopped
2 heads garlic, peeled and thinly sliced
2 potatoes, peeled and thinly sliced
8 cups chicken stock (see page 519)
or water
2 zucchini
1 tablespoon finely chopped fresh basil

One Heat 4 tablespoons of olive oil in a
large heavy-bottomed saucepan, add the
onion and garlic and cook over medium
heat for 5–10 minutes, or until golden
brown. Add the potatoes and cook for
2 minutes, stirring continuously. Add the
stock, season to taste and simmer for 30
minutes. Allow to cool a little.

Two Trim the ends from the zucchini.
Cut into quarters lengthwise, then cut
into short pieces. Set aside.

Three Purée the soup in a blender or food
processor until smooth. Return to the
saucepan and bring to a boil. Skim
any foam from the top if necessary,
then add the zucchini and cook for
20–25 minutes, or until the zucchini is
tender. Just before serving, stir in the
basil and adjust the seasoning. Serve
garnished with a few extra basil leaves.

Creamy garlic soup with black olive crostini

This unusual recipe has its roots in the garlic-based soups of the Mediterranean. The black olive crostini would also go beautifully with many of the other cream soups in this book.

***Preparation time** 20 minutes*
***Total cooking time** 45 minutes*
Serves 4

⅓ cup unsalted butter
2 heads garlic, peeled into
individual cloves
2 onions, finely chopped
3 small russet or baking potatoes,
cut into cubes
2 cups milk
2 cups chicken stock (see page 519)
or water

BLACK OLIVE CROSTINI
4 slices day-old French baguette
½ cup pitted and finely chopped
black olives
3 tablespoons olive oil

One Melt 2 tablespoons of the butter in a medium saucepan over medium heat. Add the garlic cloves and cook for 5–7 minutes, or until the garlic is golden in color. Add the onions, cook gently for 2–3 minutes, then add the potatoes and the remaining butter and continue to cook for 7–10 minutes, or until the onions begin to soften. Stir frequently to prevent the potatoes from sticking to the saucepan. Pour in the milk and stock or water, then cook gently for 15 minutes, or until the potatoes are very soft.

Two Purée the soup in batches in a food processor or blender. Return to the rinsed pan and season to taste with salt and freshly ground black pepper. Cover to keep warm and set aside.

Three To make the black olive crostini, toast the four slices of French baguette under the broiler until golden brown on both sides. Place the finely chopped olives in a small bowl and moisten with the oil to lightly bind. Season to taste and spread onto the crostini.

Four Ladle the soup into bowls and serve with the crostini.

Cream of chicken soup

This soup is quick and easy to prepare. It is based on a simple stock made from chicken wings, which can be ready in just 30 minutes. You could also make the more traditional stock from the Chef's techniques (see page 519).

Preparation time *10 minutes*
Total cooking time *50 minutes*
Serves 6

1 leek, coarsely chopped
1 small carrot, coarsely chopped
1 small onion, coarsely chopped
1 stalk celery, coarsely chopped
12 oz. chicken wings, disjointed
2 sprigs of fresh tarragon
1 bouquet garni (see page 520)
6 black peppercorns
1 whole clove
2 tablespoons unsalted butter
1/4 cup all-purpose flour
1 cup whipping cream
1 skinned, boneless chicken breast half
sprigs of fresh tarragon,
to garnish
2 egg yolks

One Place the leek, carrot, onion, celery, chicken wings, tarragon, bouquet garni, peppercorns and clove in a large saucepan. Pour in 6 cups water to cover and bring to a boil, then turn down the heat and simmer for 30–35 minutes. Skim frequently for a clear finish.

Two Pour the stock through a fine strainer and measure 1 quart of the liquid, reserving the rest. In a medium saucepan, melt the butter, add the flour and cook gently, stirring constantly, for 1 minute, or until a smooth paste is formed and the flour is cooked. Remove from the heat. Pour the 1 quart of hot stock into the cooled butter and flour mixture, a little at a time, and stir well between each addition. Return the saucepan to the heat and continue to stir until the mixture boils and thickens. Add 3/4 cup of the cream and return to a boil. Season to taste with salt and pepper.

Three Poach the chicken breast half for 8 minutes in enough of the reserved stock to just cover it. Drain and cut into small cubes. Remove the leaves from the remaining tarragon stems, put in boiling salted water and cook for 30 seconds, then drain. Mix the egg yolks with the rest of the cream and stir into the soup. Do not boil the mixture any further. Add the chicken cubes and sprinkle with some tarragon leaves and some freshly ground black pepper to garnish.

LE CORDON BLEU ✦ COMPLETE COOK

Seafood and lemon soup

Choose from a selection of local fresh or frozen shellfish to make this very elegant and refined dish. Savor the richness of the seafood married with the tang of refreshing lemon.

Preparation time 25 minutes
Total cooking time 20 minutes
Serves 6–8

12 oz. cockles or littleneck clams
1 lb. small mussels
12 oz. cherrystone or large clams
⅓ cup dry white wine
3 shallots, finely chopped
6 fresh or frozen sea scallops
2 small squid or calamari, cleaned
1 tablespoon oil
1¼ cups fish stock (see page 519)
⅓ cup whipping cream
1 tablespoon unsalted butter, cut into pieces and chilled
1 small carrot, cut into julienne strips (see Chef's tip)
1 stalk celery, cut into julienne strips
½ leek, cut into julienne strips
6–8 small cooked shrimp, shells removed (see page 522)
finely grated zest of 1 lemon
chopped fresh chervil or parsley, to garnish

One Wash the cockles, mussels (see page 523) and clams in lots of water and repeat twice. Be especially careful when washing the cockles as they can be very sandy and will need to be rinsed thoroughly. Place the shellfish in a large pot with the wine and shallots, bring the mixture slowly to a boil and cook for 2–3 minutes, or until the shells open. Discard any shells that do not open after this time. Lift the shellfish out of the cooking liquid, remove the flesh from the shells and set aside. You may need to wash any sandy cockles again.

Two Add the scallops to the cooking liquid and poach for 1–3 minutes, then remove and cut into small cubes. Cut the squid or calamari into small cubes and fry in a skillet with the hot oil, then drain on crumpled paper towels.

Three Pour the cooking liquid from the shellfish into a clean saucepan and add the fish stock and cream. Place over high heat and boil for 3–5 minutes, or until a very light sauce is obtained. Strain, then mix in the butter, shaking the saucepan until it has blended in.

Four Cook the carrot, celery and leek in salted boiling water for 3–4 minutes. Drain, refresh in cold water to stop the cooking, then drain again and add all the vegetables and seafood, including the shrimp, to the sauce to heat through. Mix in some of the lemon zest and check the seasoning, adding more zest to taste. Serve sprinkled with the fresh chervil or parsley.

CHEF'S TIP *Julienne strips are vegetables cut to the size and shape of matchsticks.*

about shellfish...

Shellfish such as cockles, clams and mussels must be bought from a reputable source. They should always be bought live and need considerable care and attention in both storage and cooking. Buy shellfish on the day you intend to cook them and throw any suspect ones away (tap them on the work bench; if they do not close they are not live).

Cream of mushroom soup

This soup combines wild and cultivated mushrooms to create a rich, complex flavor. Try using some of the new varieties becoming more widely available to create different flavors.

Preparation time 20 minutes
Total cooking time 30 minutes
Serves 6

6 oz. wild mushrooms, such as chanterelles, enoki, oyster, shiitake or porcini
30 small button mushrooms
2 tablespoons unsalted butter
4 shallots, finely chopped
2 cups chicken stock (see page 519)
1½ cups whipping cream
5–6 sprigs of fresh chervil
2 tablespoons unsalted butter, cut into pieces and chilled

One Place the wild mushrooms in a strainer and shake off some of the sand and dirt. Thoroughly clean by tossing them in a large bowl of water, but do not leave them in the water too long as they will absorb too much liquid. Lift out and thinly slice. Clean the button mushrooms by wiping with paper towels.

Two Melt the butter in a medium saucepan. Add the shallots and cook over low heat, covered, for 1–2 minutes. Add the mushrooms, cover and cook for 2–3 minutes. Pour the chicken stock and 1¼ cups whipping cream into the saucepan and season with salt and pepper. Add three or four chervil sprigs and simmer for 12–15 minutes.

Three Pour the soup into a blender or food processor and purée. Strain the purée into a clean saucepan, heat gently and toss in the chilled butter, shaking the saucepan until it has blended in. Season to taste with salt and black pepper.

Four Beat the remaining cream until it forms soft peaks and season well.

Five Pour the soup into bowls. Just before serving, use two soup spoons to shape neat oval quenelle-like shapes from the whipped cream and then place one cream quenelle on top of the soup in each bowl. Decorate with the remaining chervil.

CHEF'S TIPS *If the wild mushrooms are only available dried, use half the weight and then soak overnight in enough cold water to just cover. The soaking liquid has a strong flavor and is an excellent substitute for stock.*

Porcini are also known as cèpes.

LE CORDON BLEU COMPLETE COOK

Chicken, bacon and lentil soup

Lentils are excellent for thickening winter soups and are here partnered with chicken and the traditional bacon. Brown and green lentils have the best texture for soups, but yellow and red lentils can also be used.

***Preparation time** 40 minutes*
+ overnight soaking
***Total cooking time** 1 hour 40 minutes*
Serves 4

1²/₃ cups brown or
green lentils
1 x 3¹/₂ lb. chicken
3 tablespoons unsalted butter
3 oz. bacon, cut into cubes
1 carrot, sliced
1 small onion, sliced
1 stalk celery, sliced
1 bouquet garni (see page 520)
2 tablespoons oil
sprigs of flat-leaf parsley,
to garnish

One Soak the lentils in cold water overnight. Rinse and drain well.

Two Remove the skin from the chicken. Then remove the breast meat and set aside. Chop up the legs, wings and the carcass. In a large stockpot, melt the butter and add the bacon and chicken legs, wings and carcass and brown over medium heat for 7–10 minutes. When nicely colored, add the vegetables, bouquet garni, 3 quarts cold water and the lentils. Place back on the heat and allow to simmer for 1 hour, occasionally skimming the scum off the top.

Three Meanwhile, season the chicken breasts with salt and pepper and pan-fry in the oil over medium heat for 5 minutes on each side, or until they are cooked to a golden brown. Set aside to cool.

Four Take the chicken pieces out of the stockpot with tongs and remove the meat, discarding the bones. Place the chicken meat back in the stockpot and simmer for 15 minutes. Remove the bouquet garni, then purée the soup in a blender or food processor. Return to a clean saucepan over low heat and season with salt and freshly ground black pepper to taste.

Five Cut the cooled chicken into small cubes and add to the soup to heat through. Serve garnished with parsley.

CHEF'S TIP *To enrich the flavor of this soup, a few spoons of cream and butter can be mixed in just before serving.*

Fish soup

*French cuisine has a number of wonderful traditional fish soups,
making good use of fresh fish simmered with herbs and wine. This is
a light soup, but with a surprising depth of flavor.*

Preparation time 30 minutes
Total cooking time 1 hour
Serves 6

1 John Dory, porgy or sea bream, total
12 oz., filleted (see Chef's tip)
4 red mullet or sea bass, total
1¼ lb., filleted
2 halibut, sole, whiting or snapper,
total 12 oz., filleted
1 lb. fresh eel, filleted
3 tablespoons olive oil
1 small carrot, finely chopped
½ small onion, finely chopped
½ leek, cut into ¾-inch squares
3 cloves garlic, chopped
2 sprigs of fresh thyme
1 bay leaf
1 tablespoon tomato paste
1⅓ cups chopped fresh parsley
4 tomatoes, quartered and seeded
¾ cup white wine
¼ cup brandy
¾ cup whipping cream
2 large pinches of cayenne
pepper
2 large pinches of saffron threads

One Wash the fish and eel thoroughly.
Pat dry with paper towels and cut into
1¼–2-inch cubes. Cover and refrigerate
until ready to use.

Two Heat the olive oil in a saucepan, add
the carrot, onion, leek and garlic and
cook over low heat for 5 minutes. Add
the thyme sprigs, bay leaf and the
tomato paste. Mix well for 5 minutes.
Stir in the pieces of fish and eel and cook
for another 5 minutes. Add 2 quarts
water, the chopped parsley and tomatoes
and simmer for about 30 minutes. Pour
in the white wine and brandy and stir
over low heat for 2 minutes.

Three Pour the mixture through a fine
strainer and press hard to extract all the
liquid. Discard the solids. Pour the
liquid into a clean saucepan and heat
gently. Add the cream, cayenne pepper
and saffron and season to taste with salt
and pepper. Cook gently for 5 minutes.
Serve sprinkled with black pepper.

CHEF'S TIPS *Ask your fish merchant to
scale, gut, head and fillet the fish and to
skin and clean the eel.*

*If one kind of fish is not available,
increase the amount of another fish to
make up the quantities. Eel can be
replaced with a high-fat fish such as
mackerel, sturgeon or herring.*

Vegetable and saffron consommé

*This beautifully light consommé is very low in fat
and would make an elegant first course for those who
are watching their weight.*

Preparation time *30 minutes*
Total cooking time *1 hour 5 minutes*
Serves 6

CONSOMMÉ
1 onion, coarsely chopped
1 carrot, coarsely chopped
1 stalk celery, coarsely chopped
1/2 bulb fennel, coarsely chopped
1 leek, coarsely chopped
1 cup chopped button mushrooms
*2 ripe tomatoes, quartered, seeded and
chopped*
2 cloves garlic, halved
6 white peppercorns
small pinch of ground nutmeg
1 tablespoon finely grated orange zest
1 bouquet garni (see page 520)
2 large pinches of saffron threads

*1/2 small leek, cut into julienne strips
(see Chef's tip)*
*1/2 small carrot, cut into
julienne strips*
1/2 stalk celery, cut into julienne strips
*1 ripe tomato, peeled, seeded and
diced (see page 534)*
6 quail eggs
*chopped fresh chives and chervil,
to garnish*

One To make the consommé, put the
vegetables in a large saucepan with
6 cups of water. Add the garlic,
peppercorns, nutmeg, orange rind,
bouquet garni and a large pinch of salt.
Bring to a boil, cover and reduce the
heat to simmer gently for 45 minutes.

Two Push the stock through a fine
strainer and discard the vegetables.
Measure 1 quart of the stock, adding
water if necessary, and pour into a large,
clean saucepan. Add the saffron.

Three Add the julienned leek, carrot and
celery to a saucepan of boiling salted
water. Cook for 5 minutes, or until the
vegetables are tender, and then drain.
Add these vegetables to the measured
stock along with the tomatoes and
season to taste with salt and pepper, then
reheat without allowing the soup to
come to a boil.

Four Bring a small saucepan of salted
water to a boil. Gently lower in the quail
eggs and simmer for 3–4 minutes.
Remove the shells and place each in a
soup dish. Pour over the hot consommé
and sprinkle with chives and chervil.

CHEF'S TIP *Julienne strips are vegetables
cut to the size and shape of matchsticks.*

Smoked salmon soup with lime chantilly cream

*If you order a smoked salmon as a whole side with skin and bones for
Christmas or another special occasion, don't throw the trimmings away.
Keep them in the freezer to make this elegant soup.*

Preparation time *30 minutes*
Total cooking time *1 hour*
Serves 8

2 tablespoons unsalted butter
1 onion, finely chopped
3 shallots, finely chopped
1/2 bulb fennel, finely chopped
1 stalk celery, finely chopped
1 leek, finely chopped
1 carrot, finely chopped
11/2 lb. smoked salmon trimmings
11/2 cups white wine
1 bouquet garni (see page 520)
10 white peppercorns
1 star anise
*1 tablespoon chopped fresh herbs, such
as parsley*
*7 cups fish stock (see page 519)
or water*
2/3 cup whipping cream
chopped fresh chives, to garnish
*2 oz. thinly sliced smoked salmon,
to garnish*

LIME CHANTILLY CREAM
2/3 cup whipping cream
finely grated zest of 1 lime

One Melt the butter in a large saucepan over medium heat and then add the onion, shallots, fennel, celery, leek and carrot. Cook, stirring constantly, for 10 minutes, or until the vegetables are soft but not colored. Remove half the vegetables from the saucepan and set them aside.

Two Add the salmon trimmings to the vegetables in the saucepan and cook gently for 2 minutes, without coloring. Add the wine, bouquet garni, peppercorns, star anise and mixed herbs and season with salt and pepper. Bring

to a boil, reduce the liquid by half, then add the fish stock. Reduce the heat and simmer for 25 minutes, skimming the surface frequently, then pass through a strainer, discarding the salmon trimmings, vegetables and the seasonings.

Three Transfer the liquid to a clean saucepan, add the reserved vegetables and cook for 10 minutes over medium heat. Strain once more, discarding the vegetables, return the soup to the saucepan and stir in the whipping

cream. Season with salt and pepper; set aside and keep warm.

Four To make the lime Chantilly cream, lightly whisk the whipping cream in a small bowl to softly hold its shape, add the grated lime zest and gently fold in.

Five Serve the soup hot or cold with the chopped chives sprinkled on top. Add a spoonful of lime Chantilly cream in the center and top with a small roll of thinly sliced salmon.

Apple and parsnip soup

Don't save your fruit for dessert—a fruit and vegetable soup makes a wonderful beginning to a meal. Granny Smiths are just right for this recipe as they are not too sweet.

Preparation time *30 minutes*
Total cooking time *40 minutes*
Serves 6

2 tablespoons unsalted butter
1 onion, chopped
2 stalks celery, chopped
5 parsnips, chopped
3 Granny Smith or other tart cooking apples, peeled and chopped
1 bouquet garni (see page 520)
6 cups chicken stock (see page 519)
sprigs of fresh thyme, to garnish
chopped walnuts, to garnish

One Heat the butter in a medium saucepan, add the onion, cover with buttered parchment paper and a lid and cook gently until the onion is transparent, but not colored. Add the celery, parsnips and apples and season with salt and pepper. Cook for a few minutes, then add the bouquet garni and cover with the chicken stock.

Two Bring to a boil, then reduce the heat and simmer gently for 25 minutes, or until the vegetables are soft. Skim the surface, remove the bouquet garni, transfer the soup to a food processor or blender and process until smooth. Return the soup to a clean saucepan, season with salt and freshly ground pepper to taste and reheat.

Three Divide the soup into individual soup bowls. Arrange a little thyme and some chopped walnuts in the center of each soup bowl to serve.

CHEF'S TIP *For a different garnish, stir 1 tablespoon of Calvados or applejack into ²/₃ cup softly whipped cream. Carefully swirl the flavored cream into the soup just before serving.*

Gazpacho

Of Arabic origin, the name of this soup means "soaked bread."
Gazpacho originates from Seville in the south of Spain, but many
Spanish regions have their own versions of the soup.

Preparation time *35 minutes*
+ 2 hours refrigeration
Total cooking time *None*
Serves 6–8

GAZPACHO
2¹/₂ oz. fresh white bread,
crusts removed
2 tablespoons red wine vinegar
2 cloves garlic
³/₄ English cucumber, unpeeled and
roughly chopped
1 onion, chopped
¹/₂ green bell pepper, coarsely chopped
3¹/₂ lb. ripe tomatoes, quartered
and seeded
¹/₂ cup olive oil

TO GARNISH
¹/₄ English cucumber, unpeeled
¹/₂ green bell pepper
4 slices bread, crusts removed, toasted

One In a food processor or blender, process the bread into fine bread crumbs and add the vinegar, garlic, cucumber, onion, green bell pepper, tomato and a teaspoon of salt. Purée and then push the mixture through a strainer.

Two Return the mixture to the food processor or blender and pour in the olive oil in a thin steady stream. Alternatively, pour the mixture into a large bowl and briskly stir or whisk in the oil.

Three Check the flavouring, season with salt and freshly ground black pepper and add a little more vinegar if required for a refreshing tang. Check the consistency— the soup should be fairly thin, so you may need to add a little more water to dilute it. Cover the bowl with two layers of plastic wrap and chill in the refrigerator for at least 2 hours.

Four To prepare the garnish, cut the remaining cucumber in half lengthwise and use the point of a teaspoon to scoop out the seeds. Cut the cucumber, green bell pepper and bread into small cubes.

Five Pour the soup into well-chilled bowls and pass round the cucumber, green bell pepper and croutons in separate dishes for garnishing.

CHEF'S TIPS *To serve, you could add two or three ice cubes to chill the soup, or for more color, chop a red bell pepper along with the green.*

This soup can be made a day in advance for a mature, well-rounded flavor, but cover it well—it has a strong smell that can affect other foods close to it in the refrigerator.

LE CORDON BLEU COMPLETE COOK

Summer shrimp and cucumber soup

*This unusual and refreshing soup has its origins in the Middle East.
Very easy to make, it should be served chilled, accompanied by
pita bread, for a perfect al fresco lunch.*

Preparation time 20 minutes
+ 30 minutes standing
+ 2–3 hours refrigeration
Total cooking time 10 minutes
Serves 6–8

1 large cucumber
1 egg, optional
1¹/₂ cups chicken stock (see
page 519)
²/₃ cup tomato or vegetable juice
3²/₃ cup Greek yogurt or crème fraîche
¹/₂ cup whipping cream
2 oz. cooked shrimp, shells removed
(see page 522) and coarsely chopped
12 medium cooked shrimp,
shells on
1 clove garlic, crushed
1 teaspoon chopped fresh mint
1 teaspoon chopped fresh chives

One Peel and cut the cucumber into
¹/₂-inch cubes, salt them lightly and keep
in a colander for 30 minutes. Rinse in
cold water, drain and dry on crumpled
paper towels.

Two Bring a small saucepan of salted
water to a boil, lower in the egg and
simmer for 7 minutes. Transfer the egg
to a bowl of iced water to stop the
cooking process and tap to just crack the
shell. Keep in the water until just cool
enough to remove the shell, then return
the egg to the cold water. When fully
cooled, chop coarsely.

Three In a large bowl, mix together the
chicken stock, tomato juice and yogurt.
When quite smooth, add the cucumber,
cream and chopped shrimp to the soup.
Season to taste with salt and freshly
ground black pepper. Cover and place in
the refrigerator to chill for 2–3 hours.

Four Meanwhile, remove the shells from
the whole shrimp, leaving any heads and
tails on, then devein them. Cover and
store in the refrigerator.

Five Rub the inside of the individual
soup bowls with the garlic. Pour in the
soup and sprinkle with the egg, chopped
mint and chopped chives. Remove the
shrimp from the refrigerator and hang

two shrimp on the side of each bowl
and serve immediately, accompanied by
fresh bread.

CHEF'S TIP *To keep a hard-boiled egg
from overcooking, it must be cooled
immediately in iced water. The quick
cooling also prevents an unsightly
green-grey ring from forming around
the yolk.*

eggs and cheese

Scrambled eggs with smoked salmon

Scrambled eggs are delicious served with toast, as a filling for croissants, or alternatively, in puff pastry shells. The key to making really creamy scrambled eggs is not to overcook them.

Preparation time 10 minutes
Total cooking time 5 minutes
Serves 4–6

¼ lb. smoked salmon
10 eggs
⅓ cup whipping cream
1 tablespoon unsalted butter
sprigs of fresh flat-leaf parsley,
to garnish

One Set aside a few whole pieces of smoked salmon for decoration. Finely chop the rest and set aside.

Two In a bowl, whisk the eggs with the cream and season with salt and pepper.

Three Melt the butter in a skillet. Add the eggs and cook over medium heat, stirring constantly, for 3–5 minutes, or until the eggs are thick and creamy but still have a flowing consistency. Stir in the chopped salmon and serve immediately, garnished with the whole pieces of salmon and some parsley. Serve with fingers of toast.

CHEF'S TIPS *Scrambled eggs will continue cooking even when the pan is removed from the heat, so it is important that everything is ready to serve as soon as they are cooked and can be tipped straight out of the pan.*

If you prefer, you can leave the salmon in whole pieces and serve it beside the eggs.

This combination also makes a good filling for warm fresh croissants.

Eggs Benedict

Toasted English muffins topped with crisp bacon, lightly poached eggs and smothered in rich buttery hollandaise sauce. This American specialty is a truly memorable breakfast or brunch treat.

Preparation time *25 minutes*
Total cooking time *10 minutes*
Serves 4

HOLLANDAISE SAUCE
2 egg yolks
2 tablespoons water
1/3 cup clarified butter (see page 520), melted
1/2 teaspoon lemon juice

8 slices bacon
4 English muffins, fork-split into halves
1/4 cup vinegar
8 eggs
4 black olives, pitted and halved, or 8 slices of truffle

One Make the hollandaise sauce, following the method in the Chef's techniques on page 521. Cover the surface with waxed paper and keep warm over the hot water, off the heat.

Two Broil the bacon until crisp and toast the muffins. Put the bacon on the muffins and keep them warm.

Three To make the poached eggs, half-fill a large skillet with water and bring to a boil. Reduce the temperature to low and add the vinegar. The water should be barely at simmering point. Crack the eggs one at a time into a small cup or bowl and then carefully slide them into the water two or three at a time. Cook for 2–3 minutes, or until the egg whites are firm but not hard. Remove with a slotted spoon and drain well.

Four Top each muffin with a poached egg. Cover with the hollandaise sauce, decorate with the olive halves and serve.

Eggs en cocotte with smoked trout and leek

*Eggs that are en cocotte are baked in the oven in ramekins
placed in a bain-marie. An excellent breakfast dish, these eggs
would also make a wonderful first course (pictured top right).*

Preparation time 15 minutes
Total cooking time 35 minutes
Serves 4

3 tablespoons unsalted butter
1 small leek, halved and thinly sliced
6 oz. smoked trout, flaked finely
1/2 cup whipping cream
4 eggs
1 teaspoon snipped fresh chives

One Melt the butter in a saucepan. Add the leek, cover and cook gently for 8 minutes, or until soft but not brown. Meanwhile, brush four 2/3-cup flameproof ramekins or soufflé dishes with a little melted butter.

Two Remove the leek from the heat and stir in the trout and a third of the cream. Season, spoon into the dishes and allow to cool. The cocottes can be prepared up to this stage the night before, covered and refrigerated.

Three Preheat the oven to 325°F. With the back of a teaspoon, make a slight indentation in the center of the mixture in each of the dishes. Break an egg into each cocotte, spoon 1 tablespoon of cream on each and sprinkle with salt and pepper and 2 teaspoons of the chives. Place the dishes in a baking dish or roasting pan and pour in enough boiling water to come halfway up the sides.

Four Bake for 20–25 minutes, or until the whites are set and the yolks are cooked but still tremble when lightly shaken. Set each cocotte on a cold plate, sprinkle with the remaining chives and serve immediately with fingers of freshly made buttered toast.

Frittata

*Unlike a French omelet, the Italian frittata (pictured bottom right) usually requires all
ingredients to be mixed with the eggs before being cooked to a fairly firm texture.*

Preparation time 20 minutes
Total cooking time 30 minutes
Serves 4–6

1/4 lb. skinned, boneless chicken
breast halves
1/4 cup unsalted butter
1 1/3 cups sliced button mushrooms
2 cloves garlic, chopped
1 red bell pepper, cut
into short strips
10 eggs, beaten and seasoned with
salt and pepper
1 cup shredded Gruyère or
Cheddar cheese

One Preheat the oven to 425°F.

Two Cut the chicken breasts into 1/2-inch cubes and season with salt and pepper. Melt the butter in a flameproof skillet over medium heat and cook the chicken for 2–3 minutes, until lightly browned.

Three Add the mushrooms and cook for 5–7 minutes, or until any liquid has evaporated. Add the garlic and red bell pepper. Season with salt and pepper and cover. Lower the heat and cook gently for 5–8 minutes, or until the red bell pepper is tender.

Four Add the beaten eggs and stir to distribute evenly. Continue stirring for 2–3 minutes, or until the eggs have started to set.

Five Sprinkle the cheese over the eggs and transfer the skillet to the oven. Cook for 5–8 minutes, or until the cheese has melted and the eggs are cooked through. Remove from the oven and slide the frittata onto a plate. Cut into wedges to serve.

Twice-baked individual cheese soufflés

A soufflé with a difference—you can relax. Prepare these individual soufflés the day before and watch them rise again ready to thrill your brunch guests.

***Preparation time** 35 minutes*
+ cooling time
***Total cooking time** 45 minutes*
Serves 8

1¼ cups milk
tiny pinch of grated nutmeg
1 small bay leaf
1 small shallot, halved
4 whole peppercorns
2 tablespoons unsalted butter
¼ cup potato starch or 2 tablespoons
all-purpose flour mixed with
2 tablespoons cornstarch
1 tablespoon unsalted butter, cut into
very small pieces
3 eggs, separated
⅔ cup shredded Cheddar cheese
¼ teaspoon mustard powder
1 egg white
⅔ cup whipping cream
3 tablespoons grated Parmesan or
Gruyère cheese

One In a small saucepan, warm the milk with the nutmeg, bay leaf, shallot and peppercorns. When bubbles form around the edge of the saucepan, remove from the heat.

Two Melt the butter in a large saucepan, remove from the heat and stir in the potato starch. Strain the milk and pour into the saucepan, blend well and return to the heat. Whisk briskly until the mixture comes to a boil. Remove from the heat and scatter the butter pieces over the surface. Cover the saucepan with a lid and allow to cool slightly. Meanwhile, preheat the oven to 350°F. Lightly butter 8 individual ⅔-cup soufflé dishes.

Three Uncover the sauce and stir in the melted layer of butter, followed by the egg yolks, Cheddar, mustard, and salt and pepper to taste. In a large bowl, beat the four egg whites until stiff. Using a large metal spoon or a spatula, stir 1 tablespoon of the egg whites into the cheese mixture to lighten it, then add the remainder all at once, carefully folding until just combined.

Four Divide the mixture among the soufflé dishes, pouring it in gently to avoid losing any volume. Place the dishes in a roasting pan or deep baking dish and pour in enough warm water to come three-quarters of the way up the sides of the dishes. Bake for 25 minutes, or until the soufflés have slightly risen and are firm to the touch. Remove from the water and allow to cool. (Cover and keep overnight in the refrigerator if you wish to prepare the night before.)

Five Just before serving, preheat the oven to 400°F. Return the soufflé dishes to their baking dish, pour some cream into each, dividing it equally, and season each one lightly. Sprinkle with Parmesan and pour enough warm water into the baking dish to come three-quarters of the way up the sides of the soufflé dishes, as before. Bake the soufflés for 10–15 minutes, or until risen and golden brown. Lift out carefully and place each dish on to a plate. Serve immediately.

about soufflés...

The secret to making soufflés is to cook the mixture at the right temperature. This allows the air to puff up the soufflé before the mixture around it cooks and sets the structure in shape. If the soufflé is then cooled and reheated, as the air expands again it will push the structure back up.

Eggs Florentine

*A classic dish made from a layer of spinach and lightly poached eggs
topped with a creamy Mornay sauce. Mornay sauce is a béchamel,
or white sauce, flavored with cheese and enriched with egg yolks.*

Preparation time *25 minutes*
Total cooking time *30 minutes*
Serves 4

MORNAY SAUCE
1 tablespoon unsalted butter
2¹/₂ tablespoons all-purpose flour
1 cup milk
pinch of ground nutmeg
¹/₃ cup shredded Gruyère cheese
2 egg yolks

¹/₄ cup unsalted butter
1 lb. young spinach leaves
¹/₄ cup vinegar
8 very fresh eggs

One To make the Mornay sauce, melt the butter in a heavy-bottomed saucepan over medium-low heat. Sprinkle the flour over the butter and cook for 1–2 minutes without allowing it to color, stirring with a wooden spoon. Remove the saucepan from the heat and slowly add the milk, whisking or beating vigorously to avoid lumps. Return to medium heat and bring to a boil, stirring constantly. Simmer for 3–4 minutes, or until the sauce coats the back of a spoon. Stir in the nutmeg, then remove from the heat. Set aside, covered, and keep warm.

Two In a large skillet, melt the butter over low heat and cook the spinach for 5–8 minutes, or until dry. Keep warm.

Three Whisk the cheese into the Mornay sauce, then whisk in the egg yolks. Season to taste with salt and pepper. Place over low heat and mix until the cheese is melted, then heat until very hot but not boiling. Set aside, cover the surface with a piece of waxed paper and keep warm.

Four To make the poached eggs, half-fill a large skillet with water and bring to a boil. Reduce the temperature to low and add the vinegar. The water should be barely at simmering point. Crack the eggs one at a time into a small cup or bowl and then carefully slide them into the water two or three at a time. Cook

for 2–3 minutes, or until the egg whites are firm but not hard. Remove with a slotted spoon and drain well.

Five Mound the spinach on warmed plates. Place two poached eggs in the center of each mound and cover with the hot Mornay sauce. Serve immediately.

Quiche Lorraine

This open tart originated in the Lorraine region around the sixteenth century. The name quiche comes from the German word Küchen, *meaning cake. A quiche can contain many fillings, but a quiche Lorraine is traditionally made with cream, eggs and smoked bacon and is considered a classic of French cuisine.*

Preparation time *30 minutes*
Total cooking time *1 hour 5 minutes*
Serves 4–6

1/2 *quantity short pastry*
(see page 544)
1 egg, beaten

FILLING
oil, for cooking
6 oz. slab bacon, rind removed and
cut into thin strips
3 eggs
nutmeg, to taste
1 cup whipping cream
2/3 *cup shredded Gruyère cheese*

One Lightly grease an 83/4 x 11/4-inch fluted tart pan with removable bottom. Roll out the dough on a lightly floured surface to a thickness of 1/8 inch and line the prepared pan (see Chef's techniques, page 547). Preheat the oven to 350°F. Bake blind for about 25 minutes, or until firm (see Chef's techniques, page 547). Remove the weights and paper, and brush the bottom of the pastry with the beaten egg. Bake for another 7 minutes.

Two To make the filling, heat a little oil in a skillet. Sauté the bacon, drain on paper towels and set aside. Whisk the eggs and season with the nutmeg, salt and freshly ground black pepper. Mix in the cream and pass through a strainer.

Three Sprinkle the bottom of the pastry with the bacon and cheese. Gently pour in the egg mixture until the pastry is three-quarters full. Bake for about 20–30 minutes, or until the filling is golden brown and set. Serve hot.

LE CORDON BLEU COMPLETE COOK

Caramelized onion, spinach and blue cheese quiche

*The delicious combination of vegetables
with blue cheese and a hint of nutmeg makes
a perfect filling for this vegetarian quiche.*

*Preparation time 30 minutes
+ 50 minutes refrigeration
Total cooking time 1 hour 45 minutes
Serves 8–10*

1 quantity short pastry (see page 544)

FILLING
2 tablespoons vegetable oil
4 onions, thinly sliced
1 teaspoon sugar
1/3 cup red wine
3 tablespoons unsalted butter
10 oz. frozen spinach, thawed and
squeezed dry
pinch of ground nutmeg
3/4 cup whipping cream
6 oz. strong blue cheese, such as
Roquefort or Stilton
4 eggs, beaten

One Brush a 9½ x 1¼-inch fluted tart pan with removable bottom with melted butter and line with the pastry, following the method in the Chef's techniques on page 547.

Two Preheat the oven to 350°F and blind bake the pastry for 10 minutes, or until firm, following the method in the Chef's techniques on page 547. Remove the weights or rice and discard the paper. Return the pastry to the oven and continue to bake for 5–10 minutes, or until the pastry is dry. Remove and cool. Raise the oven temperature to 375°F.

Three For the filling, heat the oil in a large saucepan. Add the onions and cook gently for 8 minutes, or until the onions are translucent. Increase the heat, add the sugar and cook for about 10 minutes, or until the onions begin to caramelize. Next, pour in the wine and cook until the liquid has evaporated and the onions are soft. Season well. Remove from the saucepan and set aside.

Four In the saucepan, melt the butter, add the spinach and fry over high heat, stirring constantly, until the spinach is dry when pressed with the back of a spoon. (Wet spinach will make the quiche soggy.) Season with salt, pepper and the nutmeg, turn out onto a cutting board and chop finely.

Five In a saucepan, warm the cream and cheese gently, stirring, until the cheese melts, but does not boil. Season and cool before adding the eggs. Fill the pastry shell with the onion, then the spinach. Smooth the surface a little but do not pack down. Pour in the cream mixture and bake for 30 minutes, then lower the temperature to 325°F and bake for 20 minutes to cook the center of the quiche. Cover with aluminum foil if it is getting too brown. Serve warm.

---

about blue cheese...

Blue cheese is often used for cooking because its strong taste is robust enough to compete with other flavors. Creamy soft-rind blues, such as bleu de bresse, would be lost in a recipe such as this. Blue cheeses are ripened internally by blue molds which add a particularly strong taste. True Roquefort is produced from sheep's milk and left to ripen for 3 months in the limestone caves of Les Causses in south-central France. It has all-over marbling that is more green than blue in color.

Leek and Brie flamiche

The flamiche derives its name from the Flemish word for cake, as originally it was in fact a type of cake made from bread dough and served with butter. Nowadays, however, the name usually refers to a pie filled with vegetables or cheese, or both, as in this particular recipe.

Preparation time *1 hour 5 minutes*
+ 30 minutes chilling
Total cooking time *55 minutes*
Serves 4–6

PASTRY
2 cups all-purpose flour
1 teaspoon salt
¼ cup unsalted butter
1 egg
1 egg yolk

1 egg, beaten

FILLING
¼ cup unsalted butter, cut into cubes
3½ cups leeks, white part only,
thinly sliced
5 oz. Brie
1 egg
1 egg yolk
3 tablespoons whipping cream

One To make the pastry, sift the flour and salt together into a bowl. Using your fingertips, rub in the butter until the mixture resembles fine bread crumbs. Make a well in the center and add the egg, egg yolk and 3 tablespoons water. Mix well, shape into a ball and refrigerate for 20 minutes, wrapped in plastic wrap.

Two To make the filling, melt the butter in a deep skillet and slowly cook the leeks, covered, for 5 minutes. Cook for another 5 minutes, uncovered, or until all the liquid has evaporated, being careful not to allow the leeks to brown. Transfer the leeks to a strainer and set aside to allow to cool.

Three Preheat the oven to 325°F. Lightly grease an 8¼ x 1-inch fluted tart pan with removable bottom. Following the Chef's techniques on page 547, divide the pastry in half and roll out one half on a lightly floured surface to a thickness of ⅛ inch and line the prepared tart pan leaving a ½-inch overhang. Roll out the second piece of dough on a lightly floured surface to an 8¾-inch round, and then refrigerate until needed.

Four Remove the rind of the cheese and cut the cheese into small cubes. Spread the leeks over the bottom of the pastry shell, and sprinkle with the cheese. Whisk together the egg, egg yolk and cream. Pour over the leeks and cheese. Brush the edge of the pastry with the beaten egg and place the second piece of pastry on top. Trim the top pastry sheet so that it is even with the lower sheet. Pinch the dough well to seal the two pieces together, and trim the edges by pressing down with the thumb against the fluted edge of the pan. Brush the top with the egg and refrigerate for 10 minutes.

Five Brush again with the beaten egg and cut a hole in the center using a small round cutter. Bake for 40–45 minutes, or until golden. Place on a wire rack to cool slightly before removing from the tart pan and allow to rest for 5 minutes before cutting.

about leeks...

The secret to cooking leeks is to cook them very slowly until their crunchiness turns to a sweet softness. Always wash leeks well as they often contain dirt right through their structure of layers.

Goat cheese and watercress quiche

The rather peppery flavor of the watercress complements the creamy goat cheese filling in this recipe. This quiche could also be made as individual tartlets and served either warm or cold.

Preparation time *30 minutes*
Total cooking time *1 hour 15 minutes*
Serves 4–6

FILLING
1/2 lb. watercress
3 eggs
1/3 cup whipping cream
nutmeg, to taste
5 oz. goat cheese, cut into
5/8-inch slices

1/2 quantity short pastry
(see page 544)
1 egg, beaten

One To make the filling, remove the large stems from the watercress, then rinse and pat dry with paper towels. Bring 2 quarts water to a boil, add some salt and cook the watercress for just 10 seconds. Drain, then refresh in iced water for 3 minutes, and then drain again. Squeeze out any excess water, then coarsely chop the watercress. Season with salt and pepper.

Two Preheat the oven to 350°F. Lightly grease an 8¼ x 1-inch fluted tart pan with removable bottom. Roll out the dough on a lightly floured surface to a thickness of ¹/₈ inch and line the prepared pan (see Chef's techniques, page 547). Bake blind for 25 minutes, or until firm (see Chef's techniques, page 547). Remove the weights and paper, and brush the bottom of the pastry with the beaten egg. Return to the oven and bake for another 7 minutes.

Three Whisk the eggs with the cream, and season with nutmeg, salt and pepper. Sprinkle the pastry shell with the watercress and arrange the slices of goat cheese on top. Add the egg mixture and bake for 30–40 minutes, or until set and a knife inserted into the center comes out clean. Cool slightly on a wire rack before removing from the pan. Allow to stand for 5 minutes before cutting.

LE CORDON BLEU ✦ COMPLETE COOK

Cheese and herb muffins

*Cheese and herb muffins are an excellent accompaniment
to soups and stews. Or, of course, you can eat them
on their own, spread thickly with butter.*

Preparation time 25 minutes
Total cooking time 20 minutes
Makes 12 standard muffins

1³/4 cups self-rising flour
1 cup whole wheat flour
1¹/2 teaspoons baking powder
pinch of cayenne pepper
pinch of salt
2 tablespoons finely chopped
fresh parsley
2 tablespoons finely chopped
fresh chives
2 tablespoons fresh thyme leaves
1 cup shredded Cheddar cheese
2 eggs
1 cup milk
¹/2 cup unsalted butter, melted

One Preheat the oven to 425°F. Brush a
12-cup standard muffin pan with melted
butter or oil. Sift the flours, baking
powder, cayenne pepper and salt into a
large bowl, and return the husks to the
bowl. Stir in the herbs and cheese, and
make a well in the center.

Two Whisk the eggs and milk together
and pour into the well of the dry
ingredients along with the butter. Stir
with a metal spoon until the ingredients
are just combined. Do not overmix—the
mixture should be lumpy.

Three Spoon the mixture into the muffin
pan, filling each cup about three-
quarters full. Bake for 20 minutes, or
until a skewer comes out clean when
inserted into the center of a muffin. Cool
the muffins in the pan for 5 minutes
before lifting out onto a wire rack.

CHEF'S TIP *Serve spread with butter
while the muffins are still warm.*

Brie purses with pears and almonds

A sophisticated brunch dish that may be served with broiled tomatoes, some watercress or a green salad. This would also make an elegant first course for a lunch or dinner party.

*Preparation time 25 minutes
+ 30 minutes chilling
Total cooking time 15 minutes
Serves 4*

*³/4 cup whole blanched almonds
1 large or 2 small ripe pears, peeled
and thinly sliced
2 tablespoons balsamic or tarragon
vinegar
¹/2 lb. ripe Brie
12 sheets phyllo pastry
²/3 cup unsalted butter, melted*

One Preheat a broiler. Blend the almonds in a food processor for 30 seconds, or until they resemble fine bread crumbs. Turn out onto a baking sheet and toast under the broiler. Do not walk away while this is happening as the almonds will burn very quickly. Season with a little salt and pepper.

Two Place the pear slices in a bowl and sprinkle with the vinegar, toss to coat well and set aside. Cut the Brie in half through the middle to make two large flat pieces with a rind on one side of each. Lay one piece on a work surface, rind downwards, and place the pear slices on top of the cheese in a neat layer to completely cover the top of the cheese. You may need to do several layers in order to use up all the pears. Sprinkle with any remaining vinegar, season with salt and pepper and place the second piece of Brie on top, so that the rind is on top and the edges are even all the way around. Wrap the cheese tightly in plastic wrap, place on a plate and chill for a minimum of 30 minutes. When chilled, cut into eight even-size pieces and coat them with the almonds, keeping the wedges whole.

Three Preheat the oven to 425°F. Brush one sheet of phyllo with the melted butter (see page 549), cover with another sheet, brush again, then add a third sheet. Cut into two 8-inch squares. Discard the trimmings. Place one wedge of the Brie in the center of each square and gather up the edges to form a purse, squeezing the pastry together to make a "drawstring" effect. Brush gently with a little more butter. Repeat this process with the remaining pastry and Brie, making sure the Brie remains chilled or it will melt too quickly. When ready to cook, place the purses on a greased baking sheet and bake for 10 minutes, or until golden. Serve immediately.

CHEF'S TIP *A few ripe, peeled and sliced apricots or peeled seedless grapes can be used instead of the pears, or if time is limited, omit both the fruit and the vinegar and spread the opened-out cheese with 2 tablespoons of a fruit chutney instead.*

Gougères

*In Burgundy these cheese-flavoured pastry
puffs are traditionally served cold with wine
during tastings in the local cellars.*

Preparation time 25 minutes
Total cooking time 25 minutes
Makes 25–30

*1 quantity cream puff pastry (see
page 545)*
*1/3 cup finely shredded Gruyère
or Cheddar cheese*
1 egg, beaten

One Preheat the oven to 325°F. Lightly grease two baking sheets. Mix half the cheese into the pastry dough.

Two Spoon the mixture into a pastry bag fitted with a small plain tip. Pipe out 1-inch balls of dough onto the prepared sheets, leaving a space of 1¼ inches between each ball. Using a fork dipped in the beaten egg, slightly flatten the top of each ball. Sprinkle with the remaining shredded cheese. Bake the balls for 20–25 minutes, or until they have puffed up and are golden brown. Serve hot.

CHEF'S TIP *This is a very simple and light finger food to serve with predinner drinks. Gougères are sometimes served in restaurants with drinks and referred to as* amuse-gueule, *the French term for an appetizer.*

salads

Salade niçoise

"Niçoise" indicates a dish that contains ingredients from the Nice region of Southern France, usually tomatoes, tuna and black olives. Originally this salad did not include cooked vegetables, but as it began to appear on menus around France, local chefs made their own adaptations, including the addition of potatoes.

***Preparation time** 40 minutes*
+ 20 minutes cooling
***Total cooking time** 1 hour 20 minutes*
Serves 4

3/4 cup olive oil
1 bay leaf
4 sprigs of fresh thyme
1 x 12 oz. fresh tuna fillet, skin removed
10 oz. waxy or small new potatoes
8 oz. green beans
3 tablespoons white wine vinegar
1 green bell pepper, cut into julienne strips (see Chef's tip)
1 red bell pepper, cut into julienne strips
2 red onions, thinly sliced
1 head Boston or Bibb lettuce
4 tomatoes, quartered
4 hard-boiled eggs, quartered
1 x 1³/4-oz. can anchovies, drained
30 black olives

One Preheat the oven to 300°F. In a small flameproof skillet or roasting pan, place the oil, bay leaf, thyme and tuna. Warm over low heat for 5 minutes, then place in the oven for 30 minutes, or until the tuna feels firm to the touch. Cool for 20 minutes in the oil, remove the tuna and drain on a rack. Strain the oil.

Two Put the unpeeled potatoes in a saucepan of cold, salted water. Bring to a boil and cook for 30–35 minutes, or until the tip of a knife easily pierces them. Remove and allow to cool. Peel, then slice into rounds.

Three Trim the beans and cook them in boiling salted water for 8 minutes, or until they are tender. Refresh in cold water and drain.

Four To make the vinaigrette, whisk the vinegar with a little salt, then gradually whisk in the reserved oil.

Five Toss the potatoes, green beans, bell peppers and onion with a little vinaigrette and season to taste. Break the tuna into bite-size pieces and mix with some of the vinaigrette. Arrange a few leaves of lettuce on each plate. In the center, place a mound of the potatoes. Top with the green beans, bell peppers and onion and finish with the tuna. Alternate the tomato and egg quarters around the edge and finish with the anchovies and olives. Drizzle the remaining vinaigrette over the salad.

CHEF'S TIP *Julienne strips are vegetables cut to the size and shape of matchsticks.*

LE CORDON BLEU ✠ COMPLETE COOK

Waldorf salad

Traditionally made with apple, celery, walnuts and mayonnaise, this salad was created in New York's Waldorf Astoria Hotel in the 1890s. This version is based around the same key ingredients with the addition of Parma ham.

Preparation time *30 minutes*
Total cooking time *5 minutes*
Serves 6–8

2 celery hearts
²/₃ cup walnut halves
¹/₂ lemon
4 dessert apples, such as Red Delicious
1 shallot, very finely chopped
1 clove garlic, very finely chopped
1 tablespoon vegetable oil, for frying
6 slices Parma ham or prosciutto
1 head cos or romaine lettuce

DRESSING
2 teaspoons Dijon mustard
4 tablespoons olive oil
4 tablespoons whipping cream

One Using a large sharp knife, cut the celery hearts into thin slices, wash well and set aside to drain thoroughly.

Two Preheat the broiler. Spread the walnuts out on a baking sheet and toast for 1–2 minutes, or until brown, taking care that they don't burn.

Three Grate the zest of the lemon finely into a large bowl and squeeze in all but a tablespoon of the juice. One at a time, peel, quarter and slice the apples across and toss them gently into the lemon in the bowl to prevent them from going brown. Add the shallot and garlic with the walnuts, drained celery and a little salt and black pepper.

Four To make the dressing, place the remaining tablespoon of lemon juice in a small bowl and mix with the mustard. Using a small hand whisk, beat in the olive oil a few drops at a time until the dressing is smooth and emulsified, then beat in the cream for a few seconds until blended. Taste the dressing and season with salt and black pepper.

Five Heat the vegetable oil in a heavy-bottomed, nonstick frying pan and fry the Parma ham for 30 seconds, or until shriveled slightly. Drain on paper towels, then cut into small strips using scissors or a sharp knife and allow to cool and become crispy.

Six Slice the lettuce leaves very thinly and use to line a serving bowl. Drizzle the dressing over the apples and celery, stir gently to mix and toss together with the lettuce. Sprinkle the strips of Parma ham over the salad just before serving.

Caesar salad

*This salad is often thought of as an American dish, but was actually
created by Caesar Cardini in Tijuana, Mexico in the 1920s.*

Preparation time *20 minutes*
Total cooking time *15 minutes*
Serves 4

DRESSING
2 egg yolks
1 tablespoon lemon juice, or to taste
2/3 cup olive oil
4 anchovy fillets, finely chopped
2 cloves garlic, finely chopped

2 eggs
1 head romaine lettuce
4 slices white bread, crusts removed
1/3 cup olive oil
1/3 cup freshly grated Parmesan cheese
*2 tablespoons finely chopped fresh
parsley*

One To make the dressing, beat the egg
yolks and lemon juice using a whisk or
an electric blender. Add the oil in a thin
steady stream and beat until thick and
smooth. Stir in the anchovies and garlic
and season to taste with salt, pepper and
extra lemon juice. Set aside.

Two To hard-boil the eggs, place them in
a small saucepan and cover with cold
water. Bring to a gentle boil and cook
for 10 minutes. Drain and cool in cold
water, then peel and chop finely.

Three Tear the lettuce into bite-size
pieces and set aside in the refrigerator.
To make the croutons, cut the bread into
even-size cubes. Heat the oil in a skillet

and brown the bread until nicely golden.
Remove the croutons and drain on
crumpled paper towels.

Four In a large serving bowl, toss the
lettuce in the dressing. Sprinkle with the
remaining ingredients to serve.

CHEF'S TIP *To make the salad a meal in
itself, try adding smoked duck breast,
chicken or salmon.*

LE CORDON BLEU ✠ COMPLETE COOK

Kaleidoscope salad

This attractive salad has a bold dressing of fresh ginger, olive oil and cilantro and makes an ideal side dish for outdoor or broiled food. It can be made up to 12 hours in advance to develop the flavors.

Preparation time 20 minutes
Total cooking time 25 minutes
Serves 4–6

2 ears corn
5-inch piece cucumber
1 small bulb fennel
1/2 red bell pepper
6 scallions, finely sliced
4 large ripe tomatoes
2/3 cup uncooked peas, shelled
2 tablespoons chopped fresh parsley
1 tablespoon chopped fresh cilantro
1 tablespoon chopped fresh basil

DRESSING
1-inch piece fresh ginger
1 clove garlic, crushed
1/2 cup olive oil
3 tablespoons rice vinegar
1 teaspoon Tabasco sauce
1 teaspoon ground coriander

One Preheat a broiler. Remove the papery husk and silk from the ears of corn and place the corn under the broiler for 25 minutes, turning several times, until mottled brown and tender. Remove from the broiler and, when cool, place corn upright on a cutting board and cut off the kernels using a downward action with a sharp knife. Place in a large bowl.

Two Cut the cucumber in half lengthwise, remove the seeds with a teaspoon and dice the flesh. Add to the corn. Discard any tough, outer layers of fennel. Remove the seeds, stem and membrane from the red bell pepper, then dice this and the fennel. Add to the bowl with the scallions.

Three Halve two of the tomatoes and remove the seeds with a teaspoon. Dice the flesh and add to the bowl with the peas, parsley, cilantro and basil and gently combine everything with a large spoon, taking care not to break up the tomatoes.

Four To make the dressing, finely grate the ginger and place in a bowl with the garlic. Using the back of a teaspoon, mash the ginger and garlic to a paste with 1/4 teaspoon salt. Add the olive oil, rice vinegar, Tabasco sauce, ground coriander and season with 1/2 teaspoon salt and 3/4 teaspoon freshly ground black pepper. Whisk the dressing, then pour over the vegetables and gently toss to lightly coat with the dressing. Slice the remaining tomatoes and arrange them around the plates. Place the salad inside the tomato slices to serve.

Mustard seed potato salad

A flavorful potato salad made with whole
small potatoes and a mustard mayonnaise

Preparation time *10 minutes*
Total cooking time *35 minutes*
Serves 4

4 lb. small salad or new potatoes,
scrubbed

MAYONNAISE
2 egg yolks
1 cup lightly flavored vegetable oil
1 tablespoon white wine vinegar
2 heaping tablespoons whole
grain mustard

One Bring a saucepan of salted water to a boil. Add the potatoes and boil for 30–35 minutes, or until tender to the point of a knife. Drain well and place in a bowl.

Two To make the mayonnaise, bring all the ingredients to room temperature and set a large bowl on a damp kitchen towel to prevent it from moving. Add the egg yolks and a pinch of salt to the bowl and mix with a hand whisk or electric mixer.

Three Put the oil in a pitcher that is easy to pour from. While whisking constantly by hand or with an electric mixer, pour a steady thin stream of oil into the mixture. Begin with a small amount and stop pouring periodically to allow each addition to emulsify to a thick creamy mixture. Continue until a third of the oil has been added and the mayonnaise has begun to thicken.

Four Add the vinegar to make the texture slightly thinner. Continue gradually adding the oil, then stir in the whole grain mustard. Adjust the flavor by adding more vinegar, salt and pepper if necessary. Add 1–2 tablespoons of boiling water if it curdles or separates. Add the mayonnaise to the potatoes and stir until evenly coated. Serve warm.

Celery root rémoulade

*This French classic makes a delicious first course or light lunch.
A mustard mayonnaise and some gherkins, capers and anchovies
enhance the flavor of the crunchy celery root.*

Preparation time *35 minutes
+ 1 hour resting*
Total cooking time *None*
Serves 4–6

*2½ lb. celery root
juice of 1 lemon
2 tablespoons capers
8 gherkins, finely chopped
2 ripe tomatoes, peeled, seeded and
diced (see page 534)
1 cup fresh herbs, such as chervil, basil
and dill
2⅓ cups small salad leaves
8 anchovy fillets, to garnish*

RÉMOULADE SAUCE
*2 egg yolks
2 heaping tablespoons Dijon mustard
or 1 heaping teaspoon
dried mustard powder
pinch of cayenne pepper
1 cup lightly flavored
vegetable oil*

One Cut the celery root in half and peel away the skin, cutting ⅛ inch deep into the flesh to remove all of the fibrous skin. Coarsely grate the celery root into a bowl, season and toss in the lemon juice. Cover with plastic wrap and set aside for 30–60 minutes.

Two To make the rémoulade sauce, bring all the ingredients to room temperature and set a large bowl on a damp kitchen towel to prevent it from moving. Add the egg yolks, mustard, cayenne pepper and a pinch of salt to the bowl and mix with a hand whisk or electric mixer.

Three Put the oil in a pitcher that is easy to pour from. While whisking constantly by hand or with an electric mixer, pour a steady thin stream of oil into the mixture. Begin with a small amount of oil and stop pouring periodically to allow each addition to emulsify to a thick creamy mixture. Continue until the sauce resembles whipped cream. Add 1–2 tablespoons of boiling water if it curdles or separates.

Four Squeeze out the excess liquid from the celery root and mix with the rémoulade sauce. Rinse the capers, dry them and chop if large, then stir these and the gherkins into the celery root. Serve decorated with the tomatoes, herbs and salad leaves, then top with the anchovy fillets.

Tabbouleh

This grain salad originated in Lebanon and is made with generous amounts of fresh mint, parsley and bulgur.

***Preparation time** 20 minutes
+ 30 minutes soaking
Total cooking time None
Serves 4*

1¹/₂ cups bulgur
1 English cucumber
²/₃ cup fresh mint, finely chopped
1¹/₃ cups fresh flat-leaf parsley, finely chopped
6 scallions, finely chopped
¹/₃ cup olive oil
¹/₂ cup lemon juice
cos or romaine lettuce leaves, to serve

One Place the bulgur in a bowl and pour in enough hot water to just cover. Allow the bulgur to soak for 20–30 minutes. Peel the cucumber and cut in half lengthwise. Using a teaspoon, remove the cucumber seeds from the center, then finely dice the flesh. Place the chopped cucumber, mint, parsley and scallions in a medium bowl with the olive oil and lemon juice.

Two Transfer the bulgur to a strainer to drain off any excess water. Fluff up the grains with a fork, add to the bowl with the herbs and season generously with salt and black pepper.

Three Serve with a side of lettuce leaves. To eat, place some tabbouleh in the center of each lettuce leaf and fold each leaf into a package.

Rustic Greek salad

A hearty salad with the Greek flavors of feta, oregano, black olives and ripe tomatoes.

***Preparation time** 15 minutes
Total cooking time None
Serves 4*

1 head cos or romaine lettuce
3 ripe tomatoes
²/₃ cup Kalamata olives
1 shallot, finely chopped
1²/₃ cups feta cheese
1 tablespoon fresh oregano leaves, chopped
¹/₄ cup olive oil
¹/₄ cup lemon juice

One Shred the cos or romaine lettuce finely and place on 4 plates. Cut the tomatoes into slim wedges and arrange them on top of the lettuce with the olives and shallot.

Two Cut the feta cheese into ³/₄-inch cubes and scatter these over the salads with the oregano. Season with salt and black pepper.

Three Whisk together the oil and lemon juice and pour it over the salads.

CHEF'S TIP *Greek salads are always made with wonderful fresh ingredients and often include plenty of chopped herbs for flavour. The ingredients, including the herbs, can be varied according to seasonal availability and individual preference.*

Caprese

*This lovely combination of tomato, mozzarella and
basil is an Italian classic. Balsamic vinegar and
good olive oil make up the dressing*

__Preparation time__ 15 minutes
__Total cooking time__ None
__Serves 4__ as a side dish

4–6 large ripe, full-flavored tomatoes
¾ lb. fresh mozzarella or
bocconcini cheese
1 tablespoon olive oil
2 tablespoons balsamic vinegar
⅓ cup fresh basil leaves

One Cut the tomatoes horizontally into
thin slices and slice the mozzarella to a
similar thickness. Sprinkle the bottom of
a serving plate with salt and black
pepper, then arrange the tomatoes and
mozzarella in slightly overlapping circles
on the plate.

Two Drizzle with the olive oil and
balsamic vinegar and sprinkle over the
basil leaves, tearing any large leaves with
your fingers. Season with salt and black
pepper. The salad can be served
immediately or covered and set aside at
room temperature for several hours to
allow the flavors to infuse. If you wish
to do this, drizzle only half the olive oil
and balsamic vinegar over, then drizzle
over the remainder just before serving.

CHEF'S TIP *Choose tomatoes of any
type, just as long as they have some
flavor—vine-ripened tomatoes are best.
You really need top-quality tomatoes for
this dish, so if they're not available,
choose to make another salad instead.*

Goat cheese with a watercress and mâche salad

*The bitter watercress, tangy goat cheese and homemade herb
olive oil marry beautifully to make a simple salad that
is ideal to serve as a light meal with fresh bread.*

Preparation time *25 minutes*
+ 3–4 days marinating
Total cooking time *2 minutes*
Serves 4

10 oz. goat cheese (see Chef's tips)
3 sprigs of fresh thyme
1 large sprig of fresh rosemary
15 fresh basil leaves
6 whole black peppercorns,
lightly crushed
4 juniper berries,
lightly crushed
1²/₃ cups olive oil
¹/₃ cup pine nuts
3¹/₃ cups watercress sprigs
5 cups mâche

One Place the goat cheese on a cutting board and cut off the skin with a sharp knife. Cut into roughly ¹/₂-inch cubes and place loosely in a 4-cup canning jar with an airtight lid, tucking the thyme, rosemary and basil leaves in between layers of cheese cubes. Drop the crushed peppercorns and juniper berries into the jar and pour in the olive oil. The oil must cover the cheese completely, so add a little more if the shape of your jar requires it. Place in the refrigerator for 3–4 days for the flavors of the herbs to infuse the cheese.

Two Preheat a broiler and place the pine nuts on a baking sheet. Toast for 2 minutes, turning several times and taking care not to let the nuts burn. Allow to cool.

Three Just before serving, put the watercress in a bowl with the mâche and then sprinkle with the pine nuts and the marinated goat cheese, drizzling about a quarter of the olive oil over the leaves.

Season with salt and plenty of black pepper and serve immediately.

CHEF'S TIPS *Choose a firm goat cheese like chèvre for this recipe—soft goat cheese will break down too much in the oil.*

If there is any cheese left over, it will keep for up to a month if covered completely in oil in the jar and stored in the refrigerator. If you are storing it, remove and discard the basil leaves.

Fattoush

*This Middle Eastern salad is traditionally garnished
with toasted Arab or Lebanese bread and
flavored with fresh mint and parsley.*

Preparation time *40 minutes*
Total cooking time *5 minutes*
Serves 4

4 ripe tomatoes, peeled, seeded and
diced (see page 534)
1 small head cos or romaine lettuce,
shredded
1 small cucumber
1 green bell pepper
2 shallots, finely chopped
4 scallions, finely sliced
4 tablespoons fresh mint,
finely chopped
4 tablespoons fresh flat-leaf parsley,
finely chopped
2 pita breads or other similar
flat breads

DRESSING
1 clove garlic
1 teaspoon salt
1/4 cup lemon juice
1/2 cup olive oil
few drops of Tabasco sauce

One Put the tomatoes and lettuce in a
bowl. Peel the cucumber, slice it into
quarters lengthwise and remove the
seeds with a teaspoon. Cut the flesh into
cubes and place in the bowl. Cut the bell
pepper into similar-size cubes. Add to
the bowl with the shallots, scallions,
mint and parsley. Stir gently.

Two To make the dressing, crush the
garlic and mix with the salt to form a
paste. Use a fork to whisk the lemon
juice, olive oil and Tabasco sauce into the
garlic, then season with black pepper.

Three Toast the pita bread until crisp.
Cut into 1/2-inch squares and add to the
salad. Pour in the dressing and toss.

Coleslaw

*If you have never before made coleslaw, you will be amazed
at how different real home-made slaw tastes from that
sold in plastic tubs by supermarkets.*

Preparation time *30 minutes*
Total cooking time *None*
Serves 6–8

MAYONNAISE
*2 egg yolks
1 heaping tablespoon Dijon mustard
or 1 heaping teaspoon mustard
powder
1 cup lightly flavored
vegetable oil
1 tablespoon white wine vinegar*

*¹/₂ head white cabbage
1 onion
2 carrots*

One To make the mayonnaise, first bring all the ingredients to room temperature and then set a large bowl on a damp kitchen towel to prevent it from moving. Add the egg yolks, mustard, some ground white pepper and a pinch of salt, and mix well with a hand whisk or electric mixer.

Two Put the oil in a pitcher that is easy to pour from. While whisking constantly, pour a steady thin stream of oil into the mixture. Stop pouring periodically to allow each addition to fully emulsify to a thick, creamy mixture. If the oil is added too quickly, the mayonnaise will separate. Continue until a third of the oil has been added and the mayonnaise has begun to thicken.

Three Add the vinegar to make the texture slightly thinner. Continue gradually adding the oil and adjust the flavor by adding more vinegar, salt and white pepper if necessary. If the mayonnaise curdles or separates, add 1–2 tablespoons of boiling water

Four Finely slice the cabbage and onion and coarsely grate the carrots. Place these in a large bowl and mix together gently with your hands. Using your hands or a large metal spoon (the former is a little messy, but gentler and more effective) mix in enough mayonnaise to coat the vegetables. Season and serve.

CHEF'S TIPS *Up to half the light vegetable oil can be replaced with olive oil, but the flavor of olive oil is too strong to use alone.*

Any unused mayonnaise can be covered tightly and stored in a clean canning jar in the refrigerator for up to 3 days.

Artichoke, spinach and pine nut salad

*This fresh-tasting salad could either be served
as a first course, or with crusty bread as
a light lunch on a hot summer's day.*

Preparation time 40 minutes
Total cooking time 30 minutes
Serves 4

4 large fresh artichokes
juice of 2 lemons
3 cups firmly packed baby spinach
leaves
1/2 cup pine nuts (pignoli), toasted
3 tablespoons olive oil
1/3 cup grated Parmesan
16 black olives, halved and pitted

One Prepare the fresh artichokes, following the method in the Chef's techniques on page 534. When you place the artichokes in the pan of boiling water, use the juice from one of the lemons in the water. Once you have cooked and prepared the artichokes, cut the chokes into bite-size wedges, cover and set aside.

Two In a large bowl, toss the spinach leaves with the pine nuts. Whisk the olive oil with 1 tablespoon lemon juice and freshly ground black pepper to taste, and use to dress the spinach. Divide the artichoke pieces among four bowls and pile the spinach up in the center. Top the salad with the Parmesan and black olives.

Smoked chicken salad with macadamia nut dressing

This delicious salad contains all the ingredients for a wonderful lunch or light supper—smoked chicken and asparagus with peppery arugula and baguette slices.

Preparation time *20 minutes*
Total cooking time *15 minutes*
Serves 4

12 asparagus spears
12 thin slices French baguette
4 cups arugula leaves
2 x 5¾ oz. smoked chicken breasts
sprigs of fresh chervil, to garnish

DRESSING
⅓ cup macadamia nuts
3 tablespoons white wine vinegar
2 tablespoons olive oil
3 tablespoons macadamia or hazelnut oil

One Bring a large saucepan of salted water to a boil. Use a vegetable peeler to remove the outer layer from the lower two-thirds of each asparagus spear. Snap the woody ends off at their natural breaking point and discard. Cut the spears into 1-inch pieces and simmer until tender. Remove, run under cold water and drain on paper towels.

Two To make the dressing, preheat the broiler. Put the macadamia nuts onto a baking sheet and broil for 5 minutes— they can burn very quickly after they start to brown. Allow to cool slightly before chopping with a sharp knife.

Three Place the slices of baguette on a baking sheet in a single layer and toast for 5 minutes on each side under the broiler, or until crisp and golden brown.

Four Place the vinegar, olive oil and macadamia oil in a small bowl and whisk, using a small hand whisk, until combined, then stir in the chopped macadamia nuts and season well.

Five Stir the dressing to distribute the nuts and drizzle a little over the arugula, tossing to thoroughly coat. Arrange the baguette slices and arugula on plates. Cut the chicken into bite-size pieces and put in a small bowl with the asparagus.

Stir the dressing and pour over a little to coat. Place the chicken and asparagus on the arugula and top with the chervil.

CHEF'S TIP *If making the dressing in advance, add the nuts just before using.*

Salmon salade niçoise

This typical Provençal salad from Nice is traditionally made with tuna, but here it is served with a salmon fillet. Perfect for a light summer supper.

Preparation time *20 minutes*
Total cooking time *1 hour*
Serves 4

3/4 lb. small salad or new potatoes
1/2 lb. green beans
8 quail eggs
1 green bell pepper, cut into julienne strips (see Chef's tip)
1 red bell pepper, cut into julienne strips
2 shallots, finely sliced
4 ripe tomatoes, cut into 6 pieces
4 x 5 oz. salmon fillets, skin removed
1 small head Boston or Bibb lettuce
2 3/4 cups arugula leaves
20 black olives

VINAIGRETTE
2 tablespoons balsamic vinegar
1/2 cup olive oil

One Bring a large saucepan of salted water to a boil and add the potatoes in their skins. Return to a boil and simmer for 30–35 minutes, or until tender to the point of a knife. Drain, then plunge into a bowl of iced water for 5 minutes to stop the cooking process. Drain again and cut into quarters.

Two Bring a large saucepan of fresh salted water to a boil and trim the ends off the beans. Put in the saucepan and boil for 8 minutes, or until tender, then place into iced water as above to stop the cooking process and retain the color of the beans. Drain well.

Three Bring a small saucepan of salted water to a boil and boil the quail eggs for 4 minutes, or until hard-boiled. Run the eggs under cold water, set aside to cool, then peel and cut them in half.

Four To make the vinaigrette, place the balsamic vinegar into a small bowl and whisk in the olive oil and some salt and black pepper with a small hand whisk. Place the potato quarters, green beans, peppers, shallots and tomatoes into a large bowl and toss very gently with half the vinaigrette.

Five Heat a lightly oiled grill pan or frying pan over high heat and when hot, cook for 10 minutes, or until cooked through, turning once. Remove from the pan and keep warm. Place the lettuce and arugula leaves on four plates and arrange the potato mixture, quail eggs and olives on top. Place a portion of salmon on top of each salad and drizzle with the remaining vinaigrette.

CHEF'S TIP *Julienne strips are vegetables cut to the size and shape of matchsticks.*

Seared scallop and mango salsa salad

*A very pretty appetizer for a special occasion. The scallops
and salsa can be prepared ahead, leaving just the brief
cooking of the scallops to the last minute.*

Preparation time *30 minutes*
Total cooking time *5 minutes*
Serves 4

16 large scallops
1 tablespoon olive oil
1 tablespoon unsalted butter
young salad leaves, to serve
sprigs of cilantro, to garnish

MANGO SALSA
2 ripe mangoes
*6 ripe tomatoes, peeled, seeded and
diced (see page 534)*
¹/₄ cup cilantro leaves, finely chopped
2 large shallots, finely chopped
2 green chiles, finely chopped
juice of 2 limes

One If the scallops are in their shells,
remove them by sliding a knife
underneath the white muscle. Wash the
scallops to remove any grit or sand, then
pull away the small tough shiny muscle
and the black vein. Dry the scallops on
paper towels, cover and chill.

Two To make the mango salsa, dice the
mangoes into ¹/₂-inch cubes and mix
with the tomatoes, cilantro leaves,
shallots, chiles and lime juice. Season
with salt and pepper. Cover and place in
the refrigerator until ready to serve.

Three Heat the olive oil in a nonstick
frying pan, add the butter and when it
has melted and starts foaming, place the
scallops in the frying pan. Cook for

3–4 minutes, or until lightly golden on
both sides and just tender to the touch.
Arrange a bed of salad leaves on 4 plates
and spoon over the salsa. Top with the
warm scallops, any juices and the
cilantro sprigs and serve immediately.

LE CORDON BLEU COMPLETE COOK

Duck salad with plum dressing

*This easy and unusual salad has a wonderful flavor
and is glamorous enough for a dinner party appetizer.*

Preparation time *20 minutes*
Total cooking time *10 minutes*
Serves 4

DRESSING
*1 cup canned plums in syrup,
pitted
1 tablespoon honey
1 teaspoon Worcestershire sauce
1 tablespoon dark soy sauce
1/2 teaspoon Tabasco sauce*

*4 x 7 oz. duck breasts
4 slices white bread
4 tablespoons unsalted butter
1 tablespoon olive oil
2 cloves garlic, crushed
4 scallions
4 cups curly endive*

One To make the dressing, place the plums and their syrup, the honey and the Worcestershire, soy and Tabasco sauces in a small saucepan. Bring to a boil over medium heat and simmer for 5 minutes, then remove from the heat and allow to cool. Once cooled, put the plum mixture with all the liquid into a blender or food processor and process until completely smooth. Check the seasoning, adding salt and black pepper only if necessary, and transfer to a small bowl. Cover and put in the refrigerator to chill.

Two Prick the duck breasts all over with a fork and place them skin side down in a hot frying pan. Cook for 5 minutes, or until the skin is well browned and the fat has melted out. Turn them over and cook the other side for 2 minutes, or until cooked through.

Three Remove the crusts from the bread and cut the bread into 3/4-inch cubes. In a large heavy-bottomed frying pan, heat the butter, oil and garlic over medium heat until the butter has melted, then raise the heat a little, and add the cubes of bread and cook them for 2–3 minutes, stirring frequently to ensure that they cook to an even golden color, taking care that they do not burn. Remove the frying pan from the heat, drain the croutons on crumpled paper towels and sprinkle them with a little salt and black pepper.

Four Remove the skin from the duck breasts if you prefer and cut across into 1/4-inch thick slices. Cut the scallions diagonally and tear the curly endive into bite-size pieces. Toss the scallions, endive and half the croutons in about 1 tablespoon of the plum dressing just to coat, and then pile into a dish. Arrange the duck slices on top and scatter over the remaining croutons. Serve immediately with the remaining plum sauce offered on the side.

Chicken liver salad with bacon and croutons

Chicken liver has a delicate flavor and soft moist texture when cooked. When pan-fried it is best served slightly pink in the center. Here, the sherry vinegar dressing cuts its richness.

Preparation time *15 minutes*
Total cooking time *15 minutes*
Serves 4

6–8 cups mixed salad leaves
6 oz. slab bacon, rind removed, cut
into thin strips
1/3 cup oil
2 slices bread, crusts removed, cut into
small cubes
14 oz. chicken livers
2 tablespoons unsalted butter
3 shallots, finely chopped
2 1/2 tablespoons vinegar

VINAIGRETTE DRESSING
2 tablespoons Dijon mustard
1/4 cup sherry vinegar
1/3 cup oil

One Wash and dry the salad leaves and then refrigerate, covered with a clean dish towel, to prevent wilting.

Two Fry the bacon in a dry skillet over medium heat. Remove and drain on crumpled paper towels. Set aside.

Three Heat the oil in a shallow skillet, add the bread cubes and fry, stirring, until golden brown. Remove and drain on crumpled paper towels. Sprinkle lightly with salt and keep warm.

Four Clean the chicken livers, removing the small green area that can be bitter, and cut into small pieces. Heat the butter in a skillet and toss the liver over high heat for 2 minutes. Add the shallots and fry for another 2 minutes, then season with salt and pepper and transfer to a plate. The liver should be barely pink and juicy inside. Add the vinegar to the pan and heat to dissolve any of the sticky juices. Pour the juice over the liver and keep warm.

Five To make the vinaigrette dressing, put the mustard and sherry vinegar with salt and pepper to taste in a bowl and add the oil in a slow, steady stream, mixing continuously with a fork or small whisk until fully blended.

Six Put the salad leaves in a bowl, pour the dressing over and carefully toss to coat thoroughly without bruising the leaves. Serve topped with the bacon, croutons and liver with its juices.

Warm lentil salad with mustard vinaigrette

This traditional regional salad, high in protein, may be served with shellfish, such as shrimp. Normally, the small French Puy lentils are used as they hold their shape well. However, other green or brown lentils could be used instead. Red lentils are not suitable as they soften to a purée.

Preparation time *15 minutes*
+ overnight soaking
Total cooking time *40 minutes*
Serves 6

1½ cups brown or green lentils
3 tablespoons unsalted butter
⅔ cup diced carrots
½ onion, diced
3 oz. bacon, diced
1¼ cups chicken stock (see page 519)
1 head Boston or Bibb lettuce

VINAIGRETTE
2 tablespoons whole grain mustard
2 teaspoons white wine vinegar
⅓ cup olive or peanut oil
¼ cup chopped fresh parsley

One Soak the lentils in cold water overnight. Drain.

Two Melt the butter in a large saucepan, add the vegetables and bacon and cook gently until soft but not brown.

Three Add the lentils and chicken stock to the saucepan. Cover and simmer very gently for 30–35 minutes, or until the lentils are tender. Season to taste. Pour the mixture into a strainer and allow the liquid to drain off. Transfer the lentils, vegetables and the bacon to a bowl.

Four To make the vinaigrette, whisk together the mustard and white wine vinegar. Season and very slowly add the olive oil or peanut oil, whisking constantly. Finally, add the parsley.

Five Toss the warm lentils, vegetables and bacon with the vinaigrette. Arrange a bed of lettuce leaves on a plate and pile the warm salad in the center.

Warm fennel and cherry tomato salad

The dressing for this salad is an aromatic herb oil, made a week in advance to allow the flavors to infuse. If making extra, the oil keeps well and is perfect for drizzling over grilled meat and fish.

Preparation time *10 minutes*
+ 1 week infusing
Total cooking time *30 minutes*
Serves 4

AROMATIC OIL
¼ cup sesame oil
1 cup olive oil
½ cup hazelnut oil
1 bay leaf
1 sprig of fresh thyme
1 sprig of fresh rosemary

3 large or 4 small bulbs fennel with feathery leaves
1 sprig of fresh thyme
¾ lb. ripe cherry or small plum tomatoes
½ cup Pecorino or Parmesan cheese, freshly shaved

One Begin by making the aromatic oil at least 1 week in advance. Place the oils, bay leaf, thyme and rosemary in a saucepan and heat gently for 5 minutes without boiling. Season well. Cool, then transfer to a sterilized screwtop bottle or jar and store the oil in the refrigerator for a week, turning the bottle occasionally. After a week, decant the oil into a clean bottle, discarding the herbs.

Two To make the salad, trim the feathery leaves from the top of the fennel bulbs and reserve for garnish, then cut each fennel bulb into eight, leaving a little of the bottom on each section to hold it together. Brush generously with about ¼ cup of the aromatic oil.

Three Heat a grill until it is very hot and brush with a little of the oil. Alternatively, the vegetables can be placed under a preheated broiler, but then they will not have the attractive charred lines. Place the fennel on the pan and cook on high heat for 10 minutes on each side, or until tender, caramelized and lightly charred. When the fennel is cooked, set aside and keep warm.

Four Heat the remaining oil in a large shallow pan until very hot. Carefully place the thyme and tomatoes in the hot oil and fry for 2–3 minutes, or until the skins are just splitting. Remove with a slotted spoon, discarding the thyme and reserving the oil, and pile up on a plate with the fennel and any juices. Top with the Pecorino or Parmesan and reserved fennel leaves. Season with some salt and black pepper and drizzle over some of the oil from cooking the tomatoes. Serve immediately with fresh bread.

Warm chicken and mushroom salad

*The warmth of the chicken and mushroom brings
out the tangy flavor of the Dijon dressing.*

***Preparation time** 20 minutes*
***Total cooking time** 15 minutes*
Serves 4

*2 skinned, boneless chicken breast
halves
oil, for cooking
3 tablespoons unsalted butter
7 oz. mixed wild mushrooms,
trimmed
1 shallot, finely chopped
5–6 cups mixed salad leaves
2 teaspoons Dijon mustard
2 teaspoons red wine vinegar
1/3 cup olive oil
sprigs of fresh chervil or parsley,
to garnish*

One Season the chicken with salt and pepper, then heat a little oil in a skillet and fry for 4 minutes on each side, or until tender. Remove from the pan, cover with aluminum foil and set aside.

Two Heat a little more oil in the pan, add the butter and fry the mushrooms for 3–5 minutes, or until tender and lightly colored. Add the shallot and cook for 1 minute. Season to taste and remove with a slotted spoon.

Three Wash and dry the salad leaves and tear into bite-size pieces. Set aside in a large bowl. Remove the foil from the chicken and slice at an angle lengthwise.

Four Whisk together the mustard and vinegar. Continue whisking and slowly add the oil. Pour half the dressing over the salad leaves and toss well; place a mound in the center of each plate. Toss the mushrooms in half of the remaining dressing and sprinkle over the salad. Arrange the chicken on top. Drizzle with the remaining dressing and garnish with sprigs of fresh chervil or parsley.

fish and seafood

Salmon kedgeree

An old English favorite with a twist: fresh salmon and dill replace the traditional smoked haddock. Prepare the ingredients the day before.

Preparation time 20 minutes
Total cooking time 16 minutes
Serves 4

2 eggs, at room temperature
3 tablespoons unsalted butter
¾ lb. salmon fillet, cooked and flaked
1¼ cups long-grain rice, cooked and well drained
1 egg, beaten
¼ cup whipping cream
1–2 teaspoons chopped fresh dill or snipped fresh chives

One Bring a small saucepan of water to a boil, gently put in the 2 eggs, return to a boil and simmer for 7 minutes. Remove the eggs with a spoon and place in a bowl of iced water to cool. Tap the shells with the back of a spoon to craze them, then peel. Coarsely chop the eggs—the yolks should still be a little moist.

Two Melt the butter in a skillet, add the cooked salmon and heat for 30 seconds. Add the rice and the chopped egg and, using a wide spatula, toss over high heat for 2 minutes, or until hot. Keep your movements light and the mixture loose as you do not want to compact the rice.

Three Add the beaten egg with the cream. Toss for 3–5 minutes, scraping the bottom of the pan, until the egg has set. Season with salt and pepper. Pile onto a warm serving dish and sprinkle with the fresh dill or chives to serve.

CHEF'S TIPS *For the best result, the rice needs to be quite dry, so cook it the day before, drain well, cover and refrigerate.*

Don't worry that the boiled eggs initially seem underdone as they will continue to cook in the kedgeree.

Gravlax

This method of curing salmon in salt, sugar and dill is Scandinavian.
The salmon is left to marinate for 1½ days and is then
served with a traditional sweet dill and mustard dressing.

***Preparation time** 1 hour*
+ 36 hours refrigeration
***Total cooking time** None*
Serves 10

1 x 3³/₄ lb. salmon fillet, skin on but
scales removed
¹/₃ cup rock, kosher or sea salt
¹/₃ cup sugar
4 tablespoons chopped fresh dill
1¹/₂ tablespoons black peppercorns,
crushed
2 teaspoons coriander seeds, crushed
1 teaspoon ground allspice
6 tablespoons roughly chopped fresh
dill leaves

DILL AND MUSTARD DRESSING
2 teaspoons sweet mustard (German)
or 2 teaspoons whole grain mustard
mixed with 2 teaspoons honey
2 teaspoons chopped fresh dill
2 teaspoons white wine vinegar or
cider vinegar
1 cup vegetable oil

One Wash the salmon fillet, dry it with paper towels and lay on a baking sheet or plate, skin side down. Mix together the salt, sugar, dill, peppercorns, coriander seeds and allspice and spoon over the fish. Cover with plastic wrap, top with a baking sheet and then a 1-lb. weight to press the salmon lightly (this could be cans spaced out along the fish). Refrigerate for 24 hours.

Two Remove the weight and covering, discard the solids from the marinade, then rinse the remaining marinade off with cold water and pat the salmon dry with some paper towels. Place the salmon on a clean baking sheet or plate, skin side down.

Three Press the dill onto the salmon, then cover with plastic wrap and press over it with your fingers to make the dill stick. Refrigerate for 12 hours.

Four To make the dill and mustard dressing, mix all the ingredients except the oil in a bowl with some salt and black pepper, then slowly drizzle the oil into the bowl, whisking to emulsify with the other ingredients.

Five Uncover the salmon, removing any excess dill, and place on a cutting board.

With a long, thin-bladed knife held at an angle of 45 degrees and 2¹/₂–3 inches from the tail, cut a slice toward the tail and continue working to produce short, thin slices. Serve with the dressing.

CHEF'S TIP *For a variation, try this beet and mustard mixture. Follow the recipe to the end of Step 2, then combine ¹/₃ cup mustard seeds (first soaked in cold water for 30 minutes, then drained) and 2 cups very finely chopped cooked beets. Press onto the salmon and continue as above.*

LE CORDON BLEU ✤ COMPLETE COOK

Spinach and crab roulade

*Thick slices of light spinach roulade with
a creamy crab filling are perfect for brunch,
a light lunch or served as a first course.*

Preparation time 45 minutes
Total cooking time 40 minutes
Serves 6

FILLING
1 tablespoon unsalted butter
1 tablespoon all-purpose flour
3/4 cup milk
7 oz. white crab meat, fresh, frozen or
canned
pinch of cayenne pepper

ROULADE
1 lb. young spinach, large stems
removed
1 tablespoon unsalted butter, melted
4 eggs, separated
pinch of ground nutmeg

One To make the filling, melt the butter in a heavy-bottomed saucepan over low-medium heat. Sprinkle the flour over the butter and cook for 1 minute without allowing it to color, stirring constantly with a wooden spoon. Remove the saucepan from the heat and slowly add the milk, whisking or beating vigorously to avoid lumps. Return to low heat and briskly stir with a wooden spoon or whisk until the mixture is smooth and begins to thicken, then turn up the heat and stir briskly until boiling. Simmer for 3–4 minutes, or until the sauce coats the back of a spoon. Cover with a piece of buttered waxed paper pressed onto the surface and set aside.

Two To make the roulade, line a jelly roll pan, about 15½ x 10½ inches, with parchment paper. To cook the spinach, half-fill a large saucepan with water and bring to a boil, add a generous pinch of salt and the spinach. Return to a boil and cook for 1–2 minutes, then drain the spinach in a strainer, run under cold water and squeeze out the excess water. Chop finely, using a large sharp knife. Put the spinach in a large bowl and add the butter.

Three Preheat the oven to 400°F. Stir the egg yolks and nutmeg into the spinach and season well. In a large bowl, beat the egg whites until stiff and forming peaks, then stir a large tablespoon of egg

whites into the spinach mixture to lighten it. Add the remaining egg whites in one addition, then using a large metal spoon, carefully fold into the spinach. Pour into the prepared pan, lightly smoothing it to the edges with a flexible bladed knife. Bake for about 10 minutes, or until the mixture is just set and springs back to the light touch of a finger. Meanwhile, spread a clean towel onto the work surface and cover it with parchment paper.

Four Reheat the filling mixture, then stir in the crab, cayenne pepper and salt and freshly ground black pepper to taste, and heat through.

Five Turn the spinach roulade out onto the paper and towel and remove the pan and the paper lining. Quickly spread with the crab filling, then, with the shortest edge facing towards you, pick up the towel and the paper and push the roulade away from you, holding it very low, so that the roulade rolls up like a jelly roll. Stop when the last of the roulade is underneath, then transfer it onto a dish. Cut the roulade into thick slices and serve immediately.

CHEF'S TIPS *This is perfect to serve alone, but can also be served with a sauce such as hollandaise or Béarnaise.*

Parchment paper, for lining the tin, is now widely available.

Ceviche

*Ceviche originated in South America and is the perfect way to show off
the freshest fish. The acidity of the lime dressing magically "cooks"
the raw fish until it is opaque, just as if heat had been used.*

Preparation time *55 minutes
+ 4 hours refrigeration*
Total cooking time *1 minute*
Serves 6

*1¹⁄₄ lb. snapper, sea bass or any firm
white fish fillets, skin removed (see
Chef's tips)
juice of 6 limes
1 small onion, finely chopped
1 green bell pepper, halved, seeded and
finely chopped
¹⁄₂ red chile, seeded and finely
chopped
¹⁄₂ cucumber, cut into ¹⁄₄-inch cubes
1 small avocado, peeled and cut into
¹⁄₄-inch cubes
4 tomatoes, peeled, seeded
and diced (see page 534)
sprigs of fresh parsley or chervil,
to garnish*

WATERCRESS VINAIGRETTE
*3 cups watercress leaves, tough
stems removed
1¹⁄₄ tablespoons white wine vinegar
¹⁄₃ cup olive oil*

One Cut the fish fillets into ¹⁄₄-inch-wide slices, pour the lime juice over the top, cover and refrigerate for about 2 hours.

Two Drain the fish, then add some salt and black pepper, the onion, green bell pepper, chile, cucumber and avocado and mix gently to combine. Cover with plastic wrap and refrigerate for 1–2 hours. Chill six serving plates.

Three To make the vinaigrette, add the watercress to a saucepan of boiling salted water and cook for 1 minute, then drain and run the watercress under cold water. Pat dry with paper towels to remove excess water, then purée in a blender or food processor with the white wine vinegar and olive oil. Season with some salt and black pepper.

Four To serve, place a 3-inch egg ring or cookie or pastry cutter in the center of a chilled plate and spoon the ceviche into it until full, packing down lightly with the back of a spoon. Remove the ring and repeat on the other plates. Decorate the plates with the watercress vinaigrette and garnish with the diced tomatoes and parsley or chervil. Serve with bread.

CHEF'S TIPS *If you can only buy a whole snapper, sea bass or red porgy, buy a 1¹⁄₂-lb. fish and remove the bones yourself following the method in the Chef's techniques on page 526.*

For a creamier variation, add 1 cup coconut milk with the vegetables.

Smoked salmon and leek terrine with sauce verte

*Beautifully light but with a good depth of flavor, this dish makes a
perfect appetizer or lunch. Cooking the leeks in fish stock helps them
to press together better, and makes it easier to slice the terrine.*

Preparation time 1 hour
+ 4 hours refrigeration
Total cooking time 20 minutes
Serves 10

6 cups fish stock (see page 519)
30 very small whole leeks, tough green
leaves and roots removed
10–15 large spinach leaves, stems
removed
1–1 1/4 lb. long slices smoked salmon
arugula leaves, to garnish

SAUCE VERTE
3 1/2 cups watercress, tough stems
removed
3/4 cup fresh chervil leaves, chopped
3/4 cup fresh dill leaves, chopped
3/4 cup fresh parsley leaves, chopped
few drops of lemon juice
1 1/3 cups crème fraîche or sour cream

One In a large saucepan, bring the fish
stock to a boil. Put the leeks in the stock,
reduce the heat and simmer gently for
20 minutes, or until tender. Drain well,
then set aside to cool.

Two Blanch the spinach in boiling water
for 30 seconds. Drain, then plunge into
iced water. Carefully remove the leaves
individually and place on paper towels
or a cloth towel and pat dry.

Three Line a 4-cup, 8 1/2 x 4-inch terrine
mold with plastic wrap, then line the
bottom and sides with some smoked
salmon, allowing a long overhang at one
end. Add a layer of spinach, allowing for
an overlap over one side of the terrine.

Four Tightly pack 2 layers of leeks
lengthwise into the bottom of the lined
terrine and season well, then add a layer

of half the remaining salmon, followed
by one layer of leeks and seasoning.
Cover with the remaining salmon and
top this with 2 layers of leeks and
seasoning. Fold over the salmon and
spinach overhangs to enclose the filling
and cover with plastic wrap. Cut a piece
of cardboard to fit inside the terrine,
cover it twice with foil and place a 2-lb.
weight on top (use cans if you like).
Refrigerate for 4 hours.

Five To prepare the sauce verte, put the
watercress, herbs and a little water into
a blender and blend to a fine purée. Push

through a coarse strainer, add the lemon
juice and salt and black pepper and fold
in the crème fraîche or sour cream.
Cover with plastic wrap and place in the
refrigerator until ready to serve.

Six To serve, slice the terrine and arrange
neatly on plates with a spoonful of
the sauce verte and some arugula leaves
to garnish.

Creamy and salsa oysters

Two versions of classic oyster dishes. The creamy version is made with white wine and bacon
and is flashed under the broiler to create a golden topping. If you prefer less heat, just omit the chile.
The salsa oysters are not cooked and come with a fiery tomato, red onion and lime dressing.

***Preparation time** 50 minutes*
***Total cooking time** 15 minutes*
(Creamy oysters)
Serves 4

24 oysters

CREAMY
2 teaspoons Tabasco sauce
1/4 lb. bacon slices
4 egg yolks
1/3 cup white wine
1/3 cup whipping cream, lightly
whipped
1/2 red chile, seeded and
finely chopped
1 tablespoon olive oil
1 small red bell pepper, cut into
julienne strips (see Chef's tip)

OR

SALSA
2 cups peeled, seeded, and diced
tomatoes (see page 534)
1 red onion, finely chopped
juice of 2 limes
1 teaspoon Tabasco sauce
1 teaspoon roughly chopped fresh
cilantro
1 tablespoon roughly chopped fresh
flat-leaf parsley
fresh cilantro leaves, to garnish

salad leaves or crushed ice, to serve

One Shuck the oysters following the method in the Chef's techniques on page 522. Add the oysters to their liquid in the bowl and refrigerate until needed. Clean the deeper half of the shells thoroughly and discard the flat halves.

Two To make the creamy oysters, add half the Tabasco to the oysters before refrigerating. Place the bacon in a small saucepan, cover with cold water, bring to a boil and simmer for 4 minutes. Drain, then run under cold water to remove excess salt. Drain the bacon on paper towels, then cut into matchsticks.

Three Put the egg yolks, wine and remaining Tabasco in a heatproof glass bowl over a saucepan of simmering water, ensuring the bowl is not touching the water. Whisk vigorously until the mixture has increased to three or four times the original volume and leaves a trail across the surface when the whisk is lifted. Remove the bowl from the saucepan, whisk until it cools to room temperature, then fold in the cream and chile and set aside.

Four Preheat the broiler. Heat the oil in a saucepan and fry the bacon until golden. Add the red bell pepper and cook for 1 minute, or until soft but not colored.

Five Heat the oysters and their juices in another saucepan over low heat for 1 minute. Do not overheat or the oysters will toughen. Put the warm oysters back in their shells and place in a flameproof dish (a layer of rock salt underneath will help them stay balanced). Pour over the juices and place the bacon and bell pepper mixture on top. Spoon the egg mixture over them and place under the broiler for 2 minutes, or until golden. Serve immediately.

Six To make the salsa, mix together all the ingredients except the whole cilantro leaves with some salt and black pepper. Cover with plastic wrap and set aside for 20 minutes at room temperature.

Seven Place an oyster in each shell and spoon over some juices and a little salsa, then garnish with a cilantro leaf. Arrange on a bed of salad leaves or crushed ice.

CHEF'S TIP *Julienne strips are vegetables cut to the size and shape of matchsticks.*

about oysters...

Oysters need to be bought from a reliable source as they have a reputation for harboring toxins. There are several different varieties available including Pacific oysters, Portuguese oysters, American oysters and "natives". Like any other fresh produce, oysters are at their best when in season. Ask your fish merchant if you need advice.

Dressed crab

In Britain, the most traditional way to enjoy fresh crab is to "dress" it.
This enduring favorite is well worth the effort and evokes
the feeling of an old-fashioned English seaside vacation.

***Preparation time** 40 minutes*
***Total cooking time** 10 minutes*
Serves 1–2

2 eggs, at room temperature
1 x 1½–2 lb. cooked crab (see Chef's tip)
1–2 tablespoons mayonnaise
1 cup fresh bread crumbs
Worcestershire or Tabasco sauce
¼ cup chopped fresh parsley
3 canned anchovy fillets, to garnish
3 teaspoons drained capers, to garnish
2 tablespoons sliced stuffed green olives, to garnish
4 slices whole wheat bread
1 tablespoon unsalted butter, at room temperature
1 lime or lemon, cut into wedges

One To hard-boil the eggs, place them in a small saucepan and cover with cold water. Bring to a gentle boil and cook for 10 minutes. Drain and cool in cold water. Peel the eggs and push the whites and the yolks separately through a fine metal strainer.

Two Prepare the crab, following the method in the Chef's techniques on page 523. Scrape all the creamy brown meat from the shell and flake it into a bowl. Stir in the mayonnaise and bread crumbs to bind, adding more of each if the flavor of the dark meat is too strong. Season with salt, freshly ground pepper and Worcestershire or Tabasco sauce.

Three Crack open the claws and remove all the white meat, checking that there are no shell splinters left. Season to taste with salt and white pepper.

Four Place the white meat from the claws and body of the crab towards the two outer sides of the cleaned and dried shell. Spoon the brown meat into the center, then arrange the chopped parsley on the seams in between. Cover half of the white meat with the egg whites; spoon the egg yolks on the dark meat. Garnish with anchovies, capers and sliced olives. Butter the bread thinly, and serve the dressed crab with the bread and butter, and lime or lemon wedges to the side.

CHEF'S TIP *When choosing a crab, select one that feels heavier than it looks. If possible, buy a fresh crab, as frozen crabs tend to lose a lot of flavor and liquid as they defrost. Male crabs have larger claws than females.*

Coquilles Saint-Jacques Mornay

*Coquilles Saint-Jacques, the French term for scallops, literally means
"Saint James's shells." Here the scallops are baked in the half shell
beneath a crown of piped potato and a Gruyère cheese sauce.*

Preparation time 25 minutes
Total cooking time 45 minutes
Serves 4

8 sea scallops, preferably in
their shells
1/2 cup finely grated Gruyère cheese

DUCHESSE POTATOES
2 lb. baking potatoes, peeled and
cut into pieces
1 1/2 tablespoons unsalted butter
2 egg yolks
pinch of freshly grated nutmeg

MORNAY SAUCE
1 tablespoon unsalted butter
2 tablespoons all-purpose flour
1 cup milk
1 egg yolk
1/2 cup grated Gruyère cheese

One Prepare the scallops, following the method in the Chef's techniques on page 524. Place the scallops flat on a cutting board and slice each one into 3 circles, leaving the orange roe (if available) whole. Cover and refrigerate.

Two If you have purchased scallops in their shells, scrub the shells, put them in a saucepan of cold water and bring to a boil. Simmer for 5 minutes, then drain and allow to cool and dry. If you do not have scallops in their shells, use scallop shells purchased in a specialty cookware shop or 4 small shallow gratin dishes.

Three To make the duchesse potatoes, put the potatoes in a large saucepan of salted, cold water. Cover and bring to a boil, reduce the heat and simmer for 15–20 minutes, or until tender. Drain, return to the saucepan and shake over low heat for 1–2 minutes to remove excess moisture. Mash the potatoes, then stir in the butter and egg yolks and season with nutmeg, salt and black pepper. Spoon the mixture into a pastry bag with a 5/8-inch star tip. Preheat the oven to 400°F.

Four To make the Mornay sauce, melt the butter in a heavy-bottomed saucepan over medium-low heat. Sprinkle over the flour and cook for 1 minute without allowing it to color, stirring continuously with a wooden spoon. Remove from the heat and slowly add the milk, blending thoroughly. Return to the heat and bring slowly to a boil, stirring constantly. Lower the heat and cook for 3–4 minutes, or until the sauce coats the back of a spoon. Remove from the stove and stir in the egg yolk and cheese, then season with salt and black pepper.

Five Pipe shell shapes or overlapping circles of duchesse potato to form a border around the edge of each shell or dish. Place on a baking sheet that has a rim so that the round edge of each shell rests on the rim to prevent the filling from running out. Place a sliced scallop and whole roe in each shell, season and spoon the Mornay sauce over the top. Sprinkle with the cheese and bake for 12–15 minutes, or until golden brown.

Asparagus, artichoke and lobster salad

*This is an elegant salad for a special occasion. The walnut oil adds
a delicious nuttiness to the dressing, but don't be tempted
to increase the quantity because it has a strong flavor.*

Preparation time *1 hour + chilling*
Total cooking time *35 minutes*
Serves 4

COURT BOUILLON
1 large carrot, thinly sliced
2 onions, thinly sliced
2 stalks celery, thinly sliced
1 leek, white part only, thinly sliced
3 sprigs of fresh thyme
1 bay leaf
10 black peppercorns
2 cups white wine
1/4 cup salt

3 uncooked lobster tails
24 spears asparagus
1/3 cup salt, extra

DRESSING
1/4 cup sherry vinegar
1 shallot, finely chopped
1/4 cup walnut oil
1/2 cup vegetable oil
*1 tablespoon chopped fresh chervil
or chives*

*4 large artichoke hearts, from a jar
or can*
*20 whole fresh chervil leaves,
to garnish*

One To make the court bouillon, place all the vegetables with the thyme sprigs, bay leaf, peppercorns and wine in a large kettle or stockpot and bring to a boil. Cook for 5 minutes over high heat. Add the salt and 4 quarts water and return to a boil. Add the lobster tails, bring to a boil and cook for 12 minutes. Remove the kettle from the heat and allow the lobster to cool slightly.

Two When the lobster is cool enough to handle, remove it from the bouillon. Discard the bouillon. Remove the tail flesh in a single piece, following the method in the Chef's techniques on page 524, then slice into medallions. Cover and refrigerate.

Three Wash the asparagus under cold, running water. Using a small knife, remove the spurs from the asparagus spears, starting from the top and working down, then peel the outer layer from the lower two-thirds of the spear using a vegetable peeler. Lining up the tips, tie the spears in bundles of six to eight and cook in 4 quarts of salted water, following the method in the Chef's techniques on page 535. When cooked, place the asparagus in a bowl, cover and refrigerate.

Four To make the dressing, whisk together the vinegar and shallot. Gradually whisk in the oils, then the chervil or chives. Season and set aside. Rinse the artichokes well, pat dry, toss them in a little dressing and season to taste. Repeat with the asparagus, being careful not to break the tips. Refrigerate the vegetables until ready to use. To serve, arrange the artichokes, asparagus and lobster medallions on serving plates. Drizzle the remaining dressing around the artichokes, then garnish with the chervil leaves.

*CHEF'S TIP The cooked lobster tail
shells can be frozen and used another
time when preparing a seafood bisque
or stock.*

about lobsters...

True lobsters have large front pincers but as this recipe just calls for the tails you can use rock lobster or crayfish instead. Buy live lobsters so you know they are fresh and then kill them humanely by putting them in the freezer for a couple of hours beforehand, following the method in the Chef's techniques on page 524.

Garlic shrimp

Ideal as an appetizer or light summer lunch,
serve this Spanish-inspired dish with lots of crusty
bread to soak up the lemony garlic butter.

***Preparation time** 20 minutes*
***Total cooking time** 10 minutes*
***Serves** 4*

1/4 lb. curly endive, escarole or frisée
1 red chile, seeded and thinly sliced
1 tablespoon fresh chervil leaves
24 large shrimp, shells on
2 teaspoons vegetable or olive oil
4 cloves garlic, crushed
1/2 cup unsalted butter,
cut into cubes
finely grated zest and juice of 1 lemon
1 tablespoon finely chopped fresh
parsley

One Mix together the endive, escarole or frisée, chile and chervil leaves and pile onto the center of four plates.

Two Shell and devein the shrimp, removing the heads but leaving the tails intact, following the method in the Chef's techniques on page 522. Place the shrimp on a plate and season lightly.

Three Heat the oil in a large, heavy-bottomed frying pan over medium-high heat. Fry the shrimp for 1 minute on each side, or until they are cooked through. Remove and keep warm.

Four Add the garlic to the frying pan and cook for 1 minute, then add the cubes of butter and cook for 4 minutes, or until the butter is nut brown. Remove from the stove and add the lemon zest and juice and the parsley.

Five Quickly shake the frying pan once or twice to combine all the ingredients, then add the shrimp and toss briefly to warm through. Arrange around the salad and drizzle with any pan juices.

Crab cakes

*These crispy crab cakes make a perfect light lunch with salad,
or you can make lots of small ones to serve as appetizers
at a barbecue or as part of a summer picnic.*

Preparation time *55 minutes
+ 20 minutes cooling + 30 minutes
refrigeration*
Total cooking time *20 minutes*
Serves 4–6

2 tablespoons vegetable oil
1 onion, finely chopped
2 cloves garlic, crushed
1½ tablespoons grated fresh ginger
1 small red bell pepper, halved, seeded
and cut into fine dice
8 scallions, finely chopped
1 lb. crabmeat, drained well if frozen
or canned
2 teaspoons Tabasco sauce
2 tablespoons chopped fresh
flat-leaf parsley
3 tablespoons fresh bread crumbs
½ teaspoon Dijon mustard
1 egg, beaten
1⅔ cups all-purpose flour, seasoned
with salt and pepper
1¼ cups fresh bread crumbs
⅔ cup grated Parmesan cheese
2 eggs
oil, for deep-frying
lemon wedges, to serve

One Heat the oil in a frying pan and add
the onion, garlic and ginger. Cook for
1 minute, then add the bell pepper and
scallions and cook for 2 minutes, or
until soft. Transfer to a plate and leave
for 20 minutes to cool completely. Stir in
the crabmeat, Tabasco, parsley, bread
crumbs, mustard and some salt and
black pepper. Add the beaten egg and
bind together.

Two Divide the mixture into 4, 6 or
12 portions, depending on desired size
of cakes. Using lightly floured hands and
a lightly floured surface, shape into

cakes. Put on a baking sheet, cover and
refrigerate for 30 minutes, or until firm.

Three Place the flour on a large piece of
waxed paper. Combine the bread
crumbs and Parmesan on another piece
of paper. Beat the eggs in a shallow dish.
One at a time, place cakes in the flour,
then pat off any excess. Put in the eggs
and use a brush to help coat. Remove

with a fish turner or spatula and coat in
the bread crumbs and Parmesan.
Reshape the cakes, pressing the crumbs
on, then place on a baking sheet.

Four Heat ½ inch oil in a nonstick frying
pan and cook the crab cakes in batches
over medium heat for 1–2 minutes each
side, or until golden. Drain on paper
towels and serve with lemon wedges.

Fritto misto with a garlic dip

*There are a number of ways to prepare Italy's well-known mixed fry.
Here the fish is simply dipped in flour, egg and then bread crumbs
before being fried to a crispy golden brown.*

***Preparation time** 1 hour*
***Total cooking time** 20 minutes*
Serves 6 as a starter or
2 as a main course

2 shallots, finely chopped
2/3 cup dry white wine
1 bay leaf
1 sprig of fresh thyme
10 oz. fresh mussels, scrubbed and
beards removed (see page 523)
5 oz. fresh squid (calamari)
oil, for deep-frying
4 eggs, lightly beaten
3/4 cup all-purpose flour, seasoned
with salt and pepper
2 1/2 cups fresh bread crumbs
5 oz. plaice, sole or flounder fillet,
cut into strips
5 oz. cod, ling cod or haddock fillet,
cut into large, bite-size cubes
3/4 cup mayonnaise
1 tablespoon plain yogurt
2 cloves garlic, finely chopped
fresh parsley and lemon wedges,
to garnish

One Put the shallots, wine, bay leaf and thyme in a large saucepan, cover and bring to a boil. Add the mussels, discarding any that are already open, cover and reduce to medium heat. Cook for 2 minutes, shaking the pan occasionally, until the mussels open (discard any that do not open). Drain and remove from the shells.

Two To prepare the fresh squid, remove the wings from the tube, peel off the skin and remove the head. Remove the clear cartilage quill from the opening of the tube, cut off the tentacles and rinse the tube under running water. Drain, dry, then slice into rings.

Three Fill a large heavy-bottomed saucepan one-third full with oil and heat to 375°F. Put the eggs, flour and bread crumbs into separate dishes. Toss the fish, mussels and squid in the flour, shake off the excess, then dip into the egg and finally coat with the bread crumbs, shaking off the excess. Deep-fry the breaded seafood in batches (see page 537) until golden brown, drain on paper towels and sprinkle lightly with salt. If keeping warm for a few minutes, do so on a wire rack in a warm oven, uncovered to keep them crisp.

Four To make the garlic dip, stir together the mayonnaise, yogurt and garlic and serve in a bowl to accompany the seafood. Garnish with the parsley and lemon wedges.

Sardines with walnut and parsley topping

A crisp walnut topping gives these broiled fresh sardines a lovely texture.
They can be served as a main course or appetizer with warm olive oil,
lemon wedges, arugula leaves and plenty of fresh bread.

Preparation time *40 minutes*
Total cooking time *20 minutes*
Serves 4

WALNUT AND PARSLEY TOPPING
2/3 cup unsalted butter
4 shallots, finely chopped
2 cloves garlic, crushed
4 tablespoons fresh white bread
crumbs
1 cup walnuts, finely chopped
2 teaspoons chopped fresh parsley

16 x 1³/4 oz. fresh sardines, cleaned
and scales removed
2 tablespoons all-purpose flour
1/4 cup olive oil

One To make the topping, melt the butter in a saucepan over moderate heat. Add the shallots and garlic, cover and cook for 3 minutes, or until soft and translucent. Remove from the stove, season, then add the bread crumbs, walnuts and parsley and mix thoroughly.

Two Preheat the broiler to high. Wash the sardines and dry on paper towels. Put the flour and oil on separate plates. One at a time, roll the sardines in flour to coat, shaking off the excess. Coat both sides in oil, then transfer half the sardines to a baking sheet or shallow roasting pan. Place under the broiler and cook for 3 minutes on each side. Keep warm while you cook the second batch.

Three Sprinkle the walnut and parsley topping over the sardines and press firmly onto the skin. Grill again in two batches until the topping is golden brown. Serve drizzled with a little warmed olive oil and with lemon or lime wedges on the side.

Trout flans with chive and lemon sauce

*These delicately flavored and finely textured flans, served with
a smooth lemon butter sauce, make an elegant first course
to impress your friends and dinner guests.*

***Preparation time** 30 minutes*
***Total cooking time** 30 minutes*
Serves 4

TROUT FLANS
*fresh flat-leaf parsley leaves,
to garnish
10 oz. trout, skin and bones removed
and trimmed
1/4 teaspoon salt
pinch of cayenne pepper
1 egg
2/3 cup whipping cream
3/4 cup milk*

CHIVE AND LEMON SAUCE
*1 shallot, finely chopped
juice of 1 lemon
2/3 cup unsalted butter, chilled and cut
into small cubes
1 tablespoon very finely chopped
fresh chives*

One Preheat the oven to 325°F. Prepare four 3 x 1½-inch individual soufflé dishes or custard cups by cutting four rounds of waxed paper to the same diameter. Grease the molds, then line them with the rounds of waxed paper and brush the lining with softened butter, pressing out any air holes. Press one or two parsley leaves onto the waxed paper, then refrigerate.

Two To make the flan mixture, cut the trout into ½-inch cubes and place in a food processor with the salt, cayenne pepper and the egg. Blend until smooth. Scrape down with a spatula and process again. With the machine still running, add the cream and milk, stopping the moment the liquid is incorporated—the mixture should resemble a cake batter. Push the mixture through a strainer into a pitcher.

Three Pour the mixture into the molds, tapping them on a work surface to remove any air bubbles. Smooth the tops and transfer the molds to a small roasting pan lined with one or two sheets of paper towel, spacing them evenly apart. Fill the pan with boiling water to come halfway up the sides of the molds; transfer to the oven and bake for 15–20 minutes. Insert a small knife in the center of a mold for 3 seconds. If the blade comes out hot, the flans are cooked. Remove from the hot water bath and allow to rest. Keep warm.

Four To make the chive and lemon sauce, place the shallot and lemon juice in a small saucepan. Add 2 tablespoons water, bring to a boil and reduce for about 5–7 minutes, or until almost dry. Reduce the heat to low, then whisk in the butter, a few pieces at a time, without letting the sauce boil. Strain into a clean saucepan and season to taste with salt and white pepper. Just before serving, whisk in the chives.

Five Loosen the flans from the inside of the molds using a knife. Gently unmold the flans onto individual serving plates. Carefully remove the paper, drizzle the sauce around and serve immediately.

CHEF'S TIP *When making a lightly colored sauce, use ground white pepper rather than black pepper as the white pepper will not show.*

Shrimp with stir-fried bell peppers

*This colorful dish is perfect as a starter or a light main course.
It derives its superb flavor from the sweetness of the
bell peppers, spiked with lemon oil and fresh ginger.*

Preparation time *30 minutes*
+ 1 hour infusion
Total cooking time *5 minutes*
Serves 4

LEMON OIL
¹/₄ cup oil
finely grated zest of ¹/₄ lemon

2¹/₂ lb. uncooked extra large or
jumbo shrimp, with heads attached
if possible
1 red bell pepper
1 yellow bell pepper
1 tablespoon grated fresh ginger
1 tablespoon crushed garlic
¹/₄ cup dry sherry
2 tablespoons lemon juice
2 teaspoons light soy sauce

One To make the lemon oil, gently warm
the oil until lukewarm. Add the lemon
zest, then allow the oil to cool and infuse
for 1 hour. Strain before using.

Two Leaving the heads attached, remove
the shells and tails from the shrimp.
Remove the eyes then devein the shrimp
(see Chef's techniques on page 522). Pat
dry on paper towels.

Three Halve the bell peppers and remove
stems and seeds. Dice the bell peppers
into ¹/₄-inch cubes.

Four Heat the lemon oil in a wok or deep
heavy-bottomed skillet over high heat
until it begins to smoke. Add the ginger,
garlic and bell peppers and stir-fry for
1 minute. Add the shrimp and stir-fry for
1 minute. Stir in the sherry, lemon juice
and soy sauce; stir-fry for 3 minutes, or
until the shrimp are just tender. Serve hot
with crusty bread and a green salad.

Moules marinière

*This is a classic French way to prepare mussels,
cooked simply in white wine and onions
and enriched with cream.*

Preparation time *15 minutes*
Total cooking time *10 minutes*
Serves 4

*1/4 cup unsalted butter
2 onions, chopped
4 lb. fresh mussels, scrubbed and
beards removed (see page 523)
1 1/2 cups dry white wine
1 bay leaf
1 large sprig of fresh thyme
3/4 cup whipping cream
1 cup chopped fresh parsley*

One In a deep stockpot, melt the butter, add the onions and cook over medium heat until transparent and soft, stirring constantly to prevent the onion from coloring. Stir in the mussels, wine, bay leaf and thyme and place a tight-fitting lid on the stockpot. Turn the heat to high and cook rapidly for 2–3 minutes, shaking the stockpot occasionally, until all the mussels have opened. Discard any mussels that do not open.

Two Remove the mussels from the liquid and set aside. Strain the liquid through a fine strainer into a clean saucepan and reheat. Stir in the cream and season to taste with salt and freshly ground black pepper. Divide the mussels among four bowls and pour the liquid over them. Just before serving, sprinkle with the chopped parsley.

Three Provide a finger bowl and a spare bowl for the shells. Serve with hot crusty bread to soak up the juices.

CHEF'S TIP *Mussels can be kept alive overnight by placing in a bowl in the refrigerator covered with a damp cloth to keep them closed and moist.*

Seared tuna with chickpea salad

*These tuna steaks are infused with Asian flavors and are seared quickly
to great effect. The chickpea salad is very versatile and is also
lovely with broiled or barbecued vegetables or chicken.*

Preparation time 10 minutes + overnight
soaking + 3–4 hours marinating
Total cooking time 1 hour 5 minutes
Serves 4

²⁄₃ cup dried chickpeas (garbanzos)
(see Chef's tip)
4 x 5–6 oz. tuna steaks
1 bay leaf
1 shallot, chopped
1 small clove garlic, crushed
1 red chile, seeded and chopped
1 red bell pepper, chopped
1 avocado
2 tablespoons chopped fresh
cilantro leaves
4 lime wedges, to serve

MARINADE
⅓ cup olive oil
finely grated zest and juice
of 1½ limes
6 stems fresh cilantro, coarsely
chopped or slightly bruised

One Soak the chickpeas overnight in
plenty of cold water.

Two Combine the marinade ingredients
and mix well. Place the tuna steaks in a
shallow glass or nonreactive dish and
pour in a third of the marinade, turning
to coat both sides. Cover with plastic
wrap and refrigerate for 3–4 hours,
turning the tuna occasionally.

Three Drain the chickpeas and place in a
large saucepan and cover with water.
Add the bay leaf, bring to a boil, then
reduce the heat and simmer for 1 hour,
or until tender. Drain and set aside.

Four To make the chickpea salad, place
the chickpeas, shallot, garlic, chile and

bell pepper in a bowl and toss well. Peel
and dice the avocado and fold into the
salad with the cilantro. Strain the
remaining marinade into the salad and
season to taste.

Five Preheat the broiler or barbecue grill
to high. When the broiler is hot, cook

the tuna for about 2 minutes on each
side, or grill for 1 minute on each side.
Serve on warmed plates with a wedge of
lime, and the chickpea salad on the side.

CHEF'S TIP *To save time, you can use
1½–2 cups canned chickpeas. Drain
well and add to the salad in step 4.*

Whole baked salmon with watercress mayonnaise

*Baked in aluminum foil to retain the salmon's flavor and moist texture,
this impressive centerpiece is the perfect dish for a large summer
gathering, served with new potatoes and summer vegetables.*

Preparation time *1 hour 10 minutes
+ 1 hour refrigeration*
Total cooking time *40 minutes*
Serves 10–12

*1 x 3–3¹/₂ lb. whole salmon, cleaned
and scales removed (ask your fish
merchant to clean the fish and
remove the scales)
1 small onion, thinly sliced
1 small bay leaf
1 sprig of fresh thyme
5 sprigs of fresh parsley
¹/₃ cup dry white wine
sprigs of watercress, to garnish
lemon wedges, to garnish*

WATERCRESS MAYONNAISE
*4 cups watercress, tough stems
removed
1¹/₄ cups whole-egg
mayonnaise
few drops of lemon juice*

One Lift up the gill flap behind the cheek
of the salmon head and, using kitchen
scissors, remove the dark, frilly gills.
Repeat on the other side of the fish. If
any scales remain, hold the tail and,
using the back of a knife, scrape the skin
at a slight angle, working toward the
head. Trim the fins. Cut across the tail to
shorten it by half, then cut a V shape
into the tail. Wash the salmon under
cold water and open it on the belly side
where the fishmonger has slit it. Remove
the blood vessel lying along the
backbone using a spoon. Rinse and wipe
inside and out with paper towels.

Two Preheat the oven to 350°F. Butter a
piece of aluminum foil large enough to
wrap around the fish and place on a
large baking sheet. Lay the salmon just
off center and place the onion and herbs
inside the belly. Season with salt and
black pepper, then pour over the wine.
Quickly cover with foil and seal the
edges tightly.

Three Bake for 30–40 minutes, or until
the fish feels springy and firm to the
touch. Open the foil and allow to cool.
Remove the onion and herbs and
transfer the salmon onto waxed paper,
draining off any liquid. Prepare the
salmon for serving following the Chef's
techniques on page 527, then cover with
plastic wrap and refrigerate for 1 hour,
or until it is needed.

Four To make the watercress
mayonnaise, add the watercress to a
saucepan of boiling salted water and
cook for 1 minute, then drain and run
under cold water. Pat dry with paper
towels to remove excess water, then
purée in a blender or food processor.
Beat the purée gradually into the
mayonnaise. If it is too dry, add a few
drops of lemon juice. Season with salt
and black pepper.

Five To serve, decorate the fish with
some mayonnaise and serve the
remainder separately. Garnish with the
watercress sprigs and lemon wedges.

Broiled lobster with a buttery Pernod sauce

*Seafood gains a wonderful new dimension when served with a buttery
sauce brightened with a dash of Pernod. The anise flavor of the
sauce is enhanced with the infusion of star anise.*

Preparation time 15 minutes
Total cooking time 30 minutes
Serves 4

PERNOD SAUCE
1 star anise
2 tablespoons Pernod
3/4 cup unsalted butter, cubed

4 uncooked lobster tails
3 tablespoons unsalted butter, melted

One To make the Pernod sauce, place
1/2 cup water in a small saucepan with
the star anise and bring to a boil. Reduce
the heat to low and simmer the sauce for
10 minutes, or until reduced to about
2 tablespoons. Stir in half the Pernod.
Whisking constantly, gradually add the
butter, a few pieces at a time. Season
with salt and ground white pepper, then
place the pan in a bowl of hot water to
keep warm or transfer the sauce to the
top of a double boiler over hot water.
(The sauce will separate if placed back
over direct heat.)

Two Add the lobster tails to a large
saucepan of boiling water and cook for
2 minutes, or until the shells turn bright
orange. Drain and refresh in cold water.
Place the lobster tails on a cutting board
with the soft undershells facing down.
Using a large knife, but without cutting
all the way through, split the tails in half
lengthwise down the back, then open
them up.

Three Preheat the broiler to high. Brush
the lobster flesh with the melted butter,
season lightly, then broil cut side down
for 5 minutes. Turn and broil the other
side for 5–10 minutes, or until the flesh
is firm.

Four Transfer to serving plates. Stir the
remaining Pernod into the sauce, then
spoon a little sauce over the tails and
serve the remainder on the side.

CHEF'S TIP *You could also use cooked
whole Maine lobsters in this recipe. First
remove the claws by twisting where they
meet the body, then crack them using a
nutcracker or meat mallet and set aside
to serve later with the broiled lobsters.*

*Place the lobsters face down on a
cutting board. Using a large knife, but
without cutting all the way through,
split the lobsters in half lengthwise down
the back, then open them up. Remove
the vein along the tail, the small sac just
behind the mouth, and any coral or
grey-green liver (tomalley). Brush the
flesh with melted butter, season lightly
and broil under a hot broiler until
heated through, turning during cooking.*

Roast salmon with a basil and sweet pepper sauce

*The smoky sweetness of roasted bell peppers marries with peppery basil
in this inspirational sauce that makes salmon fillets, simply cooked,
so sumptuous. Enjoy in the garden with a glass of chilled wine.*

***Preparation time** 15 minutes*
***Total cooking time** 8–12 minutes*
Serves 4

2 red bell peppers
⅓ cup olive oil
*4 x 6 oz. salmon fillets, scaled but
skin on*
2 tablespoons vegetable oil
2 tablespoons unsalted butter
*2 tablespoons shredded fresh
basil leaves*

One Preheat the oven to 425°F. Lightly brush the whole bell peppers with some olive oil, then place them on a baking sheet and roast for 15–20 minutes, or until the skin is blackened and blistered and the peppers are soft.

Two Cover the peppers with plastic wrap, or place in a plastic bag. The peppers will sweat, making the skins peel off more easily. Allow to cool. Peel away the skin, then halve and seed the bell peppers.

Three To make the sauce, place the peppers in a blender or food processor, add the remaining olive oil and process to a smooth purée. Season to taste with salt and freshly ground black pepper, and transfer to a small saucepan.

Four Season the salmon fillets with salt and freshly ground pepper. Heat the vegetable oil and butter in a roasting pan over high heat. Place the salmon in the pan skin side up, then bake for 2 minutes. Turn and bake for 6 minutes, or until the salmon is cooked through and the skin is lightly colored.

Five Gently heat the sauce, then add the basil. Transfer the salmon to warm plates and pour the sauce around. Serve at once with a mixed green salad.

Smoked trout gougère

Here, a cheese-flavored crown of pastry holds a filling of smoked trout, leek, tomato and dill. For a variation, you could try a mixture of fish such as salmon and monkfish, or perhaps some shellfish.

***Preparation time** 35 minutes*
***Total cooking time** 45 minutes*
Serves 6

CREAM PUFF PASTRY
1¼ cups all-purpose flour
⅓ cup unsalted butter, cut into cubes
pinch of salt
4 eggs, lightly beaten
1 cup coarsely grated Cheddar cheese
1 teaspoon Dijon mustard

FILLING
½ lb. smoked trout fillet
1 tablespoon unsalted butter
1 small leek or 4 scallions, white part only, sliced
2 tablespoons all-purpose flour
¾ cup milk
1 large tomato, peeled, seeded and cut into ½-inch strips (see page 534)
1 teaspoon chopped fresh dill

1 egg, beaten
1 tablespoon grated Parmesan cheese
1 tablespoon lightly toasted fresh bread crumbs
1 tablespoon unsalted butter, melted chopped fresh dill, to garnish

One Brush six 5¾ x 1¼-inch round gratin dishes with melted butter and refrigerate to set.

Two Make the pastry following the method in the Chef's techniques on page 545) and using 1 cup of water. When the pastry is smooth, thick and glossy, beat in the cheese and mustard and season well with salt and black pepper. Cover and set aside.

Three To make the filling, place the smoked trout flat in a shallow saucepan and pour in enough cold water to cover. Slowly bring to a boil, covered, then turn off the heat and leave for 7 minutes.

Four Melt the butter in a deep saucepan, add the leek and cook over low heat for 3 minutes to soften. Sprinkle with the flour, stir in using a wooden spoon and cook for 1 minute. Remove from the heat, mix in the milk, then return to the heat and bring to a boil, stirring constantly. Simmer for 1 minute, or until the mixture thickens.

Five Preheat the oven to 400°F. Remove the fish from its cooking liquid, pat dry with paper towels, then use a fork to take the fish lightly off its skin in flakes.

Gently fold the flakes into the filling so they do not break up too much, along with the tomato, dill and salt and black pepper.

Six Fill a pastry bag with a ½–⅝-inch tip with the pastry dough. Pipe a circle around the bottom of each prepared dish, then a second circle on top to cover the side of the dish. Spoon the filling into the middle of the gratin dishes and brush the top of the pastry lightly with the beaten egg. Combine the Parmesan and bread crumbs, sprinkle over the filling, then drizzle with the melted butter. Place on a baking sheet and bake for 15–20 minutes, or until the pastry is risen and crisp. Sprinkle with chopped dill before serving.

CHEF'S TIPS *You can also spoon in the pastry to cover the sides of the dish and give a more peaked surface.*

To make one large gougère, use a deep 8-inch round flameproof dish and bake for 30–35 minutes.

Snapper with fennel en papillote

*Cooked in a package of parchment paper or foil to retain all the juices
and flavors, the white wine, basil leaves and gentle anise
aroma of fennel infuse the sweet snapper.*

Preparation time 40 minutes
Total cooking time 35 minutes
Serves 4

2 x ³⁄4 lb. snapper fillets
2 large bulbs fennel
4 tablespoons unsalted butter
16 fresh basil leaves
4 tablespoons dry white wine
4 teaspoons Pastis or Ricard (optional)

One Wash the fish, dry on paper towels and refrigerate until needed. With a small, sharp knife, trim off the small stalks at the top of the fennel bulbs, keeping the leaves and discarding the thick stalks. With a large, sharp knife, cut the bulb in half from the top down through the root, then cut away and discard the root. Cut the fennel into ¹⁄4-inch-thick slices.

Two Heat the butter in a saucepan, add the fennel slices, cover and cook over low heat for 25 minutes, or until tender to the point of a sharp knife. Remove from the stove and season with some salt and black pepper. Preheat the oven to 425°F.

Three Fold a piece of parchment paper or aluminum foil in two, then cut out a large half teardrop shape 2 inches bigger than the fish. Unfold the paper or foil and you should have a heart shape. Repeat to make 4 total, then lay the shapes flat and brush with melted butter. Spoon the fennel onto one side of each heart and spread to the size of the fish. Place a fish fillet on top and lightly season with salt and black pepper. Arrange 4 basil leaves on each piece of fish, then sprinkle each fish with a tablespoon of white wine and a teaspoon of Pastis or Ricard. Top with the reserved fennel leaf sprigs.

Four Immediately fold over the empty side of paper or foil and seal the edges by twisting and folding tightly. Place on a baking sheet or in a shallow flame-proof dish and bake for 5–8 minutes. Place the fish packages on serving plates and let your guests open them at the table to release the aroma.

CHEF'S TIP *Other fish can be cooked by this method, such as perch, mackerel or cod. The cooking times will vary according to the thickness and shape of the fish.*

LE CORDON BLEU ✠ COMPLETE COOK

Fish and chips

Tradition at its best: firm white fish that flakes at the touch of a fork, cooked in a crisp batter and served with homemade chips—French fries. For best results, make sure the fish is very fresh and eat piping hot.

Preparation time 20 minutes
+ 30 minutes resting
Total cooking time 20 minutes
Serves 4

1¼ lb. baking potatoes, peeled
oil, for deep-frying
¼–½-lb. firm white fish fillet pieces,
skin removed
2–3 tablespoons all-purpose flour,
seasoned with salt and pepper
lemon wedges, to garnish

BATTER
1¼ cups cornstarch
1¼ cups all-purpose flour
1 tablespoon baking powder
1¼–2 cups beer

One Cut the potatoes into batons ¼–½ inch wide, ½ inch deep and 2½–3 inches long. Put in a bowl and cover with cold water.

Two To make the batter, sift the cornstarch, all-purpose flour, baking powder and some salt and black pepper into a bowl and make a well in the center. Gradually pour in the beer, using a wooden spoon to beat it into the flour, until the mixture becomes a smooth batter the consistency of cream (the amount of liquid you need will depend on the flour you use). Cover and rest for 30 minutes at room temperature.

Three Meanwhile, fill a deep fryer or heavy-bottomed saucepan one-third full of oil and heat to 315–325°F (a cube of bread dropped into the oil will brown in 30 seconds). Drain the fries and pat dry, then fry until the bubbles subside and the fries form a thin, light golden skin. Lift out the fries, allowing excess oil to

drip back into the fryer, and transfer to crumpled paper towels.

Four Increase the temperature of the oil to 350°F (a cube of bread dropped into the oil will brown in 15 seconds). Wash the fish and dry thoroughly on paper towels.

Five Place the seasoned flour on a plate and coat the fish, shaking off the excess. Dip the fish into the batter until it is evenly coated, then lift out using fingers or forks to allow any excess mixture to

drip off. Lower the fish into the fryer or saucepan and fry, in batches if necessary, for 5 minutes, or until golden and crisp. Do not crowd the saucepan or the temperature will lower. Remove and drain on crumpled paper towels. Season with salt, place on a wire rack and keep warm.

Six Put the fries in the oil again and fry until golden and crisp. Remove and drain, season with salt and serve with the fish, lemon wedges and tartar sauce or ketchup.

"Lasagna" of salmon with tomato and spinach

There is no pasta in this special dish, but the effect is like a lasagna, with layers of pink salmon, dark green spinach leaves, and white and tomato sauces, making for a stunning dinner-party recipe.

Preparation time 1 hour
Total cooking time 1 hour 15 minutes
Serves 4

4 x ¼–½ lb. thick center cuts salmon
fillet, skin removed and cut into
3 slices horizontally (ask your fish
merchant to do this)
⅓ cup olive oil
2 onions, finely chopped
2 lb. ripe tomatoes, peeled,
seeded and diced (see page 534)
2 cloves garlic, crushed
1 bouquet garni (see page 520)
3 tablespoons unsalted butter
1½ lb. spinach, tough stems removed
small pinch of grated nutmeg
12 small black olives, halved and
pitted, to garnish
sprigs of fresh chervil, to garnish

BEURRE BLANC (WHITE
BUTTER SAUCE)
3 shallots, finely chopped
1¼ cups dry white wine
3 tablespoons cider vinegar
1 tablespoon whipping cream
or crème fraîche
¾ cup unsalted butter, cut into small
cubes and chilled
2 tablespoons finely chopped
fresh chives

WHITE SAUCE
1 tablespoon unsalted butter
2 tablespoons all-purpose flour
1 cup milk

One Separate the slices of salmon, brush with olive oil, cover and place in the refrigerator. Heat the oil in a saucepan, add the onions, cover and cook for 4 minutes, or until soft and translucent. Stir in the tomatoes, garlic, bouquet garni and some salt and pepper. Cook for 40 minutes, stirring occasionally, until the mixture is thick. Discard the bouquet garni, reseason and keep warm.

Two To make the beurre blanc (white butter sauce), put the shallots, wine and vinegar in a saucepan, bring to a boil and cook to reduce by one-quarter. Add the cream and remove from the heat, then whisk in the butter a piece at a time to form a creamy, flowing sauce that coats the back of a spoon. Strain the sauce into a bowl, stir in the chives, cover with plastic wrap and place over a saucepan of warm water.

Three To make the white sauce, melt the butter in a heavy-bottomed saucepan over low-medium heat. Sprinkle the flour over the butter and cook for 1–2 minutes without allowing it to color, stirring continuously with a wooden spoon. Remove the saucepan from the heat and slowly add the milk, whisking to prevent lumps. Return to medium heat and bring to a boil, stirring. Cook for 3–4 minutes, or until the sauce coats the back of a spoon. Cover and keep warm. Preheat the broiler.

Four Melt the butter in a large frying pan or wok, add the spinach and toss over high heat for 2 minutes, or until wilted. Add nutmeg, salt and black pepper and place in a strainer over a bowl to drain. Season the fish and broil for 1 minute each side.

Five To serve, take four plates and place a salmon slice on each one. Using half the spinach, spread a layer on each slice, then add half the white sauce, followed by half the tomato sauce. Cover with another slice of fish, the remaining spinach, white and tomato sauces, and finish with the remaining salmon. Spoon the beurre blanc around the bottom of the plate and garnish with the olive halves and chervil leaves.

---

about tomatoes...

Tomatoes have become remarkably popular since their arrival in Europe in the sixteenth century. The best flavored are those that have been left to ripen on the vine. For immediate use they should be firm and brightly colored with no wrinkles or cracks. Pale red tomatoes can be left to ripen naturally in the light, but not in the sun. Uniformity of shape or color bears no relation to the flavor.

Trout braised in Riesling wine

*The Alsace region of France, which borders Germany, is well known
for its preparation of the freshwater fish caught in its rivers. In this
recipe, the fish is braised in Riesling, a typical Alsatian wine.*

Preparation time 35 minutes
Total cooking time 1 hour 10 minutes
Serves 4

1/3 cup unsalted butter
3 onions, thinly sliced
1 2/3 cups sliced button mushrooms
1 tablespoon chopped fresh parsley
2 large shallots, chopped
1 cup Riesling wine
1 cup fish stock (see page 519)
*8 x 5 oz. freshwater trout fillets, skin
and all bones removed*
1 cup whipping cream
*chopped fresh parsley, to
garnish*

One Preheat the oven to 350°F.

Two In a heavy-bottomed skillet, melt
1/4 cup of the butter over low heat. Add
the onions with a pinch of salt and cook,
covered, for 15 minutes without
coloring, or until the onions are soft and
translucent. Stir in the mushrooms and
3/4 cup water and cook uncovered until
almost all the liquid has evaporated. Stir
in the parsley, season to taste and set
aside to cool.

Three In a medium saucepan, melt the
remaining butter over low heat and cook
the shallots for 3 minutes without
coloring. Add the wine and increase the
heat to high. Bring to a boil and cook
for 5 minutes. Pour in the stock, remove
from the heat and set aside to cool.

Four Butter a flameproof casserole or
baking dish large enough to hold the
trout fillets in a single layer. Place a fillet
skinned side down onto a flat surface
and sprinkle with some salt and freshly
ground black pepper. Place 1–2 spoons
of the onion and mushroom mixture
onto the wide (head end) part of the
fillet. Fold the tail end over and place the
stuffed fillet in the buttered dish. Repeat
with the remaining fillets, making sure
to leave a little space between each one.

Five Pour over the cooled wine and fish
stock, place the casserole onto the stove
top and bring the liquid just to a boil.
Immediately cover and place in the oven
for 5–8 minutes, or until the fish is
opaque and feels firm to the touch.

Carefully remove the fish onto a plate,
cover and keep warm while finishing
the sauce.

Six Pass the cooking liquid through a
fine strainer into a saucepan. Place over
medium heat and simmer until reduced
in volume by three-quarters, to about
1/4 cup. Add the cream and simmer for
5 minutes, then season. Arrange the
trout fillets on a platter or individual
plates, coat with the sauce and sprinkle
with the parsley just before serving.

Sole meunière

A stylish classic: the sole is quickly pan-fried, then butter and lemon juice are poured on top and the fish is eaten hot with parsley and lemon wedges. Dover sole is recommended for its firm texture and succulence, but any flat fish could be substituted.

Total preparation time 10 minutes
Total cooking time 10 minutes
Serves 4

4 x 1/4–1/2 lb. sole fillets,
skin removed
6 1/2 tablespoons clarified butter
2/3 cup all-purpose flour, seasoned
with salt and pepper
6 1/2 teaspoons unsalted butter,
cut into cubes and chilled
1 tablespoon lemon juice
2 teaspoons finely chopped fresh
parsley, to garnish
1 lemon, cut into wedges,
to garnish

One Wash the fish, then dry well on paper towels. In a large frying pan, heat the clarified butter until hot.

Two Place the seasoned flour on a plate and roll the fillets in it to coat thoroughly, then pat off any excess. Place in the pan skinned side up and fry for 2 minutes, turning once, or until the fish is lightly golden. Remove and place on hot plates.

Three Drain off the hot butter used for frying and wipe out the pan with paper towels before returning to the heat. Add the chilled butter to the pan and cook until golden and frothy. Remove from the heat, immediately add the lemon juice and, while still bubbling, spoon or pour over the fish.

Four Garnish with some parsley and serve with the lemon wedges.

Lobster à l'Américaine

In this famous lobster dish, the lobster is cooked in the shell in a tomato and wine sauce. There is much dispute on the origin of the name—whether it should be Armoricaine, the ancient name for Brittany, or Américaine, after a French chef who had worked in the United States.

Preparation time *30 minutes*
Total cooking time *50 minutes*
Serves 4

4 x 1 lb. lobsters or 2 x 1³/₄–2 lb. lobsters
¹/₃ cup vegetable oil
3 tablespoons unsalted butter
1 onion, diced
1 carrot, diced
2 stalks celery, diced
¹/₂ cup dry white wine
2¹/₂ tablespoons brandy
2 cups fish stock
3 tablespoons tomato paste
1 lb. ripe tomatoes, halved and seeded
1 bouquet garni (see page 520)
sprigs of fresh parsley, to garnish

One If you have bought live lobsters, kill them according to the method in the Chef's techniques on page 524. If you prefer not to do this, ask your fish merchant to do it.

Two Prepare the lobster following the method in the Chef's techniques on page 525. To fry the lobster claws and tails, heat the oil in a large frying pan and add the claws and tails. Fry quickly, turning with long-handled tongs, until they turn red and the tail flesh shrinks visibly from the shell. Remove them from the pan onto a plate and continue according to the method on page 525.

Three Heat half the butter in the pan and fry the pieces of lobster head shell quickly until the color has changed, as before. Remove any of the flesh and set aside. Add the reserved shell from the tail with the onion, carrot and celery and cook for 5 minutes, or until lightly browned. Add the wine and reduce by half, then add the brandy and the stock.

Four Stir in the tomato paste and cook for 1 minute before adding the tomato halves. Cover the pan with a lid and, over gentle heat, cook for 20 minutes, or until the tomatoes are pulpy. While this is cooking, put the reserved coral and tomalley (liver) from the lobster into a blender with the remaining butter and blend until smooth.

Five Remove the lid from the pan, add the bouquet garni and the reserved fried claws and cook for 10 minutes. Remove the claws and cool before cracking to remove the flesh.

Six Strain the tomato mixture into a clean pan, discarding the shell, tomato skins, bouquet garni and diced vegetables. Cook, stirring occasionally, for 4 minutes, or until lightly syrupy.

Seven Whisk the coral and tomalley flavored butter into the sauce until smooth, then add the lobster tail flesh and simmer very gently for 1 minute (if overcooked, the flesh with be tough). Remove the pan from the stove and allow the lobster tail to rest for 5 minutes in the sauce before removing and slicing into round slices. Gently rewarm the lobster slices in the sauce with all the cracked claw and head meat. To serve, spoon onto hot plates and garnish with the parsley.

CHEF'S TIP *Lobsters generally have two large front claws. Although in some countries crayfish are also called spiny lobsters, they do not have the large front claws.*

Sole Véronique with potato galettes

This classic French recipe uses white grapes in a white wine sauce to accompany poached lemon sole. Here the dish is served on crisp potato galettes.

Preparation time 1 hour
Total cooking time 1 hour 15 minutes
Serves 4

POTATO GALETTES
1 lb. baking potatoes, peeled and cut into even-size pieces
4 egg whites
clarified butter (see page 520), for frying

8 x ¼ lb. sole fillets, skin removed
2 shallots, finely chopped
⅓ cup dry white wine
¾ cup fish stock
1 cup seedless white grapes
1¼ cups whipping cream

One To make the potato galettes, put the potatoes in a large saucepan of salted, cold water. Cover and bring to a boil, then reduce the heat and simmer for 15–20 minutes, or until the potatoes are tender to the point of a sharp knife. Drain, return to the saucepan and shake over low heat for 1–2 minutes to remove excess moisture. Mash or push through a fine strainer, season with salt and black pepper and allow to cool.

Two Meanwhile, wash the sole and dry well on paper towels. Fold the skinned side under at each end of the fillets to create 8 fillets 4 inches long. Butter a shallow 12 x 8½-inch flameproof dish and sprinkle half the shallots over the bottom. Place the sole fillets on the shallots, drizzle with 1 tablespoon each of the wine and the stock and season lightly with some salt and black pepper. Cover with plastic wrap and set aside in the refrigerator.

Three Put the grapes in a saucepan of boiling water and cook for 15 seconds, then drain and plunge into iced water to cool. Remove from the water, peel away their skins and reserve the grapes and skins separately.

Four Preheat the oven to 350°F. In a bowl, whisk the egg whites until they form stiff peaks. Stir one-quarter of the egg whites into the potatoes then, using a spatula or large metal spoon, gently fold in the remaining egg white.

Five Pour ½ inch clarified butter into a large heavy-bottomed frying pan and place over moderate heat. Lightly oil the inside of a 3-inch round plain egg ring or cookie or pastry cutter and place in the pan. Put a ¼-inch layer of the potatoes inside the ring. Gently loosen around the sides with a thin-bladed knife and lift the ring away. Repeat to fill the pan, leaving enough space between the galettes to turn them over. Fry for 5 minutes on each side, or until golden brown. Drain on paper towels, then remove to a wire rack in a low oven and keep warm.

Six Put the remaining shallots, the wine and the stock in a saucepan. Add the grape skins, bring to a boil, then simmer for 20 minutes, or until the mixture is syrupy. Meanwhile, bake the sole for 10–12 minutes, or until the flesh is opaque and cooked through. Stir the cream into the sauce and simmer for 5 minutes, or until syrupy, then strain into a clean saucepan, discarding the grape skins. Strain the cooking liquid from the fish into the sauce, reduce until syrupy, then add the grapes and warm through.

Seven To serve, place a galette on each plate, arrange two sole fillets on top and coat with the sauce.

CHEF'S TIP *For a richer finish, mix together 3 tablespoons lightly whipped cream and 1 egg yolk. Coat the sauced fillets with the mixture, then broil until golden brown.*

Marmite dieppoise

A marmite is a covered metal or earthenware pot traditionally used for making soups and stews. This fish soup comes from Dieppe on the Normandy coast of France, which is renowned for its excellent fishing. Dieppoise dishes often include mussels, shrimp and mushrooms.

Preparation time 1 hour
Total cooking time 25 minutes
Serves 4

1 large shallot, chopped
1½ cups white wine
2 sprigs of fresh thyme
1 bay leaf
1 lb. fresh mussels, scrubbed and
debearded (see page 523)
12 large shrimp, shells removed
12 scallops, cleaned (see page 524)
8 oz. monkfish or salmon, diced
8 oz. button mushrooms, sliced
1¼ cups whipping cream
⅔ cup chopped fresh flat-leaf parsley

One Put the shallot, white wine, thyme, bay leaf and mussels in a flameproof casserole or stockpot. Bring to a boil, reduce the heat and simmer, covered, for 2–3 minutes, stirring once or twice. Remove the mussels (discarding any the haven't opened), saving the liquid.

Two Bring the cooking liquid back to a simmer and add the shrimp. Stir, then add the scallops. Cover and cook gently for 2–3 minutes, or until firm. Remove from the liquid and set aside. Bring the liquid back to a simmer and poach the fish for 5 minutes, or until firm and cooked through. Remove the mussels from their shells.

Three Strain the cooking liquid through cheesecloth, place in a saucepan and bring to a boil. Add the mushrooms and cook until the liquid has evaporated. Stir in the cream and boil for 5 minutes, or until thick enough to coat the back of a spoon. Add the mussels, shrimp, scallops and fish and simmer until hot. Season and add the parsley before serving.

LE CORDON BLEU ✤ COMPLETE COOK

Salmon, leek and potato gratin

*This wonderful recipe, combining fresh and smoked salmon, is perfect
for a special lunch or supper. A more economical version, also
delicious, could be made using a cheaper fresh fish, or even salt cod.*

Preparation time 20 minutes
Total cooking time 50 minutes
Serves 6

1¾ lb. potatoes
¾ cup unsalted butter, softened
3 small leeks, thinly sliced
5 oz. fresh salmon fillet, skin removed
6 oz. smoked salmon, diced
1¼ cups whipping cream
¾ cup shredded Gruyère cheese
3 tablespoons unsalted butter, chopped
sprigs of fresh dill, to garnish

One Peel the potatoes and place them in
a large saucepan of salted water. Bring to
a boil, then reduce the heat and simmer
for 20–25 minutes, or until the potatoes
are tender to the point of a knife. Drain
and finely mash the potatoes, or purée
them using a food mill or ricer. Mix in
half the softened butter, then set them
aside and keep warm.

Two Melt the remaining softened butter
in a skillet over low heat. Gently cook
the leeks for 2–3 minutes without
coloring. Drain the excess butter and
spread the leeks evenly in an oval gratin
dish. Set aside.

Three Remove any fine bones from the
salmon using a pair of tweezers (see page
527). Place the fillet in a steamer basket,
then cover and steam for 5–10 minutes,
or until the fish changes color and begins
to break apart when pressed with a fork.
Break the fish into pieces and mix into
the potatoes with the smoked salmon.

Four Preheat the broiler to hot. Bring the
cream to a boil in a small saucepan, then
stir into the salmon and potato mixture.
Mix well and season to taste with salt
and pepper. Transfer to the gratin dish
and sprinkle with the shredded cheese.
Dot with the butter and brown under
the broiler for 2–3 minutes, or until
golden. Before serving, garnish with
sprigs of dill.

CHEF'S TIPS *To use salt cod in this
recipe, rinse and soak it overnight, then
poach in milk with a few sprigs of fresh
thyme, a bay leaf and a few garlic cloves
until tender. Drain, break into small
pieces, then add to the potato mixture.*

*You can also use smoked haddock for
this recipe, but there is no need to soak
it overnight before poaching.*

Coulibiac

This Russian fish pie is packed with salmon, rice, hard-boiled eggs and mushrooms, then wrapped in puff pastry to form a pillow shape. A great dish for a party, especially when served with warm beurre blanc (white butter sauce).

Preparation time 50 minutes
+ 15 minutes refrigeration
Total cooking time 1 hour 40 minutes
Serves 8

1/4 cup long-grain rice
4 eggs
3 tablespoons unsalted butter
6 small scallions, finely sliced
3 large shallots, finely chopped
4 1/2 cups finely chopped mushrooms
juice of 1/2 lemon
1 lb. salmon fillet, skin on
1 quantity puff pastry (see page 542)
2 1/2 tablespoons finely chopped fresh dill
1 egg yolk
1/3 cup plain yogurt

COURT BOUILLON
1 small carrot, roughly chopped
1 small onion, roughly chopped
1 bay leaf
4 sprigs of fresh parsley
1 sprig of fresh thyme
6 black peppercorns
large pinch of salt
2 tablespoons white wine vinegar

One Cook the rice until tender, then drain well. Hard-boil 3 of the eggs for 10 minutes, put in a bowl of iced water to cool quickly, then coarsely grate or finely chop.

Two Melt half the butter in a saucepan and add the scallions. Cover and cook for 4 minutes over low heat until soft and translucent. Season and set aside.

Three Melt the remaining butter, add the shallots and cook gently for 2 minutes. Add the mushrooms, lemon juice, salt and pepper and cook until the mushrooms are dry.

Four To make the court bouillon, put all the ingredients except the wine vinegar in a saucepan with 6 cups water. Bring to a boil, then simmer, covered, for 15 minutes. Add the vinegar and simmer for 5 minutes.

Five Add the salmon fillet to the court bouillon and poach covered for 5 minutes. Remove from the heat, uncover and let the salmon cool in the liquid before transferring to a plate. Remove the flesh in large flakes from the skin and cover with plastic wrap. Discard any skin and bones.

Six Cut the pastry in half and on a lightly floured surface roll out one half to a 1/8-inch-thick rectangle. Transfer to a cookie sheet without a lip and trim down to a rectangle big enough to contain the salmon, about 9 x 14 inches. Wrap and chill the trimmings, layering them flat. Leaving a 1-inch border on all sides, spread the rice in the center of the pastry. Sprinkle with 1/2 tablespoon of dill, then the salmon, salt and pepper, mushroom mixture, chopped eggs and scallions in separate layers.

Seven Beat the remaining egg and brush over the pastry border. Roll the remaining pastry to 18 x 12 inches, then pick the pastry up on the rolling pin and place over the filling. Press the edges together to seal the top and bottom, then trim neatly and brush with egg. Roll out the reserved trimmings and cut strips to decorate the pie. Lay them on as a lattice and place the pie in the refrigerator for 10–15 minutes.

Eight Preheat the oven to 400°F. Beat the egg yolk and any remaining egg together and brush over the pie. Wipe off any egg from the baking sheet and make 3 small holes down the center of the pie with a skewer. Bake for 30 minutes, until well risen, crisp and golden.

Nine Before serving, stir the remaining dill into the yogurt and serve with slices of the coulibiac.

Sole normande

This classic dish from Normandy was originally prepared by a Parisian chef in the early nineteenth century using cider rather than white wine and braising the fish in cream. Today, the dish usually includes mushrooms and seafood.

Preparation time 1 hour
Total cooking time 1 hour
Serves 4

8 x ¼ lb. sole fillets, skin removed
2 cups dry white wine
2 shallots, chopped
1 lb. fresh mussels, scrubbed and beards removed (see page 523)
2 tablespoons unsalted butter
1 cup sliced button mushrooms
1 lemon
1 cup whipping cream
4 oz. small cooked shrimp, shells removed
1 tablespoon chopped fresh parsley, to garnish

One Place the sole fillets skinned side up on a flat surface. Lightly season with salt and pepper and carefully roll up, starting at the wide end. Secure with a cocktail pick. Cover with plastic wrap and chill until ready to use.

Two In a large saucepan, bring the wine and shallots to a boil and then simmer for 5 minutes. Add the mussels, cover and cook for 2–3 minutes. Discard any mussels that do not open. Strain and reserve the liquid. Remove the mussels from their shells, set aside to cool and discard the shells.

Three Preheat the oven to 400°F. In a large saucepan, melt half the butter, then add the mushrooms, a little lemon juice and ¼ cup water and simmer for 5 minutes. Add the cooking liquid from the mussels and cook until the liquid has reduced in volume by three-quarters. Add the cream and simmer for another 5 minutes, or until the mixture has thickened enough to coat the back of a

spoon. Season the sauce with salt and white pepper.

Four Grease a flameproof dish with the remaining butter and place the rolled sole fillets into it. Sprinkle the shrimp and the mussels around the sole fillets and then coat all the seafood with the sauce. Cover with aluminum foil and bake for 7–10 minutes, then remove the picks. Sprinkle with the parsley just before serving.

Cioppino

This superb Italian-sounding dish is said to have been created in
San Francisco by Italian immigrants. A combination of fish and seafood
with tomatoes and herbs, it is delicious served with crusty bread.

Preparation time 45 minutes
Total cooking time 35 minutes
Serves 6–8

3 cups white wine
2 onions, finely chopped
2 bay leaves
4 sprigs of fresh thyme
2 lb. fresh mussels, scrubbed and
beards removed (see page 523)
1 tablespoon fresh basil
1/3 cup olive oil
1 green bell pepper, chopped
1 stalk celery, chopped
1 carrot, chopped
4 cloves garlic, chopped
3 tablespoons tomato paste
3 x 16-oz. cans chopped tomatoes
2 x 8 oz. frozen lobster tails,
thawed
1 lb. firm white fish fillets
1 lb. frozen crab claws,
thawed
2 lb. large uncooked shrimp,
shells on
1 lb. scallops, cleaned (see page 524)
4 cloves garlic, finely chopped
3 tablespoons extra virgin
olive oil

One Place the wine, half the onions, one bay leaf, two sprigs of thyme and the mussels in a large saucepan. Cover, bring to a boil and cook for 5 minutes. Remove the mussels from the saucepan with a slotted spoon and discard any that have not opened. Strain and reserve the cooking liquid.

Two Separate the leaves from the stems of basil and set aside. Make an herb bundle by tying the basil stems, remaining thyme and bay leaf together with string.

Three Heat the oil in a large saucepan and cook the remaining onion, bell pepper, celery, carrot and garlic for 3 minutes. Add the tomato paste and cook for another 2 minutes, stirring frequently. Add the tomatoes, herb bundle and mussel liquid to the saucepan and bring to a boil. Reduce the heat and simmer for 10 minutes.

Four Meanwhile, cut each lobster tail into three or four pieces. Cut the fish fillets into bite-size pieces and crack the crab claws with a mallet. Remove the mussels from their shells. Following the method in the Chef's techniques on page 522, shell and devein the shrimp, keeping the tails intact. Remove the herb bundle, then add all the seafood except the mussels to the saucepan. Simmer for 10 minutes, and then add the mussels and heat them through.

Five To make the basil sauce, chop the reserved basil leaves and mix with the garlic and olive oil.

Six Season the Cioppino with salt and freshly ground black pepper, stir in the basil sauce and serve with bread.

Seafood pie

*A classic family dish, this seafood pie is made with white fish,
mussels and shrimp in a light wine sauce and topped with a purée
of potato that is baked until lightly golden in the oven.*

Preparation time 50 minutes
Total cooking time 1 hour 10 minutes
Serves 6

*1 lb. mussels, scrubbed and beards
removed (see page 523)*
1/4 lb. shrimp, shells on
4 tablespoons unsalted butter
2 shallots, finely chopped
*1 leek, white part only, cut into
julienne strips (see Chef's tip)*
1 cup dry white wine
2 cups milk
1 onion, studded with 1 whole clove
1 bouquet garni (see page 520)
*1 1/4 lb. mixed firm white fish fillets
such as sole, cod and halibut, skin
removed and cut into
1 1/4-inch cubes*
1/4 cup all-purpose flour
*2 lb. baking potatoes, peeled and cut
into even-size pieces*
*additional 3 1/2 tablespoons unsalted
butter*
1 egg yolk
4 tablespoons whipping cream
small pinch of grated nutmeg

One Place the mussels in a cool place covered with a damp cloth. Shell and devein the shrimp, following the method in the Chef's techniques on page 522.

Two In a saucepan, melt 2 tablespoons of the butter over low heat, add the shallots, cover the saucepan and cook for 2–3 minutes, or until the shallots are soft. Add the leek and cook, uncovered, for 2 minutes, then add 1 tablespoon of wine and simmer until the liquid evaporates. Place in a shallow, oval 11 x 8-inch flameproof dish.

Three Put the mussels and remaining wine in a saucepan, cover, bring slowly to a boil and cook for 2–3 minutes, or until all the mussels are open. Discard any unopened mussels. Drain, reserving the cooking liquid, then remove the mussels from their shells and scatter into the dish. Pass the liquid through a strainer lined with cheesecloth or damp paper towels and set aside.

Four Add the milk, onion and bouquet garni to a saucepan, bring to a slight simmer and cook for 5 minutes. Remove the onion and bouquet garni and add the cubes of fish, shrimp and reserved mussel liquid. Heat to just simmering and poach the seafood for 2 minutes. Drain, reserving the liquid and keeping it hot, and add the seafood to the dish.

Five Melt the remaining 2 tablespoons butter in a saucepan over low heat, sprinkle in the flour and cook, stirring, for 1 minute without coloring. Remove from the heat and blend in the hot poaching liquid. Return to medium heat, bring to a boil, stirring constantly, and cook for 3–4 minutes, or until it thickens and coats the back of a spoon. Season with salt and pepper, then pour over the fish. Cover and refrigerate.

Six Preheat the oven to 350°F. Put the potatoes in a saucepan of salted, cold water, cover and bring to a boil, and then reduce the heat and simmer for 15–20 minutes, or until the potatoes are tender to a sharp knife. Drain, return the potatoes to the saucepan and shake over low heat for 1–2 minutes to remove the excess moisture.

Seven Mash or push through a fine strainer back into the pan, then beat in the 3 1/2 tablespoons butter, egg yolk and cream. Season with nutmeg, salt and black pepper, spoon into a pastry bag with a large star tip and pipe a pattern over the fish. Or spread the potatoes, then use a fork to peak. Bake for 30 minutes, or until light golden.

CHEF'S TIPS *Julienne strips are pieces of vegetables cut to the size and shape of matchsticks.*

poultry

Chicken liver pâté

Chicken livers have a mild flavor and soft creaminess. Take care not to overcook a pâté—this one should be moist and juicy, with the bacon wrapping adding a contrast of flavor and texture.

Preparation time 35 minutes
+ marinating + resting twice overnight
Total cooking time 1 hour 15 minutes
Serves 4–6

1½ tablespoons unsalted butter
1 small shallot, finely chopped
6 oz. chicken livers, trimmed and
    halved
10 oz. boneless pork blade, cubed
1 teaspoon brandy
1 teaspoon port
⅛ teaspoon five-spice powder
6 slices bacon
¼ cup whipping cream
1 small egg, beaten

One Heat the butter in a large skillet, add the shallot and heat through for 2 minutes. Remove from the heat, add the livers and pork and stir over very low heat for 3 minutes, or until the meat and liver are warm. Mix in the brandy, port and five-spice, season well with salt and pepper and cover with plastic wrap. Cool slightly, then refrigerate overnight.

Two Preheat the oven to 500°F. Line a 2½-cup deep terrine or mold with some of the bacon and refrigerate until ready to use. Grind the marinated livers and meat through a meat grinder set with a fine disk or in a food processor. Mix in the cream and egg, spoon into the terrine and cover with the remaining bacon.

Three Bake for 30 minutes, or until the top has begun to brown, then turn the oven to its lowest temperature. Cook for another 30–40 minutes, or until the tip of a small knife inserted into the center of the pâté for a few seconds comes out hot. Remove from the oven and allow to cool for 20 minutes. Cut a piece of cardboard or wood to a size just smaller than the terrine and cover with aluminum foil. Place this directly onto the pâté (just inside the edge of the terrine), weigh down with heavy cans and refrigerate for 8 hours or overnight.

Four To unmold, first loosen the edges with a knife and then place the terrine in hot water for 30 seconds. Unmold onto a serving dish and lift off the terrine. Slice the pâté and serve with small gherkins and salad.

Deep-fried chicken with cumin and sesame

*Sesame seeds give this chicken a crisp crunchy batter and
the tangy dipping sauce adds an eastern twist.*

Preparation time 20 minutes
Total cooking time 20 minutes
Serves 4

2/3 cup all-purpose flour
1/2 cup potato starch
1 teaspoon baking powder
2 teaspoons oil
1/2 cup sesame seeds
1/4 teaspoon ground cumin
3 small skinned boneless chicken
breast halves
oil, for deep-frying

DIPPING SAUCE
1/2 teaspoon grated fresh
ginger
1 teaspoon finely chopped scallion
1 tablespoon vinegar
1 tablespoon soy sauce
2 tablespoons ketchup
1 teaspoon sesame oil

One Sift together the flour, potato starch,
baking powder and a good pinch of salt
into a bowl. Add the oil and whisk while
adding 2/3 cup water in a steady stream.
Whisk until the batter is smooth, add the
sesame seeds and cumin and cover with
plastic wrap.

Two To make the dipping sauce, mix
together all the ingredients and set aside.

Three Trim the chicken of excess fat and
cut lengthwise into thin strips. Season to
taste with salt and freshly ground
pepper, dip in the batter and deep-fry in
moderately hot oil at 375°F until golden
(see page 537). Drain on paper towels
and serve immediately with the dipping
sauce on the side.

LE CORDON BLEU ✤ COMPLETE COOK

Smoked chicken and sun-dried tomato pâté

*Pâtés baked in terrines are an impressive and elegant way to dress
your dinner or buffet table, but a few slices served with a
salad would also make an ideal first course or lunch.*

Preparation time *1 hour 20 minutes*
+ overnight refrigeration if possible
Total cooking time *1 hour 30 minutes*
Serves 12

1 x 2 lb. smoked chicken
4 large chicken drumsticks
2 egg whites
1¼ cups whipping cream
*⅔ cup thinly sliced sun-dried
tomatoes*
1½ cups chopped mixed fresh herbs

BLACK OLIVE AND
CAPER RELISH
¾ cup sliced pitted black olives
½ cup capers, coarsely chopped
1 clove garlic, chopped
⅔ cup chopped fresh chives
1 tablespoon olive oil

One With a sharp knife, cut down each side of the breastbone of the smoked chicken, remove the wings and set aside the two breast pieces. Remove the skin and cut away the leg meat from the chicken, discarding the bones. Grind or finely chop the leg meat in a food processor and set aside.

Two With a small sharp knife, scrape the flesh from the raw drumsticks, following the method in the Chef's techniques on page 530. Trim away the fine, shiny, white nerves and tendons—these will not break down during cooking and will spoil the smooth texture of the pâté. Work the raw meat to a fine purée in the food processor, then blend in the egg whites. Transfer the meat mixture to a bowl, cover and place in the refrigerator for 15 minutes.

Three Preheat the oven to 325°F. Place the bowl of puréed chicken over ice and slowly mix in the cream to just blend. Season with salt and pepper. Gently mix in the smoked leg meat, sun-dried tomatoes and herbs.

Four Line the length of the bottom of a 6-cup terrine with a strip of doubled waxed paper or aluminum foil that overhangs the sides to help you unmold the pâté after cooking. Half-fill the terrine with the chicken mixture, place the smoked chicken breasts on top and cover with the remaining chicken mixture. Cover the terrine with foil, firmly turning under to seal the edges.

Five Place the terrine in a baking dish and create a water bath by pouring hot water into the dish to come halfway up the side of the terrine. Bake in the oven for 1½ hours, or until the juices run clear when tested with a skewer. Remove from the water bath and allow to cool in the terrine. The pâté is best left in the refrigerator overnight to make slicing easier.

Six To make the relish, mix the olives with the capers, garlic and chives, then stir in the olive oil to bind. Loosen the edges of the pâté with a sharp knife, then unmold and cut into 12 slices. Serve with the relish on the side.

CHEF'S TIP *In step 3, it is very important that the cream and meat purée be chilled. If not, there is a risk of the cream separating. If the cream separates, the smooth light texture of the pâté is spoiled.*

about sun-dried tomatoes...

Sun-dried tomatoes are available completely dried or stored in oil. If you buy the ones stored in oil, rinse them in boiling water before chopping to remove any excess oil.

Coronation chicken

Originally created by Rosemary Hume of The Cordon Bleu Cookery School, London, for the foreign dignitaries at the coronation luncheon of Queen Elizabeth II, this dish now appears on menus around the world. Here is an updated version of the traditional recipe.

Preparation time *30 minutes + cooling*
Total cooking time *1 hour*
Serves 4

1 x 3 lb. chicken
1 carrot, sliced
1 onion, halved
1 bouquet garni (see page 520)
6 peppercorns
oil, for cooking
2 shallots, finely chopped
1 teaspoon curry powder
2 teaspoons tomato paste
¼ cup red wine
pinch of sugar
1 slice lemon
few drops of lemon juice
1 tablespoon mango chutney
1 cup mayonnaise
¼–⅓ cup whipping cream
chopped scallion, to garnish

One Place the chicken, carrot, onion, bouquet garni, peppercorns and a pinch of salt in a large saucepan, add enough water to cover and bring to a boil. Reduce the heat and simmer for about 40 minutes, or until tender. Allow the chicken to cool in the liquid. When cold, remove the chicken and discard the skin and bones. Cut the chicken meat into bite-size pieces and set aside.

Two Heat a little oil in a large saucepan, add the shallots and cook gently for 3–4 minutes. Add the curry powder and continue to cook for 1–2 minutes. Add the tomato paste, wine and 2 tablespoons water and bring to a boil. Add the sugar, salt and pepper to taste, and the lemon and lemon juice. Reduce the heat and simmer for 5–10 minutes, or until reduced by half. Stir in the mango chutney, strain and cool.

Three Once the mixture has cooled, gradually add to the mayonnaise, to taste. Adjust the seasoning, adding a little more lemon juice if necessary. Stir in the whipped cream and chicken. Garnish with a little scallion. Delicious served with rice salad.

CHEF'S TIP *For a rice salad to serve with Coronation chicken, mix 1 cup cooked rice with cubes of cooked carrot, strips of red bell pepper, sliced celery, cooked peas and peeled, seeded and quartered tomatoes (see page 534). Toss with an oil and vinegar dressing.*

Chicken Kiev

*You can pan-fry or deep-fry your Chicken Kiev to produce
a crisp coating for the chicken and garlic butter, which bursts
with succulence and flavor as you cut into it.*

Preparation time *40 minutes*
Total cooking time *40 minutes*
Serves 4

*4 skinned boneless chicken breast
halves
1 cup all-purpose flour, seasoned with
salt and pepper
3 eggs, beaten
2½ cups fine dry bread crumbs
oil, for cooking and deep-frying*

GARLIC BUTTER
*⅔ cup unsalted butter
3 cloves garlic, minced
¾ cup chopped fresh parsley*

One Remove the thin tenderloin strips from the underside of the chicken breasts and place on lightly greased plastic wrap or waxed paper. Gently flatten with a meat mallet or small heavy-bottomed pan and refrigerate.

Two To make the garlic butter, soften the butter, then mix with the garlic, parsley and seasoning. Spoon the butter along one end of a piece of greased plastic wrap or waxed paper and roll it up into a sausage shape, twisting the ends. Refrigerate until firm.

Three Cut a short slit into the top of each chicken breast and make a pocket by cutting just under either side of the slit with the tip of a small sharp knife. Place a slice of garlic butter into each pocket. Place a flattened chicken strip over the top of each breast to cover the butter.

Four Put the flour, egg and bread crumbs in separate dishes. Coat the chicken with flour, egg and then bread crumbs. Coat again with egg and bread crumbs.

Five Preheat the oven to 400°F. To pan-fry, heat enough oil in a skillet to come halfway up the sides of the chicken. Cook the Kievs over medium heat for 6 minutes each side, or until they are golden brown and cooked through. Transfer the breasts to a wire rack in the oven for a few minutes to allow the coating to crisp.

Six To deep-fry, preheat the oil in a deep saucepan to 325°F (see page 537). Add two of the chicken breasts and fry for 8–12 minutes, or until golden brown. Remove from the oil and drain on crumpled paper towels. Keep warm in the oven on a wire rack while cooking the rest. Serve Chicken Kievs with a crisp salad and fresh bread.

Chicken en croûte

*These succulent chicken breasts are married with mushrooms and bacon
and encased in crisp braided pastry. This dish requires a little
patience in the making, but the results are spectacular.*

Preparation time *1 hour
+ 40 minutes chilling*
Total cooking time *1 hour 30 minutes*
Serves 4

*oil, for cooking
4 skinned boneless chicken breast
halves
2 tablespoons unsalted butter
1 shallot, finely chopped
1 clove garlic, finely chopped
2³/4 cups finely chopped mushrooms
12 oz puff pastry (see page 542) or
2 sheets frozen puff pastry, thawed
4 thin slices slab bacon or pancetta,
rind removed
1 egg, lightly beaten*

SAUCE
*¹/4 cup oil
4 chicken wings, disjointed
1 onion, finely chopped
2 carrots, finely chopped
1 stalk celery, finely chopped
1 mushroom, finely chopped
1 bay leaf
1 tablespoon sherry vinegar
¹/3 cup dry Madeira or sherry
2 cups chicken stock (see page 519)*

One Heat about ¹/4 cup oil in a skillet and fry the chicken for 1 minute on each side to seal. Remove from the pan and set aside.

Two Heat the butter in a medium-size saucepan, add the shallot and garlic, cover with parchment paper and a lid and cook very gently until transparent and soft. Add the mushrooms and increase the heat. The mushrooms will produce juice, so cook uncovered until dry. Season with salt and pepper, then transfer to a plate to cool.

Three Roll out each sheet of pastry on a lightly floured surface to a 12 x 10-inch rectangle, then cut in half to make two 10 x 6-inch rectangles. Transfer to two lightly floured baking sheets and chill for 20 minutes. Slide each off the sheet onto a lightly floured work surface and make cuts at ³/4-inch intervals down the two short sides of each rectangle. Make the cuts 3 inches long, towards the center of the rectangle.

Four Place a chicken breast down the center of each pastry rectangle. Put a quarter of the mushroom mixture on each chicken breast and lightly flatten, then cover with bacon or pancetta, folding around to hold the mushroom in place. Brush the pastry strips with egg.

Take the top strip of pastry from one side and place over the chicken. Take the top strip from the other side and place on top, as if to braid. Continue down the chicken, overlapping slightly and leaving small gaps between the braiding to let the steam escape and the pastry to crisp. Trim the strips at the bottom of the chicken or tuck underneath. Place on a buttered baking sheet and chill for 20 minutes. Preheat the oven to 400°F.

Five To make the sauce, add the oil to a roasting pan and heat on top of the stove. Add the wings then roast in the oven for 30 minutes, or until golden brown. Transfer to the stove top, add the chopped vegetables, bay leaf and vinegar and simmer for 5 minutes, or until reduced by three-quarters and the pan juices are sticky. Add the Madeira or sherry and bring to a boil, add the stock, reduce the heat and simmer gently for 10 minutes, or until reduced by half. Skim frequently with a spoon. Strain into a clean saucepan and season to taste.

Six Brush the pastry packages with egg, avoiding the cut edges or they will not rise. Bake for 25–30 minutes, or until golden and crisp. If the underside is not crisp, cover the top with foil and cook a little longer. Serve with the sauce and steamed asparagus spears.

Chicken brochettes with vegetable rice

Brochette is a French word for skewer or kebab and is also the term for this method of cooking. Marinating the chicken before broiling on the skewers makes the meat more tender and flavorful.

Preparation time *30 minutes*
+ refrigeration (1 hour or overnight)
Total cooking time *1 hour*
Serves 4

4 skinned boneless chicken breast halves
1 large red bell pepper, halved
12 button mushrooms
1 onion
3/4 cup corn oil
1/3 cup soy sauce
juice of 1 lemon
1 onion, chopped
1/3 cup white wine vinegar
2 cups chicken stock (see page 519)
2 tomatoes, peeled, seeded and diced (see page 534)
1 teaspoon chopped fresh thyme
2 tablespoons capers, coarsely chopped

VEGETABLE RICE
oil, for cooking
1 onion, thinly sliced
1 cup long-grain rice
1/2 red bell pepper, diced
1/2 green bell pepper, diced
1/3 cup frozen baby peas, thawed

One Cut each chicken breast into six cubes. Cut the bell pepper into 12 rough squares. Remove and discard the mushroom stems. Halve and then cut the onion into large pieces to match the bell pepper. Thread the chicken, bell pepper, mushroom and onion alternately onto skewers and place in a shallow glass dish. Mix together the corn oil, soy sauce and lemon juice, spoon over the brochettes and baste well. Cover and refrigerate for at least 1 hour but preferably overnight.

Two To make the vegetable rice, preheat the oven to 400°F. Heat 2 tablespoons oil in a flameproof casserole or Dutch oven on the stove top, add the onion and cook gently until transparent. With a wooden spoon, stir in the rice and cook for 1 minute. Add 1½ cups water and bring to a boil, stirring constantly. Season to taste. Cover the casserole and bake for 15 minutes, or until the rice is tender. Lightly mix in the red and green pepper and the peas and season. Turn the oven to very low, cover the rice and return to the oven to keep warm.

Three Remove the brochettes from the marinade, reserving the liquid, and broil for 4 minutes on each side, or until the chicken juices run clear when pierced with a skewer. Transfer to a serving plate, cover and keep warm in the oven.

Four Add the onion to the juices in the broiler pan and place over low to medium heat on the stove top, stirring until lightly colored. Add the vinegar and stir until reduced by half. Add the reserved marinade and cook for 2 minutes. Add the stock and cook for another 10–15 minutes, or until reduced to a syrup. Stir in the tomatoes, thyme and capers and season to taste with salt and pepper. Serve the brochettes with the sauce spooned over the top.

CHEF'S TIP *The brochettes may be prepared the day before and kept in the refrigerator overnight.*

Southern-fried chicken

Breaded chicken, fried to crisp perfection, is one of the classic dishes from the Deep South. A great family favorite for eating with your fingers.

Preparation time 1 hour + marinating
Total cooking time 1 hour
Serves 4

1 x 3¹/4 lb. chicken
5 cups buttermilk
2 tablespoons Tabasco sauce
1¹/3 cups all-purpose flour
1 teaspoon sweet paprika
1 teaspoon dried oregano
¹/2 teaspoon cayenne pepper
2 eggs
2 tablespoons oil
3 cups fresh bread crumbs
2 tablespoons unsalted butter
oil, for pan-frying

One Cut the chicken into eight pieces, following the method in the Chef's techniques on page 528. In a large bowl, combine the buttermilk with the Tabasco sauce and season with salt. Marinate the chicken for at least 1 hour, or overnight in the refrigerator.

Two Drain the chicken and pat dry. Mix together the flour, paprika, oregano, 1 teaspoon salt and cayenne pepper in a dish and use to coat the chicken. Shake off the excess and set the chicken aside.

Three Beat the eggs with the oil and 2 tablespoons water. Dip the chicken pieces into the egg mixture, then roll in the bread crumbs and press well. Place on a plate lined with paper towels. Preheat the oven to 300°F.

Four Heat the butter with about 1 inch oil in a large heavy-bottomed skillet over medium-high heat. Add the chicken skin side down and reduce the heat to medium. Cook for 10 minutes, or until nicely browned. If necessary, cook in batches—do not crowd the pan, and leave enough space between the pieces to ensure even cooking. Turn the pieces over and cook until browned. Transfer to a baking dish or roasting pan, cover loosely with aluminum foil and bake for 45 minutes. Drain on paper towels and serve immediately.

CHEF'S TIPS *If you want to make a spicier dish, simply add a tablespoon of curry paste to the marinade.*

Curry paste is available from gourmet supermarkets and specialty stores.

Lime-marinated chicken with Mediterranean bread

This refreshing dish combines the flavors of the Mediterranean and the tropics. Lime, yogurt and cilantro blend especially well together and are complemented by a light, crusty bread.

***Preparation time** 50 minutes
+ rising + marinating*
***Total cooking time** 55 minutes*
Serves 4

MEDITERRANEAN BREAD
(SEE CHEF'S TIPS)
1³/4 cups lukewarm water
1 oz. fresh yeast
5¹/2 cups bread flour or all-purpose flour
¹/2 cup extra virgin olive oil
1 tablespoon salt
²/3 cup pitted black olives, coarsely chopped
²/3 cup sun-dried tomatoes, soaked, drained and coarsely chopped (see Chef's tips)

3 cups plain yogurt
2 fresh green chiles, seeded and chopped
2 cloves garlic, chopped
¹/4 cup coarsely chopped fresh cilantro
grated zest of 3 limes
juice of ¹/2 lime
8 skinned boneless chicken thighs

One To make the Mediterranean bread, combine the warm water and yeast in a small bowl and stir together until smoothly blended. Sift 3¹/2 cups of the flour into a bowl and make a well in the center. Pour the yeast and water into the well, followed by the olive oil. Using your hand with fingers slightly apart, gradually begin to draw the flour into the liquid in the well. Continue until all the flour has been incorporated and a loose batter forms. Beat for 5 minutes in a slapping motion to develop its elasticity and free it from lumps. Clean the sides of the bowl with a scraper, cover with a damp cloth and allow to rise at room temperature for 1–1¹/2 hours, or until doubled in volume. Add the remaining flour, salt, olives and sun-dried tomatoes and mix well. Scrape down the side of the bowl, cover with a fresh damp cloth and allow to double in volume.

Two Preheat the oven to 400°F. Lightly butter and flour two medium-size baking sheets. Divide the very soft dough in half (do not be alarmed by the very loose texture—this is quite normal). Be careful not to overhandle the dough or it will lose volume. Place on the sheets and, with wet hands, gently pat and shape each piece to a rectangle about 1 inch thick. Sprinkle with cold water and dust heavily with extra flour. Bake in the oven for 35–40 minutes, or until a skewer inserted into the center of the bread comes out clean. Transfer to a cooling rack and allow to rest for 20 minutes before serving.

Three For the marinated chicken, combine the yogurt, chiles, garlic, cilantro and lime rind and juice in a blender until smooth. Season with salt and freshly ground pepper. Place half the mixture in a dish and lay the chicken on top. Cover with the remaining mixture and allow to rest in a cool place for 30 minutes. Arrange the chicken on a broiler pan. Broil slowly, turning often, for up to 15 minutes, or until cooked through. Serve with the Mediterranean bread in slices on the side.

CHEF'S TIPS *The Mediterranean bread is a perfect complement to the marinated chicken, but be sure to prepare it well in advance to allow time for the dough to rise. The nature of this rustic bread is for it to have an uneven, crusty texture. The olive oil gives the bread its unique crustiness and not punching down the dough during rising creates the holes in the loaf.*

If you are using sun-dried tomatoes in oil, there is no need to soak them before draining and chopping.

Roast chicken

Roast chicken is an all-time favorite with many families—the tantalizing smell, crisp golden skin and snowy-white flesh all add up to a traditional Sunday lunch. Use free-range for a wonderful rich flavor.

Preparation time *30 minutes*
Total cooking time *1 hour 40 minutes*
Serves 4

1 x 3½ lb. chicken
¼ cup oil
¼ cup unsalted butter
3 chicken wings
1 shallot, chopped
1 tablespoon chopped celery
1 tablespoon chopped carrot
1 tablespoon chopped onion
1 bouquet garni (see page 520)

One Preheat the oven to 400°F. Truss the chicken for roasting by following the method in the Chef's techniques on page 529. Coat the bottom of a roasting pan with a tablespoon of oil. Season the chicken with salt and pepper and rub with the remaining oil. Put the chicken on its side in the roasting pan and place the butter on top. Put in the oven and roast, basting every 5 minutes. After 15 minutes, turn the chicken onto its other side, continuing to baste every 5 minutes. After 15 minutes, turn the chicken onto its back and add the chicken wings. Roast, basting as before, for another 20–30 minutes, or until the juices run clear.

Two Transfer the chicken and wings to a flameproof plate, cover with aluminum foil, set aside and keep warm in a 250°F oven. Place the roasting pan on the stove top over low heat to clarify the fat. After 10 minutes, without stirring, the fat should be clear. Pour off the excess fat. Strain the chicken wings of excess fat and return to the roasting pan. Add the chopped vegetables and cook for 2 minutes, then add 2 cups water and the bouquet garni. Stir to loosen any bits stuck to the roasting pan, then pour into a saucepan. Bring to a boil, reduce the heat and simmer, skimming off the fat occasionally, for 35 minutes, or until the liquid has reduced in volume by three-quarters. Strain and season to taste with salt and pepper.

Three To serve, remove the string and place the chicken on a platter. Serve the roasting juices in a gravy boat.

CHEF'S TIP *To check that a chicken is cooked doesn't require any fancy gadgets or thermometers. Simply lift the chicken by inserting a carving fork into the cavity and allow the juices to drain. If the juices run clear, the chicken is cooked. If the juices have a pink tinge, give the bird another 5–10 minutes in the oven before testing it again.*

LE CORDON BLEU ✠ COMPLETE COOK

Cider apple chicken with mushroom sauce

The traditional French name for this recipe is Poulet Vallée d'Auge. The Auge Valley is in Normandy and this recipe makes good use of local ingredients: butter, Calvados, cider, cream and apples from the dairy farms and apple orchards.

Preparation time *25 minutes*
Total cooking time *1 hour*
Serves 4

1 x 3¹/₂ lb. chicken
¹/₄ cup unsalted butter
oil, for cooking
¹/₄ cup Calvados or applejack
2 shallots, finely chopped
2 cups hard cider
1²/₃ cups sliced button mushrooms
1 cup whipping cream
1–2 Golden Delicious apples
3 tablespoons clarified butter (see page 520)
¹/₄ cup chopped fresh parsley

One Cut the chicken into four or eight pieces, following the method in the Chef's techniques on page 528, and season with salt and pepper. Heat half the butter and a little oil in a skillet and sauté the chicken in batches skin side down until lightly browned. Pour off the excess fat, return all the chicken to the pan, add the Calvados or applejack and light with a match to flambé (keep a saucepan lid on one side in case of emergency). Add the shallots and cook gently until softened but not brown. Add the cider, cover and cook for 15 minutes, turning the chicken after 10 minutes.

Two Meanwhile, sauté the mushrooms in the remaining butter, covered, for 4 minutes. Add the mushrooms, together with their cooking juices, and the cream to the chicken and cook for 5 minutes. Remove the chicken and keep warm.

Three Continue cooking the mushroom sauce for 10 minutes, or until it is reduced enough to coat the back of a spoon. Season to taste with salt and black pepper. Return the chicken to the pan, bring to a boil, then reduce the heat and simmer for 2 minutes to heat the chicken through.

Four Core the unpeeled apples and cut across into thin slices. Fry in clarified butter until golden brown on both sides. Garnish the chicken with the apples and chopped parsley to serve.

Date-stuffed chicken breast with Madeira sauce

*Although the finished dish appears complicated, this recipe is actually
relatively quick to prepare and would make a wonderful special occasion dinner.
The date and pistachio stuffing and rich Madeira sauce keep the chicken breasts moist.*

Preparation time 45 minutes
Total cooking time 50 minutes
Serves 4

DATE STUFFING
2 tablespoons unsalted butter
1/2 cup shallots, finely chopped
1/2 cup dates, pitted
*1/2 cup shelled pistachios, skins
removed, and roughly chopped*

*4 boneless chicken breasts, skin on (see
Chef's tip)*
*2 tablespoons unsalted butter
or 1 1/2 tablespoons oil*
fresh chervil or parsley, to garnish

MADEIRA SAUCE
1 2/3 cups shallots, thinly sliced
3/4 cup Madeira wine
2 cups chicken stock (see page 519)
1/3 cup whipping cream, optional
2 tablespoons chopped fresh chives

One To make the date stuffing, heat the butter in a small saucepan and cook the shallots over low heat for 4 minutes, or until soft but not colored. Finely chop all but 3 of the dates. Remove the shallots from the heat and stir in the chopped dates and pistachios, then set aside to cool. Preheat the oven to 350°F.

Two Remove the thin tenderloin fillets from the underside of the breasts and place between lightly greased pieces of plastic wrap. Gently flatten them with a meat pounder or small heavy-bottomed saucepan. On the underside of the breasts, cut a central horizontal slit to half the depth of the flesh. Slide the knife flat inside the slit and to each side to form a pocket, then fill each pocket with the stuffing. Remove the plastic wrap from the small fillets. Place a fillet lengthwise on each breast to cover the filling, bringing the edges of the pocket flesh over to seal, then secure with skewers or toothpicks by pushing them through across the top of the seal. Season with salt and black pepper.

Three Heat the butter or oil in a large frying pan and place the chicken in the pan skin side down. Cook over high heat for 4 minutes, or until just golden. Lift the chicken onto a baking sheet or shallow flameproof dish and roast skin side up for 10–12 minutes, or until the juices from the thickest part of the flesh run clear when pierced with a skewer.

Four To make the Madeira sauce, use the saucepan and the oil that the chicken was fried in to cook the shallots over medium-high heat, turning frequently, for 15 minutes, or until golden brown. Pour off excess fat and pour in three-quarters of the Madeira. Bring to a boil, then reduce the heat and simmer for 3–5 minutes, or until reduced to 2 tablespoons of light syrupy liquid. Add the stock and simmer until reduced by three-quarters, then stir in the remaining Madeira and cream, if using. Reduce once again to a light coating consistency. Season with some salt and black pepper, then strain the sauce through a fine strainer into a pitcher. Stir in the chives, cover and keep warm.

Five Cut the reserved dates lengthwise into quarters. Lift the chicken onto a cutting board, remove the skewers and cut on the diagonal into slices. Lift and fan out on 4 plates, pour the sauce around and garnish with the dates and a sprig of chervil or parsley. Serve with green vegetables and new potatoes.

CHEF'S TIP *If you can't find chicken breasts with skin on, then buy breasts on the bone and, using a small sharp knife, remove the bone.*

Deviled Poussin

*Poussin is the French name for baby chicken. You can use
either baby chickens (squab) or small Cornish hens for
this treatment with equally moist and tender results.*

Preparation time *30 minutes*
Total cooking time *1 hour*
Serves 4

*4 x 14 oz. baby chickens (squab) or
small Cornish hens
melted butter or oil, for cooking
1/4 cup Dijon or mild English mustard
3/4 cup fresh bread crumbs
chopped fresh parsley,
to garnish*

One Remove the wishbones from the
chickens, following the method in the
Chef's techniques on page 529, and
preheat the oven to 350°F.

Two To open and flatten the chickens,
rinse out the inside cavity, then with the
breast side down, use poultry shears to
cut along each side of the backbone and
remove it. Turn the chickens breast side
up and push down with the weight of
two flat hands to break the breastbone.
Tuck the wing tips under the breast. Run
a metal skewer between the two bones
of one of the middle wing joints, then
through the breast and out through to
the wing on the other side. Push another

skewer through from one thigh to the
other. Lay the chickens flat breast side
up on a greased broiler pan.

Three Brush with the butter or oil and
season lightly with salt and freshly
ground black pepper. Place under a slow
broiler to lightly color, then roast in the
oven for 40–50 minutes, or until the
juices run clear.

Four Spread the chicken skin evenly with
the mustard, sprinkle with bread
crumbs, then drizzle with a little melted
butter or oil. Place under a hot broiler
until golden brown and garnish with
chopped parsley to serve.

Roasted baby chickens with herb butter

*This is a deliciously simple variation on a plain roast chicken.
Use whichever fresh herbs you happen to have and pick up
the same flavors in the buttery sauce.*

Preparation time 40 minutes
Total cooking time 1 hour 15 minutes
Serves 4

2 x 14 oz. baby chickens (squab) or
small Cornish hens
1/3 cup unsalted butter, softened
1/4 cup chopped mixed fresh herbs
(tarragon, chervil, parsley)
2 tablespoons oil
3–4 chicken wings, disjointed
2 1/2 tablespoons chopped carrot
2 1/2 tablespoons chopped shallot
2 1/2 tablespoons chopped onion
1 tablespoon chopped celery

One Preheat the oven to 400°F. Prepare the chickens by gently sliding a finger under the skin at the neck end and loosening the skin from the flesh. Be careful not to tear the skin.

Two In a small bowl, mix together the butter and herbs and season to taste. Using a pastry bag with a small tip, pipe 2 tablespoons herb butter under the skin of each chicken, using your fingers to spread out the butter as much as possible. If you do not have a pastry bag, you can simply use the handle of a fork or spoon to spread the herb butter under the skin. Truss the chickens for roasting, following the method used in the Chef's techniques on page 529. Reserve the remaining herb butter to serve with the chicken as an accompanying sauce.

Three Heat a roasting pan on the stove top over medium-low heat. Add the oil and place the chickens on their side in the pan. Once the oil is hot, place the roasting pan in the oven and roast the chickens for 10 minutes, basting with the pan juices every 5 minutes. Turn the chickens onto their other side and roast for 10 minutes, basting every 5 minutes. Turn the chickens onto their backs, add the chicken wings and roast for about 10 minutes, or until the chicken juices run clear, basting every 5 minutes.

Four Transfer the chicken and wings to a flameproof plate, cover with aluminum foil and keep warm in a 250°F oven. Put the roasting pan on the stove top over low heat to clarify the fat, if necessary. After 5–10 minutes, without stirring, the fat should be clear. Pour off the excess fat. Strain the chicken wings of excess fat and return to the roasting pan. Add the vegetables and cook for 2 minutes, then add 2 cups water. Stir to loosen the cooking juices from the roasting pan, then pour into a saucepan. Bring to a boil, reduce the heat to simmer, skimming off the fat. Simmer for 35 minutes, or until reduced by three-quarters. Strain into a smaller saucepan, discarding the chicken wings and vegetables. Whisk in the remaining herb butter, season with salt and pepper and pour into a gravy boat. Remove the string and cut the chickens in half. Serve the chickens with the sauce poured over the top.

Roast turkey with bread sauce and gravy

The classic Christmas turkey dinner in Britain includes bread sauce, as well as gravy from the turkey juices. The cooked turkey can rest for up to 45 minutes while the juices seep back into the meat to keep it moist.

***Preparation time** 35 minutes*
***Total cooking time** 2 hours 50 minutes*
+ 30 minutes resting
Serves 8

1 x 12 lb. turkey, plus the neck from the giblets if available
⅓ cup vegetable oil
watercress to garnish

GRAVY
1 small onion, roughly chopped
1 small carrot, roughly chopped
2 stalks celery, roughly chopped
1 tablespoon all-purpose flour
2 cups chicken stock

BREAD SAUCE
2½ cups milk
½ onion, studded with 3–4 cloves
1 bouquet garni (see page 520)
2 cloves garlic, peeled and lightly crushed
1⅓ cups fresh white bread crumbs
grated fresh nutmeg
2½ tablespoons whipping cream or 3 tablespoons unsalted butter, optional

One Clean the turkey inside and out, removing any feathers. With a sharp knife, cut off and reserve the end wing joints. Lift up the flap of skin at the neck and, using a small sharp knife, scrape the meat away from the wishbone and remove the wishbone. Tie the legs together with ordinary household string. Preheat the oven to 350°F.

Two Place a large roasting pan over medium heat and heat the oil. Add the end wing joints and neck and cook until lightly browned, then arrange the turkey on top and roast for 1½–2 hours, basting with the juices and oil every 20 minutes. If the turkey begins to overbrown, cover with aluminum foil. The turkey is cooked if the juices run clear when you pierce a leg and thigh with a skewer. If the juices are pink, continue roasting until they are clear. Transfer the turkey to a large plate and keep in a warm place.

Three To make the gravy, pour off the excess fat from the pan, retaining about a tablespoon with all the juices. Add the onions, carrots and celery and cook over moderate heat, stirring occasionally, for 3–5 minutes, or until tender. Sprinkle with the flour, then stir in to mix evenly and cook for 1 minute. Add the stock gradually and stir over low heat to produce a smooth texture. Bring to a boil, then reduce the heat and simmer for 10 minutes. Strain, skim off the excess fat and season with some salt and black pepper.

Four To make the bread sauce, pour the milk into a small saucepan, add the onions, bouquet garni and garlic and bring slowly just to a boil. Remove from the heat and let stand for 20–30 minutes. Strain and discard the bouquet garni and garlic, then return the milk to the saucepan and bring to a boil. Whisk in the bread crumbs to produce a thick sauce and season with the nutmeg and salt and black pepper. Stir in the cream or butter. Serve immediately, as the sauce will thicken while resting.

Five Carve the turkey following the method in the Chef's techniques on page 531. Serve with the bread sauce, gravy, stuffing and some roast vegetables.

---

about turkeys...

When buying a turkey, allow about 1 lb. of weight per person. Frozen turkeys have often been stored for some considerable time—for a more flavorful bird, buy turkey fresh. Often turkeys are available with small thermometers that will ensure the bird reaches the right internal temperature to cook through safely.

Breast of duck with winter vegetables

This would be a great alternative to the Christmas roast turkey, especially if you don't want lots of leftovers. Delicious served with a homemade cranberry sauce.

Preparation time *40 minutes*
Total cooking time *35 minutes*
Serves 4

4 x ¼–½ lb. duck breasts
1 parsnip, cut into julienne strips (see Chef's tips)
1 cup small Brussels sprouts
1 small celery root, cut into large cubes
1 small sweet potato, cut into large cubes
⅓ cup vegetable oil
⅔ cup unsalted butter
8 chestnuts, cooked, peeled and halved
4 shallots, chopped
1 cup balsamic vinegar
1 cup chicken stock (see page 519)
fresh rosemary sprigs, to garnish

One Remove any feathers or stubble from the duck breasts, keeping the skin intact. Using a small, sharp knife, trim away and discard any shiny white skin or sinew from the flesh side, then pat dry on paper towels. Lightly score a crisscross pattern in the skin to allow fat to run out during cooking, then season with salt and black pepper.

Two Bring a small saucepan of water to a boil and separately cook the parsnips for 1 minute, then the sprouts, celery roots and sweet potatoes for 2 minutes, or until just tender. Remove each one after cooking with a slotted spoon into a colander and run with cold water to stop the cooking. Drain well.

Three Heat half the oil in a large frying pan, add half the butter and, when melted and foaming, add the chestnuts and drained vegetables and fry for 7 minutes, or until golden. Season with

salt and black pepper, remove from the saucepan and keep warm.

Four Heat the remaining oil and butter in the frying pan and add the duck breasts skin side down. Cook over medium heat for 7 minutes, then turn over and cook for another 2–3 minutes, or until the skin is crisp and the meat is moist but still slightly pink in the center.

Five Remove the duck from the pan and set aside in a warm place. Pour the excess fat from the pan, leaving about 1 teaspoon behind with any duck juices. Add the shallots and cook gently for 3 minutes, or until soft, then pour in the balsamic vinegar and boil for

1–2 minutes, or until reduced by one third. Add the stock and cook for 3–4 minutes, or until reduced again by one-third. Season with some salt and black pepper, strain and keep warm.

Six To serve, slice the duck breasts diagonally into thin slices and serve with the vegetables and sauce. Garnish with small rosemary sprigs and accompany with cranberry sauce or a chutney.

CHEF'S TIPS *The duck breasts can be served whole, especially if you need to keep them warm while eating a first course.*

Julienne strips are vegetables cut to the size and shape of matchsticks.

Stuffed chicken breast with cucumber

*The cucumber's origin dates back to Roman times and with its cool
and refreshing qualities it is included in many of today's recipes. This dish
is beautifully light and brings a taste of summer all year-round.*

*Preparation time 35 minutes
+ 20 minutes chilling*
Total cooking time 40 minutes
Serves 6

*1 skinned chicken leg and
thigh quarter
1 egg white
2¼ cups whipping cream
1 cup chopped mixed fresh herbs
6 x 6 oz. skinned boneless chicken
breast halves
1 large cucumber, not waxed
3 shallots, finely chopped
⅓ cup dry white wine
2 cups chicken stock (see page 519)*

One Cut the chicken flesh from the bones of the leg and thigh (see page 530), and purée in a food processor. Lightly beat the egg white and add just over half of it to the chicken (discard the remainder). Season with salt and freshly ground black pepper, then use the pulse button to mix in ¾ cup cream and the herbs. Do not overprocess or the cream may separate. Cover and chill for 15–20 minutes to firm up slightly.

Two Remove the thin tenderloin strips from the underside of the chicken breasts and place on lightly greased plastic wrap or waxed paper. Gently flatten them with a meat mallet or small heavy-bottomed pan and store them in the refrigerator until needed.

Three Make a short slit on the top of each chicken breast and make a pocket by cutting just under either side of the slit with the tip of a sharp knife. Using a spoon or pastry bag, fill each pocket with the chicken purée; do not overfill or it will burst during cooking. Place a flattened chicken strip over the top of each breast to completely cover the chicken purée. Wrap each breast in buttered aluminum foil, twisting the ends tightly to seal. Poach in gently simmering water for 20–30 minutes. Remove from the heat and leave to rest in the hot poaching liquid.

Four Cut the unpeeled cucumber in half lengthwise and, using the point of a teaspoon, scrape out the seeds. Cut three-quarters of the cucumber into 2-inch pieces and cut into strips about the thickness of a little finger. Blanch in a small saucepan of boiling salted water for 2–3 minutes, rinse under cold water and drain. Coarsely chop the remaining cucumber and set aside.

Five To make the sauce, place the shallots, wine and chicken stock in a wide saucepan and quickly bring to a boil. Boil the sauce for 5 minutes, or until it has reduced to a light syrupy consistency. Add the remaining 1½ cups cream and boil until the mixture thickens slightly. Add the chopped cucumber and boil the sauce for another 5 minutes.

Six Transfer the sauce to a blender or food processor and purée well. Season with salt and pepper and strain through a sieve.

Seven Serve the chicken breasts immediately, either whole or sliced, with the cucumber strips and sauce.

Duck à l'orange

The rich, moist meat of a duck is perfectly complemented by the sharpness of oranges in this classic French recipe. You can prepare the orange sauce in advance, then put the dish together quickly just before serving.

Preparation time 30 minutes
Total cooking time 1 hour 45 minutes
Serves 4

4 oranges
1 lemon
2 tablespoons unsalted butter
3/4 cup sugar
1 tablespoon Grand Marnier, optional
2 cups duck or chicken stock
4 x 6 oz. duck breasts
1 teaspoon arrowroot
chopped fresh chervil, to garnish

One Using a vegetable peeler, thinly peel the colored zest from 2 of the oranges and the lemon. Then, with a small, sharp knife, cut away the white pith and discard it. Chop the orange and lemon flesh and set aside in a small bowl. Heat the butter in a saucepan, add the orange and lemon zest and toss gently for 2–3 minutes over low heat. Add 1/3 cup of the sugar, increase the heat to medium and cook until the sugar has melted and just caramelized to a light golden brown. Stir in the chopped orange and lemon flesh and the Grand Marnier and cook gently until the juice from the flesh has evaporated and the pan is dry.

Two Pour in the duck or chicken stock and stir to combine. Bring to a boil, reduce the heat, cover and simmer for 1 hour. Pass through a fine strainer, discarding the zest and remnants of the fruit, then cover the sauce and set aside.

Three Thinly peel the zest from the remaining 2 oranges, without the white pith, into long strips. Put into a saucepan, cover with cold water and bring slowly to a boil. Drain the zest, refill the pan with cold water and repeat this procedure twice more to soften the zest and to remove any bitterness. With a small sharp knife, cut the zest into very thin, needlelike shreds, about 1/16 inch thick, and set aside. Put 1/3 cup water and the remaining sugar into a small saucepan and slowly bring to a boil,

stirring to dissolve the sugar. Add the shreds of zest and cook gently for 20 minutes to candy it. Lift the zest from the syrup using a fork and place on an overturned strainer to drain, taking care to separate the strands.

Four Heat a wide, shallow skillet over medium-high heat. Season the duck breasts with salt and freshly ground black pepper, then place them in the hot pan skin side down, and cook until most of their fat has melted and run out, and the skin is crisp and brown. Turn the breasts over and cook briefly for 1–2 minutes on the second side. Remove from the pan, cover and allow to rest for 5–10 minutes before serving.

Five Reheat the sauce to boiling. In a small bowl, mix the arrowroot with 1 tablespoon water, stir in a little of the hot sauce, then pour back into the pan and stir until boiling. The milky appearance of the arrowroot mixture will become clear as it comes to a boil. The sauce should coat the back of a spoon. Add a little more arrowroot and water if necessary, or pour in a few drops of water or stock if too thick. If too sweet, add a little lemon juice. Season to taste.

Six To serve, cut each breast into slices and fan out on a warm plate. Drizzle the sauce around the plate and garnish with a sprinkling of the candied orange zest and some chervil.

Chicken cacciatore

Literally meaning "hunter-style" chicken, this ever popular dish combines the flavors of mushrooms, bell peppers and onions with herbs in a rich tomato sauce.

Preparation time *30 minutes*
Total cooking time *1 hour*
Serves 4

¼ cup olive oil
1 x 3¼ lb. chicken, cut into 8 pieces (see page 528)
2 onions, thinly sliced into rings
1 clove garlic, finely chopped
1¼ cups thinly sliced button mushrooms
1 small green bell pepper, thinly sliced
¼ cup tomato paste
¾ cup dry white wine
1 x 16 oz. can plum tomatoes
½ teaspoon dried rosemary
½ teaspoon dried oregano

One Heat the olive oil in a large skillet. Season the chicken and fry skin side down for 5 minutes, or until lightly browned. Turn over and brown the other side. Remove and set aside.

Two Add the onions to the pan and cook for 5 minutes, then add the garlic, mushrooms and pepper. Cook for another 3–4 minutes, or until the onions are golden. Mix in the tomato paste and cook for 1–2 minutes, then add the wine. Bring to a boil, stirring constantly, then add the tomatoes, breaking them down with a wooden spoon. Sprinkle in the rosemary and oregano and return the chicken to the pan. Season with salt and pepper, cover and simmer for 20 minutes, stirring occasionally.

Three If the chicken is tender, transfer with a slotted spoon to a serving plate—if not, cover and cook for 10 minutes. If the sauce appears too liquid, allow to boil uncovered for 5 minutes. Season, then pour over the chicken and serve.

LE CORDON BLEU ✠ COMPLETE COOK

Stuffed chicken with celery root purée

*A perfect combination of delicate and robust flavors
with a syrupy mango chutney sauce—the finished dish
is even greater than the sum of its delicious parts.*

Preparation time *40 minutes*
Total cooking time *1 hour*
Serves 4

STUFFING
2 chicken thighs
½ cup plain yogurt
2–3 tablespoons chopped celery

2 cups celery root, peeled and chopped
few drops of lemon juice
¼ cup plain yogurt
*4 x 4 oz. skinned boneless chicken
breast halves*
1 tablespoon oil
1 tablespoon mango chutney
2 tablespoons sherry vinegar
2 cups chicken stock (see page 519)
1 tablespoon unsalted butter
*2 tablespoons each of diced carrot,
onion, celery and apple*

One To make the stuffing, remove the skin from the thighs and scrape the meat from the bones (see page 530), reserving the bones. Weigh 6 oz. of the meat and work until smooth in a food processor. Add the yogurt, process until combined and transfer to a bowl. Add the celery and season with salt and black pepper. Mix and set aside.

Two Add the celery root and lemon juice to a saucepan of boiling salted water and simmer for 20 minutes, or until the celery root is tender. Drain, return to the pan and shake over the heat for 1 minute. Purée in a food processor with the yogurt, season with salt and pepper and keep warm.

Three Preheat the oven to 375°F. Cut a slit in the side of each chicken breast, about two-thirds of the way through, and spoon in the stuffing, avoiding overfilling. Heat the oil in a flameproof casserole or Dutch oven and fry the chicken breasts until lightly brown. Add the thigh bones to the casserole and bake in the oven for 10 minutes. Remove the chicken breasts, set aside and keep warm. Pour off the fat from the casserole, then add the chutney and vinegar and cook on the stove top until syrupy. Add the stock and cook for 10 minutes, or until reduced by a third. Season the sauce to taste with salt and freshly ground black pepper, strain and set aside.

Four Melt the butter in a skillet, add the carrot, onion and celery and cook gently for 5 minutes, or until softened but not colored. Add the apple and cook for 2 minutes. Spoon the vegetables onto plates and top with the chicken breasts and sauce. Serve with the celery root purée alongside.

Roast quail

This small game bird makes a lovely choice for a special dinner with a whole quail for each guest. Here the quail are stuffed with a rice and bacon filling and served with a wine sauce.

Preparation time 1 hour
Total cooking time 1 hour
Serves 4

RICE AND BACON STUFFING
2 tablespoons unsalted butter
1 onion, finely chopped
1/2 cup basmati rice
2 slices bacon, diced
1 tablespoon fresh flat-leaf parsley, finely chopped
2 teaspoons golden raisins

4 quails
1 tablespoon peanut oil
3 tablespoons unsalted butter

WINE SAUCE
2 tablespoons unsalted butter
2 shallots, finely chopped
1/2 cup sweet white wine, such as Sauternes
1 cup chicken or veal stock (see pages 518-9)

One To make the stuffing, melt the butter in a saucepan, add the onion and cook covered over low heat for 5 minutes, or until soft and translucent. Add the rice and 1/2 cup water. Bring to a boil, then reduce the heat and cook, covered, for 15–20 minutes, or until the rice has absorbed all the water. Remove from the heat and set aside. Heat a small heavy-bottomed saucepan, add the bacon and dry-fry until golden brown. Add to the rice with any fat that has run out. Stir in the parsley and golden raisins, season with salt and black pepper, then set aside to cool.

Two Remove the bones from the quails following the method in the Chef's techniques on page 530. Preheat the oven to 400°F. Lay the boneless quails out flat, skin side down, season lightly, then spoon the stuffing into the center of each bird. Draw the neck skin down over the stuffing and the sides in to cover. Hold the 2 cut edges of skin and zig-zag a skewer or toothpick through their length to hold them together. Turn the quails over and, using the side of your little finger, gently plump the body cavity of each and make a division between it and the legs to give a good shape. Tuck the wing tips under at the neck end and pull the ends of the legs together by skewering through the thighs with a skewer or toothpick.

Three Heat the oil in a baking sheet over medium heat, add the butter and, when melted and foamy, put in the quails breast side down and the reserved carcass bones. Turn to brown the quails and bones evenly on all sides, then bake for 15 minutes, basting every 5 minutes with the pan juices. Place the quails and bones on a plate to rest for 5 minutes.

Four To make the wine sauce, melt the butter in a saucepan, add the shallots and roasted quail bones and cook for about 1 minute, then add the wine and cook for 5 minutes, or until the liquid has reduced by about three-quarters. Pour in the stock and cook until reduced by half. Skim any excess fat from the saucepan, then strain the sauce and season with salt and black pepper. Cover the surface with a piece of plastic wrap to prevent the sauce forming a skin and keep warm.

Five To serve, remove and discard the skewers, cut off the wing tip joints and place the birds on a serving platter or plates. Spoon the sauce around and serve with vegetables.

CHEF'S TIP *Quails vary in size, so you may have some stuffing left over. If so, place it in a lightly buttered small flameproof dish, cover with buttered aluminum foil and cook in the oven with the quails.*

Chicken with mushrooms and onions

The lovely flavors of the onions, bacon and mushrooms combine perfectly with the chicken to produce this popular dish. The chicken will cook slowly in the oven, leaving you time to spend on other things.

Preparation time 25 minutes
Total cooking time 1 hour 20 minutes
Serves 4–6

12 small boiling onions
2 slices bacon, cut into ½-inch strips
⅓ cup clarified butter (see page 520)
1 x 3 lb. chicken, cut into 8 pieces (see page 528)
1¼ cups quartered button mushrooms (leave whole if very small)
¼ cup all-purpose flour
2⅓ cups chicken stock (see page 519)
1 bouquet garni (see page 520)
chopped fresh parsley, to garnish

One Preheat the oven to 325°F. Place the onions in a small saucepan with the bacon strips, cover with cold water and bring to a boil. Drain and rinse with cold water. Melt ¼ cup of the butter in a 2½-quart, deep flameproof casserole or Dutch oven on the stove. Add the chicken pieces in batches skin side down and fry for 10 minutes, or until well browned. Remove from the pan and pat dry with paper towels.

Two Spoon off the excess fat from the casserole, leaving about 2 tablespoons, then add the bacon, onions and mushrooms. Fry for 3 minutes, or until lightly browned, then remove. Melt the remaining butter in the casserole, add the flour and stir with a wooden spoon, scraping the bottom to prevent sticking. Cook for 3 minutes, or until lightly golden. Gradually add the chicken stock and stir constantly until smooth and heated through. Do not allow to boil.

Three Return the chicken to the casserole with the bouquet garni, season and place the bacon, onions and mushrooms on top. Bring just to a boil, cover and bake for 45 minutes, or until the chicken is tender and when pierced the juices are clear, not pink.

Four Transfer the chicken to a serving dish, then with a slotted spoon, lift out the bacon and vegetables and sprinkle over the chicken. Cover to keep warm and, if necessary, reduce the sauce to a syrupy consistency. Season the sauce to taste and pour over the chicken. Sprinkle with the parsley and serve with rice, pasta, dumplings or boiled potatoes.

Tarragon and tomato chicken

This recipe comes from Lyon, France's third largest city and its gastronomic capital, situated close to the Burgundy vineyards.

Preparation time *20 minutes*
Total cooking time *45 minutes*
Serves 4

1 x 2¹/₂ lb. chicken, cut into 4 or 8 pieces (see page 528)
oil or butter, for cooking
³/4 cup tarragon vinegar (see Chef's tip)
1 tablespoon unsalted butter, softened
2 tablespoons all-purpose flour
2 lb. tomatoes, peeled, seeded and cut into wedges (see page 534)
sprig of fresh tarragon, to garnish

One Season the chicken pieces. Heat a little oil or butter in a skillet and brown the chicken on all sides, skin side down first. Remove the chicken and pour off any excess oil from the pan.

Two Return all the chicken to the pan and add half the tarragon vinegar. Cover and simmer for 10 minutes. Turn the chicken pieces, cover and cook for 10 minutes, or until the juices run clear. Remove the chicken from the pan. Cover the pan and keep the sauce warm.

Three Put the remaining vinegar in a saucepan and boil for 4 minutes. Mix together the softened butter and flour, whisk into the reduced vinegar and then whisk this into the sauce. Return the chicken to the sauce, add the tomatoes and simmer for 10 minutes, or until the sauce just coats the back of a spoon. Chop the tarragon, sprinkle over the chicken and serve with rice.

CHEF'S TIP *Make tarragon vinegar by placing a sprig of fresh tarragon into a bottle of red or white wine vinegar. After a week, strain out the tarragon.*

LE CORDON BLEU ❀ COMPLETE COOK

Chicken fricassee with spring vegetables

*The word fricassee is French in origin and may have been
a marriage of two culinary terms:* frire, *which means to fry,
and* casse, *meaning ladle or dripping pan.*

***Preparation time** 25 minutes*
***Total cooking time** 1 hour*
Serves 4

1 x 3½ lb. chicken
*¼ cup all-purpose flour, seasoned with
salt and pepper*
oil, for cooking
2 tablespoons unsalted butter
6 shallots, thinly sliced
⅓ cup dry white wine
1 cup chicken stock (see page 519)
1 bouquet garni (see page 520)
1 egg yolk
⅔ cup sour cream
8 baby carrots
8 baby turnips
4 small boiling onions
1 teaspoon sugar
2 cups trimmed snow peas
12 asparagus spears
9 button mushrooms

One Cut the chicken into eight pieces, following the method in the Chef's techniques on page 528. Coat the chicken pieces in the seasoned flour, shaking off and reserving the excess. Heat a little oil in a large skillet over medium heat, add 1 tablespoon of the butter and cook the chicken quickly to seal without coloring; remove from the pan and set aside. Lower the heat, add the shallots to the pan and cook slowly, without coloring, until softened. Stir in the reserved flour, then pour in the wine, stirring until the mixture boils and thickens. Reduce the heat and simmer for 2 minutes, then stir in the stock and bouquet garni. Return the chicken to the pan, cover and simmer for 15 minutes. Remove the wings and breast meat, keeping them covered and warm, and cook for another 5 minutes. Remove the chicken thighs and legs, leaving the cooking liquid in the pan.

Two Increase the heat and let the liquid boil for 5–10 minutes, or until reduced by half, skimming off the excess fat with a spoon. Mix the egg yolk with a tablespoon of sour cream in a bowl. Stir the remaining sour cream into the pan and bring to a boil, then simmer for 2 minutes. Remove from the heat, pour some of the hot sauce into the egg yolk mixture, blend and return to the pan, whisking or stirring until heated (do not allow to boil). Strain, season to taste and set aside.

Three Place the carrots, turnips and boiling onions in separate small pans with just enough water to cover. Add a small pinch of salt, sugar and a third of the remaining butter to each pan, then press on buttered parchment paper to cover. Cook gently until the water has nearly evaporated and the vegetables are cooked and shiny, shaking the pan occasionally. Transfer to a lightly buttered dish, arrange in separate piles and keep warm.

Four Cook the snow peas, asparagus and mushrooms in salted boiling water for 3–5 minutes, or until tender but still crisp. Drain well.

Five Lay a piece of chicken breast and dark meat on each serving plate and coat with the sauce. Serve with the cooked vegetables on the side.

Roasted duck with turnips

*Roasting a duck on each side before turning it onto its back will
make sure the meat does not dry out. The salty bacon and
sweetened turnips perfectly complement this succulent dish.*

Preparation time *40 minutes*
Total cooking time *1 hour 40 minutes*
Serves 4

*1 x 2³/4 lb. duck, trussed (ask your
butcher to do this)
oil, for cooking
¹/4 cup unsalted butter, softened
6 oz. duck trimmings (wings or necks),
chopped
6 large turnips
10 oz. lean bacon, cut into
¹/2-inch cubes
1 tablespoon unsalted butter
1 teaspoon sugar
1 shallot, chopped
1 tablespoon chopped celery
1 tablespoon chopped carrot
1 tablespoon chopped onion
3 cups chicken stock
(see page 519)
1 bouquet garni (see page 520)*

One Preheat the oven to 400°F. Coat a
roasting pan with 2 tablespoons of oil.
Season the duck, rub it all over with oil
and place it on its side in the pan. Dot
with the softened butter, transfer to the
oven and roast for 20 minutes, basting
every 5 minutes. Turn the duck onto its
other side and roast for 20 more
minutes, basting as before. Turn the
duck on its back, add the duck
trimmings, then roast and baste for
another 15 minutes.

Two Peel the turnips and use a melon
baller to scoop the flesh into little balls.
Place the balls in cold water until ready
to use.

Three In a skillet, heat some oil and
brown the bacon over medium heat.
Strain and set aside. Drain and dry the
turnips; place in the pan with the butter,
sugar and some salt. Cover with cold
water and cook over high heat until
evaporated. Roll the turnips until coated
and shiny. Remove from the heat, add
the bacon and set aside.

Four Remove the duck from the roasting
pan; cover and keep warm. Remove and
drain the trimmings. Drain the pan of all
but 2 tablespoons of the oil and duck
juices and place over low heat for
10 minutes, or until the juices are sticky
and the fat is clear.

Five Add the trimmings and vegetables
and cook for 2 minutes. Add the stock
and bouquet garni; stir well and pour
into a saucepan. Bring to a boil, reduce
the heat and simmer, skimming
occasionally, for 20–30 minutes, or until
the sauce is reduced by half. Strain,
discarding the solids; season to taste
with salt and freshly ground black
pepper and keep warm.

Six Remove the string and place the duck
on a platter. Reheat the bacon and
turnips and arrange around the duck.
Drizzle half the sauce over the bacon
and turnips and serve the remaining
sauce on the side.

CHEF'S TIP *For the best method to
carve the duck, follow the technique for
carving turkey on page 531.*

LE CORDON BLEU ✠ COMPLETE COOK

Chicken chasseur

This classic French pan-fried chicken with a mushroom sauce is easy to prepare and will fully satisfy any guest. The recipe may be traditional but it's also versatile—try adding onions, wild mushrooms, tomatoes or bacon to the sauce. Delicious with crusty bread or roast potatoes.

***Preparation time** 30 minutes*
***Total cooking time** 1 hour 30 minutes*
Serves 4

1 x 2½ lb. chicken, giblets optional
1½ cups chicken stock (see page 519)
oil, for cooking
1⅔ cups sliced button mushrooms
1 large shallot, finely chopped
2 tablespoons brandy
2 tablespoons white wine
2–3 large sprigs fresh tarragon
2–3 sprigs fresh chervil

One Preheat the oven to 400°F. Cut the chicken into four or eight pieces, following the method in the Chef's techniques on page 528, then coarsely cut up the remaining carcass with a knife or poultry shears.

Two Put the carcass pieces and giblets, if using, into a roasting pan and roast for 25 minutes, or until browned. Remove from the oven and add the stock. Use a wooden spoon to loosen any bits stuck to the pan and simmer gently on the stove top for 30 minutes. Strain and reserve the liquid. Skim off any excess fat.

Three On the stove top, heat a little oil in the clean roasting pan, add the chicken pieces skin side down and brown quickly and lightly on both sides. Transfer to the oven to finish cooking: the legs will need 20 minutes, the breast and wings 15 minutes. Check that the chicken is cooked by piercing with a fork or fine skewer—the juices should run clear. Remove the chicken from the pan and keep warm.

Four Pour the excess fat from the pan, leaving 1 tablespoon and any chicken juices. Reheat on top of the stove, then add the mushrooms and cook until lightly browned. Add the shallot and cook without browning. Increase the heat if necessary and, when the pan is very hot, add the brandy. Bring to a boil and light with a match to flambé. Add the white wine and reduce the heat to simmer for 1–2 minutes, or until reduced by half. Add the reserved chicken stock and reduce for 4–5 minutes. Season to taste. Finely chop the herbs and add to the sauce—do not allow to boil again. Spoon over the chicken to serve.

Coq au vin

The long list of ingredients is not as daunting as it appears. The chicken is marinated overnight in wine, vegetables and herbs to tenderize and flavor it, and the dish can quickly be put together the next day. This traditional recipe originated in the Burgundy region, famous for its fine red wines.

Preparation time *50 minutes*
+ overnight marinating
Total cooking time *2 hours*
Serves 6–8

MARINADE
1 onion, chopped
1 carrot, chopped
5 juniper berries
10 peppercorns
1 whole clove
1 clove garlic
2 quarts red wine
¼ cup brandy
2 tablespoons red wine vinegar
1 bouquet garni (see page 520)

6 lb. chicken pieces
clarified butter (see page 520) or oil,
for cooking
⅓ cup all-purpose flour
3 cups chicken stock (see page 519)
6 oz. slab bacon
3 small boiling onions
4 teaspoons sugar
1 tablespoon unsalted butter
15 button mushrooms

CROUTONS
4 slices bread, crusts removed
⅔ cup clarified butter or oil
1 tablespoon chopped fresh parsley

One To make the marinade, place all the ingredients into a large nonreactive bowl. Add the chicken pieces, cover and marinate overnight in the refrigerator.

Two Remove the chicken pieces and dry with paper towels. Strain the marinade and reserve the vegetables and herbs separately from the liquid. Preheat the oven to 400°F.

Three Heat a little clarified butter or oil in a deep flameproof casserole or Dutch oven and sauté the chicken over high heat skin side down first until well browned on all sides. Add the reserved marinated vegetables and herbs. Cook for 5 minutes, or until softened, stirring occasionally. Pour off any excess fat. Sprinkle the flour into the casserole and mix well. Add the reserved marinade, hot stock and salt and pepper. Cover with parchment paper and a lid and bake in the oven for 45 minutes, or until the chicken is cooked through. Reduce the oven temperature to 300°F. Transfer the chicken to a clean casserole, strain the sauce and skim off the excess fat.

Season to taste. Pour over the chicken and return to the oven to heat through.

Four Meanwhile, put the bacon in a saucepan, cover with water and bring to a boil. Drain, rinse under cold water and trim off the rind. Cut into small pieces and fry in a little oil until golden; drain on paper towels. Put the onions, sugar and butter in a saucepan with just enough water to cover. Bring to a boil, then simmer until all the water has evaporated and the onions are tender (if necessary, add a little extra water and continue cooking). Glaze the onions by tossing them in the butter and sugar until golden. Fry the mushrooms in hot oil and drain. Sprinkle the bacon, onions and mushrooms over the chicken, cover and keep warm.

Five To make croutons, cut each slice of bread into four triangles and pan-fry in very hot clarified butter or oil until golden brown—be careful as the bread browns quickly. Dip the tips of the croutons in the parsley and arrange over the dish.

---

about cooking with wine...

Wine for cooking should be of a reasonable quality—one that you would be happy to drink. Cheaper wines will not add a good flavor to food and the flavor of expensive wines will be lost in the cooking process.

Breast of chicken with tarragon and mustard sauce

The perennial aromatic herb French tarragon has a subtle anise-like flavor, which perfectly complements other gently flavored foods such as eggs, fish and chicken. The Latin name means "little dragon," from the belief that the herb could cure the bites of venomous creatures.

Preparation time 15 minutes
Total cooking time 50 minutes
Serves 4

oil, for cooking
4 skinned boneless chicken breast halves
4 shallots, thinly sliced
1/3 cup dry white wine
2 cups chicken stock (see page 519)
3/4 cup whipping cream or crème fraîche
2–3 tablespoons Dijon or tarragon mustard, to taste
2–3 tablespoons fresh tarragon leaves

One Preheat the oven to 350°F. Heat 1 tablespoon oil in a roasting pan on the stove top and fry the chicken breasts for 5 minutes on each side, or until they are golden brown. Transfer the chicken breasts to the oven and cook for another 5–10 minutes, or until the juices run clear when a skewer is inserted into the center.

Two Remove the chicken from the pan and keep warm. Spoon off the excess fat and transfer the roasting pan to the stove top. Add the shallots and fry until soft and lightly browned, then add the wine and reduce until almost dry. Add the stock and simmer for 5–10 minutes, or until syrupy.

Three Strain the sauce into a clean saucepan, add the cream and simmer for 5 minutes. Stir in the mustard and season with salt and pepper to taste. Chop the tarragon and sprinkle into the sauce at the last minute to prevent it discoloring. Pour the sauce over the chicken before serving.

CHEF'S TIP *The shallots, which have a lovely flavor, could be left in the sauce. If you wish to do this, simply add the cream without straining the sauce first.*

Chicken Basque

The Basque country is located in the south-west of France and northern Spain. This traditional recipe uses local produce such as onions, bell peppers and tomatoes but we have substituted the more readily available Parma ham or prosciutto for the local cured ham from Bayonne, and olive oil instead of the traditional goose fat.

***Preparation time** 30 minutes*
***Total cooking time** 1 hour 15 minutes*
Serves 4

2 red bell peppers
2 green bell peppers
1 x 2 lb. 6 oz. chicken
oil, for cooking
1 large onion, thinly sliced
3 cloves garlic, crushed
2 tomatoes, peeled, seeded and
quartered (see page 534)
1/3 cup white wine
3 oz. Parma ham or prosciutto,
cut into strips
1 tablespoon chopped fresh parsley,
to garnish

One Halve the red and green bell peppers, remove the seeds and membrane and slice the flesh into long thin strips.

Two Cut the chicken into eight pieces, following the method in the Chef's techniques on page 528. Season to taste with salt and freshly ground black pepper. Heat 2 tablespoons oil in a large deep skillet. Add the chicken pieces skin side down first and fry until they are light golden brown all over. Remove and drain on crumpled paper towels while making the sauce.

Three Spoon off the excess oil, leaving just 1 tablespoon in the pan. Add the onion, garlic, peppers and tomatoes and simmer for 10 minutes. Add the white wine, cover and simmer for another 30 minutes. Add the chicken, season lightly with salt and pepper, cover and simmer for 15–20 minutes. Check that the chicken is fully cooked by piercing it with a fork (the juices should run clear).

Lift out the chicken pieces, cover with aluminum foil and keep warm. Season the sauce with salt and pepper to taste.

Four Pan-fry the ham or prosciutto in a little oil, lifting directly from the pan with a slotted spoon, without draining on paper towels. Pour the sauce over the chicken, sprinkle with the ham or prosciutto and garnish with the parsley.

Chicken pie

Serve this delicious pie with simple boiled or mashed potatoes to mop up the chicken juices. Brussels sprouts or spinach would also be delicious accompaniments. Alternatively, for a crisper bite, serve with a mixed green side salad.

Preparation time 45 minutes
+ 30 minutes resting
Total cooking time 1 hour 35 minutes
Serves 4–6

1 x 3 lb. chicken
8 slices pancetta, rind removed
1/4 cup unsalted butter
1 hard-boiled egg, coarsely chopped
12 button mushrooms, quartered
1 onion, finely chopped
1/4 cup white wine
1 cup chicken stock (see page 519)
1/2 quantity puff pastry (see page 542)
or 1 sheet frozen puff pastry, thawed
1 egg, beaten
large pinch of chopped fresh herbs,
such as parsley, tarragon or chervil

One Cut the chicken into eight pieces, following the method in the Chef's techniques on page 528, and remove the bones and skin. Season with salt and pepper, then wrap each piece of chicken in a slice of pancetta and secure with wooden cocktail picks or string.

Two Heat half the butter in a skillet over medium heat and lightly brown the chicken in batches, turning regularly to seal on all sides. Remove the chicken from the pan and drain on crumpled paper towels. Discard the cocktail picks or string and place the chicken in a 6-cup pie plate with the hard-boiled egg. Pour off the excess fat from the pan, add the remaining butter and cook the mushrooms and onion over low heat for 5 minutes without coloring.

Three Add the white wine to the pan and simmer until only a little liquid is left. Pour over the chicken. Add sufficient stock to almost cover the chicken pieces.

Four Roll out the pastry so that it is a little bigger than the top of the pie plate. Brush the rim of the plate with beaten egg and line with 1/2 inch of spare pastry cut from around the pastry edge, pressing onto the plate firmly and brushing with beaten egg. Fold the pastry over a rolling pin and cover the pie plate. Be careful not to stretch the pastry or it will shrink out of shape while baking. Press the edges together to seal. With a small sharp knife, trim off the excess pastry. Do not angle the knife in towards the dish or it will encourage shrinkage later. With the back of the knife, notch the cut pastry edge. Brush the top surface with egg, but not the edges. Make a small hole for steam to escape, then decorate with pastry trimmings and brush them with egg.

Five Chill the pie for 30 minutes to prevent it shrinking during baking and preheat the oven to 375°F. Bake the pie for 20 minutes, or until the pastry is risen and golden. Reduce the oven to 250°F and cover the pie with aluminum foil to maintain its golden brown color. Cook for 45 minutes. Break the crust in the center, or loosen and lift off from the side, and add the chopped fresh herbs. Serve immediately.

CHEF'S TIPS *This pie has a thin gravy; if you prefer a thicker sauce, roll the chicken pieces in seasoned flour after sealing and before putting them in the pie plate.*

Frozen puff pastry can be purchased in 17 1/4 oz. packages, each containing two sheets, from gourmet or specialty food stores.

meat

Carpaccio with arugula and Parmesan

*Beef carpaccio is a classic Italian first course consisting
of very thin slices of raw beef served with a vinaigrette and
often topped with onions or capers as in this recipe.*

Preparation time *15 minutes
+ 30 minutes freezing*
Total cooking time *None*
Serves 4

*¾ lb. beef tenderloin steak
(see Chef's tips)
3 tablespoons lemon juice
3 tablespoons extra virgin olive oil
3 oz. piece Parmesan cheese,
at room temperature
3 cups arugula leaves or watercress
sprigs
¼ cup drained capers*

One To prepare the carpaccio, trim the beef of all fat and sinew. Wrap tightly in plastic wrap and freeze for at least 30 minutes, or until very firm but not rock solid. Remove the plastic wrap and using a very sharp, thin knife, slice the meat as thinly as possible. Place each slice between two layers of plastic wrap and lightly pound the slices to flatten.

Two Divide the beef among four plates, arranging the slices in a single layer, overlapping them slightly. Cover with plastic wrap and refrigerate until ready to serve.

Three To make the dressing, whisk together the lemon juice and olive oil. Season to taste with salt and freshly ground pepper and set aside.

Four Using a vegetable peeler, shave cheese curls from the piece of Parmesan, allowing six shavings per plate. Set aside until ready to use.

Five Just before serving, toss the arugula leaves or watercress in half the dressing and arrange on the plates with the carpaccio. Sprinkle with the Parmesan and capers. Drizzle with the remaining dressing and serve at once with freshly ground black pepper.

CHEF'S TIPS *When making your own carpaccio, it is very important to use a good-quality cut of very fresh meat. Alternatively, for the thinnest possible slices of beef, your butcher may be able to prepare the carpaccio for you. Order the meat several days in advance of the day you plan to serve it and specify how you would like it prepared. Ask your butcher to lay out the slices on a sheet of plastic wrap for easier handling.*

This recipe can be adjusted to taste by adding freshly chopped herbs such as basil, as well as olives, anchovies or roasted and skinned red bell peppers.

English corned beef with vegetables and dumplings

This delicious corned beef is served with onions, carrots, turnips and light dumplings cooked in a well-flavored beef stock. The marrow may be extracted from the bone with a teaspoon and is particularly good sprinkled with a little salt.

Preparation time 20 minutes
+ 3 hours soaking
Total cooking time 4 hours 30 minutes
Serves 6

2 lb. piece corned beef
6 x 2-inch pieces marrow bone
1 bouquet garni (see page 520)
6 peppercorns
½ onion
6 onions, quartered
4 large carrots, quartered
2 turnips, quartered
2 teaspoons chopped fresh parsley

DUMPLINGS
2 cups self-rising flour
pinch of salt
3 tablespoons suet, coarsely grated
½ cup cold water

One Soak the beef in cold water for at least 3 hours, remove and rinse.

Two Place the marrow bones and beef in a large saucepan, cover with water and bring to a boil slowly, skimming off the impurities as necessary. Reduce the heat to a simmer. Add the bouquet garni, peppercorns and the ½ onion. Partially cover the saucepan and simmer for 3 hours. Check regularly and skim off any fat and impurities. Remove and discard the bouquet garni, peppercorns and onion. Add the quartered onions, carrots and turnips and simmer for 40 minutes.

Three Begin to prepare the dumplings 30 minutes before the beef is cooked. Sift the flour and salt into a bowl and stir in the suet. Make a well in the center, add a little water, and mix in the flour using a fork. Add enough of the water to make a soft, but not sticky dough, then knead gently until smooth. Shape, with floured hands, into about 20 dumplings. Add to the saucepan of beef and simmer for 20 minutes, or until they float and have puffed up. Remove with a slotted spoon.

Four Place the beef in a large dish surrounded with vegetables from the pot, dumplings and marrow bones. Cover and keep warm. Reduce the stock for 30 minutes, skimming as necessary, until it has a good flavor. Ladle onto the meat and sprinkle with chopped parsley.

CHEF'S TIP *These dumplings could be served with stews. Simply poach in 2¼ cups of simmering beef stock or well salted water.*

Beef Wellington

*Beef Wellington is the name given to loin of beef, lightly covered
with duxelles (shallots and mushrooms cooked in butter) and sometimes
liver pâté, then wrapped in puff pastry and baked until golden.*

*Preparation time 1 hour
+ 15 minutes chilling*
Total cooking time 1 hour 15 minutes
Serves 6

3¼ lb. beef rib-eye roast
½ cup oil
1 small carrot, chopped
1 small onion, chopped
1 small leek, chopped
3 tablespoons dry Madeira or sherry
2 cups brown stock (see page 518)
3 tablespoons unsalted butter
2 shallots, finely chopped
1 clove garlic, finely chopped
*1 lb. button mushrooms,
finely chopped*
*1 lb. 10 oz. puff pastry (see page 542)
or 2–3 sheets frozen puff pastry,
thawed*
10 slices prosciutto
1 egg, beaten

One Preheat the oven to 425°F. Remove and reserve the thin muscle from the side of the beef. Remove and discard the shiny surface membrane and tie the meat with string at ¾-inch intervals.

Two Coarsely chop the beef trimmings. Heat 1 tablespoon of the oil in a skillet, then add the beef trimmings and chopped carrot, onion and leek. Gently fry until the mixture browns. Stir in the Madeira, scraping up the sticky juices from the bottom of the pan, then simmer for a few minutes, or until reduced to a syrup. Stir in the stock. Bring to a boil, then reduce the heat and leave for 1 hour to simmer to a syrupy sauce while preparing the Beef Wellington.

Three Place a roasting pan over high heat and add the remaining oil. When it begins to smoke, add the beef roast and brown quickly all over. Season well, then transfer to the oven and roast for about 5 minutes for medium rare, 10 minutes for medium and 15 minutes for well done. (The actual roasting time will depend on the thickness of the beef.) Remove from the pan to allow the beef to cool completely.

Four Melt the butter in a saucepan and gently cook the shallots for 1–2 minutes, or until soft but not browned. Add the garlic and mushrooms and cook gently until the saucepan looks dry when scraped with a spoon. The mixture should be barely moist. Set aside.

Five On a lightly floured work surface, slightly overlap the pastry sheets and roll out into a rectangle measuring 24 x 14 inches. Transfer to a baking sheet, cover with plastic wrap and chill in the refrigerator for 15 minutes.

Six Transfer the pastry to the work surface. To reduce excess overlap, cut away each corner, reserving the pastry trimmings and leaving the center large enough for the beef—the pastry will resemble a cross. Flatten each flap of pastry with a rolling pin.

Seven Lay the prosciutto slices on the pastry and spread thinly with half the mushrooms. Untie the beef, season well, place it on the pastry and spread with the remaining mushrooms. Bring the flaps of prosciutto over the beef. Brush the pastry edges with a little beaten egg and fold them over each other to completely encase the beef.

Eight Turn onto a lightly buttered baking sheet seam side down. Cut the excess pastry into strips and crisscross a lattice pattern over the top. Brush with more beaten egg, then pierce a small slit in the top for a crisp finish. Place in the oven for 5 minutes to set, then lower the heat to 400°F and bake for 20 minutes.

Nine Remove from the oven and allow to rest for 10 minutes in a warm place. Skim any impurities from the simmering sauce, then strain into a gravy boat. Slice the Beef Wellington and serve at once with the gravy served on the side.

Beef stroganoff

Thin strips of tenderloin, shallots and mushrooms sautéed in butter and served in a sour cream sauce.

***Preparation time** 20 minutes*
***Total cooking time** 30 minutes*
Serves 4

¼ cup olive oil
*1¼ lb. beef tenderloin steak,
cut into 2- x ½-inch strips*
2 tablespoons unsalted butter
3 large shallots, finely chopped
1 tablespoon sweet paprika
²/₃ cup thinly sliced button mushrooms
2 tablespoons white wine vinegar
3 tablespoons brandy
1 cup chicken stock (see page 519)
³/₄ cup sour cream
*3–4 pickled gherkins, cut into julienne
strips (see Chef's tip)*
*1–2 slices canned beets,
cut into julienne strips*

One Heat the oil in a skillet over high heat until very hot. Add the meat and fry in batches for 3–5 minutes, stirring constantly, until the meat is lightly browned. Remove from the pan, set aside and keep warm.

Two Melt the butter in the pan, add the shallots and cook for 2 minutes or until soft but not colored. Stir in the paprika for 45 seconds, then add the mushrooms and cook over high heat until dry. Add the vinegar and cook for 1 minute, or until the pan is nearly dry. Add the brandy, cook until the liquid is reduced to half, then add the stock and reduce to half again. Finally, add half the sour cream and return the meat to the pan to reheat. Serve with a rice pilaf, dot with the remaining sour cream and garnish with the gherkins and beets.

CHEF'S TIP *Julienne strips are vegetables cut to the size and shape of matchsticks.*

Estouffade of beef with green and black olives

An estouffade is a type of stew where the ingredients are slowly simmered.
It is usually made with beef, wine, carrots and onions. The addition
of ripe olives here gives the recipe its Provençal flavor.

Preparation time 40 minutes
Total cooking time 2 hours 30 minutes
Serves 4–6

4 lb. beef for stew, cut into cubes
2 carrots, chopped
1 large onion, chopped
2 tablespoons all-purpose flour
2 tablespoons tomato paste
3 cups white wine
1 quart brown stock (see page 518)
3 fresh tomatoes, halved, seeded and
chopped (see page 534)
3 cloves garlic, chopped
1 bouquet garni (see page 520)
6 oz. mushrooms, thinly sliced
1 x 16 oz. can chopped tomatoes
6 oz. slab or sliced bacon, rind
removed and cut into batons
½ cup pitted and chopped
green olives
½ cup pitted and chopped
black olives
2 tablespoons chopped fresh parsley

One Preheat the oven to 350°F. Season the beef with salt and freshly ground black pepper. Heat a 1-inch depth of olive oil in a large flameproof casserole or Dutch oven. Add the beef, in batches, brown on all sides, then remove from the casserole. Add the carrots and onion and cook until lightly golden. Lower the heat, then sprinkle over the flour and cook, stirring, for 2 minutes. Stir in the tomato paste and cook for 1 minute. Pour on the wine and blend in until smooth, then stir to a boil and simmer for 3–4 minutes. Stir in the stock, fresh tomatoes, garlic and bouquet garni. Return the meat to the casserole, bring just to a boil, then cover, transfer to the oven and bake for 1 hour 45 minutes, or until the meat is tender.

Two Heat a little oil in a skillet and fry the mushrooms over high heat for about 3–4 minutes, or until dry. Season the mushrooms with salt and black pepper, remove them from the oil and set aside. Clean the pan, add a few drops of olive oil, allow the oil to warm, then add the canned tomatoes and boil until thick and the liquid has evaporated; set aside. Place the bacon in a saucepan of cold water, bring to a boil, then drain, rinse with cold water and dry. Fry the bacon in a little oil until it is golden, drain on paper towels and set aside.

Three Once the beef is tender when pierced with a fork, remove it and strain the sauce. Discard the vegetables and bouquet garni, then return the meat and sauce to the cleaned casserole with the mushrooms, tomato, bacon and olives. Bring to a boil and check the seasoning. Serve sprinkled with the parsley.

Boeuf bourguignon

*The Burgundy region of France is famous for its fine wines and sophisticated cuisine.
Dishes à la bourguignonne generally include a sauce made of red wine
and a garnish of small onions, mushrooms and pieces of bacon.*

***Preparation time** 1 hour
+ marinating overnight*
***Total cooking time** 2 hours 30 minutes*
Serves 4

MARINADE
*1 large carrot, cut into ½-inch pieces
1 onion, cut into ½-inch pieces
1 stalk celery, cut into ½-inch pieces
2 cloves garlic
1 bouquet garni (see page 520)
¼ cup brandy
10 black peppercorns
6 cups good red wine
2 tablespoons oil*

*2 lb. beef chuck steak, trimmed and
cut into 1½-inch cubes
1 heaping tablespoon tomato paste
2 tablespoons all-purpose flour
1½ cups brown stock
(see page 518)
32 small boiling onions, peeled
1 tablespoon unsalted butter
2 teaspoons sugar
5 oz. mushrooms, quartered
2 tablespoons chopped garlic
8 oz. slab or sliced bacon, cut into
cubes or short batons
2 slices white bread, crusts removed,
cut in triangles
2 tablespoons chopped fresh parsley*

One Place all the ingredients for the marinade in a bowl with the cubes of beef. Cover and refrigerate overnight.

Two Preheat the oven to 400°F. Strain the marinade into a saucepan, remove the beef and set aside, and keep the vegetables and bouquet garni separate. Bring the marinade to a boil, skim off the impurities and cook for 6–8 minutes. Pass through a fine strainer.

Three In a large, heavy-bottomed flameproof casserole or Dutch oven, heat a little oil and butter. Pat dry the meat and brown on all sides in batches, remove and keep to one side. Add the well-drained vegetables from the marinade, lower the heat slightly and cook, stirring occasionally, until lightly browned. Return the meat to the casserole with the tomato paste and stir over medium heat for 3 minutes. Sprinkle with the flour, place in the oven for 6–8 minutes, then remove and mix in the flour. Place over medium heat, add the marinade and bring to a boil, stirring constantly, then add the stock and bouquet garni. Return to a boil, cover the casserole and bake in the oven for 1 hour 30 minutes, or until the meat is tender.

Four Place the onions, butter, sugar and some salt in a deep skillet and pour in enough water to cover. Cook over medium heat until the water has almost evaporated and swirl the skillet until the onions are golden. Fry the mushrooms in some sizzling butter until golden, season, drain and add to the onions. Fry the garlic and bacon in a little oil, drain and add to the onions and mushrooms.

Five Brush the bread with melted butter and toast in the oven for 3–5 minutes, or until brown.

Six Once the beef is cooked, skim off excess fat. Transfer the beef to a clean flameproof casserole or serving dish, cover and keep warm. Strain the sauce and return it to the pan, discarding the vegetables and bouquet garni. Bring the sauce to a boil and simmer for about 15 minutes, or until the sauce coats the back of a spoon, skimming frequently. Season, strain over the meat and simmer or return to the oven for 5 minutes. Add the onions, mushrooms and bacon. Dip a corner of each bread crouton in the sauce, then into the parsley. Sprinkle the remaining parsley over the beef and serve with the croutons on the edge of the dish or on the side.

---

about beef...

For long, slow-cooked dishes such as boeuf bourguignon it is important that you use cuts of meat such as chuck or rump which will become very tender as they cook. These cuts contain a certain amount of fat and connective tissue which melts into the dish and gives a rich, smooth quality to the sauce.

Roast beef and Yorkshire puddings

Roast beef served with crisp, golden Yorkshire puddings and tangy horseradish cream is a traditional favourite for English Sunday lunch. Carve the beef at the table for the greatest effect.

Preparation time *40 minutes*
+ 30 minutes resting
Total cooking time *1 hour 40 minutes*
Serves 4–6

YORKSHIRE PUDDINGS
3/4 cup milk
1 1/2 cups all-purpose flour
2 eggs

oil, for cooking
3 lb. boneless beef roast (round tip or rib)

HORSERADISH CREAM
1/2 cup whipping cream
2–3 tablespoons grated fresh or prepared white horseradish
a few drops of lemon juice

JUS
1 carrot, chopped
1 onion, chopped
1 stalk celery, chopped
1 leek, chopped
1 bay leaf
2 sprigs of fresh thyme
3 peppercorns
2 cups brown stock (see page 518)

One Preheat the oven to 425°F. To make the Yorkshire puddings, combine the milk with 1/2 cup water. Sift the flour and some salt into a bowl and make a well in the center. Add the eggs and begin to whisk. As the mixture thickens, gradually add the milk and water, whisking until a smooth batter forms. Pour into a pitcher, cover and let rest for 30 minutes.

Two On the stove top, heat about 1/4 cup of oil in a roasting pan over high heat. Add the beef fat side down and brown all over, turning with tongs. Transfer the beef to the oven and, turning and basting every 15 minutes, roast for 30 minutes for rare, 45 minutes for medium rare and 1 hour for well done.

Three To make the horseradish cream, lightly whip the cream until soft peaks form. Gently fold in the horseradish and season to taste with salt, pepper and the lemon juice. Do not overfold or the mixture will become too thick. Transfer to a serving bowl, cover and chill.

Four Transfer the beef to a plate, cover lightly with aluminum foil and allow to rest for 10–15 minutes before carving. Reserving a tablespoon of fat in the roasting pan, drain the excess fat and use it to brush a deep 12-cup muffin pan and to make the jus.

Five Heat the muffin pan in the oven for 2–3 minutes until lightly smoking. Divide the pudding batter between the cups and bake for 15–20 minutes, or until puffed and golden.

Six To make the jus, heat the remaining fat in the roasting pan over the stove top. Add the vegetables and gently fry over medium heat for 5 minutes, or until golden, stirring constantly. Drain the pan of any excess fat; add the bay leaf, thyme, peppercorns and a little hot stock, scraping the bottom of the pan with a wooden spoon. Add the remaining hot stock and simmer to reduce by half, skimming off any impurities or fat. Strain into a saucepan, discard the vegetables and seasonings, and skim again. Season, then cover and keep warm. (Pour into a warm gravy boat just before serving.)

Seven Serve the beef and puddings on warm plates, with the jus and horseradish cream on the side. Green vegetables and roast potatoes are traditional accompaniments.

CHEF'S TIP *Allowing a roast to rest makes the meat easier to carve and helps prevent the juices from running. Any juices from the resting can be poured over the meat, but do not add them to the jus: they will spoil its texture.*

Carbonade à la flamande

Although the word carbonade *comes from the Italian for "charcoal cooked," the beef is not grilled but browned in a skillet then transferred to the casserole. The dish first appeared in the Flemish area of northern France, where beef and onions were cooked in beer.*

Preparation time *30 minutes*
Total cooking time *2 hours 30 minutes*
Serves 4

¼ cup lard or oil
2 lb. beef chuck or round steak, cut into eight ½-inch slices
4 small onions, thinly sliced
¼ cup all-purpose flour
1 tablespoon tomato paste
1 quart beer (brown ale)
1 bouquet garni (see page 520)
3 juniper berries
1 tablespoon brown sugar
5 cups brown stock (see page 518)

One Preheat the oven to 350°F. Heat the lard or oil in a large skillet and add the beef in batches. Over high heat, quickly fry to seal and brown. Remove and set aside. Lower the heat, add the onions and cook for 10 minutes, or until soft and golden.

Two Transfer the onions to a 6-quart flameproof casserole or Dutch oven, stir in the flour and cook over low heat for 2 minutes. Add the tomato paste and cook for 1–2 minutes. Add the beer, bouquet garni, juniper berries and sugar and stir to a boil. Add the stock, bring back to a boil, then add the beef and simmer for 5 minutes, skimming off any impurities. Season, cover and bake for 1 hour 45 minutes.

Three The beef should be tender when pierced with a fork; if not, return to the oven. Once cooked, transfer the beef to a serving dish. On the stove top, bring the sauce to a boil, skimming off any impurities, and cook for 10 minutes until it thickens. Pour the sauce over the beef to serve.

Steak au poivre

This is a simple method for the traditional French pepper steak that has quite controversial origins. At least four chefs claimed to have invented this dish at various times between 1905 and 1930.

Preparation time *10 minutes*
Total cooking time *30 minutes*
Serves 4

4 x 5–6 oz. filet mignon or rib-eye steaks
1/3 cup clarified butter (see page 520)
3 1/4 cups brown stock (see page 518)
2 shallots, finely chopped
2 tablespoons crushed black peppercorns
3 tablespoons white wine
1/4 cup brandy
small sprigs of fresh parsley, to garnish

One Season the steaks with salt. In a shallow skillet big enough to fit the four steaks, heat the clarified butter until it is smoking. Add the steaks and brown for 3–4 minutes on each side for medium rare and a little longer for medium. Remove from the pan, cover with aluminum foil to keep warm and set aside. For well-done steak, brown on each side for 3 minutes, then transfer to a roasting pan and bake in a 400°F oven for 8–10 minutes. Remove from the oven and cover with aluminum foil.

Two Put the brown stock in a saucepan and reduce down to 1 1/2 cups. Add the shallots to the skillet and lightly color for 3–4 minutes before adding the peppercorns. Add the white wine and half the brandy, stir well with a wooden spoon and gently boil for 1 minute until syrupy. Stir in the reduced stock and bring to a boil. Cook for 7 minutes, or until syrupy. Add the remaining brandy.

Three Return the steaks to the sauce in the pan and reheat for 3–4 minutes, without boiling. Serve garnished with sprigs of parsley.

Beef stew with herb biscuits

*Just below the well-risen, golden brown biscuits is
a rich, tender beef and mushroom stew, which is
guaranteed to bring warmth to a cold winter day.*

Preparation time *30 minutes*
Total cooking time *2 hours*
Serves 4–6

3 tablespoons olive oil
*1½ lb. beef chuck or round steak, cut
into 1-inch cubes*
2 onions, thinly sliced
1 clove garlic, crushed
1 tablespoon all-purpose flour
¾ cup red wine
1 teaspoon tomato paste
3⅓ cups quartered button mushrooms

HERB BISCUITS
2 cups self-rising flour
¼ teaspoon salt
*¼ cup unsalted butter, cut into cubes
and chilled*
*1 tablespoon chopped fresh herbs, such
as parsley, rosemary or thyme*
½ cup buttermilk (see Chef's tip)
1 egg, beaten

One Preheat the oven to 300°F. Heat the oil in a flameproof casserole or Dutch oven until it is very hot. Brown the meat in batches, taking care not to crowd the pot, for 3–4 minutes each side, then remove from the pot and set aside.

Two Add the onions to the casserole with the garlic and cook for 2 minutes. Sprinkle the flour on top and stir in with a wooden spoon, scraping the bottom of the pot. Cook for 1 minute, stirring constantly, until the mixture is golden brown. Gradually stir in the wine, ¾ cup water and the tomato paste, and season with salt and freshly ground black pepper. Continue stirring until the mixture begins to thicken, then return the meat to the pot, add the mushrooms and bring to a boil. Cover and either cook gently on the stove or bake in the oven for 1½ hours.

Three Begin preparing the biscuits no more than 10 minutes before the beef has finished cooking. Sift the flour and salt into a wide bowl, then add the butter. Using your fingertips, rub the butter into the flour until the mixture resembles fine bread crumbs. Add the herbs. Stir in the buttermilk, using a wooden spoon or rubber spatula, until the flour has disappeared and the mixture is in large lumps, then bring together quickly into a rough ball. Place the ball on a lightly floured surface and knead quickly until the dough is just smooth. Roll or pat out the dough with the palm of your hand to a ⅝-inch thickness, then cut out about 10 rounds using a 2-inch biscuit cutter.

Four Remove the stew from the oven, then increase the temperature to 400°F. Arrange the biscuits on the surface of the stew and brush the tops with the egg. Place the stew at the top of the oven, uncovered, to bake for 12 minutes, or until the biscuits have risen and turned golden brown.

CHEF'S TIP *If you don't have any buttermilk, add 1 teaspoon lemon juice to fresh milk.*

Braised beef in dill sauce

Slowly braised beef served with a creamy dill sauce makes a welcome change from the more traditional recipes for beef. Delicious served with crisp green vegetables and new potatoes.

Preparation time 25 minutes
Total cooking time 2 hours 15 minutes
Serves 4

*2 lb. boneless beef roast for braising,
such as chuck eye,
round tip or round rump, tied
1 large carrot, quartered and cut
into 1½-inch lengths
3 onions, quartered
1 stalk celery, cut into
1½-inch lengths
1 large clove garlic, quartered
2½ cups brown stock (see page 518)
1 small bay leaf
2 tablespoons unsalted butter
¼ cup all-purpose flour
⅔ cup sour cream (see Chef's tips)
2–3 tablespoons chopped fresh dill or
1–1½ teaspoons dried dill*

One Preheat the oven to 350°F. On the stove top heat a little oil in a 2½-quart flameproof casserole or Dutch oven until the oil is lightly smoking.

Two Place the beef in the casserole and brown quickly on all sides, including the ends, then transfer to a plate. Reduce the heat, add the carrot, onions and celery and cook until golden brown, turning frequently. Add the garlic, place the meat on the vegetables and pour in the stock—it will come about halfway up the meat. Season with salt and freshly ground black pepper and add the bay leaf. Bring to a boil, reduce the heat and cover with parchment paper and the lid. Simmer on top of the stove or bake in the oven for 1½ hours, turning the meat every 30 minutes. After 1½ hours, check for tenderness by piercing with a sharp knife—cook for another 15–30 minutes if necessary.

Three To make the sauce, melt the butter in a saucepan, add the flour and cook over low heat until the mixture turns from butter yellow to a pale straw color. Remove from the heat and allow the mixture to cool.

Four Transfer the meat from the casserole onto a plate and cover with the parchment paper to keep moist. Strain 2½ cups of the cooking liquid into a glass measure, discard the vegetables and bay leaf and skim the fat from the surface of the liquid.

Five Gradually add most of the measured liquid to the butter and flour mixture and whisk until blended and smooth. Return to the stove, heat gently until slightly thickened, then increase the heat and bring to a boil, stirring. Cook, gently, boiling for 3 minutes, or until the sauce is reduced and slightly syrupy. Stir in the sour cream and reduce for another 3 minutes, or until it lightly coats the back of a spoon. Stir in the dill, add more seasoning as necessary and cover.

Six Remove the string and slice the beef into ¼-inch-thick slices, then drizzle over the remaining cooking liquid to keep it moist. Pour a light coating of the sauce into a clean baking dish or shallow serving dish. Place the meat in the dish and coat with the sauce. Cover and keep warm for 5 minutes before serving.

CHEF'S TIPS *For a lighter sauce, use half-and-half instead of sour cream.*

To prepare in advance, leave the sliced meat in a little cooking liquid and press a piece of buttered parchment paper onto the surface. To serve, warm the meat in its liquid and reheat the sauce.

Pot-au-feu

Pot-au-feu literally means "pot on the fire," and the long, slow cooking of this classic French dish will fill your kitchen with sumptuous aromas as it gently simmers to perfection. The traditional vegetables used in this recipe could be changed to suit the season or your personal taste.

***Preparation time** 30 minutes*
***Total cooking time** 2 hours 45 minutes*
Serves 6–8

2 small leeks
1 stalk celery or ½ small celery root
8–10 black peppercorns
5–6 coriander seeds
½ small green cabbage, cut into quarters
8 oz. oxtail, cut into small pieces
1½ lb. beef ribs
1 small veal shank (see Chef's tips)
1½ tablespoons salt
1 small onion, studded with 2 whole cloves
1 clove garlic
1 bouquet garni (see page 520)
2 carrots, cut into 2-inch pieces
1 turnip or rutabaga, peeled and quartered

One Tie the leeks and celery or celery root into a bundle. Place the peppercorns and coriander seeds in a small piece of cheesecloth, tie it up and set aside. Place the cabbage in a large saucepan and cover with cold water. Bring to a boil, cook for 3 minutes, then drain the cabbage and rinse in cold water and set aside.

Two Rinse all the meat and bones, place them in a large pot and cover with cold water. Bring to a boil, then remove from the heat and drain. Rinse the meat again, return to the pot and cover with 3½ quarts cold water. Add the salt and bring to a boil. Skim off the impurites and any fat that rise to the surface. Add the onion, garlic, bouquet garni and the bag of peppercorns and coriander seeds. Simmer over low heat for at least 1 hour 45 minutes.

Three Add the carrots, turnip, cabbage, leeks and celery bundle. Cook for another 30 minutes, or until the meat is tender. Remove and discard the bouquet garni and bag of spices. Strain the meat and vegetables, reserving the broth. Arrange the meat on a platter with the vegetables around. Serve the broth in a soup tureen.

CHEF'S TIPS *This dish is traditionally served with gherkins or sweet pickles, and salt for the meat.*

Boiled potatoes may be added to the broth. You can also replace the veal shanks with ham or bacon bones but do not season the meat as it is already quite salty.

Venetian-style liver

*Tender calf's liver, rich in iron, protein and vitamin A,
has a mild flavor that is perfectly enhanced by the soft
caramelized onions in this Venetian recipe.*

Preparation time *20 minutes*
Total cooking time *30 minutes*
Serves 4

*1 lb. calf's liver, sliced
vegetable oil, for cooking
2 medium onions,
thinly sliced*

One Make sure the liver is completely free of veins and remove any of the thin skin that may still be attached.

Two Heat 2–3 tablespoons of oil in a large nonstick skillet and add the onion and a large pinch of salt. Cook over medium heat for 20–30 minutes, or until the onions are very soft and golden brown. Remove the onions with a slotted spoon, leaving the oil in the skillet.

Three Add a little more oil to the skillet if necessary and heat until lightly smoking. Fry the liver in small batches, just enough to cover the bottom of the pan, for 1 minute, or until it has changed color from pink to brown. Toss and cook for a moment more. Transfer each batch to a warm plate and season to taste with salt and black pepper.

Four Return all the liver to the pan, add the cooked onions and toss to combine, but not to cook further. Transfer to a warm serving plate and serve immediately with steamed spinach and a simple risotto on the side.

CHEF'S TIP *The liver must fry quickly to retain its succulence, therefore it is important that the pan is hot or the liver will stick and fry for too long. Don't try to rush by cooking the liver in large batches—too much meat will crowd the pan, making the temperature drop and the liver stew rather than fry.*

Blanquette de veau

*A blanquette is a classic French "bourgeois" dish, which derives
its name from* blanc, *the French word for white. It is always made from
white meat cooked in a white stock or water, then enriched with cream.*

Preparation time *20 minutes*
Total cooking time *2 hours 10 minutes*
Serves 4

2³/4 lb. boneless veal shoulder
1 carrot, quartered
1 small onion, quartered
1 stalk celery, quartered
1 bouquet garni (see page 520)
1 teaspoon salt
10–12 peppercorns
10–12 small boiling onions
1²/3 cups sliced button mushrooms
1 teaspoon lemon juice
3 tablespoons unsalted butter
¹/4 cup all-purpose flour
1¹/4 cups whipping cream

One Remove excess fat from the veal and cut into 1¹/4-inch cubes. Place in a large heavy-bottomed saucepan with the carrot, onion, celery, bouquet garni, salt and peppercorns. Cover with about 2 cups cold water and bring to a boil on the stove top, skimming off any impurities that come to the surface. Reduce the heat and simmer for 1¹/2 hours, or until tender, skimming regularly. Add boiling water if necessary to keep the meat covered in liquid.

Two Cook the boiling onions for about 10 minutes in boiling salted water, drain well and set aside. Cook the mushrooms for 5 minutes in 2–3 tablespoons boiling salted water with the lemon juice and just under half of the butter. Drain well and set aside.

Three After 1¹/2 hours, check if the meat is cooked by piercing it with a fork—it should not resist and should slip easily from the fork. Remove the veal from the cooking liquid. Strain the liquid,

discarding the solids, return to the heat and cook for 30 minutes, or until it has reduced by two-thirds of its volume, skimming off excess fat. Cool slightly. Melt the remaining butter in a large saucepan, add the flour and cook for 1 minute. Stir in the reduced liquid and cook over low heat, whisking constantly, until the sauce has thickened. Add the cream, mix until smooth and season to taste with salt and pepper.

Four Add the meat, onions and mushrooms to the saucepan and simmer for 5 minutes. Serve the veal in a deep serving dish.

LE CORDON BLEU 🍲 COMPLETE COOK

Veal chops grand-mère

*Grand-mère, "grandmother" in French, refers to the garnish of
glazed onions, fried bacon, mushrooms and small potato balls that melt
in the mouth, making this dish a nourishing and succulent meal.*

Preparation time *30 minutes*
Total cooking time *1 hour 15 minutes*
Serves 4

⅓ cup oil
2 tablespoons unsalted butter
4 x 6 oz. veal chops
8-oz. Canadian bacon, finely diced
25 button mushrooms
20–24 small boiling onions
1 teaspoon sugar
5 potatoes
2 tablespoons white wine
⅓ cup brown stock (see page 518)

One Preheat the oven to 325°F. In a large heavy skillet, heat 1 tablespoon of the oil, then add the butter. Cook the chops for 2–3 minutes on each side, or until well browned. Remove from the pan, arrange in a baking dish and set aside. Cook the bacon in a skillet until browned, and add to the chops. Cook the mushrooms in the skillet, stirring occasionally, for about 2 minutes and scatter over the chops. Add the onions to the skillet with the sugar and cook, stirring occasionally, until light golden. Add to the chops.

Two Peel the potatoes and scoop out small balls with a melon baller. Heat the remaining oil in a separate skillet and cook the potatoes until golden brown, then drain on paper towels.

Three Pour the wine into the first skillet and stir well, scraping the bottom of the pan with a wooden spoon until the pan juices have dissolved. Cook until the wine has reduced by three-quarters. Add the stock and ⅓ cup water, bring to a boil and cook until the liquid has reduced by half.

Four Pour the liquid over the meat and vegetables in the baking dish and toss to coat in the liquid. Season with salt and freshly ground black pepper. Cover and bake for about 30–40 minutes, or until the chops are tender and cooked through. Serve immediately.

Veal chops with Chablis en cocotte

A cocotte is a round or oval cooking pan with two handles and a tight-fitting lid that was traditionally used to cook slow-cooking dishes. Now "en cocotte" refers to braised dishes in which the meat is first browned and then cooked in a liquid at a low simmer either in the oven or on the stove top.

Preparation time *15 minutes*
Total cooking time *50 minutes*
Serves 4

4 x 6 oz. veal loin chops
¼ cup unsalted butter
½ lb. veal trimmings or bones, finely chopped (ask the butcher)
1 cup Chablis wine
1 bouquet garni (see page 520)
3 oz. Canadian bacon, finely diced
1 small onion, finely chopped
1 carrot, finely diced
1 turnip, finely diced
1 tablespoon chopped fresh parsley

One Season the veal chops with salt and pepper. In a large skillet over medium heat, melt two-thirds of the butter and brown the veal for 2–3 minutes on both sides. Once browned, transfer the chops to a plate. Add the trimmings to the pan and brown, then return the veal chops to the pan. Cover, reduce the heat and cook slowly for 4 minutes on each side. Transfer the chops and trimmings back to the plate and set aside.

Two Increase the heat to medium-high and cook the meat juices, stirring constantly, for 3–4 minutes, or until they have caramelized onto the bottom of the pan. Strain the trimmings to remove the excess fat and return to the pan. Add the Chablis and stir well, scraping the bottom, until the cooking juices have dissolved. Cook for 5 minutes, or until the wine has reduced in volume by three-quarters. Add 2 cups water and the bouquet garni and simmer for 30 minutes. Strain the sauce into a glass measure and discard the veal trimmings and bouquet garni.

Three Meanwhile, melt the remaining butter in another skillet and brown the bacon for 2–3 minutes. Add the onion and carrot and cook them for another 2 minutes before adding the turnip. Reduce the heat, cover and cook for 8 minutes.

Four Add the sauce to the vegetables, bring to a boil and cook for 10 minutes. Return the veal chops to the hot sauce, reduce the heat and allow to simmer for 5 minutes, or until the veal is heated through. Serve immediately, sprinkled with the chopped parsley.

Osso buco

*A specialty of Milan, this dish is best made using shank from the hind leg and
the pieces should be cut no thicker than suggested to guarantee tenderness.
Savor the bone marrow, supposedly the best part of the dish.*

Preparation time 45 minutes
Total cooking time 2 hours 30 minutes
Serves 4

4 veal shank cross cuts,
1½ inches thick (osso buco)
all-purpose flour, seasoned with salt
and pepper
oil, for cooking
3 tablespoons unsalted butter
1 carrot, sliced
1 stalk celery, sliced
1 onion, sliced
4 cloves garlic, chopped
8 tomatoes, peeled, seeded and
chopped (see page 534)
1 cup white wine
1 bouquet garni (see page 520)
l quart beef stock or water
2 tablespoons chopped fresh parsley
zest of ¼ orange, finely chopped
zest of ¼ lemon, finely chopped

One Preheat the oven to 350°F. Trim the
meat of all sinew and skin and lightly
coat with the seasoned flour. Heat a little
oil in a small nonstick skillet and brown
the veal on both sides, in batches if
necessary. Set aside.

Two Melt the butter in a flameproof
casserole or Dutch oven and cook the
carrot, celery and onion over medium
heat for 3 minutes. Add the garlic and
mix well, then add the chopped
tomatoes and cook for 5 minutes. Add
the white wine and bouquet garni and
cook for another 5 minutes. Add the
stock and the browned meat, bring to
a simmer, season, cover and bake for
1½ hours, or until the meat is tender.

Three Transfer the meat to a serving
platter, cover and keep warm. Heat the
cooking liquid and vegetables and bring
to a boil. Skim off any fat or impurities
that rise to the surface and cook for
about 20 minutes, or until the sauce has
thickened and coats the back of a spoon.
Stir in the parsley, orange and lemon zest
and season to taste. Simmer for another
5 minutes, then pour over the meat and
serve immediately.

CHEF'S TIP *If you prefer a milder citrus
flavor, blanch the orange and lemon zest
before using. Place the rinds in a small
saucepan and cover with cold water,
bring to a boil for 30 seconds, then
strain and refresh. Use as instructed in
the recipe.*

Veal parmigiana

*This dish from northern Italy successfully combines the delicacy
of veal with the strong, tangy flavor of Parmesan cheese. If you can find it
Parmigiano Reggiano is the best-quality Parmesan.*

Preparation time 45 minutes
Total cooking time 1 hour 40 minutes
Serves 4

2–3 small sprigs of fresh basil
1 bay leaf
2 sprigs of fresh thyme
olive oil, for cooking
1 onion, finely chopped
2 lb. large ripe tomatoes, peeled,
seeded and diced (see page 534)
3 cloves garlic, finely chopped
4 x 4 oz. veal scallops
all-purpose flour, seasoned with salt
and pepper, to coat
2 eggs, lightly beaten
1²/₃ cups fresh bread crumbs
¹/₃ cup grated Parmesan
1 tablespoon finely chopped
fresh parsley
¹/₂ cup unsalted butter
8 oz. mozzarella cheese, sliced

One Pull the basil leaves from their
stems. Tie the stems with the bay leaf
and thyme to make a bouquet garni.

Two Heat ¹/₄ cup olive oil in a saucepan
and slowly cook the onion for 5 minutes
without coloring. Add the tomatoes,
garlic and bouquet garni. Season and
simmer covered for 20 minutes, then
uncovered for 45 minutes. Remove the
bouquet garni and adjust the seasoning
again to taste.

Three Pound the veal with a meat mallet
until ¹/₈ inch thick. Coat in the flour,
shaking off the excess. Dip the coated
veal in the beaten egg.

Four Mix together the bread crumbs,
Parmesan and parsley in a shallow dish.
Drain any excess egg from the veal and

then coat with the bread crumb mixture,
pressing well with your fingers to make
it stick.

Five Preheat the oven to 400°F. Heat ¹/₂
cup oil in a large nonstick skillet. Add
half the butter and, when it is foaming,
cook two pieces of veal for about
3 minutes, or until golden brown,
turning once. Drain on paper towels.

Discard any leftover oil and butter from
the pan and cook the remaining veal in
fresh oil and butter. Arrange the veal in a
baking dish, cover with the mozzarella
and bake for 10 minutes, or until the
cheese has melted. Serve with the tomato
sauce on top, garnished with the fresh
basil leaves.

LE CORDON BLEU ✠ COMPLETE COOK

Veal with lemon and capers

*The capers and lemon provide a sharp contrast
to the buttery sauce in this classic Italian dish.*

***Preparation time** 20 minutes*
***Total cooking time** 25 minutes*
Serves 4

4 x 4 oz. veal scallops
all-purpose flour, seasoned
with salt and pepper
2 eggs, beaten
3 tablespoons oil
3 tablespoons unsalted butter
1 cup white wine
¼ cup capers, rinsed and drained
1 cup chicken or brown veal stock (see
pages 518–9)
1–2 tablespoons lemon juice
½ cup unsalted butter, cut into cubes
and chilled

One Pound the meat with a mallet until it is ⅛ inch thick, then cut into thirds and coat with the seasoned flour. Put the beaten egg in a bowl and mix with 2 tablespoons water. Coat the veal in the egg mixture, draining off any excess.

Two Heat the oil and butter in a nonstick skillet. Cook the veal, in batches, for 3–5 minutes, until golden brown on both sides. Drain on paper towels, cover and keep warm while cooking the other veal slices.

Three Pour off the oil from the pan, add the wine and capers and cook for 8 minutes, or until almost dry. Add the stock and cook for 5 minutes, or until reduced by half. Add 1 tablespoon lemon juice, then transfer the sauce to a small saucepan (keeping the skillet on one side). Whisk in the cubes of butter, without allowing the sauce to boil. Adjust the seasoning, adding more lemon juice if necessary. Transfer the veal to the skillet, pour in the sauce, cover and allow to rest for 2 minutes before serving.

Veal kidneys sautéed in white wine

A simple and delicious dish of veal kidneys cooked with wine, shallots and herbs.
The recipe may be adjusted according to personal preference by adding mustard or cream.
Follow the Chef's tip to transform this one recipe into three different meals.

Preparation time 25 minutes
Total cooking time 25 minutes
Serves 4

3 fresh veal kidneys, outer
fat removed
¼ cup unsalted butter
4 shallots, finely chopped
1 cup white wine
2 cups brown stock (see page 518)
1 tablespoon chopped
fresh parsley

One Cut the kidneys in half and remove the central core, then cut them into bite-size pieces. Melt 3 tablespoons of the butter in a heavy-bottomed skillet over high heat and brown the kidneys in batches for 2–3 minutes—taking care not to overcook. Remove the kidneys from the pan, set aside and keep warm.

Two Reduce the heat to medium and, using the same pan, melt the remaining butter. Add the shallots and cook for 1 minute, without coloring, then add the wine and cook for 5 minutes, or until it is almost completely evaporated. Add the stock and cook for 8–10 minutes, or until the sauce is thick enough to coat the back of a spoon. Season to taste with salt and black pepper. Add the kidneys and heat through for 1 minute without boiling. Remove from the heat, stir in the parsley and serve.

CHEF'S TIP *This is a basic recipe that can be changed to suit different tastes. A tablespoon of Dijon or whole grain mustard can be added to the sauce before it is seasoned. For a richer dish, some of the stock can be replaced by some cream, with or without the addition of the mustard.*

Rack of lamb with herb crust

The Mediterranean region of Provence is known for its sunny climate and wonderful fresh vegetables and herbs. The herb crust in this Provençal dish features aromatic thyme, found growing wild in the hills.

Preparation time 1 hour
Total cooking time 1 hour 30 minutes
Serves 4

2 x 6-rib racks of lamb, trimmed and cleaned, reserving the trimmings (see Chef's tip)
2 tablespoons oil

LAMB JUS
1/2 onion, chopped
3 cloves garlic, coarsely chopped

HERB CRUST
1 1/2 cups fresh bread crumbs
5 cloves garlic, finely chopped
1/3 cup finely chopped fresh parsley
1 tablespoon fresh thyme leaves
1/3 cup unsalted butter, softened

One Preheat the oven to 400ºF. Score the fat on the outside of the racks in a crisscross pattern. Heat the oil in a skillet over medium-high heat, season the lamb, place in the pan and cook quickly to seal and brown the surface. Remove from the pan and set aside. Place the lean trimmings in a roasting pan and roast them in the oven for 20–30 minutes, then remove to cool. Increase the oven temperature to 500ºF.

Two To make the lamb jus, remove the trimmings from the roasting pan, leaving the fat behind, and place them in a saucepan with the onion, garlic and 1 1/2 cups water. Bring to a simmer and simmer for 30 minutes.

Three To make the herb crust, mix together in a bowl the bread crumbs, chopped garlic, parsley and thyme leaves. Season and mix in the softened butter to form a paste.

Four Firmly press a layer of the herb crust onto the fat side of the racks, leaving the bones and the bottom clean. Place the crusted racks in a roasting pan and lightly brown in the oven for 20–25 minutes. Set aside and keep warm.

Five Strain the jus into another saucepan and cook until reduced in volume by three-quarters, skimming off the fat or impurities that float to the surface. Serve on the side in a gravy boat.

CHEF'S TIP *Ask your butcher to trim and clean the racks for you. You can also do it yourself by cutting away the fat and meat to expose the bones, then scraping the bones until perfectly clean.*

Lamb rib chops with pea fritters and garlic cream sauce

*Lean pink lamb served with bright green pea
fritters and a creamy garlic sauce make an unusual,
appetizing and colorful summer's meal.*

*Preparation time 35 minutes
+ 40 minutes refrigeration
Total cooking time 1 hour
Serves 4*

1 teaspoon salt
5 cups fresh shelled or frozen peas
2 teaspoons unsalted butter
1 egg yolk
2 teaspoons finely chopped
fresh mint leaves
all-purpose flour, seasoned with salt
and pepper
2 eggs
2/3 cup dry bread crumbs
1/3 cup finely chopped
blanched almonds
oil, for deep-frying
12 lamb rib chops, frenched and
trimmed of excess fat
2 tablespoons unsalted butter, melted

GARLIC CREAM SAUCE
10 cloves garlic, halved
1/3 cup white wine (not too dry)
1 1/4 cups whipping cream

One Half-fill a medium saucepan with water and bring to a boil. Add the salt and peas, return to a boil, then reduce the heat and simmer for 3 minutes, or until the peas are tender. Drain well, then purée the peas in a food processor. Push the purée through a fine metal strainer to remove the skins.

Two Melt the butter in a skillet, add the pea purée and cook over low heat for 7 minutes, or until the mixture is dry. Remove from the heat, stir in the egg yolk and chopped mint, and season with salt and freshly ground pepper. Allow to cool, then refrigerate for 20 minutes, or until firm.

Three Place the seasoned flour on a sheet of waxed paper. Beat the eggs in a shallow dish. Mix together the bread crumbs and almonds and place them on another sheet of waxed paper. Divide the pea mixture into 12 portions and roll each portion between your palms into a ball, or shape them into patties. Coat the fritters with the flour, dip them in the beaten egg, then roll them in the almond mixture. Refrigerate for 20 minutes.

Four To make the garlic cream sauce, place the garlic in a small saucepan,

cover with cold water and bring to a boil. Reduce the heat and simmer for 3 minutes, then drain. Return the garlic to the saucepan, add the white wine and cream, then cover and simmer gently for 25 minutes, or until the garlic is soft. Pour the garlic mixture into a food processor or blender and process until smooth. Transfer the garlic to a clean saucepan to keep warm and season to taste with salt and black pepper. Preheat the broiler and then, when it's very hot, set the oven to its lowest setting.

Five Preheat a deep-fat fryer or deep saucepan, one-third full of oil, to 350°F (see page 537). Deep-fry the fritters in small batches, stirring gently to make sure they brown evenly. When they are golden, remove the fritters and drain on crumpled paper towels. Place on a wire rack and keep warm in the oven.

Six Brush the lamb chops with the melted butter and season with salt and freshly ground black pepper. Broil for 3 minutes on each side for pink, or longer if preferred.

Seven Divide the cutlets and fritters among warm serving plates and serve with a little garlic cream sauce.

about garlic...

Garlic has different strengths according to how fresh it is and how it is prepared and cooked. Fresh, young garlic has a much less harsh flavor than older garlic. The strongest garlic flavor is gained by crushing the garlic as this breaks down the majority of the cell walls. However, finely chopped garlic will also be strongly flavored. Sliced garlic will give a milder flavor and cooked whole cloves of garlic, either roasted or simmered, will be sweet rather than strong.

Deviled kidneys with sage polenta rounds

*These herb and polenta rounds are a modern
alternative to the more usual toast when serving
deviled kidneys for breakfast or brunch.*

Preparation time *40 minutes
+ 1 hour resting*
Total cooking time *25 minutes*
Serves 4–6

SAGE POLENTA DISKS
*2 1/2 cups milk
1 tablespoon unsalted butter
1 1/4 cups precooked or instant polenta
(yellow cornmeal)
1/2 cup freshly grated Parmesan cheese
2/3 cup finely chopped fresh sage leaves*

oil, for deep-frying

DEVILED KIDNEYS
*8 lamb kidneys
2 tablespoons tomato chutney
1/2 teaspoon mustard
dash of Worcestershire sauce
small pinch of cayenne pepper
1/4 cup unsalted butter
1 shallot, chopped
1/4 cup beef stock (see page 518) or
vegetable stock*

One To prepare the sage polenta rounds, heat the milk and butter in a large saucepan until nearly boiling. Using a whisk, briskly stir in the polenta and stir constantly over medium heat for 2–3 minutes, or until thick. Remove and allow to cool for 1 minute.

Two Add the Parmesan and sage, season well and cool for another 5 minutes. Lightly flour the work surface and roll or press out the polenta to a thickness of 1/2 inch. Allow to cool and become firm for 1 hour. Using a 2-inch plain biscuit cutter, cut out 25–30 rounds. Place the rounds in a single layer on two baking sheets lined with parchment paper and cover until they are needed.

Three To prepare the deviled kidneys, remove the fat and fine membrane from around the kidneys, then lay them flat, hold in place with one hand and cut each through sideways with a sharp knife. Using the tip of a sharp knife or scissors, trim the core from the cut side of each kidney half. In a small bowl, stir together the tomato chutney, mustard, Worcestershire sauce and cayenne pepper. In a wide skillet, melt half the butter and, over medium heat, cook the shallot for 3–4 minutes, or until golden. Transfer the shallot to a plate, wipe out the pan with paper towels and set aside.

Four Heat the oven to 250°F. Fill a deep-fat fryer or large saucepan one-third full of oil and heat to 350°F (see page 537). Deep-fry the sage polenta rounds in small batches for 2–3 minutes, then remove from the oil and drain on crumpled paper towels. Transfer to a wire rack and keep the rounds warm in the oven, uncovered so that they retain their crispness.

Five Melt the remaining butter in the skillet. When sizzling hot, add the kidneys, skin side down first. Cook over high heat for 20 seconds, turn over and cook for another 20 seconds. Transfer to the plate with the shallot. Lower the heat, add the mustard mixture from the bowl to the pan and stir to blend. Return the kidneys and the shallot to the pan and toss for 1–2 minutes, or until cooked through. Put four or five polenta rounds on each plate and divide the kidneys among them. Add the stock to the pan and cook for 1 minute, stirring to blend in the kidney juices. Pour the sauce over the kidneys and serve immediately.

CHEF'S TIP *The deviled kidneys could be served just on toast. The sage and polenta rounds would be an excellent accompaniment to serve with fried or scrambled eggs, grilled tomatoes or sautéed chicken livers.*

Lamb medallions with cilantro sauce

Toasted pine nuts add a wonderful texture to these
medallions of pink lamb, presented on a bed of spinach,
with a syrupy sauce of shallots and herbs.

Preparation time *30 minutes*
Total cooking time *30 minutes*
Serves 4

2 x 6–7-chop lamb rib roasts,
tenderloins removed (ask the
butcher)
1 tablespoon oil or clarified butter (see
page 520)
2 large shallots, chopped
2 cups lamb stock (see page 518)
or light beef stock
1/2 cup chopped fresh cilantro leaves
1 tablespoon chopped fresh mint
leaves
1 tablespoon hazelnut oil
3 lb. young spinach leaves
2 large tomatoes, peeled, seeded and
diced (see page 534)
2/3 cup pine nuts, toasted

One Remove the "eye" or long round tenderloin of meat at the thick end of each rack by running a small, sharp knife along the bone. Trim off the fat and sinew.

Two Heat the oil or clarified butter in a skillet. Season the lamb with salt, then fry over gentle heat, turning often, for 10–12 minutes, or until it is still just pink inside, yet browned outside. Remove the lamb from the pan; keep warm and set aside to rest.

Three Drain the pan of any excess fat, then add the shallots and cook for about 2 minutes, or until lightly colored. Add the stock, bring to a boil, then reduce the heat and simmer rapidly for about 10 minutes, or until the mixture is syrupy. Remove from the heat, season, then stir in the cilantro and mint. Cover the sauce and keep warm.

Four In another skillet, heat the hazelnut oil and quickly cook the whole spinach leaves over high heat until just wilted. Drain and season to taste. Pack the spinach into four flat 1-cup molds or ramekins, then unmold onto the center of a warm plate.

Five Carve the lamb into medallions about 1/4-inch thick. Arrange on the spinach beds and swirl the sauce around; sprinkle the chopped tomatoes and pine nuts over the sauce.

Navarin of lamb

This traditional French lamb and potato stew has existed for over 180 years and is said to have been named after one of the main ingredients, navet, *the French word for "turnip". Other vegetables may also be added to the stew if desired, as in this recipe.*

Preparation time *45 minutes*
Total cooking time *2 hours*
Serves 4

2 lb. boneless lamb shoulder
⅓ cup oil
3 tablespoons unsalted butter
1 large onion, finely chopped
1 tablespoon tomato paste
2 large tomatoes, peeled, seeded and chopped (see page 534)
3 cloves garlic, chopped
1 tablespoon all-purpose flour
1 bouquet garni (see page 520)
1 cup shelled fresh peas
1 large carrot, cut into 2-inch pieces
2 turnips, peeled and quartered
12 new potatoes
1 tablespoon chopped fresh parsley

One Preheat the oven to 400°F. Trim any excess fat from the meat and cut into 1-inch cubes. Heat the oil in a skillet and cook the lamb in batches until brown. Remove from the pan, drain off the oil, and set aside.

Two Place a 3-quart flameproof casserole or Dutch oven on top of the stove and melt the butter. Gently cook the onion for 5 minutes without coloring. Add the tomato paste and cook over medium heat for 2 minutes. Add the tomatoes and cook for another 3 minutes. Add the garlic and mix well. Add the lamb and any juices to the mixture and sprinkle the top with flour. Without mixing in the flour, place the casserole in the oven for 5 minutes.

Three Remove the casserole from the oven and place over medium heat. Mix in the flour, then gradually add 6 cups boiling water. Mix well by scraping down the sides and bottom of the casserole. Simmer for a few minutes, skimming off the impurities, then add the bouquet garni, season to taste with salt and pepper, cover and return to the oven. Bake for 1 hour. Bring a saucepan of salted water to a boil and cook the peas for 3 minutes. Drain, refresh with cold water, drain again, and set aside.

Four Remove the casserole from the oven and place over medium heat. Add the carrot, turnips and potatoes and cook for 15 minutes, then add the peas. Cook for another 10–15 minutes, or until the meat and potatoes are tender. Remove the bouquet garni and discard, then season to taste with salt and black pepper. Stir in the chopped parsley just before serving.

Roasted lamb with vegetables

*This memorable roast is served with a classic French garnish of bacon, mushrooms,
glazed onions and golden brown potatoes. It makes a special dish
for a Sunday lunch with all the family.*

Preparation time *1 hour 15 minutes*
Total cooking time *1 hour*
Serves 6

⅓ cup oil
1 x 3 lb. boneless lamb shoulder roast,
(ask your butcher to reserve some of
the bones and trimmings)
1 carrot, chopped
1 onion, chopped
½ stalk celery, chopped
2 cloves garlic, crushed
1 sprig of fresh thyme or
¼ teaspoon dried thyme
1 bay leaf
10 oz. bacon
12 tiny boiling onions, peeled
⅓ cup unsalted butter
1 tablespoon sugar
24 button mushrooms
4 potatoes, peeled
1½ cups chicken stock (see page 519)
2 tablespoons chopped fresh parsley

One Preheat the oven to 400°F. Heat half the oil in a roasting pan over high heat. Season the lamb and brown on all sides in the hot oil. Remove and set aside. Add the bones and trimmings to the pan and brown all over.

Two Add the carrot, onion, celery, garlic, thyme and bay leaf to the pan. Rest the lamb on the bones, then transfer to the oven and roast for 40 minutes for rare, or 1 hour for medium, basting two or three times.

Three Cut the bacon into ⅛-inch pieces. In a skillet, lightly brown the bacon, then drain. Place the onions in a medium saucepan and cook over high heat with 1 tablespoon of the butter, the sugar, 3 tablespoons water, and salt and freshly ground pepper to taste. Cook until the water has evaporated and the onions are a light blond color.

Four Cut the mushrooms into quarters, then sauté them in 2 tablespoons of the butter over high heat until browned. Season to taste and drain.

Five Using a melon baller, carve the potatoes into balls, placing them in cold water to prevent them from browning, then transfer to a saucepan of cold water. Bring to a boil, boil for 1 minute, then drain.

Six Heat the remaining oil in a flame-proof skillet over high heat. When the oil is hot, add the potatoes, tossing to coat them evenly with oil. Cook for 2–3 minutes, or until well colored, then transfer to the oven and roast for 20 minutes, or until tender. Drain off the excess oil, toss the potato balls in the remaining butter and season with salt and freshly ground black pepper.

Seven Remove the lamb from the oven and place on a wire rack to rest. Drain the pan of excess fat, remove the bones and trimmings, and place the pan on the stove top over medium-high heat. Cook for 2–3 minutes, or until the vegetables have colored, then add the stock and stir to dissolve the cooking juices. Cook for about 10 minutes, or until reduced in volume by a third. Strain and season to taste with salt and pepper.

Eight Toss together the onions, potatoes, mushrooms and bacon and reheat if necessary. Sprinkle with the chopped parsley. Carve the lamb into slices about ½ inch thick and serve surrounded with the vegetables and bacon with the sauce on the side.

---

about lamb...

The flavor of lamb varies according to where it was raised and how young it is. Baby lamb is the tastiest (and most expensive) lamb. It can be under a month old, weighing only a few pounds. Spring lamb is next best, and is butchered at 3–5 months. Spring lamb is now available all year round.

LE CORDON BLEU COMPLETE COOK

Lancashire hot pot

*A traditional regional British dish, the exceptional
flavor of this casserole comes from the meat cooked on the
bone adding to the flavor of the stock as it cooks.*

Preparation time *30 minutes*
Total cooking time *2 hours 20 minutes*
Serves 4

*2 lb. lamb shoulder blade
or arm chops
1 tablespoon unsalted butter
5 potatoes, peeled
2 large onions, thinly sliced
2 carrots, sliced into
⅛-inch-thick rounds
½ teaspoon chopped fresh thyme
1 bay leaf
1½ cups brown stock
(see page 518)
¼ cup unsalted butter,
melted*

One Preheat the oven to 350°F. Brush a 3½-quart baking dish with butter. Trim the excess fat from the lamb, melt the butter in a skillet and, over high heat, quickly fry the chops until lightly browned and just sealed, but not cooked through. Remove from the pan and transfer the chops to a plate.

Two Slice the potatoes into ⅛-inch-thick rounds and cover the bottom of the baking dish with about a third of the slices. Season lightly with salt and pepper. Place the chops neatly on the potatoes, scatter with the onions, carrots and thyme, season lightly and add the bay leaf. Put the remaining potato slices into the dish, neatly overlapping the very top layer. Pour in enough of the stock to come up to just under the top layer by pouring the stock down one side of the dish so that the top layer is not wet. Brush well with melted butter and season lightly. Cover with a lid or aluminum foil and bake on the middle shelf of the oven for 1½ hours.

Three Remove the lid, then add a little more stock or water if the liquid has been taken up by the potatoes and you would like it to be more moist. Return the dish to the oven for 45 minutes, uncovered, or until the meat is cooked and the potato top is crisp and brown. Serve hot with green vegetables of your choice.

CHEF'S TIPS *Do not slice the peeled potatoes until required or they will discolor. Also, do not keep sliced potatoes in cold water, because the* starch that is needed to help thicken the hot pot will be washed out.

If you wish, add one lamb kidney, halved, trimmed of its core and cut into ½-inch pieces. Scatter it raw onto the lamb as it goes into the baking dish.

LE CORDON BLEU ✦ COMPLETE COOK

Braised lamb with tomato sauce

A simple yet delicious lamb stew, flavored with garlic, bacon and tomatoes, which can be served with rice or fresh pasta.

***Preparation time** 25 minutes*
***Total cooking time** 1 hour 45 minutes*
Serves 4

2¹/₂ lb. boneless lamb shoulder,
trimmed and cut into
small pieces
3 tablespoons oil
3 tablespoons unsalted butter
2 oz. Canadian bacon, diced
1 small onion, chopped
1 small carrot, chopped
2–3 tablespoons tomato paste
1 tablespoon all-purpose flour
3 tomatoes, peeled, seeded
and chopped (see page 534)
1 bouquet garni (see page 520)
4 cloves garlic, chopped
2 cups brown stock (see page 518)
or water
1 tablespoon chopped fresh parsley
or basil

One Preheat the oven to 350°F. Season the lamb with salt and pepper. Heat the oil in a heavy-bottomed skillet over medium-high heat, add the lamb and brown it, in batches, for 6–8 minutes, or until well colored on all sides. Drain on paper towels.

Two Melt the butter in a large flameproof casserole or Dutch oven over medium heat. Add the bacon and cook until golden brown. Add the onion and carrot and cook for 3 minutes. Stir in the tomato paste and cook for another 2 minutes. Sprinkle with the flour and bake for 5 minutes. Remove from the oven and mix in the flour. Add the tomatoes, bouquet garni and garlic. Place on the stove top and cook for 5 minutes, stirring constantly, then add the stock or water. Bring to a boil,

stirring constantly. Add the lamb, cover and bake for 1 hour, or until the meat is tender when pierced.

Three Remove the meat from the sauce, cover and keep warm. Pass the sauce through a fine strainer, pressing well to extract as much liquid as possible. Discard the contents of the strainer and pour the sauce into a saucepan.

Four Bring the sauce back to a boil, skimming if necessary. Simmer for 10 minutes, or until the sauce is thick enough to coat the back of a spoon. Add the lamb and stir until heated through. Season with salt and pepper. Sprinkle with the parsley or basil and serve.

Cassoulet

Dried white beans are the essential ingredient in this dish from the Languedoc region of France and give the cassoulet its creaminess. Some sort of meat, depending on the region, and a gratin topping are added near the end of cooking. The name comes from cassole, *an earthenware pot traditionally used for cooking this dish.*

Preparation time *1 hour 30 minutes*
+ soaking overnight
Total cooking time *4 hours 30 minutes*
Serves *4–6*

1¼ cups dried white beans (such as navy or pea beans), soaked overnight in cold water
3 oz. fresh pork rind
3 oz. slab bacon
½ carrot
½ onion, studded with a whole clove
2 bouquets garnis (see page 520)
1 clove garlic
3 tablespoons goose fat, duck fat or lard
6 oz. boneless lamb shoulder, cut into 8 pieces
7 oz. boneless pork shoulder, cut into 8 pieces
1 small onion, chopped
2 tomatoes, peeled, seeded and cubed (see page 534) or 1 tablespoon tomato paste
1 clove garlic, crushed
10 oz. fresh garlic sausage, sliced
4 small fresh garlic pork sausages
2-leg duck or goose confit or
1 x 12 oz. cooked duck leg and thigh quarter, cut into 2 pieces
1 cup fresh bread crumbs

One Rinse the soaked beans and cover generously with fresh cold water in a large saucepan. Add the pork rind and slab bacon and bring to a boil. As soon as it boils, remove from the heat, strain and refresh in cold water. Cover the beans, pork rind and bacon once more with fresh water, return to the heat and add the carrot, cloved onion, 1 bouquet garni and the garlic. Simmer for about 1½ hours (do not add salt, as this will interfere with the cooking of the beans and make them tough).

Two Preheat the oven to 350°F. While the beans are simmering, melt 2 tablespoons of the goose fat, duck fat or lard in a large flameproof casserole or Dutch oven. Season the lamb shoulder and pork shoulder and brown in the casserole. Remove the meat and set aside. In the same dish, cook the chopped onion until soft but not colored. Add the tomatoes or tomato paste, crushed garlic and second bouquet garni. Heat until bubbling, return the meat to the casserole, then cover and bake for 1 to 1½ hours, or until the meat is tender. Remove the meat from the casserole.

Three Reduce the oven temperature to 325°F. Add the sausages and confit to the casserole, bring to a simmer on the stove, then bake in the oven for 20 minutes. Transfer the confit and the sausages to a bowl and keep warm and set the sauce aside. Reduce the oven temperature to 300°F.

Four When the beans are almost cooked (they should be tender with a slight resistance), drain and add the beans' cooking liquid to the reserved sauce in the casserole. Remove and discard the vegetables and bouquet garni. Remove the slab bacon and pork rind and allow to cool. Keeping the bacon and pork separate, cut into bite-size pieces.

Five Warm a large baking dish. Cover the bottom with some of the pork rind and then cover with a layer of beans. Add the lamb shoulder, pork shoulder, sausages, confit and about 1–1½ cups of the reserved liquid. Cover with another layer of beans and top with the pieces of bacon, the remaining pork rind and liquid. Sprinkle with bread crumbs and drizzle with the remaining melted goose fat. Bake for 1 hour, or until the bread crumbs are lightly colored, then serve.

about cassoulet...

The ingredients used in cassoulet vary depending on where it is made. Several different cities in the Languedoc region have their own version. You can vary the types of sausage if you prefer or use just lamb or pork rather than both.

Country-style terrine

This coarsely textured pâté derives its name from the deep rectangular dish in which it is cooked. Meat terrines often contain a high proportion of pork, and some pork fat, to prevent the meat from becoming dry.

Preparation time 30 minutes
+ 2 nights refrigeration
Total cooking time 50 minutes
Serves 6–8

1½ tablespoons unsalted butter
2 cloves garlic, chopped
2 shallots, chopped
3 sprigs of fresh thyme
1 small bay leaf
6 oz. pork fat, finely diced
5 oz. calf, lamb or ox liver,
finely diced
12 oz. pork tenderloin,
finely diced
3 tablespoons brandy
3 tablespoons white wine
½ teaspoon salt
¼ teaspoon ground nutmeg
⅔ cup fresh bread crumbs
1 tablespoon milk
1 egg, beaten
20 slices bacon,
for lining

One Melt the butter in a deep skillet over low heat. Warm the garlic, shallots, thyme and bay leaf with the pork fat, liver and diced pork. Gently cook for 3–5 minutes. Add the brandy, wine, salt, nutmeg and some pepper, stirring well to coat the meat—the mixture should be warm, not hot. Allow to cool, then refrigerate overnight.

Two Preheat the oven to 350°F. Wrap a small piece of wood or stiff cardboard (the same size as the top of a 1-quart terrine) in aluminum foil. Soak the bread crumbs in milk.

Three Remove the thyme and bay leaf from the terrine mixture. Process the meat in a food processor in short bursts until coarsely chopped, then transfer to a bowl. Mix together the bread crumbs and egg and add to the meat. Mix well.

Four Line a greased terrine mold with bacon, letting the slices hang over the sides. Add the meat mixture, fold the slices over and cover with a layer of bacon, then a sheet of greased parchment paper. Place the terrine in a baking pan half-filled with hot water and bake for 30–40 minutes. To check the temperature, insert the tip of a small knife into the center of the terrine for a few seconds. If the blade comes out hot, the terrine is cooked; if not, cook for another 5 minutes, or until the knife comes out hot.

Five Remove from the oven and allow to cool for 20 minutes. Place the wood or cardboard across the top, then weight it down with a heavy can. Refrigerate overnight. Leave the terrine at room temperature for at least 30 minutes before serving. The terrine can be served in the mold, or unmolded onto a board or plate.

LE CORDON BLEU COMPLETE COOK

White bean stew with Italian sausages

Dried white beans—full of protein, calcium and iron —are cooked with fennel-flavored Italian sausages in a creamy herb sauce, making this stew a complete meal.

Preparation time 25 minutes
Total cooking time 1 hour 30 minutes
Serves 4

1¾ cups dried white beans (such as
    navy or cannellini)
1 small onion, diced
1 small carrot, diced
1 small stalk celery, diced
sprig of fresh thyme
sprig of fresh rosemary
1 teaspoon black peppercorns
4 Italian sweet or hot sausages
    with fennel
¼ cup whipping cream
chopped fresh parsley,
    to garnish

HERB BUTTER
1 clove garlic, coarsely chopped
1 tablespoon chopped fresh parsley
1 tablespoon fresh rosemary leaves
1 tablespoon fresh thyme leaves
½ cup unsalted butter,
    softened

One Place the beans and vegetables in a flameproof casserole or Dutch oven with the sprigs of thyme and rosemary. Tie the peppercorns in a piece of cheesecloth and add to the dish. Cover with 1½ quarts cold water. Place on the stove and bring to a boil, then reduce the heat to low and simmer for 55 minutes.

Two To make the herb butter, use a mortar and pestle or a blender to purée the garlic, parsley, rosemary, thyme and butter until smooth. Season to taste with salt and black pepper and set aside.

Three Preheat the oven to 350°F. Heat a little oil in a skillet and brown the sausages. Cut diagonally into four pieces and add to the beans after they have finished simmering. Cover and bake in the oven for 30 minutes, or until the beans are tender. There should be just enough liquid left to cover the beans. If not, add some boiling water.

Four Remove the sausages and set aside. Remove the bag of peppercorns and the sprigs of herbs and discard. Mix in the herb butter and the cream and season to taste with salt and freshly ground black pepper. Transfer the beans to a serving dish, then arrange the sausages on top, sprinkle with some chopped fresh parsley and serve immediately.

LE CORDON BLEU ❦ COMPLETE COOK

Roast pork with prunes and Armagnac

*This recipe for roast pork, with its stuffing of sweet prunes
and French brandy, is a good holiday choice. Use loin
of pork—it is a cut that is easy to carve into neat slices.*

*Preparation time 30 minutes
+ 1 hour soaking*
Total cooking time 1 hour 50 minutes
Serves 4–6

1/4 cup pitted prunes
1 1/2 tablespoons Armagnac
*3 lb. loin of pork, bone removed, with
a long rib flap if possible*
2 teaspoons oil
1 tablespoon unsalted butter

HERB SAUCE
2 1/2 tablespoons unsalted butter
2 large shallots, chopped
2 cups chicken stock (see page 519)
1 cup whipping cream
*1 1/2 tablespoons fresh sage, finely
chopped*
*1 1/2 tablespoons fresh parsley, finely
chopped*

One Put the prunes in a bowl and pour in the Armagnac. Cover and soak for at least 1 hour.

Two Preheat the oven to 400°F. Remove the skin and excess sinew from the pork, leaving a thin layer of fat. Spread out the loin, and, on the side of the round muscle of meat where it joins the flat flap that once held the ribs, cut a long slit down the length of the muscle to halfway through the meat. Remove the prunes from the Armagnac, reserving the Armagnac, and gently push them into the slit. Close and roll the flat flap around the loin. Tie pieces of string 1 inch apart along the loin to hold it together.

Three Heat the oil in a frying pan, add the butter and heat until frothy. Add the pork and fry over medium-high heat for 5–8 minutes, or until sealed and browned all over. Transfer to a flameproof dish or roasting pan and roast for 1–1 1/4 hours, or until the juices run clear when pierced with a skewer.

Four To make the herb sauce, melt the butter in a saucepan, add the shallots and cook covered over low heat for 5 minutes, or until soft and translucent. Add the reserved Armagnac and cook uncovered until the liquid has reduced to 1 tablespoon. Pour in the stock and simmer for 15–20 minutes, or until reduced to 1/4 cup, then stir in the cream and simmer until the sauce lightly coats the back of a spoon. Remove from the heat, cover the surface with plastic wrap and keep warm.

Five Transfer the pork from the oven to a plate and let rest for 5 minutes, then place on a cutting board. Gently reheat the sauce, but do not allow it to bubble for more than 1 minute. Add the sage and parsley and season with salt and black pepper just before serving. Remove the string from the meat and, using a thin, sharp knife, cut the pork into slices. Arrange the slices on plates and pour the sauce around. Serve with a green salad or vegetables and potatoes.

about prunes...

Prunes are dried plums. The plums are usually dried and then rehydrated by different degrees to produce semi-dried or dried prunes. The semi-dried variety are softer and do not need to be soaked for as long. Some of the best are prunes d'Agen from Aquitaine in France. However, all types are suitable for this recipe.

Honey-glazed spiced ham

A whole ham is perfect for feeding a large Christmas gathering. This version is served hot with a mustard cream sauce, and any leftovers make a delicious holiday lunch with a green salad and pickles.

Preparation time 30 minutes
+ overnight soaking
Total cooking time 6 hours
Serves 20

1 x 14 lb. uncooked ham, smoked
or unsmoked
2 onions
2 stalks celery
3 carrots
3–4 bay leaves
3 sprigs of fresh thyme
1 clove
4 allspice berries

HONEY GLAZE
1/2–2/3 cup light brown, Demerara
or turbinado sugar
1/4–1/3 cup honey
1 1/2 teaspoons pumpkin pie spice
1 tablespoon English mustard
cloves, for decorating

MUSTARD CREAM SAUCE
2 cups whipping cream
1/3 cup English mustard
2 tablespoons whole mustard seeds,
soaked in water

One Soak the ham overnight in cold water, changing the water once or twice.

Two Preheat the oven to 315°F. Remove the ham from the soaking liquid and rinse it under cold water. Pat dry, place the ham in a large roasting pan and distribute the vegetables, herbs and spices around it. Pour 1 pint cold water into the pan and cover the pan with aluminum foil. Bake for 20 minutes per pound, plus an extra 20 minutes.

Three Remove the ham from the oven and lift it out of the liquid. Reserve the cooking liquid and discard the vegetables. Prepare the ham, following the method in the Chef's techniques on page 531. Raise the oven temperature to 350°F.

Four To make the honey glaze, mix together all the ingredients except the cloves in a bowl and spread the glaze over the ham with a flexible bladed knife. Push a clove into the center of each diamond. Place the ham fat side up on a rack over a roasting pan into which 1/2 inch of water has been poured (this will make the pan easier to clean later on). Bake the ham for 20 minutes, or until the surface of the ham is lightly

caramelized. Allow the ham to rest for 30 minutes before carving it.

Five To make the mustard cream sauce, boil the ham's cooking liquid in a saucepan over high heat for 30 minutes, or until the liquid is reduced to a light syrup. Add the cream and return to a boil, then remove from the heat and stir in the mustard and drained mustard seeds. Do not reboil or the mustard will lose its fresh flavor. Taste and season only if necessary.

Six To carve the ham, follow the method in the Chef's techniques on page 531. Serve the ham with the hot mustard cream sauce, some new potatoes and a choice of vegetables.

CHEF'S TIPS *If you want to serve the ham cold, allow to cool after removing from the oven. Rather than serving with the hot mustard cream sauce, mix 1 cup mayonnaise with 2 tablespoons whole grain mustard to accompany the ham. Serve with hot new potatoes, mixed salad leaves and pickles or chutneys.*

If a whole ham is too big, buy a half ham or smaller piece. Prepare in the same way, calculating the cooking time at 30 minutes per pound.

Saucisson de Lyon with warm potato salad

*Lyon is renowned for its hearty dishes, often featuring onions, potatoes and charcuterie.
The Lyonnais sausages used in this recipe need to be carefully poached to prevent
them from bursting, and can be bought or made with or without pistachios.*

Preparation time *35 minutes*
Total cooking time *55 minutes*
Serves 4

COURT BOUILLON
1 carrot, thinly sliced
2 onions, thinly sliced
2 stalks celery, thinly sliced
*2 small leeks, white part only,
thinly sliced*
3 sprigs of fresh thyme
1 bay leaf
10 black peppercorns
1 teaspooon salt
2 cups white wine

*4 large potatoes (total weight
1¹/2–1³/4 lb.)*
*1 lb. Lyonnais or pure pork sausages
(see Chef's tip)*

MUSTARD DRESSING
¹/3 cup Dijon mustard
¹/3 cup finely chopped shallots
1 cup oil
2 tablespoons chopped fresh parsley

One To make the court bouillon, place the carrot, onions, celery, leeks, seasonings and white wine in a large saucepan and bring to a boil. Boil for 5 minutes. Remove the saucepan from the heat and set aside to cool.

Two Place the potatoes in a large saucepan of salted water. Bring to a boil, then reduce the heat and simmer for 20–30 minutes, or until tender to the point of a knife. Drain, rinse with cold water and peel, then slice into ¹/4-inch-thick slices. Cover and keep warm.

Three Meanwhile, place the sausages in the cooled court bouillon. Pour in 2 quarts water to completely cover the sausages, bring to a simmer and poach for 20 minutes. Do not allow to boil or the sausages will burst. Remove from the heat and set aside until you are ready to serve.

Four To make the mustard dressing, mix the mustard and shallots in a bowl, slowly whisk in the oil until smooth and thick, then stir in the chopped parsley. Season the warm potato slices with salt and freshly ground black pepper and mix with the dressing.

Five Transfer the potatoes to a large platter. Remove the sausages from the court bouillon, dry with paper towels and cut into 16 slices. Arrange around the potato salad.

CHEF'S TIP *To make the Lyonnais sausages from scratch, finely grind 14 oz. pork loin and 5 oz. lean veal shoulder and mix together in a bowl with 5 oz. pork fat (lard), salt and pepper. Add ²/3 cup shelled and skinned pistachios and mix well. Using a large sausage funnel, fill a large sausage casing to make a 12–14-inch-long sausage. Tie off the ends with kitchen string.*

Venison stew

Venison is the most common large game animal and has a distinctive strong flavor. In this recipe, the venison is slowly cooked to perfection with onions, mushrooms and garlic in red wine. It is then combined with red currant jelly and juniper berries to produce a truly memorable dish.

Preparation time 30 minutes
Total cooking time 2 hours
Serves 4

1½ lb. boneless venison, for braising
10–12 small boiling onions
3 tablespoons olive oil
3⅓ cups whole button mushrooms
1 clove garlic, crushed
1 tablespoon all-purpose flour
1 cup red wine
1 tablespoon red currant jelly
6 juniper berries, crushed

One Preheat the oven to 325°F. Cut the meat into 1½-inch pieces and trim off all the fat.

Two Place the onions in a small saucepan with just enough cold water to cover them. Bring to a boil, reduce the heat, simmer for 2 minutes, then drain. Heat the oil in a 2½-quart flameproof casserole or Dutch oven over high heat. When it is very hot, add the meat in batches and fry for 1–2 minutes each side, or until brown on all sides. Remove the meat from the pan and keep warm.

Three Add the onions to the casserole and toss gently until just beginning to color. Add the mushrooms and garlic and cook for 1 minute. Sprinkle in the flour and cook, stirring, for 1 minute. Stir in the wine, 1 cup water and some salt and bring to a boil. Return the meat to the casserole, cover and place in the oven to bake for 1½ hours.

Four Remove the casserole from the oven and strain off the liquid into a small saucepan. Bring to a boil and cook for 1 minute to reduce the liquid. Stir in the red currant jelly, add the juniper berries and return to a boil. Season to taste, then pour the liquid over the stew. Return to the oven and bake for another 15 minutes to heat through. Serve the venison piping hot with a potato and celery root purée on the side.

Braised rabbit with mushrooms

Rabbit meat is very lean, which makes this tasty dish even more attractive. Combined with mushrooms, shallots and tomatoes, slowly cooked in white wine and enhanced with the flavor of fresh herbs, this rabbit dish is perfect for a special occasion.

Preparation time *25 minutes*
Total cooking time *1 hour 20 minutes*
Serves 4

1 x 3½ lb. rabbit, cut into 8 pieces
⅓ cup unsalted butter
1½ cups sliced button mushrooms
2 shallots, chopped
1 cup white wine
3 large tomatoes, peeled, seeded and chopped (see page 534)
2 cups brown stock (see page 519)
1 bouquet garni (see page 520)
1–2 teaspoons chopped fresh tarragon
1 tablespoon chopped fresh chervil

One Season the rabbit with salt and pepper and preheat the oven to 350°F. Melt half the butter in a large flameproof casserole or Dutch oven over medium heat and brown the rabbit in batches. Remove the meat from the pan and set aside. Discard the butter left in the pan, then return the pan to the heat and add the remaining butter. Add the mushrooms and cook for 3 minutes, then add the shallots and cook for 3 minutes. Add the wine and continue cooking for 3 minutes, or until almost all the liquid has evaporated.

Two Add the tomatoes and mix well. Bring to a boil, reduce the heat and simmer for 10 minutes. Add the stock and bouquet garni and return to a boil. Boil for 5 minutes, skimming off any impurities or fat from the surface.

Three Return the rabbit to the casserole and bring to a simmer. Cover and bake for 20–25 minutes, or until the rabbit is tender. To test the meat, pierce a thick piece with a fork and lift it up. If tender, it should slide easily from the bone. Transfer the rabbit to a serving platter, cover and keep warm. Place the casserole on the stove top and remove the bouquet garni. Bring the sauce to a boil and cook for 5–10 minutes, skimming as necessary. Adjust the seasoning and check the consistency of the sauce. If the sauce is not thick enough, continue to boil for 5 minutes, or until it is the desired consistency.

Four Stir in the chopped tarragon and chervil and pour the sauce over the rabbit. Serve immediately.

Rabbit and marjoram stew with herb biscuits

*Italians are very fond of game, and rabbit, with its light and tender flesh,
is definitely a favorite. Here it is teamed with fresh herbs, both in the
stew and in the biscuits placed on top to soak up the flavorful juices.*

Preparation time *40 minutes*
Total cooking time *1 hour 30 minutes*
Serves 4

1 x 2½ lb. rabbit, cut into 8 pieces
*all-purpose flour, seasoned with salt
and pepper*
butter or oil, for cooking
1 onion, finely chopped
1²⁄₃ cups sliced button mushrooms
1 teaspoon tomato paste
1 clove garlic, chopped
2 cups chicken stock (see page 519)
*8 ripe tomatoes, peeled, seeded
and chopped (see page 534)*
1 tablespoon chopped fresh rosemary
2 tablespoons chopped fresh marjoram
1 tablespoon chopped fresh parsley

HERB BISCUITS
2 cups self-rising flour
2 teaspoons sugar
*¹⁄₃ cup unsalted butter, cut into cubes
and chilled*
*1 tablespoon chopped fresh herbs,
such as parsley, rosemary, thyme
or marjoram*
½ cup buttermilk
1 egg, beaten

One Coat the rabbit in the flour. Heat a little butter or oil in a skillet, brown the rabbit on all sides, then remove from the pan and drain on paper towels. Add the onion to the pan and cook over low heat until soft. Add the mushrooms, increase the heat and stir in the tomato paste and garlic. Transfer to a flameproof casserole or Dutch oven, add the rabbit and season with salt and black pepper.

Two Pour in the stock (it should be enough to barely cover the rabbit) and simmer gently for 30 minutes. Add the

tomatoes and cook for 10 minutes. Add the rosemary, marjoram and parsley. Check the meat is tender and season.

Three To make the biscuits, preheat the oven to 400°F. Sift the flour, sugar and a good pinch of salt into a large bowl, add the butter and cut it in until crumbly. Toss in the herbs, then stir in the milk until the dry flour has disappeared and the mixture is in large lumps. Turn out

onto a lightly floured surface and gather together into a smooth ball. Roll or pat out to a ⁵⁄₈-inch thickness. Work quickly—you want the dough to rise in the oven, not waste its rising power while it's being rolled. Cut into 1½-inch rounds, brush the tops with the egg and arrange immediately over the rabbit stew. Place the casserole on the top rack of the oven and bake for 12 minutes, or until the biscuits are golden.

pasta and rice

Pesto with spaghetti

This classic, uncooked basil, Parmesan and pine nut sauce is traditionally served with pasta, as pictured (top right). The recipe makes enough for about 25 serves of pesto and can be stored in the refrigerator (see Chef's tip).

Preparation time 15 minutes
Total cooking time None
Makes approximately 3¼ cups

1¾ cups firmly packed fresh basil leaves
1 cup shredded Parmesan cheese
2 cloves garlic
⅓ cup pine nuts
⅓ cup olive oil
spaghetti, to serve

One Wash the basil leaves well and dry thoroughly in a salad spinner or gently pat dry using a paper towel.

Two Process the Parmesan in a food processor until it resembles fine bread crumbs. Add the garlic and pine nuts and process briefly to coarsely combine the ingredients. Add the basil at this point and process to combine.

Three While the machine is still running, slowly add the olive oil until a paste is formed. Season to taste with salt and black pepper, then continue to add the oil until it reaches a thick consistency. Serve a small amount of the pesto stirred into spaghetti (cook about 4 oz spaghetti per person according to the manufacturer's instructions), or with char-grilled vegetables or meats. To store the pesto, cover and refrigerate for up to 3 days.

CHEF'S TIP *If you wish to store the pesto for a longer period, transfer it to a sterilized jar, cover the surface with olive oil and store the jar in the refrigerator. Once opened, the pesto must be used within 2–3 days.*

Tomato concassée with ravioli

This is a classic vegetable preparation. "Concassée" is also used to describe finely diced tomato used as a garnish. It is shown here (bottom right) with ravioli.

Preparation time 15 minutes
Total cooking time 15 minutes
Serves 4

olive oil or good vegetable oil, for cooking
2 large shallots, finely chopped
1 clove garlic, finely chopped
1 tablespoon tomato paste, optional
3 ripe tomatoes, peeled, seeded and diced (see page 534)
1 bouquet garni (see page 520)
500 g fresh ravioli (see page 533)

One Heat a little oil in a skillet and add the shallots and garlic. Cook gently until softened, but not brown. Stir in the tomato paste if the fresh tomatoes are not particularly ripe.

Two Add the tomatoes to the pan with the bouquet garni and cook rapidly, stirring constantly with a wooden spoon, for 7 minutes, or until the mixture is dry. Remove the bouquet garni and season to taste with salt and pepper.

Three Cook the ravioli in a saucepan of rapidly boiling water for 5 minutes or until it floats to the surface. Drain and serve the sauce over the top.

Tortellini with creamy mushroom sauce

Fresh tortellini, small pasta packages containing meat, cheese or vegetable fillings, are available in supermarkets, making this delicious dish very easy to put together.

Preparation time 15 minutes
Total cooking time 35 minutes
Serves 4

3 tablespoons unsalted butter
2 shallots, finely chopped
1 lb. button mushrooms, thinly sliced
1 tablespoon lemon juice
2 tablespoons port
2 cups whipping cream
1 lb. fresh tortellini

One Over low heat, melt the butter in a skillet and cook the shallots with a pinch of salt for 3–5 minutes without coloring. Toss the mushrooms in the lemon juice, add to the pan with another pinch of salt and cook over medium heat for about 10–15 minutes, or until the mushrooms are dry and all the liquid has evaporated. Add the port and cook for 2–3 minutes, or until almost dry, being careful to not let the mixture scorch. Stir in the cream and simmer for 5–10 minutes, or until the sauce is thick enough to coat the back of a spoon. Check for seasoning.

Two Meanwhile, bring a large saucepan of salted water to a boil. Add a splash of oil to prevent the pasta from sticking and cook the tortellini according to the manufacturer's instructions. Drain well and divide the tortellini among four warm plates. Spoon the sauce over the top and serve with some freshly ground black pepper.

CHEF'S TIP *For a stronger flavor, mix some reconstituted dried mushrooms, such as porcini (cèpes) or shiitake, with the button mushrooms.*

Ziti Amatriciana

The ziti used in this recipe are very long thin tubes.
If unavailable, use macaroni or penne.

Preparation time *15 minutes*
Total cooking time *50 minutes*
Serves 4–6

3 tablespoons olive oil
12 oz. pancetta or bacon, cut into
¼-inch-thick pieces
1 onion, thinly sliced
2–3 fresh red chiles, thinly sliced or
½ teaspoon dried hot red chile
flakes
2 x 16-oz. cans chopped
plum tomatoes or 3½ lb. fresh
tomatoes, peeled and chopped (see
page 534)
1 lb. ziti
grated Parmesan cheese, to serve

One In a heavy-bottomed saucepan, heat half the oil and slowly brown the pancetta or bacon for 5 minutes, then drain and set aside on paper towels. Add the onion and lightly brown for about 3 minutes, then add the chiles or hot chile flakes and cook for 2 minutes. Add the pancetta or bacon and the tomatoes, cover and cook over medium heat for about 20 minutes, then cook uncovered for another 10–15 minutes, or until the sauce is thick.

Two Bring a large saucepan of salted water to a boil. Add a splash of oil to prevent the pasta from sticking and cook the ziti according to manufacturer's instructions.

Three Drain the pasta and divide among the serving bowls. Serve with the sauce and freshly grated Parmesan.

CHEF'S TIP *The degree of spiciness depends on the strength of the chiles. Remember that most of the heat is in the seeds and membranes. Be careful when handling the chiles and keep your fingers away from your face.*

Spaghetti bolognese

Spaghetti bolognese, which reflects the rich style of the cooking of Bologna in northern Italy, is both one of the best-known and best-loved Italian pasta dishes, as pictured top right.

Preparation time *50 minutes*
Total cooking time *1 hour 10 minutes*
Serves 6–8

1/2 cup olive oil
2 lb. lean ground beef
1 large onion, finely chopped
3 tablespoons tomato paste
1/3 cup red wine
8 cloves garlic, finely chopped
5 lb. fresh tomatoes, peeled, seeded (see page 534) and puréed in a food mill or food processor
4 sprigs of fresh thyme
1 bay leaf
1 1/2 lb. spaghetti
grated Parmesan cheese, to serve

One In a large saucepan, heat half the oil until very hot. Add the beef to the saucepan, season with salt and pepper, and brown for 10 minutes, pressing out any lumps with the back of a fork, or until the liquid from the meat has evaporated. Strain off the fat and set the meat aside.

Two Heat the remaining oil in the saucepan, add the onion and cook for 5 minutes, without coloring. Add the tomato paste and cook for 1–2 minutes. Add the wine and cook for 5 minutes.

Transfer the meat back to the saucepan, add the garlic, tomatoes, thyme and bay leaf and simmer for 45 minutes, or until the liquid has reduced by half. Remove the thyme and bay leaf.

Three Meanwhile, bring a large saucepan of salted water to a boil. Add a splash of oil to prevent the pasta from sticking and cook the spaghetti according to the manufacturer's instructions. Drain well and transfer to individual plates. Pour the sauce over the pasta and sprinkle with the Parmesan.

Fettuccine Alfredo

A delicious creamy dish (pictured bottom right) that is simple and quick to make. For good results, however, it is essential to use freshly grated Parmesan cheese, as store-bought grated Parmesan is usually a poor substitute.

Preparation time *5 minutes*
Total cooking time *15 minutes*
Serves 4

1 1/2 cups whipping cream
2 1/4 cups grated Parmesan cheese
1/4 cup chopped fresh flat-leaf parsley
1 lb. fettuccine
grated Parmesan cheese, to serve

One Place the cream in a heavy-bottomed saucepan and bring to a boil. Gradually whisk in the grated Parmesan cheese. Add the parsley, salt and freshly ground black pepper to the saucepan and stir until well combined.

Two Meanwhile, bring a large saucepan of salted water to a boil. Add a splash of oil to prevent the pasta from sticking and cook the fettuccine according to the manufacturer's instructions. Drain well and divide among individual bowls. Toss with the cream sauce. Serve with freshly grated Parmesan on the side.

Winter squash ravioli with basil butter

The unusual and delicate flavor of the squash and herb filling is perfectly complemented by the basil and garlic butter. When making ravioli, it is important to roll the pasta as thinly as possible, making sure that it doesn't tear when handled.

Preparation time *1 hour 30 minutes*
Total cooking time *1 hour 20 minutes*
Serves 6–8

12 oz. piece butternut or hubbard squash
2 tablespoons olive oil
3 oz. prosciutto, finely chopped
1/2 cup grated Parmesan cheese
3 tablespoons chopped fresh basil
1/4 cup chopped fresh sage
1 egg yolk
2 tablespoons whipping cream
pinch of nutmeg

PASTA
3 1/3 cups all-purpose flour
1 teaspoon salt
3 tablespoons olive oil
4 eggs, lightly beaten

HERB SAUCE
3/4 cup unsalted butter or olive oil
6 cloves garlic, halved
2/3 cup firmly packed fresh basil leaves

One Preheat the oven to 375°F. Place the squash on a lightly greased baking sheet and brush with the olive oil. Bake for 1 hour, or until the flesh is soft when pressed lightly with a spoon. Set aside.

Two Make the pasta, following the method in the Chef's techniques on page 532, dividing the dough into four pieces before passing it through the machine. Pass the pieces through the thinnest setting, making sure they are at least 6 1/2 inches wide, then trim horizontally into 5-inch-wide strips.

Three Once the squash has cooled, scrape out the flesh and mash in a bowl. Stir in the prosciutto, Parmesan, basil, sage,

egg yolk and cream. Season with the nutmeg and salt and pepper. Cover.

Four Spoon heaping teaspoons of the squash mixture at 2 1/2-inch intervals along the pasta strips. Lightly brush with water around the edges of the squash. Lay another sheet of pasta on top and press firmly around each mound to seal. Cut out the ravioli by pressing a 2 1/2-inch biscuit cutter down firmly, then flour lightly. Place in a single layer between sheets of waxed paper and refrigerate until ready to use.

Five Bring a large saucepan of salted water to a boil. Add a splash of oil to prevent the pasta from sticking and cook

the ravioli in batches for 5–6 minutes, or until they float to the surface. Drain.

Six To make the herb sauce, melt the butter over low heat, then add the garlic and let infuse for a few minutes without browning. The longer you do this, the stronger the garlic flavor. Take the saucepan off the heat and remove the garlic with a slotted spoon. Tear the basil leaves and add to the sauce.

Seven Toss the ravioli with the basil sauce to reheat and coat well.

CHEF'S TIPS *For an extra garnish, scatter some roasted, lightly salted pumpkin seeds around the ravioli.*

Classic lasagna

Although you can make this very popular classic Italian dish with store-bought lasagna noodles, the flavor and texture of thinly rolled fresh pasta is quite unique and well worth the effort.

Preparation time 1 hour
+ 20 minutes resting
Total cooking time 2 hours 15 minutes
Serves 10–12

olive oil, for cooking
2 lb. lean ground beef
1 large onion, finely chopped
8 cloves garlic, finely chopped
4 x 16 oz. cans peeled plum tomatoes,
undrained and puréed in a food mill
or processor
1/2 cup red wine
1/4 cup tomato paste
4 sprigs of fresh thyme
1 bay leaf
1 1/4 lb. ricotta cheese
1/3 cup whipping cream
4 eggs
12 oz. mozzarella cheese, thinly sliced
1/2 cup grated Parmesan cheese

PASTA
3 1/3 cups all-purpose flour
1 teaspoon salt
3 tablespoons olive oil
4 eggs

One Heat 2 tablespoons oil in a large saucepan until very hot. Add the beef and brown for 10 minutes, or until the liquid has almost evaporated. Strain off the fat and set the meat aside. Reduce the heat to low, heat a little more oil and cook the onion for 5 minutes without coloring. Add the garlic, tomatoes, wine, tomato paste, thyme, bay leaf and beef and simmer for 45 minutes to 1 hour, or until the liquid has reduced by half.

Two Make the pasta, following the method in the Chef's techniques on page 532, dividing the dough into four pieces before passing it through the machine.

Drain the ricotta in a sieve, then mix with the cream and eggs in a large bowl. Season, cover and set aside. Preheat the oven to 375°F.

Three Roll out the pasta dough to 1/16 to 1/8 inch thick and cut into 5 x 4-inch rectangles. Blanch two or three noodles at a time briefly in boiling salted water, then drain on clean towels.

Four Spread about 3/4 cup of the meat sauce in a 9 x 13-inch baking dish. Arrange a layer of pasta on top and

cover with a third of the cheese mixture, then another layer of meat sauce. Repeat the layers twice more and finish with a layer of pasta covered with meat sauce. Cover with mozzarella and sprinkle with Parmesan. Bake for 45 minutes, or until golden brown. Rest for 20 minutes before cutting.

Pasta with prosciutto and Parmesan

This simple pasta dish makes the most of two of Italy's most famous ingredients—prosciutto, a salt-cured ham, and the rich, grainy Parmesan. As both of these ingredients are salty, particular care should be taken when seasoning this dish.

Preparation time *20 minutes*
Total cooking time *20 minutes*
Serves 4

¼ cup olive oil
12 oz. farfalle bow tie pasta
1 large onion, thinly sliced
18 button mushrooms, thinly sliced
3 zucchini, cut into short sticks
1 large clove garlic, chopped
5 oz. prosciutto, cut into strips
1¼ cups crème fraîche
1 cup grated Parmesan cheese
fresh basil leaves, to garnish

One Bring a large saucepan of salted water to a boil. Add a splash of oil to prevent the pasta from sticking and cook the bow tie pasta according to the manufacturer's instructions. Drain well and keep warm.

Two Heat a saucepan over high heat and add the rest of the olive oil. When the oil is hot, add the onion, mushrooms, zucchini and garlic and fry for about 2 minutes, or until the vegetables are lightly colored. Reduce the heat, add the prosciutto strips and fry for 2–3 minutes. Stir in the crème fraîche and heat the mixture for another 2 minutes. Stir in the grated Parmesan and season to taste with salt and freshly ground black pepper.

Three Add the pasta to the saucepan, stir to combine and cook briefly to make sure the pasta is heated through. Serve immediately with the fresh basil leaves sprinkled over the pasta.

LE CORDON BLEU COMPLETE COOK

Linguine vongole

*Linguine, the Italian word for "little tongues," are long flat noodles.
Here they are teamed with fresh clams in a creamy white wine and parsley
sauce. A little time-consuming to make, but well worth the effort.*

Preparation time *25 minutes
+ 1 hour soaking*
Total cooking time *50 minutes*
Serves 4–6

*4 lb. fresh littleneck or cherrystone
clams (see Chef's tip)
1/3 cup plus 1 tablespoon
unsalted butter
1 large onion, finely chopped
1 large stalk celery,
thinly sliced
2 sprigs of fresh thyme
1 bay leaf
8 stems of fresh parsley
8 cloves garlic, chopped
1 cup sliced button mushrooms
3 cups dry white wine
1 lb. linguine
3 tablespoons all-purpose flour
1 1/2 cups whipping cream
1/3 cup chopped fresh flat-leaf parsley*

One Wash the clams, then soak for 1 hour in cold water, changing the water several times. While the clams are soaking, melt the 1/3 cup butter in a large stockpot. Add the onion and cook over low heat for 5 minutes, then add the celery, thyme, bay leaf, parsley stems, garlic, mushrooms and wine. Bring to a boil and cook for 5 minutes. Add the drained clams and cook, covered, for 5–8 minutes (15–20 minutes for large clams), or until they open. Remove the clams with a slotted spoon, discarding any that are unopened, and set aside to cool. Remove the meat from half the clam shells, rinse well under cold water, drain and coarsely chop. Boil the sauce for another 10 minutes, then strain through a strainer lined with damp cheesecloth. Measure out 1 1/2 cups of the cooking liquid.

Two Bring a large saucepan of salted water to a boil. Add a splash of oil to prevent the pasta from sticking and cook the linguine according to the manufacturer's instructions. Drain the pasta well, toss with a little olive oil and keep warm.

Three Melt the 1 tablespoon of butter in a saucepan over low heat. Stir in the flour and cook for 2 minutes. Remove from the heat and gradually whisk in the

reserved cooking liquid. Return to the heat and bring to a boil, stirring. Reduce the heat to low and simmer for 5 minutes, or until thickened. Whisk in the cream and simmer for another 5 minutes. Add the whole and chopped clams, parsley and season well. Cook for 30 seconds and serve over the linguine.

CHEF'S TIP *Use the smallest clams you can find—they are less tough than the larger varieties.*

LE CORDON BLEU COMPLETE COOK

Spaghetti alla diavola

Diavola, meaning devil in Italian, refers to any dish that has been enlivened with hot pepper and garlic. Sometimes simple is better, so here is a recipe that is simply spicy, garlicky and good (pictured top left).

Preparation time *15 minutes*
Total cooking time *15 minutes*
Serves 4

1 lb. spaghetti
1 cup olive oil
2 heads of garlic, peeled and sliced
1/2–1 teaspoon dried hot red chile flakes, or to taste
chopped fresh flat-leaf parsley, to serve
grated Parmesan cheese, to serve

One Bring a large saucepan of salted water to a boil. Add a splash of oil to prevent the pasta from sticking and cook the pasta according to the manufacturer's instructions.

Two While the pasta is cooking, heat the oil in a deep skillet over medium heat. Add the garlic and chile flakes and cook for 10–15 minutes, or until the garlic starts to brown slightly. Drain the pasta thoroughly and toss with the hot sauce. Season to taste.

Three Sprinkle with chopped parsley and serve with the freshly grated Parmesan.

CHEF'S TIP *Use the dried red chile flakes with discretion—some are much hotter than others.*

Linguine with Gorgonzola sauce

If Gorgonzola is unavailable, any mild blue cheese could be used in its place (pictured bottom left).

Preparation time *10 minutes*
Total cooking time *15 minutes*
Serves 4–6

1 lb. linguine
1 1/4 cups whipping cream, at room temperature
10 oz. Gorgonzola or similar blue cheese, cut into cubes

One Bring a large saucepan of salted water to a boil. Add a splash of oil to prevent the pasta from sticking and cook the pasta according to the manufacturer's instructions.

Two Meanwhile, in a heavy-bottomed saucepan, bring the cream to a boil. Remove from the heat and whisk in the cheese until smooth. Pass through a fine strainer.

Three Drain the linguine and toss it with the hot sauce. Serve immediately.

Mushroom ravioli in rosemary garlic cream

*Ideal as a first course or for a light lunch,
the creamy sauce in this dish truly complements
the ravioli with its tasty mushroom filling.*

Preparation time *1 hour*
+ 20 minutes cooling
Total cooking time *45 minutes*
Serves 4 as a starter

PASTA
*1 cup all-purpose flour
pinch of salt
1 teaspoon oil
1 egg, lightly beaten*

MUSHROOM FILLING
*olive oil, for cooking
2 shallots, finely chopped
5 oz. button or wild mushrooms,
chopped
3 tablespoons fresh bread crumbs
1/4 cup each chopped fresh chervil,
thyme, flat-leaf parsley and basil*

*2 cups chicken stock (see page 519)
8 cloves garlic, coarsely chopped
large sprig of fresh rosemary,
cut into pieces
2 cups whipping cream
beaten egg, to glaze
shavings of Parmesan cheese, to
garnish*

One To make the pasta, follow the method in the Chef's techniques on page 532, dividing the dough into two pieces before passing through the pasta machine.

Two To make the mushroom filling, heat a little oil over low heat and cook the shallots for 3 minutes. Add the mushrooms and a good pinch of salt. Cook, stirring, for 10 minutes, or until the mushrooms are dry. Season to taste, then mix in the bread crumbs, herbs and enough olive oil to just bind the mixture. Set aside.

Three To make the sauce, cook the chicken stock and chopped garlic in a saucepan over high heat for 20 minutes, or until the mixture is syrupy. Remove from the heat, add the sprig of rosemary and allow to cool for about 20 minutes. Remove the rosemary, transfer the sauce to a blender or food processor and blend until the mixture is smooth. Strain into a small saucepan, add the cream and simmer over low heat for 5 minutes, or until the sauce is thick enough to coat the back of a spoon. Season, to taste, and keep warm.

Four Make the ravioli, following the method in the Chef's techniques on page 533 and using a round 1½-inch biscuit cutter to cut and seal the dough.

Five Bring a large saucepan of salted water to a boil. Cook the ravioli for 2–3 minutes, or until *al dente*. Strain and serve with the sauce and shavings of Parmesan.

Italian meatballs

Tasty meatballs cooked in a rich tomato sauce and served with spaghetti make a warming winter dish. The meatballs may be made from ground beef or a combination of ground pork and veal if preferred.

Preparation time *50 minutes*
Total cooking time *1 hour 25 minutes*
Serves 4

⅓ cup olive oil
1 onion, finely chopped
2 cloves garlic, finely chopped
¼ teaspoon chopped fresh oregano
1 lb. lean ground beef
1 egg, lightly beaten
1 lb. spaghetti
grated Parmesan cheese, to serve

SAUCE
3 tablespoons olive oil
1 large onion, finely chopped
3 x 16-oz. cans whole peeled plum tomatoes, undrained and puréed in a food mill or food processor
5 cloves garlic, finely chopped
1 bay leaf
2 sprigs of fresh thyme

One Heat half the oil in a small skillet over low heat and cook the onion for 5–7 minutes, or until soft. Off the heat, add the garlic and oregano and stir well. Strain off any excess oil and allow to cool. Add to the meat and mix well. Season and add enough of the egg to bind the mixture together.

Two Divide the meat into eight portions and roll into smooth balls. Heat the remaining olive oil in a large skillet and cook the meatballs until browned. Drain on a plate lined with paper towels.

Three To make the sauce, heat the olive oil in a saucepan and slowly cook the onion for 5 minutes without coloring. Add the tomatoes, garlic, bay leaf, thyme and the meatballs and simmer over low heat, covered, for 20 minutes.

Remove the lid and simmer for another 30–40 minutes, skimming as needed. Remove the bay leaf and thyme and season to taste with salt and pepper

Four Bring a large saucepan of salted water to a boil. Add a splash of oil to prevent the pasta from sticking and cook the pasta according to the manufacturer's instructions.

Five Drain well and transfer the pasta to plates. Top with the sauce and meatballs. Serve with grated Parmesan.

Vegetable lasagna

Try this deliciously different lasagna with its crunchy vegetables and cheese sauce with a hint of nutmeg. Making your own pasta is both enjoyable and satisfying.

***Preparation time** 1 hour*
+ 30 minutes resting
***Total cooking time** 1 hour 30 minutes*
***Serves** 6*

PASTA
2¹/2 cups all-purpose flour
1 teaspoon salt
2 tablespoons olive oil
3 eggs, lightly beaten

CHEESE SAUCE
1¹/2 tablespoons unsalted butter
3 tablespoons all-purpose flour
2 cups milk
¹/4 teaspoon ground nutmeg
¹/4 cup whipping cream
1 cup shredded Gruyère cheese

TOMATO SAUCE
1¹/2 tablespoons unsalted butter
1 small onion, sliced
4 ripe tomatoes, peeled, seeded and chopped (see page 534)
1 sprig of fresh thyme
1 bay leaf
1¹/4 cups diced carrots
3¹/3 cups small broccoli florets
¹/2 cauliflower, cut into florets
³/4 cup shredded Gruyère cheese

One Make the pasta, following the method in the Chef's techniques on page 532.

Two To make the cheese sauce, melt the butter in a saucepan, stir in the flour with a wooden spoon and cook gently for 3 minutes, stirring constantly. Remove from the heat and whisk in the cold milk. Blend thoroughly, season and stir in the nutmeg. Return to the heat and bring slowly to a boil, stirring constantly. Lower the heat and cook for 7 minutes, stirring occasionally. Stir in the cream and cheese. Set aside, covered with buttered parchment paper.

Three Heat the butter in a skillet and cook the onion slowly without browning. Add the tomatoes, thyme and bay leaf. Season with salt and pepper. Simmer for 15 minutes, or until pulpy. Discard both the bay leaf and the thyme.

Four Bring a large saucepan of salted water to a boil. Add the carrot, reduce the heat and simmer for 4 minutes. Add the broccoli and cauliflower and simmer for 3 minutes. Drain and refresh in cold water to stop the cooking process. Drain well and set aside.

Five Preheat the oven to 375°F. On a lightly floured surface, roll out the pasta dough to ¹/16 inch thick. Cut with a sharp knife into long strips 6 x 3 inches and cook a few strips at a time, in a large saucepan of boiling salted water with a dash of oil, for 2–3 minutes, or until *al dente*. Transfer to a bowl of cold water, drain and put between layers of a clean dish towel.

Six Mix the cheese sauce and tomato sauce together and simmer for 15 minutes. Add the vegetables to the sauce. Season to taste.

Seven Butter a 2–2¹/2-quart baking dish and alternate layers of pasta and vegetable mixture, finishing with pasta. Sprinkle with cheese and bake for 35 minutes.

Ricotta shells

The extensive cooking time for this dish may seem alarming at first glance; however, it is worth noting that, in fact, both the rich tomato sauce and the finished cheese-and-herb stuffed pasta shells spend much time cooking in the oven, leaving you free to do other things.

Preparation time *1 hour*
Total cooking time *2 hours 30 minutes*
Serves 4

3 tablespoons unsalted butter
2 oz. slab bacon, diced
1 small onion, chopped
1 small carrot, chopped
3 tablespoons tomato paste
1 tablespoon all-purpose flour
1 lb. tomatoes, peeled, seeded and chopped (see page 534)
1 bouquet garni (see page 520)
4 cloves garlic, chopped
2 cups chicken stock (see page 519) or water
32–40 conchiglioni (large pasta shells)
1 lb. ricotta cheese
¼ cup grated Parmesan cheese
2 eggs
1 tablespoon chopped fresh parsley
1 tablespoon chopped fresh basil
¼ teaspoon grated nutmeg
8 oz. fresh mozzarella cheese or bocconcini, sliced or shredded

One Preheat the oven to 350°F. To make the tomato sauce, melt the butter over medium heat in a large flameproof casserole or Dutch oven. Add the bacon and cook until golden brown. Add the onion and carrot and cook for 3 minutes. Add the tomato paste, stir well and cook for another 2 minutes. Sprinkle with the flour and place in the oven for 5 minutes. Remove and stir well until the flour disappears, then add the tomatoes, bouquet garni and garlic. Cook on the stove for 5 minutes, stirring well, then add the stock or water, bring to a boil, stirring, and cook for 2 minutes. Cover and bake for 1 hour.

Two Bring a large saucepan of salted water to a boil. Add a splash of oil to prevent the pasta from sticking and cook the shells according to the manufacturer's instructions. Drain and drizzle with a little olive oil. Arrange on a damp towel.

Three Lightly oil a large baking dish. In a bowl, mix together the ricotta, Parmesan, eggs, herbs and nutmeg and season with salt and pepper. Spoon the mixture into a pastry bag with a plain tip, fill each shell and arrange in a single layer in the prepared dish.

Four Pass the tomato sauce through a strainer, pressing well to extract as much liquid as possible. Discard the contents of the strainer. Bring the sauce back to a boil and skim if necessary. Simmer for 20 minutes, or until the sauce thickens. Pour over the stuffed shells. Sprinkle the mozzarella over the sauce and bake for 30–40 minutes, or until the cheese is melted and browned.

Herb tagliatelle with mushrooms and olive oil

This recipe calls for herb tagliatelle. However, if time is short, it could be made with fresh, plain or spinach tagliatelle bought from a specialty market or good supermarket. Serve with a crisp green salad.

***Preparation time** 30 minutes*
***Total cooking time** 15 minutes*
Serves 6

HERB TAGLIATELLE
2¹/₂ cups all-purpose flour
1 teaspoon salt
2 tablespoons olive oil
3 eggs, lightly beaten
3 tablespoons finely chopped fresh herbs, such as tarragon, parsley or basil leaves

2 tablespoons unsalted butter
3 shallots, chopped
12 oz. mushrooms (button or a mixture of button and wild mushrooms), sliced
1 tablespoon sherry or Marsala
¹/₃ cup olive oil
5 large tomatoes, peeled, seeded and chopped (see page 534)
¹/₂ cup chopped mixed fresh herbs
2 tablespoons shredded basil leaves or chopped oregano, to garnish
shavings of Parmesan cheese, to serve

One Make the pasta, following the method in the Chef's techniques on page 532, and add the chopped herbs with the eggs. Divide the dough into four pieces before passing through the pasta machine. When the pasta has passed through the thinnest setting, pass the sheets through the ¹/₄-inch cutters to make tagliatelle (see Chef's techniques, page 532).

Two Heat the butter in a skillet over medium heat, add the shallots and cook until soft but not colored. Turn up the heat, toss in the mushrooms and fry until they start to color. Continue to cook for 2–3 minutes. Add the sherry or Marsala and cook for 30 seconds. Season and set aside.

Three Bring a large saucepan of salted water to a boil. Add a splash of oil to prevent the pasta from sticking and cook the tagliatelle for 2–3 minutes, or until *al dente*. Drain well and set aside.

Four Heat the olive oil in a large saucepan over medium heat and add the mushroom mixture, the herb tagliatelle, tomatoes and mixed herbs. Heat the mixture through and season generously with salt and freshly ground black pepper. Serve immediately, garnished with the shredded basil or chopped oregano and serve immediately with the Parmesan shavings.

Sicilian-style pasta

*Tuna and sardines are the most common fish in Sicily,
hence the name of this tuna pasta (pictured top right).*

Preparation time *30 minutes*
Total cooking time *50 minutes*
Serves 6

½ cup olive oil
2 small onions, finely chopped
*1½ lb. tomatoes, peeled, seeded and
chopped (see page 534)*
3 cloves garlic, crushed
1 bouquet garni (see page 520)
*½ cup pitted and chopped
black olives*
2 cups sliced button mushrooms
1 lb. fresh tuna, cut into ½-inch cubes
1 lb. pappardelle (wide noodles)
3 tablespoons chopped fresh parsley
3 tablespoons grated Parmesan cheese

One Heat a third of the olive oil in a heavy-bottomed saucepan and cook the onions until translucent. Add the tomatoes, garlic and bouquet garni and cook gently for 30–35 minutes. At the end of the cooking, mix in the black olives. In a skillet, sauté the mushrooms in a third of the olive oil. Season and transfer to a strainer to drain.

Two In the skillet, heat the remaining oil over high heat. Lightly season the tuna, then sauté in the hot oil.

Three Bring a large saucepan of salted water to a boil. Add a splash of oil to prevent the pasta from sticking and cook the pasta according to the manufacturer's instructions. Drain and place in a large bowl. Add the tomato sauce, tuna and mushrooms and toss well. Sprinkle with the parsley and Parmesan and serve immediately.

Spaghetti puttanesca

*A piquant combination of garlic, tomatoes, capers, olives and anchovies
make up this popular Italian sauce (pictured bottom right).*

Preparation time *35 minutes*
Total cooking time *50 minutes*
Serves 4

¼ cup olive oil
4 cloves garlic, chopped
*1¾ lb. tomatoes, peeled, seeded and
chopped (see page 534)*
*¼–½ teaspoon dried hot red chile
flakes*
3 tablespoons capers, drained
1 cup pitted black olives
¾ cup chicken stock (see page 519)
*1–1¼ oz. can of anchovy fillets,
drained and coarsely chopped*
3 tablespoons chopped fresh basil
3 tablespoons chopped fresh parsley
1 lb. spaghetti

One In a medium saucepan, heat the oil over low heat and cook the chopped garlic for 1 minute without browning. Add the tomatoes, red chile flakes, capers, olives and stock or water. Bring to a boil and cook over medium heat, covered, for 20 minutes. Remove the lid and simmer for 25 minutes. Once the sauce is cooked, mix in the anchovies, basil and parsley.

Two Bring a large saucepan of salted water to a boil. Add a splash of oil to prevent the pasta from sticking and cook the pasta according to the manufacturer's instructions. Drain well and toss with the hot sauce and serve.

Spinach pasta salad

*Combining Roquefort, bacon and walnuts with
the bright green tagliatelle creates a winning formula.*

Preparation time *20 minutes*
Total cooking time *10 minutes*
Serves 4

PASTA
1²/₃ *cups all-purpose flour*
¹/₂ *teaspoon salt*
4 *teaspoons olive oil*
2 *eggs, lightly beaten*
3 *tablespoons frozen spinach,
thawed, squeezed dry and
very finely chopped*

4 *slices bacon*
¹/₂ *cup walnuts*
3 *oz. Roquefort cheese,
cut into cubes*
1 *small red onion, thinly sliced*
1 *tablespoon chopped fresh parsley*

VINAIGRETTE
1 *shallot, finely chopped*
1 *clove garlic, finely chopped*
3 *tablespoons white wine vinegar*
¹/₂ *cup walnut oil*

One Make the pasta following the method in the Chef's techniques on page 532, adding the spinach with the eggs. Divide the dough in half and pass through the pasta machine. When the pasta sheets have passed through the thinnest setting, pass through the ¹/₄-inch cutters to make tagliatelle (see Chef's techniques, page 532).

Two Heat a skillet and dry-fry the bacon until very crisp and browned. Remove from the skillet, leaving the fat behind, drain well on crumpled paper towels and crumble into small pieces. Reheat the skillet containing the fat and fry the walnuts for 2 minutes, or until well browned. Drain well.

Three To make the vinaigrette, combine the shallot, garlic, vinegar, oil, salt and pepper and whisk until blended.

Four Bring a large saucepan of salted water to a boil. Add a splash of oil to prevent the pasta from sticking and cook the tagliatelle for 2–3 minutes, or until *al dente*. Drain, run under cold water, then drain once more.

Five Toss the pasta and vinaigrette in a bowl. Add the bacon, walnuts, cheese, onion and parsley and toss again.

Pasta primavera

Bursting with the fresh flavors of spring vegetables and the delicate taste of parsley and mint, this pasta dish is a truly wonderful way of celebrating the arrival of spring.

Preparation time 40 minutes
Total cooking time 35 minutes
Serves 4

2 cups vegetable stock
12 scallions or baby leeks, cut
into 2-inch pieces
12 very small boiling onions
1/4 cup shelled fresh or frozen baby
lima beans
12 asparagus tips, cut into
2-inch pieces
12 baby carrots, cut into
2-inch pieces
2/3 cup fresh shelled baby peas
1 lb. spaghetti
3 egg yolks
3/4 cup whipping cream
1 tablespoon unsalted butter
1/2 cup grated Parmesan cheese
3 tablespoons chopped fresh
flat-leaf parsley
1 tablespoon shredded fresh mint
grated Parmesan cheese, to serve

One Place the vegetable stock in a saucepan and bring to a boil. Cook the vegetables in batches in the stock, until they are just cooked or *al dente*. Remove the vegetables from the stock with a slotted spoon, refresh with cold water and set aside. Retain the stock and keep it warm.

Two Bring a large saucepan of salted water to a boil. Add a splash of oil to prevent the pasta from sticking and cook the spaghetti according to the manufacturer's instructions, or until *al dente*. Drain well and keep warm.

Three Bring a large saucepan of water to a boil and remove from the heat. Set a large bowl over the pan, making sure the bottom of the bowl isn't touching the water. Place the egg yolks and 3 tablespoons of the reserved stock in the bowl and whisk until the mixture thickens slightly. Add the cream, butter and Parmesan to another 3/4 cup of the stock, then gently stir into the yolk mixture. The sauce should be very light and liquid. Add the drained vegetables to the sauce to heat through, but do not allow to boil.

Four Add the spaghetti to the sauce and vegetables and toss with the parsley and mint until heated through. Season to taste and serve sprinkled with Parmesan.

Cannelloni

*These pasta tubes are stuffed with a succulent meat filling, coated with
a creamy cheese sauce and baked in the oven until piping hot and
golden brown. Perfect for lunch with a crisp green salad.*

Preparation time *50 minutes*
Total cooking time *55 minutes*
Serves 4

1/3 cup fresh bread crumbs
1 tablespoon milk
4 teaspoons unsalted butter
1 onion, finely chopped
*3 oz. pork tenderloin or lean pork
from the shoulder*
*5 oz. skinned boneless chicken breast
halves*
1/3 cup whipping cream
1/4 cup chopped fresh parsley
1/3 cup grated Parmesan cheese
1 egg white, lightly beaten
1 oz. prosciutto, diced
*12 cannelloni or manicotti tubes (see
Chef's tip)*

SAUCE
1/4 cup unsalted butter
1/3 cup all-purpose flour
2 cups milk
1/2 cup shredded Gruyère cheese

One Preheat the oven to 350°F. Soak the bread crumbs in the milk. Heat the butter in a small skillet, add the onion and cook gently until soft and translucent. In a meat grinder or food processor, grind the pork and chicken and transfer to a bowl. Add the soaked bread crumbs, cream, parsley, Parmesan and enough egg white to hold the filling together. Add the prosciutto and cooked onion. Season well.

Two Spoon the meat mixture into a pastry bag fitted with a large tip. Fill each cannelloni tube with the filling.

Three To make the sauce, melt 3 tablespoons of the butter in a saucepan over medium heat. Add the flour and whisk for 3 minutes. Remove from the heat and gradually add the milk. Return the saucepan to the heat and whisk the sauce until the mixture boils and is thick enough to coat the back of a spoon. Whisk in the cheese until melted, then stir in the remaining butter. Spread a thin layer of sauce over the bottom of an 11 x 7 x 2-inch (or 8 x 8-inch) baking dish and place the filled cannelloni tubes on top. Pour the remaining sauce over the cannelloni tubes and bake for 25 minutes covered, then bake for about 15–20 minutes uncovered, or until lightly colored.

CHEF'S TIP *If you can't find cannelloni tubes, lightly cook 12 lasagna sheets and then carefully roll them up into tubes.*

Pasta with seafood sauce

*For this recipe, you can use any variety of seafood,
but do not overcook it or it can become tough.*

Preparation time *20 minutes*
Total cooking time *1 hour 40 minutes*
Serves 4–6

*2 sprigs of fresh thyme
2 sprigs of fresh parsley
1 bay leaf
1/2 cup olive oil
1 large onion, finely chopped
1/2 cup white wine
3 x 16-oz. cans whole peeled plum
tomatoes, undrained and puréed
in a food processor
5 cloves garlic, finely chopped
8–10 small mussels, scrubbed and
debearded (see page 523)
8 oz. scallops, cleaned (see page 524)
8 oz. cleaned squid (calamari) bodies,
sliced into rings
1 lb. cooked shrimp, shells removed
(see page 522)
1/2 cup chopped fresh flat-leaf
parsley
1 lb. spaghetti*

One Tie the herbs and bay leaf in a bundle. Heat two-thirds of the oil in a saucepan and cook the onion for 5 minutes without coloring. Add the wine and simmer until reduced by three-quarters. Add the tomatoes, garlic and herbs and simmer, covered, for 20 minutes, then uncovered for 40 minutes. Add the mussels and simmer for 5 minutes until they open. Discard any mussels that have not opened during the cooking time.

Two Heat the remaining oil in a skillet and fry the scallops and squid for 1 minute, or until firm and white. Add to the sauce with the shrimp and heat through. Remove the herbs and mix in the parsley.

Three Bring a large saucepan of salted water to a boil. Add a splash of oil to prevent the pasta from sticking and cook the spaghetti according to the manufacturer's instructions. Season the sauce and pour over the drained pasta.

Pasta with Parmesan and Gruyère

*A quick, simple dish that may be made using fresh
or dried pasta, as pictured top left. It also makes
a good accompaniment to broiled meats.*

Preparation time 20 minutes
Total cooking time 25 minutes
Serves 4

PASTA
3¹/3 cups all-purpose flour
1 teaspoon salt
3 tablespoons olive oil
4 eggs, lightly beaten

¹/4 cup olive oil
¹/3 cup shredded Gruyère cheese
1 cup grated Parmesan cheese
*extra piece of Parmesan cheese, to
make shavings*

One Make the pasta, following the method in the Chef's techniques on page 532. Divide the dough into four before passing through the pasta machine. When the pasta has passed through the thinnest setting, pass the sheets through the ¹/4-inch cutters to make tagliatelle (see Chef's techniques, page 532).

Two Bring a large saucepan of salted water to a boil. Add a splash of oil to prevent the pasta from sticking and cook the tagliatelle for 2–3 minutes, or until *al dente*.

Three Drain the pasta well, place in a large bowl and pour in the olive oil. Season and toss with the Gruyère and grated Parmesan. Place in a serving dish and top with Parmesan shavings and freshly ground black pepper.

CHEF'S TIP *Parmesan shavings are an easy decoration to make. Take a piece of Parmesan and draw a vegetable peeler along one side to make thin shavings.*

Spaghetti carbonara

*The pasta must be well drained and extremely hot when
tossed in the sauce, as it is the heat of the pasta that
lightly cooks the egg yolks (pictured bottom left).*

Preparation time 10 minutes
Total cooking time 20 minutes
Serves 4–6

1¹/3 cup oil
*8 oz. slab bacon, cut into
¹/2-inch cubes*
1 lb. spaghetti
8 egg yolks
1 cup grated Parmesan cheese
3 tablespoons chopped fresh parsley

One Heat the oil in a skillet and add the bacon and brown it for 5–10 minutes, or until the bacon is crisp and evenly colored. Drain, then place on paper towels. Set aside.

Two Bring a large saucepan of salted water to a boil. Add a splash of oil to prevent the pasta from sticking and cook the pasta according to the manufacturer's instructions.

Three Just before the pasta has finished cooking, whisk the egg yolks in a large bowl and season with freshly ground black pepper. Whisk in ¹/4 cup boiling water and the Parmesan. Drain the spaghetti well and toss the hot pasta with the egg and cheese mixture. Toss in the bacon and serve immediately with a little chopped parsley sprinkled over the top.

Potato gnocchi

*These popular little dumplings may be served
as a starter, as a main course with salad,
or as an accompaniment to roast meat.*

Preparation time *30 minutes*
Total cooking time *50 minutes*
Serves 4–6

2 lb. baking potatoes, scrubbed
1³/4 cups all-purpose flour
1 teaspoon salt
small pinch of ground nutmeg

One Place the potatoes in a large saucepan of salted water. Bring to a boil, then reduce the heat and simmer for 30–35 minutes, or until the potatoes are tender to the point of a sharp knife. Drain and allow to cool a little before removing the skins.

Two Purée the potatoes directly onto a lightly floured surface (see Chef's techniques, page 536). Sift the flour, salt and nutmeg onto the warm potato mash and work together—take care not to overwork the mixture or the texture will become gluey. Clean the surface and lightly flour again. Taking a little dough

at a time, roll the mixture out into ³/4-inch pieces.

Three Bring a large saucepan of salted water to a boil and gently lower in the gnocchi. Do not crowd the pan or the gnocchi will stick together—you may have to cook them in several batches. When the gnocchi float to the surface, lift them out with a slotted spoon and place in a lightly oiled serving dish. Serve with a hot tomato pasta sauce and grated Parmesan.

LE CORDON BLEU ✠ COMPLETE COOK

Roman gnocchi

These extremely popular Italian gnocchi can be made from potatoes, pumpkin or, as in this case, semolina. Often served as a starter, gnocchi are also perfect for lunch, accompanied by a crisp green salad.

Preparation time *35 minutes
+ 30 minutes cooling*
Total cooking time *2 hours 20 minutes*
Serves 4 as a starter

*3 tablespoons unsalted butter
2 oz. bacon, diced
1 small onion, chopped
1 small carrot, chopped
3 tablespoons tomato paste
1 tablespoon all-purpose flour
1 lb. tomatoes, peeled, seeded and
chopped (see page 534)
1 bouquet garni (see page 520)
4 cloves garlic, chopped
2 cups chicken stock (see page 519)
or water*

GNOCCHI
*2 cups milk
1/4 cup unsalted butter
1 1/4 cups semolina flour
or fine semolina
1/4 cup all-purpose flour
3 tablespoons whipping cream
1 egg
2 egg yolks
1/3 cup grated Parmesan cheese
1/3 cup unsalted butter, melted*

One Preheat the oven to 350°F. Melt the butter in a small flameproof casserole and cook the diced bacon until golden brown. Add the onion and carrot to the casserole and cook for 3 minutes. Stir in the tomato paste and cook for 2 minutes. Sprinkle with the flour, place in the oven for 5 minutes, then stir until the flour disappears. Add the tomatoes, bouquet garni and garlic, return to the stove top and cook for 5 minutes, stirring. Stir in the stock and boil for 2 minutes. Cover and bake in the oven for 1 hour.

Two Strain into a clean saucepan and discard the contents of the strainer. Bring the sauce back to a boil and skim if necessary. Lower the heat and simmer for 20 minutes, or until thickened. Season, set aside and keep warm.

Three To make the gnocchi, bring the milk and butter to a boil in a large saucepan. Add the flours and stir over low heat until absorbed, then stir for 5 minutes longer, or until the mixture rolls off the side of the pan. Remove from the heat, add the cream, egg, egg yolks and half the Parmesan and stir until smooth. Season to taste and spread 1/2-inch-thick on a baking sheet lined with parchment paper. Cool for 30 minutes, then cut into rounds with a wet 1 1/2-inch biscuit cutter. Put in a baking dish, drizzle with the melted butter and sprinkle with the remaining Parmesan. Bake for 20 minutes, or until golden, and serve with the tomato sauce.

Seafood paella

This classic Spanish dish consists of rice and saffron, often combined with chicken, pork and chorizo, although here we use seafood only. The name is derived from the large, two-handled dish in which the paella is traditionally cooked and served.

Preparation time 45 minutes
Total cooking time 45 minutes
Serves 4

3 pinches of saffron threads
3 tablespoons olive oil
1 large onion, sliced
1½ cups long-grain rice
3 tomatoes, peeled, seeded and
  chopped (see page 534), or
14-oz. can diced tomatoes, drained
2 cloves garlic, crushed
2¼ cups chicken stock (see page 519)
  or vegetable stock
¾ lb. mussels, scrubbed and beards
  removed (see page 523)
16 large shrimp, shells on
1 cooked crab in its shell, prepared
  and quartered (see page 523), or
4 cooked crab claws in their shells
½–¾ lb. small clams or cockles,
  thoroughly washed
¼ lb. firm white fish fillets, skin
  removed and cut into
  1¼-inch pieces
⅔ cup frozen baby peas
1 red bell pepper, cut into 1-inch
  pieces and thinly sliced

One Place the saffron threads in a small bowl with 2 tablespoons hot water and allow to soak.

Two Heat the olive oil in a paella pan or heavy-bottomed frying pan, 12–14 inches in diameter. Add the onion and cook for 3–4 minutes, or until soft. Add the rice and saffron and cook, stirring, for 2 minutes. Add the tomatoes, garlic and stock and bring to a boil. Reduce the heat and stir in half the mussels, shrimp, crab, clams and fish with all the peas and red bell pepper. Season well.

Three Arrange the remaining seafood on top and cover with a piece of parchment paper and a lid. Cook over low heat for 30 minutes, or until the rice is tender and the liquid has been absorbed. Don't stir the paella while it cooks, as this will break up the fish and make the finished dish look messy. If the liquid has been absorbed but the rice is not cooked, add a little extra water and continue cooking until the rice is cooked through.

Discard any mussels that haven't opened during the cooking time and serve the paella immediately.

CHEF'S TIP *Paella is traditionally served directly from the pan. If you are using a frying pan, check that it is deep enough (1¼–2 inches) to hold the liquid.*

Baked mushroom risotto

Traditional risotto is cooked on top of the stove and needs to be stirred constantly. This baked risotto, however, needs little attention and yet retains the beautiful taste and texture of the classically made version.

*Preparation time 15 minutes
+ 2 hours soaking*
Total cooking time 1 hour
Serves 6

¼ cup dried morel or porcini
mushrooms
3½ cups chicken stock (see page 519)
or vegetable stock
¼ cup unsalted butter
1 onion, finely chopped
1 clove garlic, finely chopped
2¼ cups thickly sliced button
mushrooms
1 cup Arborio rice
⅓ cup dry sherry
1 sprig of fresh rosemary
3 tablespoons finely grated Parmesan
cheese
3 tablespoons coarsely grated
Parmesan cheese

One Place the dried mushrooms in a deep bowl and pour in the boiling stock. Allow to soak for 2 hours, then pass through a fine strainer, reserving the liquid. Finely chop the mushrooms.

Two Preheat the oven to 300°F. Place a 2½-inch-deep 1¾-quart baking dish in the oven to warm.

Three Melt the butter in a saucepan, add the onion and garlic and cook gently for 7 minutes. Stir in the fresh mushrooms and chopped dried mushrooms. Continue to cook gently for 15 minutes. Add the rice and stir for 1 minute. Pour in the reserved mushroom liquid, leaving the last tablespoon in the bowl with any sediment. Add the sherry and season with salt and pepper. Stir in the sprig of rosemary. Increase the heat, and when

bubbles begin to rise, transfer the mixture to the baking dish. Bake on the middle shelf of the oven for about 15 minutes. Stir in the finely grated Parmesan and return to the oven for another 20 minutes.

Four Stir the risotto as soon as it comes out of the oven. Discard the rosemary and season with salt and freshly ground black pepper to taste. Serve immediately, sprinkled with the remaining Parmesan.

Seafood risotto

Despite being a rather time-consuming dish to make, the final combination of fresh seafood with creamy risotto rice is well worth the effort.

***Preparation time** 55 minutes*
***Total cooking time** 1 hour 20 minutes*
Serves 8

1 lb. uncooked shrimp, shells on
1 lb. mussels, scrubbed and debearded
(see page 523)
3 cups white wine
1 onion, coarsely chopped
1 bay leaf
2 sprigs of fresh thyme
olive oil, for cooking
8 oz. scallops, cleaned (see page 524)
4 shallots, roughly chopped
1 stalk celery, coarsely chopped
1 small carrot, coarsely chopped
8 cloves garlic, coarsely chopped
1 onion, finely chopped
2 cups Arborio rice
1/2 cup whipping cream
2/3 cup grated Parmesan cheese
2 tablespoons chopped fresh parsley
shavings of Parmesan cheese and
lemon wedges, to garnish

One Peel and devein the shrimp, following the method in the Chef's techniques on page 522, keeping the shells and any heads.

Two Put the mussels, 2 cups of the wine, the coarsely chopped onion, bay leaf and thyme in a large saucepan, cover and bring to a boil. Cook for 5 minutes, or until the mussels have opened. Remove the mussels and set aside to cool, discarding any that haven't opened. Pass the cooking liquid through a fine strainer lined with a piece of cheesecloth.

Three Heat 1/4 cup olive oil in a large saucepan and cook the peeled shrimp over high heat for 2 minutes, or until pink. Remove with a slotted spoon and set aside. Add the scallops and cook for 2 minutes, then drain and set aside. Add the shrimp heads and shells and cook for 2–3 minutes, or until pink, crushing with a large spoon or potato masher. Add the shallots, celery, carrot and half the garlic and cook for 2 minutes. Add the cooking liquid from the mussels and boil for 15 minutes. Add 2 cups water, bring to a boil and cook for 10 minutes. Strain the liquid, pressing the contents of

the strainer to extract as much flavor as possible. Add enough water to the liquid to make up 7 cups and return to the pan. Bring to a boil, then reduce the heat and maintain the stock at a very low simmer.

Four Heat 1/4 cup of the oil over medium-low heat in a large heavy-bottomed saucepan and cook the finely chopped onion for 3–5 minutes, or until soft and translucent. Add the rice and remaining garlic and stir well with a wooden spoon, making sure the rice is coated with oil. Cook for 2 minutes, then add the rest of the wine, stirring well. Cook over low heat, stirring constantly, until the wine has been absorbed. Add 1 cup of the hot stock, stirring frequently until the liquid has been almost completely absorbed before adding another 1 cup of stock. Continue for 30–35 minutes, or until all the stock has been added and the rice is tender, stirring constantly to prevent sticking. Mix in the cream and Parmesan, season with salt and pepper and remove from the heat. Stir in the shrimp, scallops, mussels and the chopped parsley and serve with the Parmesan shavings and some lemon wedges on the side.

about risotto rice...

The are many varieties of risotto rice. The grain is medium to long and has a hard core and translucent edges. Arborio is the classic risotto rice and is the one most commonly used because it absorbs plenty of liquid without becoming too soft. You can also use carnaroli or vialone nano—the latter has a slightly shorter cooking time.

vegetables

· LE CORDON BLEU ·

Vegetable tian

Layers of vegetables with added flavor from herbs and garlic are delicious baked in a shallow dish that can be presented at the table. Suitable for lunch or dinner.

Preparation time *30 minutes*
Total cooking time *1 hour*
Serves 4

olive oil, for cooking
1 small onion, thinly sliced
1½ lb. tomatoes, peeled, seeded
and diced (see page 534)
13 oz. large mushrooms, sliced
13 oz. potatoes, thinly sliced
2 cloves garlic, finely chopped
1 lb. spinach leaves
sprig of fresh rosemary
3 tablespoons chopped fresh parsley

One Preheat the oven to 375°F. Heat a little olive oil in a skillet and gently cook the onion with a pinch of salt for 3 minutes, without coloring. Add the tomato and cook gently for 7 minutes. Season and remove from the skillet.

Two Heat a little more oil in the clean skillet and fry the mushrooms over high heat for 3–4 minutes. Drain off any excess moisture. Season to taste and remove from the skillet.

Three Heat a little more oil in the clean skillet and fry the potato in batches over medium–low heat for 3 minutes. Return all the potato to the pan, add the garlic and cook for 1 minute. Season and drain on paper towels.

Four Arrange a layer of potato in a 2-quart baking dish and cover with a layer of the mushrooms, a layer of spinach, then a layer of tomato. Cover with parchment paper and bake for 30–45 minutes. Sprinkle with rosemary and parsley to serve.

Mixed glazed vegetables

*The initial shaping of the vegetables with a melon baller may be a little
fiddly but for a special occasion you will find this beautifully
presented dish well-worth the trouble.*

***Preparation time** 40 minutes*
***Total cooking time** 30 minutes*
Serves 4

20 small boiling onions
2 zucchini
3 turnips
3 carrots
1/4 cup unsalted butter
1 tablespoon sugar

One Soak the boiling onions in a bowl of warm water for 5 minutes to make peeling easier. Lightly trim the root end, being careful not to cut off too much, since it is the root end that will keep the onions intact.

Two Using a standard 3/4-inch melon baller, make 20 balls each of the zucchini, turnips and carrots. Cook the zucchini balls for 1 minute in boiling salted water and refresh in iced water. Transfer to a small saucepan. Add one-third of the butter, 1 teaspoon of the sugar, 1/2 teaspoon salt and 2 tablespoons water and cook until the water has evaporated and a syrupy glaze remains. Check to see if the vegetables are tender. If not, add some water and cook a little longer. Roll the vegetables around to evenly coat, then set aside and keep warm.

Three Put the turnip and carrot balls together in a saucepan with half of the remaining butter, 1 teaspoon of the sugar, 1/2 teaspoon salt and enough water to just cover. Cook in the same way as the zucchini, then set aside and keep warm. Repeat with the onions.

Four Reheat by combining the vegetables in a saucepan, placing the saucepan over medium heat and rolling the vegetables around to prevent them from browning, for about 3–5 minutes. Transfer to a serving dish.

CHEF'S TIPS *Leave the vegetables at room temperature for about 1 hour before preparing.*

If you can't get boiling onions, you can also use small brown or white onions and simply remove a few of the outer layers.

Roast potatoes

Meals involving roasted meats are never quite the same without crisp, golden roast potatoes. Even the simplest ingredients—olive oil, rosemary or salt—will further enhance their wonderful flavor.

Preparation time *15 minutes*
Total cooking time *50 minutes*
Serves 4

2 lb. baking potatoes
oil, for cooking

One Preheat the oven to 375°F. Peel the potatoes and cut them into even-size pieces—halve or quarter them depending on their size. Place in a large saucepan of salted water, bring to a boil, then reduce the heat and simmer for 5 minutes.

Drain, then while the potatoes are still hot, hold each one in a cloth and lightly scratch the surface with a fork. Return to the saucepan and cover to keep hot.

Two Preheat a roasting pan over high heat and add oil to a depth of about 1/2 inch. As the oil just starts to smoke, add the potatoes in a single layer. Roll them in the hot oil to seal all sides. Bake for 40 minutes, or until the potatoes are golden, turning and basting frequently with the oil. Drain on crumpled paper towels, sprinkle with salt and serve while still hot.

CHEF'S TIPS *Boiling potatoes prior to roasting them removes excess sticky starch from the surface, leaving them dry and crisp; scratching the surface contributes texture to that crispness. Rolling hot potatoes in hot oil will then seal them nicely, leaving the centers mealy and oil free.*

If the potatoes are to accompany a roasted meat, instead of cooking them in a separate pan, place them in the hot fat around the meat as it cooks. This will give a most delicious flavor as the potatoes absorb the fat from the meat.

For special occasions, shave off the angled edges. The rounded potatoes will roll easily in the pan for all-over color and crispness: the secret of the perfect roast potato.

Potato and spinach croquettes

The flavors of spinach and Parmesan enliven the potato in these croquettes. They are great for a light lunch or supper but also work well as picnic food.

Preparation time 30 minutes
Total cooking time 45 minutes
Makes 14 croquettes

1 lb. russet potatoes
pinch of ground nutmeg
1 tablespoon unsalted butter
1 egg yolk
oil, for deep- or pan-frying
1/3 cup grated Parmesan cheese
1/4 cup finely chopped cooked spinach
1/2 cup all-purpose flour, seasoned with salt and pepper
3 eggs, beaten
1 tablespoon peanut oil
1 1/2 cups fine dry bread crumbs

One Peel the potatoes and cut them into even-size pieces—halve or quarter them depending on their size. Place in a large saucepan of salted water, bring to a boil and then lower the heat and cook for at least 20 minutes, or until quite tender.

Two Drain the potatoes and dry them by shaking them in the saucepan over low heat for 2 minutes. Purée the potatoes finely, following the method in the Chef's techniques on page 536. Season with salt and pepper to taste, and nutmeg. Add the butter and egg yolk. Spread out on a baking sheet to cool. Preheat oil for deep-frying in a large saucepan, to 360°F (see page 537).

Three Mix the Parmesan with the well-drained spinach in a bowl. Add the potato, salt and black pepper and stir to combine. On a floured surface, and using floured hands, roll the mixture beneath a flat hand to form cylinders 2 1/2 inches long and 3/4 inch wide. Even up and flatten the ends.

Four Place the seasoned flour on a plate. Combine the eggs and oil in a bowl and put the bread crumbs on a large piece of waxed paper. Roll the croquettes carefully through the flour and pat off the excess. Dip them in the egg to coat thoroughly, drain off the excess and roll in the bread crumbs, lifting the edges of the paper to make it easier. Sometimes it is necessary to coat the croquettes twice in the egg and crumbs. Do this if your mixture is a little too soft to hold its shape well. Fry in batches until evenly browned and then lift out, shaking off any excess oil. Drain well on crumpled paper towels.

CHEF'S TIPS *The potato must not be too wet or the croquettes will split and absorb the oil.*

Shake off or press on excess bread crumbs or they will burn and cling to the croquettes as dark specks.

Gratin of root vegetables

*Root vegetables go well with roast meats and this
gratin (pictured top right) baked with a golden Gruyère
topping is a perfect match for a simple roast.*

Preparation time *30 minutes*
Total cooking time *45 minutes*
Serves 4

*2 tablespoons unsalted butter
1 clove garlic, minced
1 cup milk
1 cup whipping cream
1 large boiling potato, thinly sliced
pinch of freshly grated nutmeg
1 small carrot, thinly sliced
1 small rutabaga, thinly sliced
1/2 parsnip, thinly sliced
1 small turnip, thinly sliced
3 1/2 oz. Gruyère cheese, grated*

One Melt the butter in a saucepan, add the garlic and cook over low heat for 1 minute. Add the milk, cream, potato, nutmeg, a pinch of salt and some black pepper. Bring to a boil and cook, covered, for 5 minutes. Add the carrots and cook for 3 minutes, then add the rutabaga and cook for 3 minutes. Add the parsnip and cook for another 3 minutes, then finally add the turnip and cook for 2 minutes. The vegetables should be tender, but still have a little resistance when tested with the point of a sharp knife. Strain the cooking liquid from the vegetables and reserve.

Two Preheat the oven to 350°F. Butter a 6-cup shallow gratin or flameproof dish. Layer the vegetables in the prepared dish and pour over some of the reserved cooking liquid to barely cover. Sprinkle with the cheese and bake for 20–25 minutes, or until the vegetables are tender and the surface is golden. Allow the gratin to rest for 10 minutes before serving.

Pumpkin purée

*A purée works beautifully with any meat dish.
For a change, try parsnip or rutabaga
instead of pumpkin (pictured bottom right).*

Preparation time *10 minutes*
Total cooking time *30 minutes*
Serves 4

*1 x 2-lb. pumpkin, peeled and
chopped into 2-inch cubes
3 1/2 tablespoons unsalted butter,
chilled and cut into cubes
1/4 cup whipping cream
pinch of freshly grated nutmeg*

One Bring a large saucepan of salted water to a boil, add the pumpkin cubes, then reduce the heat and simmer for 15–20 minutes, or until the pumpkin is fork tender. Drain well and return the pumpkin to the saucepan. Shake the saucepan over low heat for 1 minute to dry the pumpkin.

Two Pass the pumpkin through a food mill or food processor to purée finely, then return to a clean saucepan and, over low heat, beat in the butter followed by the cream. Add the nutmeg and some salt and black pepper and serve with meat, fish or poultry.

Cauliflower Mornay

*Perfect partners, cauliflower and cheese sauce baked
in this way make a hearty winter dish that never
has the experience of being a leftover.*

Preparation time 10 minutes
Total cooking time 30 minutes
Serves 4–6

1 lb. cauliflower florets
2 tablespoons unsalted butter
1/4 cup all-purpose flour
2 cups milk
pinch of ground nutmeg
1/3 cup whipping cream
1 cup shredded Gruyère cheese
2 egg yolks

One Preheat the oven to 350°F. Put the cauliflower florets in a large saucepan of cold salted water and bring slowly to a boil. Reduce the heat and simmer for about 10 minutes, or until the cauliflower is cooked, but still slightly firm. Drain, refresh in cold water, then drain again.

Two To make the cheese sauce, melt the butter in a saucepan, stir in the flour with a wooden spoon or whisk and cook over low heat for 3 minutes. Remove from the heat and gradually stir in the milk. Return to the heat and bring to a boil, stirring constantly. Add the nutmeg and season. Stir in the cream. Remove from the heat and add 3/4 cup of the cheese and the egg yolks. Set aside. Cover the surface with plastic wrap to prevent a skin from forming.

Three Lightly brush a baking dish with butter. Pour a thin layer of the sauce into the dish, arrange the cauliflower on the sauce and pour over the remaining sauce so that it coats the cauliflower. Sprinkle with the remaining cheese and a little ground black pepper and nutmeg and bake for 15 minutes, or until the cheese is golden brown.

CHEF'S TIPS *If the sauce looks lumpy before the cream has been added, simply whisk it until smooth. Do this before adding the cheese to prevent strands of cheese from sticking to the whisk.*

Gruyère is a strong cheese, but if you prefer to use a milder type, add a little mustard to bring out the flavors.

Green beans with bacon

This dish is very popular as a vegetable on the side, served with broiled or roasted meats or chicken. The salty flavor of bacon blends perfectly with green beans.

Preparation time *10 minutes*
Total cooking time *15 minutes*
Serves 4–6

1 lb. green or yellow wax beans
1 teaspoon salt
10 oz. bacon
¼ cup unsalted butter
¼ cup finely chopped fresh parsley

One Trim the beans. Bring a large saucepan of water to a boil. Add the salt and the beans and simmer for 10 minutes, or until tender. Drain and refresh in cold water to stop the cooking process. Drain well.

Two Meanwhile, remove any rind from the bacon and discard. Cut the bacon into small, short strips. Heat a skillet, add the bacon and fry over medium heat. There is no need to add any fat, the bacon's own fat will melt into the pan as it cooks. Remove the bacon and drain on paper towels.

Three Drain the excess fat from the pan, wipe with paper towels and then melt the butter in the pan. Toss the beans in the butter, add the bacon and season with salt and pepper. As soon as they are warmed through, transfer to a serving dish, sprinkle with the parsley and serve.

CHEF'S TIPS *To maintain the green color of the beans, simultaneously plunge the salt and the beans into the boiling water. This creates a fast bubble, which helps to fix the chlorophyll.*

As a variation, substitute the bacon with two or three canned anchovy fillets. Prepare them first by soaking in milk, draining and then drying them. Finely chop them and toss in the butter.

Sautéed potatoes

This is such a simple way to prepare potatoes,
yet it remains a firm family favorite (pictured top left).

Preparation time 20 minutes
Total cooking time 20 minutes
Serves 4

3 medium baking potatoes
1/4 cup oil, for frying
3 tablespoons unsalted butter

One Peel the potatoes and cut into ½-inch cubes. Place in a bowl of cold water until ready to use.

Two Drain the potato cubes and pat them dry—this will remove any excess starch that may make the potatoes stick to the skillet.

Three Heat a large nonstick skillet over medium-high heat. Add the oil. When the oil is hot, add the dried potato cubes and stir or toss to evenly coat them with the oil. Tossing regularly, cook for 10–15 minutes, or until the potatoes are well colored all over and cooked through. Pass them through a strainer to drain off the oil.

Four Melt the butter in the same skillet, then add the potato cubes once again. Toss them in the pan until evenly coated with the butter, then season to taste with salt and freshly ground black pepper.

Mashed potatoes

There are as many versions of mashed potato as there are cooks.
This mash is wonderfully creamy (pictured bottom left).

Preparation time 10 minutes
Total cooking time 35 minutes
Serves 4

4 medium baking potatoes
1 cup milk or half-and-half
1 tablespoon unsalted butter or
margarine

One Peel the potatoes, cut into quarters and place in a large saucepan of salted water. Bring to a boil, then reduce the heat and simmer for 30–35 minutes, or until tender to the point of a knife.

Two Heat the milk or half-and-half to a boil, then remove the saucepan from the heat and set aside.

Three Drain the potatoes and transfer to a large heatproof bowl. Mash with a large fork or potato masher, gradually mixing in enough butter and hot milk to give a good consistency, ensuring there are no lumps. Season to taste with salt and freshly ground black pepper.

CHEF'S TIP *To vary the flavor, steep your favorite herbs in the hot milk, or purée and mix in other root vegetables. Olive oil can replace the butter.*

Anna potatoes

Traditionally cooked in a copper two-handled baking dish that conducts heat to give the potatoes an even brown crust, this classic French dish is a type of potato 'cake'.

Preparation time 45 minutes
Total cooking time 45 minutes
Serves 4–6

8 medium potatoes
1 cup clarified butter (see page 520)

One Preheat the oven to 425°F. Peel and trim the potatoes, then thinly slice them using a sharp knife, or a mandoline set at 1/8 inch (see Chef's techniques, page 536). Place the slices in water until ready to cook.

Two Rinse the potato slices in cold water and pat dry with a paper towel. Heat 1/4 cup of the butter in a large, nonstick skillet over medium heat. Add some potato slices—not too many; they should be able to move around easily in the pan—and roll them in the butter for a few minutes until well coated and hot. Strain the potatoes, return the excess butter to the pan, and repeat in batches until all the potato slices are done. Set aside for about 5 minutes, or until cool enough to handle.

Three Coat the bottom of a flameproof skillet with 1/4 cup of the butter. Leaving the pan over low heat, add some of the potato slices, arranging them in slightly overlapping circles. Season with salt and black pepper, then arrange a second layer of potatoes on top, this time overlapping the slices in the opposite direction. Repeat until all the slices have been used, seasoning after each layer.

Four Drizzle the remaining butter over the top, then transfer to the oven and bake for 30 minutes, or until tender to the point of a sharp knife.

Five To unmold, pour off any excess butter. Place a heatproof plate over the skillet and, in a single motion, turn it over. Serve immediately.

Provençal stuffed tomatoes

*Olive oil, garlic, parsley and tomato predominate
in the cuisine of the Provence region of the south of France,
reflecting its close proximity to Italy.*

Preparation time *30 minutes
+ 20 minutes draining*
Total cooking time *15 minutes*
Serves 4

*4 tomatoes
¼ cup extra virgin olive oil
4 cloves garlic, finely chopped
1 tablespoon chopped fresh
thyme leaves
2 tablespoons chopped fresh parsley
¾ cup fresh bread crumbs*

One Preheat the oven to 375°F. Remove the stem ends from the tomatoes. Place the tomatoes stem side down (to make the tomatoes more secure) and cut in half horizontally. Carefully remove the seeds with a teaspoon. Season with some salt and leave cut side down on paper towels to drain for 20 minutes.

Two Gently heat the olive oil until warm. Remove from the heat and add the garlic, thyme, parsley and bread crumbs. Season with salt and pepper and mix well using a wooden spoon. Season the tomato halves with pepper and fill with the bread stuffing, making a slight dome on top of each tomato half. Place in a greased baking dish and drizzle with some extra olive oil. Bake for 5–10 minutes, or until the stuffing is golden brown.

CHEF'S TIP *This recipe would also work successfully using eight small tomatoes with the tops cut off and the seeds scooped out.*

Vichy carrots

*The water used for cooking this dish should really be Vichy water,
a natural and healthy mineral water from the springs at Vichy in France.
These carrots are a colorful accompaniment to veal and chicken dishes.*

Preparation time *15–20 minutes*
Total cooking time *20–30 minutes*
Serves 4

*1 1/4 lb. carrots
2 tablespoons sugar
1/4 cup unsalted butter
1/2 cup chopped fresh parsley*

One Peel the carrots, slice thinly and put in a saucepan with enough water to barely cover. Add a pinch of salt as well as the sugar and butter and cover with a paper lid made from a round of parchment paper (see Chef's tips).

Two Cook over high heat until almost all the water has evaporated, leaving a syrupy reduction. The carrots should be tender. If not, add 1/4 cup more water and continue cooking. Toss the carrots with the butter to evenly coat them. Sprinkle with the chopped fresh parsley and serve in a deep dish.

CHEF'S TIPS *Cut the carrots into different shapes to make a more decorative and attractive presentation.*

A paper lid serves to minimize the amount of steam escaping, allowing foods to remain moist and preventing them from cooking too quickly. To make a paper lid, prepare a piece of parchment paper larger than the diameter of the saucepan. Fold in half, then in quarters and fold once again into a fan shape. To measure the diameter of the saucepan, place the point in the center of the pan and cut at the point the folded paper reaches the edge of the saucepan. Snip off the point and unfold. The paper should now be a circle the same diameter as the saucepan with a small hole in the center.

Baked eggplant

The pronounced flavor of the eggplant is often combined with tomato, garlic and herbs. These stuffed eggplants originated in Turkey as imam bayildi.

***Preparation time** 40 minutes*
***Total cooking time** 1 hour*
Serves 4

olive oil, for cooking
2 large shallots, finely chopped
1½ lb. tomatoes, peeled, seeded and diced (see page 534)
6 cloves garlic, finely chopped
small pinch of cayenne pepper
1 cup chopped fresh basil leaves
2 small eggplants
4 small tomatoes, stems removed
1 cup shredded Gruyère cheese

One Preheat the oven to 300°F. In a heavy-bottomed skillet, heat a little oil over medium heat, add the shallots and cook for 2–3 minutes without coloring. Add the diced tomato and garlic, season with salt and cayenne pepper and simmer for 15 minutes, or until thick. Mix in the chopped basil, set aside and keep warm.

Two Meanwhile, cut the eggplants in half lengthwise. Score the flesh, being careful not to cut through the skin. Rub the surface with olive oil and season with salt. Place the eggplant cut side down in a baking dish and bake for 15 minutes, or until soft. Allow to cool. Increase the temperature of the oven to 400°F.

Three Cut the small tomatoes in half from top to bottom and thinly slice into semicircles. Set aside.

Four Carefully scoop out the flesh of the cooked eggplant. Set the empty skins aside. Chop up the pulp and remove some of the liquid by cooking in a skillet for 5–10 minutes over low heat. Transfer the eggplant pulp to a bowl and mix in

half of the cooked tomato. Season with salt and black pepper and then spoon the mixture into the eggplant skins. Return the filled eggplant to the baking dish and arrange the tomato slices on top. Sprinkle with the shredded cheese and bake until golden brown.

Five Purée the remaining cooked tomato in a blender. Dilute if necessary with some water or chicken stock. Place in a small saucepan and heat through, checking the seasoning. To serve, spoon some of the tomato sauce onto the plate and arrange the eggplant on top.

Carrot purée

*For this method of cooking, the carrots
(pictured top right) should be sliced very thinly
so they will cook quickly and evenly.*

Preparation time 10 minutes
Total cooking time 20 minutes
Serves 4–6

3 tablespoons unsalted butter
3 medium carrots, thinly sliced
pinch of nutmeg or coriander

One Melt the butter in a large shallow skillet, add the carrot and season with salt and pepper. Add the nutmeg or coriander. Cover the pan with a sheet of parchment paper and a lid. It is important to cover to prevent loss of steam made by the carrots as they cook, or they will dry and turn brown.

Two Cook over low heat for 15 minutes, or until very soft and tender enough to be mashed with a fork, then remove the paper and lid. Cook, uncovered, over high heat to reduce any excess moisture, then cool slightly. Purée in a food processor until smooth. Return to the pan, adjust the seasoning to taste and reheat to serve.

Three Serve in a neat mound or use two dessertspoons to shape the purée into oval quenelles.

CHEF'S TIP *The purée may be reheated in the microwave as long as it is in a suitable container.*

Broccoli purée with blue cheese

*Puréed broccoli (pictured bottom right) goes well with almost any dish.
Add the cheese only moments before serving.*

Preparation time 10 minutes
Total cooking time 20 minutes
Serves 4–6

1 head broccoli
3 tablespoons unsalted butter
*1¹/₂ oz. blue cheese, shredded or
crumbled*

One Trim the individual broccoli stems from the main stem, discard the main stem and check that about 4 cups of broccoli remain. Wash thoroughly and drain, then trim and slice the stems very thinly, reserving the florets.

Two Melt the butter in a medium saucepan, add the sliced stems, cover with parchment paper and a lid. Cook very gently for 10 minutes until tender, but not colored. Finely chop the florets and add them to the saucepan with ½ cup water. Cook, uncovered, for 5 minutes until tender, but still bright green. Drain well, transfer to a food processor and blend until smooth. Return to the saucepan, reheat and remove from the heat to stir in the cheese. Season to taste.

Three Serve in a neat mound or use two dessertspoons to shape the purée into oval quenelles.

CHEF'S TIP *A great accompaniment to meat, fish or poultry, and especially good with steak. Do not add the cheese until just before serving or it may become stringy from overheating.*

Tortilla

This thick potato omelet is offered in slices in tapas bars and cafés all over Spain, and each region has its own variations. The original, although seemingly plain, is delicious. This is a quick recipe that can be jazzed up with extra flavors.

***Preparation time** 15 minutes
+ 25 minutes resting*
***Total cooking time** 25 minutes*
***Serves** 4–6*

*½ cup olive oil
3–4 medium potatoes, peeled and
cut into ½-inch cubes
1 large onion, thinly sliced
8 eggs*

One Heat the oil in an 8-inch flameproof skillet. Add the potato cubes and cook over medium heat, without coloring, for 7 minutes, or until tender.

Two Add the onion and cook for 7–8 minutes without coloring. Season to taste with salt and black pepper, then strain and reserve the oil. Place the potato and onion mixture in a bowl to cool for 10 minutes.

Three Beat the eggs and season to taste with salt and freshly ground black peppe. Pour the eggs over the potato and onion mixture and mix until well coated. Allow to rest for 15 minutes. Preheat the oven to 400°F.

Four In the same pan, heat 1 tablespoon of the strained oil over medium heat. Pour in the potato and egg mixture, spreading the potato evenly in the pan. Cook for 2 minutes, then transfer the pan to the oven and cook for 4–6 minutes, or until the egg sets around the edges, yet is still soft in the center.

Five Take the pan from the oven and shake it to loosen the tortilla. To turn the tortilla over, carefully slide it onto a heatproof plate. Place the skillet over the tortilla, then flip the skillet and plate

over: the cooked side of the tortilla should be nicely colored. Cook over medium heat for 2 minutes, then bake in the oven for 2 minutes more. Remove from the oven and slide onto a clean, warm serving plate. Slice into wedges and serve hot, or at room temperature on serving plates.

CHEF'S TIP *If you want to add a dash of extra flavor to the tortilla, simply sauté some bacon or sausage—such as the spicy Spanish chorizo sausage or Italian pepperoni—along with the potatoes. Alternatively, you can add some sautéed vegetables or a little grated cheese if desired.*

Barbecued marinated vegetables

*Served cold with a vinaigrette or hot straight from
the grill, these vegetables make a delicious
light dish, full of color and flavor.*

*Preparation time 20 minutes
+ 2 hours marinating
Total cooking time 40 minutes
Serves 6*

1 eggplant
2 zucchini
2 carrots
3 red bell peppers
9 button mushrooms, washed
2 sprigs of fresh thyme,
finely chopped
2 sprigs of fresh parsley,
finely chopped
2/3 cup olive oil
1 tablespoon lemon juice
1/4 cup chopped fresh basil
3 tablespoons balsamic vinegar

One Cut the eggplant, zucchini and carrots lengthwise into long slices, about 1/2 inch thick. Halve the peppers, remove the seeds and halve into quarters. Remove the mushroom stems.

Two Spread the vegetables on a baking sheet and sprinkle with salt and black pepper, and the thyme and parsley. Reserve 2 tablespoons of the olive oil and combine the rest with the lemon juice. Pour over the vegetables and sprinkle with the basil. Leave to marinate for 2 hours.

Three Heat a barbecue or broiler and brush the rack or broiler pan with the reserved oil. Slowly cook all the vegetables on both sides until tender. (If you prefer the carrots to be less crunchy, cook them for a few minutes before adding the other vegetables.)

Four Arrange the vegetables on a dish and drizzle with the balsamic vinegar.

Braised red cabbage

*This traditional dish of northern France, chou rouge à la flamande,
is an excellent accompaniment to roast pork or game.
Slow-cooking produces a wonderful result.*

Preparation time 20 minutes
Total cooking time 1 hour 45 minutes
Serves 8

1 head red cabbage
3 tablespoons unsalted butter
1 onion, sliced
2 cooking apples
2½ tablespoons white wine vinegar
1 tablespoon sugar
2 tablespoons all-purpose flour

One Preheat the oven to 325°F. Quarter the cabbage, cut out and discard the core and shred the cabbage finely. Put the cabbage in a large saucepan of boiling salted water (there should be enough water to more than cover the cabbage), bring back to a boil and drain. The cabbage will now have taken on an inky blue color. This is normal, and it will regain its color later. You may have to do this in batches, depending on the size of the saucepan.

Two Melt 1 tablespoon of the butter in a large flameproof casserole or Dutch oven, add the onion, cover and cook gently until translucent. Peel, quarter, core and slice the apples thinly before adding to the onion. Cook for a few minutes, then remove the mixture from the casserole.

Three Add the cabbage to the casserole, layering with the onion and apple mixture and sprinkling with the vinegar, sugar and 2 tablespoons of water. Season. You will see the red color return as the vinegar is added. Cover with thickly buttered parchment paper and the lid and bake for 1½ hours, or until very tender. Stir occasionally and moisten with a little extra water if necessary.

Four Soften the remaining butter in a bowl and mix in the flour. Push the cabbage to one side of the pan. There will be some liquid at the bottom of the casserole. Add a quarter of the butter and flour and stir in. The liquid will thicken slightly. Repeat on the other side. Toss together and only add more butter and flour if any watery liquid is present. A lot of flavor and seasoning is in the liquid, so it should be just thick enough to cling to the cabbage. Taste and season. The cabbage should be gently sweet and sour. It may be necessary to add a little more sugar or vinegar, to taste.

332   LE CORDON BLEU · COMPLETE COOK

Mixed beans in sweet and sour tomato

A delicious medley of haricots verts and legumes in a piquant tomato sauce. This salad can be served warm or cold and is ideal as a light lunch with some bread and cheese.

***Preparation time** 25 minutes*
***Total cooking time** 25 minutes*
Serves 4

3/4 lb. haricots verts or green beans, trimmed
1/2 cup olive oil
2 shallots, finely chopped
2 teaspoons dark brown sugar
1 clove garlic, crushed
3 tablespoons white wine vinegar
2 red chiles, seeded and finely chopped
1/2 lb. ripe tomatoes, peeled, seeded and diced (see page 534)
1 cup canned chickpeas, rinsed
1 cup canned red kidney beans, rinsed
1/2 cup cilantro, chopped
1/4 cup fresh parsley, chopped

One Bring a saucepan of salted water to a boil and cook the haricots verts for 5 minutes, or until just tender but still a little crisp. Refresh in cold water.

Two Heat 2 tablespoons of the olive oil in a large, heavy-bottomed frying pan and cook the shallots over medium heat until softened. Stir in the brown sugar, garlic, white wine vinegar and chiles and cook, stirring, for 3–4 minutes, or until the sugar is beginning to caramelize. Add the diced tomatoes, season to taste and cover the pan. Lower the heat and simmer for 10 minutes, stirring often.

Three Gently mix the beans and pulses together in a large bowl with all but 1 tablespoon of the chopped herbs, and season with salt and black pepper. Add the sweet and sour tomato mixture and the remaining olive oil to the bowl, stir gently to combine and sprinkle with the remaining herbs. Serve warm or cold.

Vegetable cakes

These pretty layered savory "cakes" make a good accompaniment to a festive dinner, or they can be prepared in advance and served on holidays with a rich tomato sauce or pesto for vegetarian guests.

*Preparation time 25 minutes
+ 30 minutes resting
Total cooking time 35 minutes
Serves 4*

*1 small thin eggplant, sliced into
1/8-inch thick rounds
1 tablespoon kosher salt
2–3 zucchini, cut into 1/4-inch-thick
diagonal slices
1/3 cup olive oil
1 teaspoon chopped fresh thyme
1 bulb fennel
1 red onion, finely sliced*

One Layer the eggplant slices in a colander, sprinkling kosher salt between the layers as they go in. Top with a plate smaller than the colander to press the slices lightly, place in a bowl and allow to rest for 30 minutes.

Two Place the zucchini in a bowl, add half the oil and the thyme and toss to coat. With a small sharp knife, remove the woody stems at the top of the fennel bulb. With a large knife, cut the bulb in half from the top and down through the root. Cut away the root from each half then cut the fennel into 1/4-inch slices.

Three Preheat the oven to 400°F. In the colander, rinse the eggplant, then dry well on paper towels. Heat a heavy-bottomed frying pan, lightly brush with some of the remaining oil and cook the eggplant for 10 minutes, or until tender. Remove from the pan and place in a bowl. Add a little more oil if necessary, then cook the onion for 2 minutes, or until tender and remove to a separate bowl. Cook the fennel slices in batches for 10 minutes, or until tender and remove to a bowl. Finally, cook the zucchini for 5 minutes, or until tender.

Four Place 4 metal rings, 4 x 1 1/4 inches, or 4 1/2-cup ramekins on a baking sheet. If using ramekins, cut rounds of aluminum foil or parchment paper and place one in the bottom of each.

Five Beginning and ending with the eggplant, fill the rings or ramekins neatly with layers of the vegetables, draining off any excess oil and seasoning with salt and black pepper between the layers. Bake for 6–8 minutes to heat through.

Six If using rings, lift the savory cakes onto a plate and carefully remove the hot metal rings. If in ramekins, unmold onto a serving plate. Serve as a side dish or as a main-course dish with a thick tomato sauce or pesto.

CHEF'S TIPS *These savory cakes can be prepared in advance and simply heated through in a preheated moderate oven when required.*

They are also excellent served hot as a first course with a beurre blanc, hollandaise sauce or a red pepper coulis. Alternatively, serve cold with a herb mayonnaise and crusty bread.

Roasted parsnips with honey and ginger

*A very popular vegetable in Ancient Greece and
during the Middle Ages and the Renaissance,
the parsnip has a lovely sweet flavor.*

Preparation time *10 minutes*
Total cooking time *20 minutes*
Serves 6

1½ lb. parsnips
¼ cup oil
1 tablespoon unsalted butter
1 tablespoon clear honey
*1 tablespoon finely grated or
chopped fresh ginger*

One Preheat the oven to 425°F. Peel and
cut the parsnips in half lengthwise, or
quarters if they are large, to make pieces
about 3 inches long and 1 inch thick.
Remove any woody cores.

Two Put the parsnips in a large saucepan
and cover with water. Add a pinch of
salt to the saucepan and bring to a boil
over high heat. Boil for 1 minute before
draining. Return the parsnips to the pan
and dry well by shaking the pan over
low heat for 1 minute.

Three Heat the oil in a roasting pan on
the stove top. Add the parsnips and cook
quickly over high heat, turning to color
evenly. Add the butter to the pan,
transfer to the oven to roast for
10 minutes. Spoon out the excess oil.

Four Add the honey and ginger, turning
the parsnips to coat evenly, and roast for
another 5 minutes.

Five Lift the parsnips out of the pan and
serve hot with pork or chicken.

Braised Belgian endive

This is a vegetable that is wonderful braised, even though it is often thought of as simply a salad ingredient.

Preparation time *15 minutes*
Total cooking time *1 hour 30 minutes*
Serves 4

1/4 cup unsalted butter
4 Belgian endives
2 cups chicken stock (see page 519) or water
1 tablespoon lemon juice
1/2 teaspoon sugar
1 teaspoon chopped fresh parsley

One Preheat the oven to 350°F. Grease a flameproof casserole with one-third of the butter. Remove any blemished outer leaves of the endives and trim and core the root ends. This removes some of the bitterness. Wash and place the endives in the casserole.

Two Add the chicken stock or water to the casserole with the lemon juice. Season lightly with salt, pepper and the sugar. Bring to a boil on the stove top. Remove and cover with buttered parchment paper and then aluminum foil or a lid. Transfer to the oven and bake for about 1–1 1/4 hours, or until the endives are tender. Remove the endives and place on a rack to drain, reserving the cooking liquid. Cook the liquid over high heat until syrupy. Set aside and keep warm.

Three Once the endives are cooled, lightly tie in the middle with some kitchen string. Heat the remaining butter in a nonstick skillet and brown the endives until nicely colored. Remove the string, place the endives in a serving dish and cover with the reduced cooking liquid. Sprinkle with the parsley.

CHEF'S TIP *Wrap bacon around the endives before tying with string.*

Ratatouille

This is a classic French dish from the sunny area of Provence using the freshest tomatoes, zucchini, eggplant, bell peppers and onions, sautéed in olive oil with herbs.

***Preparation time** 40 minutes*
***Total cooking time** 1 hour*
Serves 4

1 onion, diced
1/3 cup olive oil, for cooking
4 tomatoes, peeled, seeded and chopped (see page 534)
2 cloves garlic, chopped
1 red bell pepper, seeded and cut into short strips
1 bouquet garni (see page 520)
2 zucchini, cut into batons
2 eggplants, cut into batons
1 cup chopped fresh basil leaves

One Preheat the oven to 350°F. In a flameproof casserole or Dutch oven, cook the diced onion in a little of the olive oil over medium-low heat for 3–5 minutes, or until soft, being careful not to let the onion color. Add the tomatoes and garlic and cook for 15 minutes, stirring occasionally.

Two In a skillet, sauté the red pepper in oil for 2–3 minutes over medium-high heat. Strain off the excess oil and add to the tomato and garlic mixture with the bouquet garni.

Three Sauté the zucchini and eggplant separately in oil, for 3–4 minutes, until slightly softened. Add to the tomato mixture. Season to taste, cover with a lid or foil and bake for 30 minutes.

Four Just before serving, remove the bouquet garni and stir in the chopped fresh basil leaves.

CHEF'S TIP *This dish can also be made on the stove top. Cook over low heat, stirring often.*

LE CORDON BLEU ✿ COMPLETE COOK

Gratin dauphinois

*This potato dish has many versions, some with onion or other vegetables added,
some with stock and different herbs. Seasoning, cheese, cream and garlic are the key
to making this particular version successful. Experiment to suit your own taste.*

Preparation time *30 minutes*
Total cooking time *1 hour*
Serves *4–6*

1 lb. potatoes
2 cups milk
freshly grated nutmeg
⅓ cup whipping cream
1 clove garlic, finely chopped
1 cup shredded Gruyère cheese

One Preheat the oven to 325°F.

Two Thinly slice the potatoes. Place in a saucepan, cover with the milk and season with some salt, freshly ground black pepper and grated nutmeg.

Three Bring to a simmer over medium-low heat and simmer until the potato is almost cooked but still firm. Strain and set the milk aside.

Four Rub an 8 x 6½-inch oblong baking dish with some butter. Arrange the potatoes in even layers in the dish.

Five Reheat the milk and allow to simmer for a few minutes. Add the cream and garlic, bring back to a simmer and check the seasoning. Simmer for a few minutes, then pour over the potatoes. Sprinkle with the shredded cheese and bake for 35–45 minutes, or until the potatoes are tender and the top is lightly browned.

CHEF'S TIP *When making a sauce to accompany a bland vegetable such as potatoes, be sure to season it well.*

sauces

White sauce

*Create a variety of sauces by adding flavors
to this basic sauce, pictured here with
broccoli and cauliflower (top right).*

Preparation time 5 minutes
Total cooking time 10 minutes
Makes approximately 2¹/4 cups

2 tablespoons unsalted butter
¹/4 cup all-purpose flour
2 cups milk
small pinch of ground nutmeg

One Melt the butter in a heavy-bottomed saucepan over medium-low heat. Sprinkle the flour over the butter and cook for 1–2 minutes without allowing it to color, stirring constantly with a wooden spoon.

Two Remove the saucepan from the heat and slowly add the milk, whisking to prevent lumps. Return to medium heat and bring to a boil, stirring constantly. Cook for 3–4 minutes, or until the sauce coats the back of a spoon. If the sauce has lumps, pass it through a fine strainer and reheat in a clean saucepan. Season with salt, pepper and nutmeg. Serve hot.

CHEF'S TIP *Flavor the sauce by adding an onion studded with cloves to the milk, then warming the milk through.*

Mornay sauce

*A white sauce enriched with cheese and egg yolks makes
a perfect topping for the scallops (pictured bottom right).
To finish, simply flash under the broiler until golden brown.*

Preparation time 10 minutes
Total cooking time 15 minutes
Makes approximately 2¹/4 cups

2 tablespoons unsalted butter
¹/4 cup all-purpose flour
2 cups milk
2 egg yolks
³/4 cup shredded Gruyère cheese
pinch of ground nutmeg

One Melt the butter in a heavy-bottomed saucepan over medium-low heat. Sprinkle the flour over the butter and cook for 1–2 minutes without allowing it to color, stirring constantly with a wooden spoon.

Two Remove the saucepan from the heat and slowly add the milk, whisking to prevent lumps. Return to medium heat and bring to a boil, stirring constantly. Cook for 3–4 minutes, or until the sauce coats the back of a spoon. If the sauce has lumps, pass it through a fine strainer and reheat in a clean saucepan.

Three Remove from the stove, add the yolks and cheese off the heat and mix. Season with salt, pepper and nutmeg.

LE CORDON BLEU ❧ COMPLETE COOK

LE CORDON BLEU COMPLETE COOK

Mayonnaise

Mayonnaise can be used as a sauce or a salad dressing. It is shown here (top left) with hard-boiled eggs, pumpernickel, olives, capers and pickles. See page 521 for step-by-step instructions to accompany this recipe.

Preparation time 10 minutes
Total cooking time None
Makes approximately 1 3/4 cups

2 egg yolks
ground white pepper, to taste
1–1 1/4 cups peanut or olive oil
1 tablespoon white wine vinegar
3 tablespoons Dijon mustard, or
1 heaping teaspoon mustard powder

One Bring all the ingredients to room temperature. Place a large deep bowl on a damp kitchen towel to prevent it moving. Put the egg yolks, ground white pepper to taste and a teaspoon of salt in the bowl and mix with a hand whisk or electric mixer.

Two Put the oil in a pitcher that is easy to pour from. While whisking constantly, pour a steady thin stream of oil into the mixture. Begin with a small amount and stop pouring periodically to allow each addition to emulsify to a thick cream mixture. Continue until a third of the oil has been added and the mayonnaise has begun to thicken.

Three Add the vinegar to make the texture slightly thinner. Continue adding the oil and then stir in the mustard.

Four Adjust the flavor of the mayonnaise by adding more vinegar, salt or pepper. Whisk in 1–2 tablespoons of boiling water if it curdles or separates.

Five The mayonnaise can be stored for up to a week in the refrigerator. Use it as a base for a number of sauces, such as Thousand Island dressing and tartar sauce.

Thousand Island dressing

This creamy dressing is full of flavor and often served over a chef's salad. Shown here (bottom left) with salad leaves and shrimp, you could also use it in sandwiches or with burgers.

Preparation time 10 minutes
+ 20 minutes refrigeration
Total cooking time None
Makes approximately 1 1/3 cups

1 cup mayonnaise
1/3 cup ketchup
1/3 cup pepper relish or chili sauce
1 small onion, grated
1 red or green bell pepper, seeded and finely chopped
1 teaspoon Worcestershire sauce, or to taste
1 teaspoon Tabasco sauce, or to taste
1 teaspoon brandy, or to taste

One Stir together the mayonnaise, ketchup and pepper relish. Stir in the onion, bell pepper, Worcestershire sauce, Tabasco and brandy, each to taste.

Two Cover the bowl with plastic wrap and refrigerate until needed. Make the dressing at least 20 minutes ahead of serving and keep covered in the refrigerator to allow all the different flavors to develop.

CHEF'S TIP *Try serving this dressing on a crisp salad of iceberg lettuce. To turn the salad into a meal, add chilled cooked shrimp and large garlicky croutons.*

Jus

A jus is gravy made from the sticky caramelized juices left in the pan after roasting veal, poultry, lamb or beef. We have shown it with lamb and steamed Asian greens (pictured top right).

Preparation time 15 minutes
Total cooking time 30 minutes
Makes approximately 1 cup

1 lb. roast of meat or poultry
2 cups brown stock for dark meats or
chicken stock for lighter meats
(see pages 518–9)
1 carrot, chopped
1 onion, chopped
1 stalk celery, chopped
1 leek, chopped
1 bay leaf
2 sprigs of fresh thyme
3 peppercorns

One When the meat or poultry is cooked, remove it from the roasting pan and allow it to rest for 20 minutes. If there is a lot of fat in the pan, spoon off most of it, leaving enough to fry the vegetables. In a saucepan, heat the stock over medium heat.

Two Add the carrot, onion, celery and leek to the roasting pan and cook gently on top of the stove for 5 minutes, stirring constantly with a wooden spoon to prevent burning, until golden brown. Spoon off the excess fat from the pan and add the bay leaf, thyme and peppercorns. Stir in some of the hot stock, scraping the bottom of the pan with a wooden spoon constantly until the stock boils.

Three Pour in the remaining stock and bring to a boil. Reduce the heat to a simmer and cook for 5–10 minutes, or until reduced by half, skimming the surface of impurities or fat throughout cooking. Season to taste with salt and pepper and strain the jus into a gravy boat. Serve immediately.

Thickened pan gravy

This recipe can be made when roasting meats such as beef or chicken. It is shown with roast beef, Yorkshire pudding, potatoes and vegetables (pictured bottom right).

Preparation time 15 minutes
Total cooking time 1–2 hours, depending on meat chosen
Makes approximately 1¼ cups

oil, for cooking
meat or poultry of your choice, for roasting
½ onion, cut into large cubes
1 small carrot, cut into large cubes
½ stalk celery, cut into large pieces
2 cloves garlic, lightly crushed
1 bay leaf
2 sprigs of fresh thyme
¼ cup all-purpose flour
2 cups brown stock for dark meats or chicken stock for lighter meats
(see pages 518–9)

One Heat ¼ inch of oil in a roasting pan on top of the stove. Add the meat and turn and baste for about 5 minutes to seal all sides. Remove the meat from the pan. Add the vegetables, garlic and herbs to the pan. Place the meat over the vegetables and roast at the temperature appropriate for the meat.

Two When the meat is cooked, remove and keep it warm. Drain off any fat, leaving the juices and sediment behind with the vegetables. If necessary, add more color to the vegetables by frying them briefly on top of the stove in the roasting pan or returning to the oven to roast.

Three Stir in the flour and cook for 1 minute over low heat. Remove from the heat and slowly add the stock, stirring to prevent lumps from forming. Return to medium heat and stir until boiling. Lower the heat and simmer for 20 minutes, skimming impurities and fat occasionally, then strain and season. Serve hot.

Mousseline sauce

An easy but delicious sauce, shown here (top right)
with steamed beans and poached white fish fillet.

Preparation time 15 minutes
Total cooking time 5 minutes
Makes approximately 2 cups

3/4 cup clarified butter
(see page 520)
3 egg yolks
small pinch of cayenne pepper
juice of 1/2 lemon
2 tablespoons whipping cream

One Melt the butter in a small saucepan. Place the egg yolks and 3 tablespoons of water in the top of a double boiler and whisk until foamy. Place the insert over barely simmering water and whisk until thick and the mixture leaves a trail on the surface when the whisk is lifted.

Two Remove the insert from the water and gradually add the melted butter, whisking constantly. When all the butter is incorporated, season with cayenne pepper, lemon juice and salt. Keep the sauce warm over the saucepan of warm water off the heat.

Three Beat the cream until the trail made by the whisk or beaters can be seen, but when the bowl is tilted the cream runs thickly. Fold the cream lightly into the sauce. This sauce is excellent with poached fish or asparagus. Mousseline sauce is always served warm.

CHEF'S TIP *At no time must this sauce be allowed to get too hot or the yolks will cook and separate from the butter. To remedy if this happens, remove the insert from the water and try adding a few drops of cold water or a chip of ice and then whisking vigorously.*

Béarnaise sauce

This creamy, tangy sauce is pictured (bottom right) with
filet mignon, potatoes and baby cauliflower.

Preparation time 20 minutes
Total cooking time 10 minutes
Makes approximately 1 1/2 cups

1 cup clarified butter (see page 520)
2 tablespoons fresh tarragon,
coarsely chopped
2 tablespoons fresh chervil,
coarsely chopped
1 shallot, finely chopped
4 peppercorns, crushed coarsely
under a heavy saucepan
1/3 cup white wine vinegar
6 egg yolks
pinch of cayenne pepper

One Melt the butter in a small saucepan. Set aside 1 tablespoon tarragon and 1/2 tablespoon chervil. Place the shallot and peppercorns in a separate small saucepan with the vinegar and remaining tarragon and chervil. Bring to a boil and simmer for 4–6 minutes, or until the liquid has reduced by three-quarters.

Two Transfer the liquid to the top of a double boiler over barely simmering water. Add the egg yolks and whisk until thick and the mixture leaves a trail on the surface when the whisk is lifted up from it.

Three Remove the insert from the water and gradually pour in the butter, whisking constantly, until all the butter in incorporated. Strain, then season with salt and cayenne pepper. Add the reserved tarragon and chervil just before serving. Serve lukewarm, don't overheat. If the sauce separates, whisk in a few drops of cold water or chips of ice to restore consistency. The sauce may be kept warm, covered with plastic wrap, over the saucepan of warm water.

White wine sauce

*This elegant sauce is shown here (top left) with poached
white fish and vegetables. It is also delicious with chicken.*

Preparation time 10 minutes
Total cooking time 40 minutes
Makes approximately 1¼ cups

1 tablespoon unsalted butter
3 shallots, finely chopped
1¼ cups white wine
1¼ cups chicken or fish stock
(see page 519)
1¾ cups whipping cream

One Melt the butter in a heavy-bottomed saucepan over low heat. Gently cook the shallots in the saucepan, without coloring, until soft and translucent.

Two Pour in the white wine, scraping the bottom of the saucepan with a wooden spoon. Turn up the heat and boil until the liquid has reduced by half. Add the stock and boil until the liquid has reduced to ⅓ cup.

Three Stir in the cream and continue to reduce the sauce until it is thick enough to coat the back of a spoon.

Four Pass the sauce through a fine strainer if you wish. Season and serve warm. It may be kept warm in the top of a double boiler over barely simmering water for up to half an hour. Do not allow the water to boil at this stage or the sauce may separate.

CHEF'S TIPS *Use a stock to complement the dish with which you serve it, for example, a chicken stock for chicken dishes.*

To prevent a skin from forming on the sauce while keeping it hot, cover the surface directly with plastic wrap.

Green peppercorn sauce

*This pungent peppery sauce, laced with brandy,
is pictured (bottom left) with steak and new potatoes.*

Preparation time 10 minutes
Total cooking time 15 minutes
Makes approximately ¾ cup

2 tablespoons drained green
peppercorns
⅓ cup brandy
1¼ cups brown or lamb stock
(see page 518)
⅓ cup whipping cream

One Place the peppercorns in a heavy-bottomed saucepan and, at a very low heat, warm through for 1–2 minutes, until dry, being careful not to burn them. Coarsely break the peppercorns against the sides of the saucepan using the back of a wooden spoon.

Two Pour the brandy into the saucepan, turn up the heat and quickly boil for 1–2 minutes, or until the brandy has evaporated. Stir in the stock, bring to a boil and boil for 5 minutes, or until the liquid has reduced by one-quarter.

Three Add the cream and continue to reduce over high heat until the sauce coats the back of the spoon. Season to taste and serve immediately with broiled or pan-fried meat such as steak or chops.

CHEF'S TIP *This sauce has quite a strong peppery taste because the green peppercorns are cooked in the sauce from the beginning. If you prefer a burst of flavor from each individual pepper-corn, proceed with steps 1 and 2 up to evaporating the brandy. In a separate saucepan, reduce the stock and cream, then add to the peppercorns and brandy. Stir and season to taste.*

Beurre fondu

The liquid used to make this classic sauce can be varied, depending on what you are intending to eat with it. It can be served with vegetables, chicken or fish. Here it is pictured (top right) with a selection of vegetables.

Preparation time 5–7 minutes
Total cooking time 10 minutes
Makes approximately 1 cup

3 tablespoons water, dry white wine or chicken stock (see page 519)
3/4 cup unsalted butter, cut into small cubes and chilled
lemon juice, to taste

One Place the liquid (water, dry white wine or chicken stock) into a small saucepan and bring to a boil.

Two While the liquid is simmering, use a whisk or an electric mixer to beat in the cubes of butter, a few at a time, to obtain a smooth consistency. Remove the saucepan from the heat and season to taste with some lemon juice, salt and pepper. Serve the sauce immediately, or keep it warm (not hot), covered with plastic wrap, in the top of a double boiler over warm water for up to 30 minutes before use.

CHEF'S TIP *If the sauce becomes too cold, it will set. Warm it by stirring over a saucepan of hot water. If it becomes too hot, it will separate. Remove the insert from the water and stir in a chip of ice or a few drops of cold water.*

Beurre blanc

Another exquisite classic, seasoned with shallots, that is ideal to serve with fish such as the poached salmon steak shown in the picture (bottom right).

Preparation time 10 minutes
Total cooking time 25 minutes
Makes approximately 1 cup

2 large shallots, very finely chopped
1/3 cup white wine vinegar
1/3 cup dry white wine
3/4 cup unsalted butter, cut into small cubes and chilled

One Add the shallots, white wine vinegar and white wine to a small wide-bottomed saucepan and heat over medium heat until the liquid has evaporated to 2 tablespoons.

Two As soon as the liquid boils, reduce the heat to very low and whisk in the butter, piece by piece. Whisk constantly to achieve a smooth and pale sauce. Season to taste with salt and pepper. Serve immediately, or transfer the sauce to the top of a double boiler, cover with plastic wrap and place over warm water until ready to serve. You may wish to strain the sauce for a smoother consistency. Serve with either fish or chicken dishes.

CHEF'S TIP *Try adding a pinch of saffron threads with the wine. Also, try adding finely grated orange, lime or lemon zest or a small amount of chopped herbs such as tarragon, chives or dill.*

Bread sauce

*A classic accompaniment to roast chicken, turkey or game,
this delicately flavored sauce is a favorite of the English.
It is shown here with turkey and vegetables (top left).*

*Preparation time 5 minutes +
15 minutes resting*
Total cooking time 15 minutes
Makes approximately 1 cup

1³/4 cups milk
1 small onion or 2 large shallots
8 whole cloves
2 bay leaves
1¹/2 cups fresh white bread crumbs

One Pour the milk into a saucepan and place the saucepan over medium heat. Stud the onion or shallots with the cloves and add to the milk with the bay leaves. Bring slowly to a boil. Remove from the heat, cover and set aside for 15 minutes to allow the flavors to infuse into the milk.

Two Strain the milk through a fine strainer and discard all the flavoring ingredients. Gradually add the bread crumbs to the milk, whisking constantly, until the sauce has thickened to a thick pouring consistency. Season to taste with salt and pepper.

Three The sauce may be made a day in advance, although some additional milk should be added when reheating because the bread crumbs will have absorbed more milk overnight. Serve the sauce warm from a gravy boat.

CHEF'S TIP *You can also add a pinch of nutmeg or infuse the milk with other flavors such as peppercorns. Stir in a few raisins if serving the sauce with game. Stir in a little cream or a tablespoon of butter at the end for a richer sauce.*

Rouille

*This is the delicious traditional accompaniment
for the bouillabaisse shown here (bottom left).*

Preparation time 20 minutes
Total cooking time 1 hour 20 minutes
Makes approximately 1¹/4 cups

1 medium baking potato
1 red bell pepper
1 egg yolk
1 teaspoon tomato paste
1 clove garlic, peeled
¹/2 cup olive oil
pinch of cayenne pepper

One Preheat the oven to 350°F. Place the potato on a baking sheet and pierce it several times with a fork. Bake for 1 hour, or until tender when tested with the point of a small knife. Alternatively, pierce the potato all over, wrap in a paper towel and microwave on high for 4–6 minutes, turning halfway through cooking. When cool enough to handle, cut in half and scoop out the flesh into a food processor.

Two Cut the bell pepper in half and remove the seeds and membrane. Lightly oil the skin and cook under a preheated broiler skin side up until the skin is blistered and blackened. Alternatively, bake for 15 minutes. Place in a plastic bag and when cool, peel off the skin. Add the flesh to the food processor with the egg yolk, tomato paste and garlic. Blend until smooth.

Three While the machine is running, gradually pour in the oil in a thin steady stream until well incorporated. Season with salt, pepper and cayenne pepper, remembering that the rouille should be quite fiery. Serve in a bowl or spread onto crisp bread croûtes. If serving as an accompaniment to a bouillabaisse, place a spoonful in the center of each serving.

Bordelaise sauce

A sauce from the Bordeaux region of France, traditionally made with wine, shallots and bone marrow. The bone marrow in this particular recipe, however, is optional; the sauce is also delicious without it. It is pictured here (top right) with grilled steak.

Preparation time 10 minutes
Total cooking time 20 minutes
Makes approximately 1 cup

3/4 lb. beef marrow bone (shank), cut into 4-inch pieces, optional
4 shallots, very finely chopped
6 peppercorns
1 sprig of fresh thyme
1/2 bay leaf
1 1/2 cups red wine
1 3/4 cups brown veal stock (see page 518)
1 tablespoon unsalted butter, cut into pieces and chilled

One If using the marrow bone, prepare it by placing the pieces of bone in enough cold water to cover, then simmer for 5 minutes, or until the marrow slips out easily. Thinly slice the marrow.

Two Place the shallots in a wide-bottomed saucepan with the peppercorns, thyme and bay leaf. Stir in the red wine and bring to a boil. Reduce by simmering briskly for about 3 minutes, or until the liquid has evaporated and the pan is almost dry.

Three Stir in the veal stock, scraping the bottom of the saucepan with a wooden spoon, and return to a boil. Reduce the heat and simmer for 10 minutes, or until the sauce is reduced to 1 cup. Skim the surface of the sauce occasionally. Season to taste and skim the surface of the sauce again. Strain through a fine strainer before whisking in the butter, piece by piece, until the sauce has thickened slightly. Finish by adding the bone marrow, reheated by simmering in water or tossing in a hot skillet. Serve hot.

Shellfish sauce

With similar ingredients to those used in a bisque, this sauce is perfect with all types of shellfish, especially lobster as shown (bottom right).

Preparation time 20 minutes
Total cooking time 1 hour
Makes approximately 1 1/3 cups

vegetable oil, for cooking
2 cloves garlic, lightly crushed
1/2 onion, coarsely diced
1 small carrot, coarsely diced
1 stalk celery, chopped
1 bay leaf
2 sprigs of fresh thyme
1 lb. seafood shells such as crab, lobster or shrimp shells
1/3 cup white wine
1/4 cup brandy
1/4 cup all-purpose flour
2 tablespoons tomato paste

2 small tomatoes, stems removed, halved and seeded
1 quart fish stock (see page 519)
1/4 cup whipping cream, optional

One Heat the oil and garlic gently in a large deep saucepan. Add the vegetables and cook, stirring occasionally, until the vegetables are soft and have become lightly colored.

Two Stir in the bay leaf, thyme and shells. Pour in the wine and brandy, scraping the bottom of the saucepan to lift all the juices. Cook until the saucepan is nearly dry. Sprinkle the flour in and stir in the tomato paste and

tomatoes. Add the stock and stir until boiling. Reduce the heat and simmer for 30–40 minutes, stirring occasionally.

Three Strain into a clean saucepan and keep warm. Season with salt and pepper and add the cream, if using. Serve hot.

Sauce verte

*This colorful, mayonnaise-based sauce complements dishes
such as the poached salmon fillet shown here (top left).*

Preparation time 20 minutes
Total cooking time 15 minutes
Makes approximately 1¹/₂ cups

1 cup firmly packed young
spinach leaves
3 tablespoons fresh tarragon leaves
1 teaspoon chopped fresh chives
³/₄ cup chopped fresh chervil or parsley
1²/₃ cups trimmed watercress leaves
1 clove garlic, coarsely chopped
1 cup mayonnaise

One Wash the spinach leaves thoroughly in cold water until all traces of sand or dirt are removed. Drain. Wash the herbs thoroughly and drain.

Two Combine all the greenery in a food processor with the garlic and 2 tablespoons water. Purée until fine.

Three Pour the mixture into a heavy-bottomed saucepan, heat gently to simmering and cook until the mixture appears to be dry and looks slightly separated. Pass immediately through a cheesecloth-lined strainer. Cool a little until you can bring the ends of the cheesecloth together and twist to squeeze out any remaining moisture. Discard the liquid.

Four In a bowl, combine a small amount of the mayonnaise with the dry purée to lighten it. Add to the remainder of the mayonnaise to make a bright green sauce. Taste and season. Serve cold with salads, cold poached poultry and fish, soups and terrines.

Marie Rose sauce

*Adjust the flavorings in this sauce to your own taste
and serve with your favorite seafood, such as the
broiled scallops and shrimp pictured (bottom left).*

Preparation time 5 minutes
Total cooking time None
Makes approximately 1¹/₃ cups

1 cup mayonnaise
¹/₃ cup ketchup
Worcestershire sauce, to taste
Tabasco sauce, to taste
brandy, to taste

One Stir the mayonnaise and ketchup together in a small bowl. Add a few drops each of Worcestershire sauce, Tabasco sauce and brandy and stir briefly to combine.

Two Cover the sauce with plastic wrap and chill in the refrigerator. Serve with seafood of your choice.

Rémoulade sauce

This sauce is traditionally served with grated celery root but it is also delicious with cold meats such as the ham, turkey and pastrami shown here (top right).

Preparation time 10 minutes
+ 10 minutes refrigeration
+ 15 minutes soaking
Total cooking time None
Makes approximately 1¼ cups

3 canned anchovy fillets
¼ cup milk
1 cup mayonnaise
2 teaspoons Dijon mustard
1 tablespoon drained capers, chopped
3 tablespoons chopped dill
or sweet pickles

One Place the anchovy fillets in a small bowl, soak in the milk for 15 minutes, then drain. Discard the milk and finely chop the anchovies.

Two Stir the mayonnaise in a small bowl with the chopped anchovies and mustard until combined. Mix the capers and the pickles into the sauce.

Three Cover with plastic wrap and place in the refrigerator to chill for 10 minutes, or until required for serving. Serve the rémoulade sauce with broiled fish, shredded raw celery root or cold meats.

Classic vinaigrette

A classic vinaigrette may be used to add a tang to all types of salads or vegetables. Here it is shown simply with mixed salad leaves (pictured bottom right).

Preparation time 5 minutes
Total cooking time None
Makes approximately 1 cup

2 tablespoons Dijon mustard
3 tablespoons white wine vinegar
¾ cup olive oil or good-quality salad oil

One Whisk together the mustard and vinegar in a bowl and season with salt and black pepper to taste.

Two Slowly drizzle in the oil, whisking constantly. This will result in an emulsification, giving a thick smooth texture, rather than the oil separating and sitting on top. If the vinaigrette is too sharp for your taste, add a little more oil.

Three The vinaigrette may be kept at room temperature in a sealed container and out of direct sunlight for up to 1 week before serving.

CHEF'S TIP *As a rule of thumb, the guide for vinaigrettes is one part acid (wine vinegar or lemon juice) to four parts oil.*

LE CORDON BLEU ❧ COMPLETE COOK

Tomato sauce

This excellent tomato sauce, full of flavor, is shown here (top left)
with deep-fried battered fish, but it would also
be delicious served with burgers or pasta.

Preparation time 20 minutes
Total cooking time 45 minutes
Makes approximately 1¾ cups

3 tablespoons olive oil
2 tablespoons tomato paste
⅔ cup diced carrots
⅔ cup diced onions
⅔ cup diced bacon
12 very ripe tomatoes, peeled, seeded
and diced (see page 534) or
4 x 16-oz. cans tomatoes,
drained and coarsely chopped
4 sprigs of fresh thyme
2 bay leaves
small pinch of cayenne pepper

One Heat the olive oil in a saucepan over medium heat. Stir the tomato paste into the oil and cook for 30 seconds, stirring constantly with a wooden spoon to prevent burning. Stir in the carrots, onions and bacon and cook gently without coloring for another 10 minutes, or until the vegetables are tender.

Two Add the tomatoes, thyme and bay leaves to the saucepan and gently cook for 30 minutes (longer if using canned tomatoes), stirring occasionally. Pass through a coarse strainer, pressing with a wooden spoon to extract as much liquid and pulp as possible. Discard the ingredients in the strainer. Season with salt and cayenne pepper and serve hot.

Apple sauce

The tartness of this sauce is the perfect accompaniment to roast pork,
as pictured (bottom left), and also for more fatty meats, such as duck or goose.

Preparation time 15 minutes
Total cooking time 15 minutes
Makes approximately 2 cups

4 medium–large tart cooking apples,
peeled and cut into small cubes
pinch of cinnamon or cumin
2 teaspoons sugar

One Combine the apple, cinnamon or cumin and sugar in a saucepan and add enough water to barely cover the bottom of the saucepan. Cover with parchment paper and a lid and cook over low–medium heat for 10–15 minutes, or until the apples have broken down to a purée. You may need to mash the apples with a fork or push through a strainer to remove any lumps.

Two If a runnier consistency is required, add some water towards the end of cooking. Also, you may adjust the sweetness with more sugar to taste. Serve hot or cold.

Three To make in the microwave, place the apples in a large microwave-safe dish with the cinnamon or cumin and sugar. Microwave on high for about 4 minutes, or until the apples break down to a purée when pressed against the side of the dish with a fork.

Hollandaise sauce

This smooth, butter-based basic sauce is famed for serving with asparagus, as shown. See page 523 for step-by-step instructions to accompany this recipe.

Preparation time *10 minutes*
Total cooking time *10 minutes*
**Makes approximately 2 cups*

*³/₄ cup clarified butter
(see page 520)
3 egg yolks, at room temperature
pinch of cayenne pepper
(see Chef's tips)
1 teaspoon lemon juice*

One Melt the butter in a small saucepan. Place the egg yolks and ¼ cup water in the top of a double boiler and whisk until foamy. Place over barely simmering water and continue whisking until thick and the mixture leaves a trail on the surface when the whisk is lifted.

Two Gradually add the butter to the sauce, whisking constantly. When all the butter is incorporated, strain the sauce into a gravy boat and season with salt to taste, cayenne pepper and lemon juice. Serve immediately.

Three Keep the sauce warm by leaving the sauce in the insert and covering the surface directly with plastic wrap. Place the insert over the pan of warm water.

CHEF'S TIPS *If the sauce becomes too cold, it will set. Warm it by increasing the heat under the saucepan of hot water. If it becomes too hot, it will separate. Remove the insert from the water and stir in a chip of ice or a few drops of cold water.*

When adding the cayenne pepper, measure out small amounts at a time using the tip of a knife. Avoid using your fingertips to measure it as the residual cayenne pepper can cause discomfort if accidentally rubbed into the eyes or onto the lips.

LE CORDON BLEU COMPLETE COOK

Crème anglaise

A rich stirred custard with a light consistency that is traditionally flavored with vanilla. Serve hot or cold to accompany all types of desserts, such as the poached peach shown in the picture.

Preparation time 5 minutes
Total cooking time 20 minutes
Makes approximately 1⅓ cups

1 cup milk
1 vanilla bean,
split lengthwise
3 egg yolks
2 tablespoons sugar

One Pour the milk into a deep, heavy-bottomed saucepan over medium heat. Scrape the seeds from the vanilla bean and add to the milk with the bean. Slowly bring to a boil, then remove from the heat and let rest to allow the flavor of the vanilla to infuse into the milk.

Two In a bowl, using a wooden spoon, beat together the egg yolks and the sugar until pale and thick. Pour the hot milk onto the yolks and mix well. Pour the mixture back into a clean saucepan and cook over very low heat, stirring constantly, for 5 minutes, or until it begins to thicken and coats the back of a spoon. If the mixture is getting too hot, remove the saucepan from the heat for a few seconds and continue to stir. Do not allow it to boil. Strain into a bowl and discard the vanilla bean. If serving cold, allow the custard to cool before chilling in the refrigerator. To reheat the sauce, transfer to the top of a double boiler and stir constantly over a saucepan of hot water, taking care not to overheat.

CHEF'S TIPS This custard sauce can be kept in the refrigerator for up to 3 days in a sealed container.

Take extra care when cooking the basic mixture. If the heat is too high, the mixture will cook too quickly around the sides of the saucepan and curdle or separate as the egg yolks become overcooked and "scramble" in the milk. The sauce may be saved by adding a dash of cold milk and rapidly whisking, which releases the heat as quickly as possible to reduce any further curdling. If the sauce has curdled and been saved in this way, it may be slightly lumpy and need to be passed through a strainer before using.

Fruit coulis

*Make this fabulous fruit sauce using any berries
in season. Ideal for serving with any dessert,
ice cream or sorbet (as pictured top right).*

Preparation time 5 minutes
Total cooking time 5 minutes
Makes approximately 1 cup

2 cups firm ripe raspberries
1/2 cup sugar
juice of 1/2 lemon
*alcohol or liqueur of your choice (see
Chef's tips)*

One Prepare the fruit by removing any that is bruised or overripe.

Two Combine the raspberries in a medium saucepan with the sugar and lemon juice and bring to a boil to soften the berries slightly. Remove from the heat and allow to cool.

Three Transfer to a food processor and blend to a smooth purée. Pass through a fine strainer to remove the seeds. At this stage your favorite alcohol can be added to taste. This fruit sauce can be kept in a covered container in the refrigerator for up to 1 week and should be served cold.

CHEF'S TIPS *Try Kirsch, Calvados, eau de vie de poivre, or Cointreau.*

When fresh berries are not available, use frozen ones instead. Thaw them before use. You may need to adjust the sugar content accordingly.

A quick, no cooking method if the fruit is very soft and will purée easily is to process with confectioners' sugar, strain and then add the lemon juice.

Orange and Grand Marnier sauce

*Crêpes or ice cream can be dressed up with this
sophisticated tangy sauce (pictured bottom right).*

Preparation time 10–15 minutes
Total cooking time 20 minutes
Makes approximately 1 1/4 cups

1 cup fresh orange juice
2 tablespoons sugar
1 teaspoon finely grated orange zest
*3/4 cup unsalted butter, cut into small
cubes and chilled*
*1/4 cup Grand Marnier, Cognac
or Cointreau*

One Bring the orange juice, sugar and orange zest slowly to a boil in a saucepan. Continue to boil the mixture, stirring occasionally, until the liquid becomes syrupy.

Two Whisk the butter into the boiling liquid, piece by piece, until a smooth consistency is obtained. Remove the pan from the heat and add the liqueur to taste. Serve the sauce immediately or keep it warm (not hot) for no more than about 30 minutes before use in the top of a double boiler over hot water.

CHEF'S TIP *If the sauce becomes too cold, it will set. If it is too hot, it will separate. To rescue the sauce from both problems, melt the former to a lukewarm heat and cool the latter to the same temperature. You can do this by bringing a small amount of water or orange juice to a boil, then whisking in a small amount of hard butter to obtain a smooth consistency. Slowly add either of the problem sauces to this mixture, whisking constantly.*

Chocolate sauce

*This is a favorite accompaniment for many desserts
and fruits, such as the poached pear and
vanilla ice cream shown here (top left).*

Preparation time 10 minutes
Total cooking time 20 minutes
Makes approximately 1 1/4 cups

3/4 cup sugar
2/3 cup chopped semi-sweet chocolate
*1/4 cup good-quality unsweetened
cocoa, sifted*

One Combine 1 1/4 cups of water with the sugar and chopped chocolate in a medium saucepan and slowly bring to a boil, stirring constantly. Remove from the heat.

Two In a bowl, mix the cocoa and 3 tablespoons water to a smooth paste. Pour this into the saucepan over medium heat and bring back to a boil, whisking vigorously and constantly. Simmer, uncovered, for 5–10 minutes, until the sauce coats the back of a spoon. Do not allow the sauce to boil over. Strain and allow to cool a little.

CHEF'S TIP *This chocolate sauce may be served hot or cold and keeps well for up to 1 week if stored in an airtight container in the refrigerator. To reheat, stir in the top of a double boiler, over hot water.*

Butterscotch sauce

*A very rich sauce ideal to serve hot with ice cream.
It also works particularly well with waffles (pictured bottom left).*

Preparation time 5 minutes
Total cooking time 15 minutes
Makes approximately 1 1/4 cups

1 vanilla bean, split lengthwise
2 cups whipping cream
3/4 cup sugar

One Scrape the seeds from the vanilla bean and add with the bean to a saucepan with the cream. Bring slowly to a boil, remove from the heat and allow the flavors to infuse into the cream, then strain and discard the vanilla bean.

Two In a separate heavy-bottomed saucepan and using a wooden spoon, stir half the sugar constantly over medium heat, until the sugar has melted. Add the remaining sugar and cook until the sugar is fluid and light golden.

Three Remove from the heat and add the cream in a slow steady stream, stirring constantly. Be careful as the sugar will splatter when the liquid is added. When all the cream has been incorporated, return to a boil and cook, stirring, until the sauce coats the back of the spoon. If you have a few lumps of sugar left in the bottom of the pan simply pass the liquid through a wire strainer. This sauce may be served either hot or cold.

CHEF'S TIP *For an adult version of the sauce, try adding a little malt whiskey to taste. You could also add a little espresso coffee to taste.*

Whiskey sauce

This is a great sauce (shown in pitcher, right) for Christmas puddings and desserts, flavored with vanilla and whiskey.

Preparation time 15 minutes
Total cooking time 25 minutes
Makes 2 1/2 cups

2 1/2 cups milk
large pinch of ground nutmeg
1 vanilla bean, split lengthwise,
or 1 teaspoon of vanilla extract
2 tablespoons unsalted butter
1/4 cup all-purpose flour
2 tablespoons sugar
2 egg yolks
2 tablespoons whipping cream or milk
3 tablespoons whiskey

One Place the milk in a saucepan with the nutmeg. Scrape the seeds from the vanilla bean and add to the milk with the bean. Heat gently until small bubbles appear around the edge of the saucepan. Set aside to cool, then strain, discard the bean and wipe out the saucepan.

Two Melt the butter in the saucepan over low heat. Sprinkle the flour over the butter and cook, stirring continuously with a wooden spoon, for 1–2 minutes, without allowing it to color.

Three Remove from the heat and slowly add the vanilla milk, whisking or beating vigorously to prevent any lumps forming. Return the sauce to low heat and bring slowly to a boil, stirring constantly. Add the sugar, then simmer for 3–4 minutes.

Four In a bowl, stir together the yolks and cream or milk, then pour in a quarter of the hot sauce, stir together to blend and return the mixture to the remaining sauce in the saucepan. Add the whiskey and vanilla extract, if using, and stir constantly over low heat to heat through, without allowing the sauce to boil. Add more sugar or whiskey, to taste, and strain the sauce. Serve warm.

Brandy butter

The classic partner for Christmas pudding, brandy butter also tastes wonderful with mincemeat pies (pictured far right).

Preparation time 20 minutes
Total cooking time None
Makes 1 cup

1/2 cup unsalted butter, at room
temperature
1/2 cup light brown sugar
2–3 tablespoons brandy

One Place the butter in a bowl and whisk using an electric mixer or beat with a wooden spoon until soft and creamy. Add the brown sugar a tablespoon at a time, whisking well each time, until the mixture is light and creamy.

Two Whisk in the brandy, half a tablespoon at a time. Do not add the brandy too quickly or the mixture will separate. Place in a serving bowl, cover with plastic wrap and refrigerate until needed. Return to room temperature before serving.

CHEF'S TIPS *For a variation, add a little orange zest, or use superfine sugar for a lighter flavor.*

If you want to make the brandy butter well in advance, place the butter in a pastry bag with a star-shaped tip and pipe small rosettes onto baking sheets lined with waxed paper. Freeze until hard and store in a bag in the freezer until needed.

desserts

Hot chocolate soufflés

*A well-risen, feather-light soufflé is one of the hallmarks of
a great chef. The real difficulty lies in transporting the soufflé
to the table before it begins to cool and collapses.*

Preparation time *20 minutes*
Total cooking time *20–25 minutes*
Serves 6

*2 oz. semi-sweet chocolate, chopped
1 cup milk
¼ cup unsalted butter
¼ cup all-purpose flour
sugar, to coat dishes
4 eggs, separated
3 tablespoons sugar
1 tablespoon unsweetened cocoa,
sifted
confectioners' sugar, to dust*

One Preheat the oven to 350°F. Put the chocolate in a bowl. Heat the milk in a saucepan until just at boiling point. Pour onto the chocolate and stir until the chocolate has melted. Melt the butter in a saucepan and add the flour. Cook over low heat for 1 minute. Add the chocolate milk gradually, stirring constantly with a wooden spoon. Bring to a boil and remove from the heat. Set aside to cool completely.

Two Brush six 4 x 2-inch, 1-cup soufflé dishes or custard cups with melted butter, working the brush from the bottom upwards. Refrigerate until the butter is firm, then repeat. Half-fill one of the dishes with sugar and, without placing your fingers inside the mold, rotate so that a layer of sugar sticks to the butter. Tap out the excess sugar and use to coat the other molds. Discard the excess.

Three Stir the egg yolks into the chocolate mixture. In a separate bowl, beat the egg whites with an electric mixer until soft peaks form. Add the 3 tablespoons sugar and beat for 30 seconds. Fold in the cocoa. Lightly beat one-third of the egg whites into the chocolate mixture to just blend. Add the rest of the egg whites and fold in very gently but quickly. Do not overmix or the mixture will lose its volume.

Four Spoon in the mixture to fill each dish completely and level the top with a flexible bladed knife. Sprinkle with sifted confectioners' sugar and then run your thumb just inside the top of the dish to create a ridge (see page 539), which will enable the soufflé mixture to rise evenly. Bake for 15 minutes, or until the soufflés are well risen and a light crust has formed. The soufflés should feel just set when pressed lightly with your fingers. Dust the tops lightly with the sifted confectioners' sugar. Serve the soufflés immediately.

Crèmes brûlées

The literal translation of this rich dessert is "burnt cream." Just before serving, chilled custard is sprinkled with sugar, which is quickly caramelized under a broiler to form a brittle topping, creating a delicious contrast in flavor and texture to the smooth, creamy custard beneath.

Preparation time *20 minutes*
+ overnight refrigeration
Total cooking time *55 minutes*
Serves 6

4 egg yolks
7 tablespoons sugar
2½ cups whipping cream
vanilla extract

One Preheat the oven to 300°F. Have ready six ½-cup soufflé dishes or custard cups.

Two Whisk the egg yolks and 3 tablespoons sugar in a large heatproof bowl. Set aside. Bring the cream and a few drops of vanilla to a boil in a heavy-bottomed saucepan, then reduce the heat and simmer for 8 minutes. Remove the saucepan from the heat and slowly pour the cream onto the egg mixture, whisking vigorously so the eggs do not scramble. Strain the custard into a large pitcher, then pour into the individual soufflé dishes.

Three Place the soufflé dishes in a baking dish. Pour enough hot water into the baking dish to reach ½ inch below the rims of the soufflé dishes. Bake the custard for 40–45 minutes, or until just firm to the touch. Remove from the oven, allow to cool, then cover and refrigerate overnight.

Four To make the caramel, evenly sprinkle some of the remaining 4 tablespoons of sugar over the top of each custard using a teaspoon. Without breaking the skin of the custard, spread the sugar out very gently using a finger or the spoon, then repeat to form a second layer of sugar. Remove any sugar

from the inside edges of the dishes as it will burn.

Five Place the dishes on a baking sheet and place under a very hot broiler for 2–3 minutes, or until the sugar has melted and is just beginning to give off a haze. Allow the glaze to harden before serving.

CHEF'S TIPS *This wonderful dessert is enhanced by fruit, which complements the sweetness of the custard with a fresh tangy flavor.*

Before pouring the custard into the soufflé dishes, arrange a few berries (strawberries or raspberries are ideal) or prunes presoaked in Armagnac or brandy in the bottom of the dish.

Apple strudel

*In Vienna it is said that to make a perfect
apple strudel, the dough must be stretched so finely that
a love letter can be read through it.*

Preparation time *40 minutes
+ 30 minutes resting*
Total cooking time *50 minutes
Serves 6–8*

*1½ cups bread flour or
all-purpose flour
1 egg, lightly beaten
½ cup unsalted butter
1 cup fresh bread crumbs
¼ cup sugar
2 teaspoons ground cinnamon
4 medium cooking or very tart dessert
apples
½ cup golden raisins
confectioners' sugar,
for dusting*

One Sift the flour and a pinch of salt into a large bowl. Make a well in the center, add the beaten egg and ¼ cup warm water, and mix with your hands to a smooth dough. With the bowl tipped to one side, and with open fingers, beat the dough, rotating your wrist. The dough is ready when it pulls away from the bowl and is difficult to beat. Place in a clean, lightly floured bowl, cover and leave in a warm place for 15 minutes.

Two Melt half of the butter in a skillet. Slowly fry the bread crumbs until golden brown, then set aside to cool in a bowl. Mix the sugar and cinnamon in a small bowl. Preheat the oven to 350°F.

Three Thoroughly flour one side of a large clean dish towel, place the pastry on top and, with your fingers, gently stretch the dough to a large rectangle about 24 x 20 inches; cover with another dish towel and set aside for 15 minutes. Melt the remaining butter and set aside.

Four Peel, quarter, core and thinly slice the apples, and combine with the bread crumbs, cinnamon mixture and raisins. Brush the dough liberally with the melted butter, then sprinkle the apple mixture all over the dough. Trim away the thick edge with a pair of scissors.

Five Pick up the dish towel from the shorter side, and push away and down from you to lightly roll the strudel up like a jelly roll. Transfer the strudel carefully onto a baking sheet, seam side down. Leave the strudel straight, or curve it lightly into the traditional crescent. Brush the pastry with any remaining butter.

Six Bake the strudel for 35–45 minutes, or until crisp and golden. Cool slightly, sprinkle with confectioners' sugar and serve warm with cream or custard.

Clafouti

This classic dessert is based on a dish originating in the French country region of Limousin, where clafouti is enjoyed when sweet, dark cherries are ripe. Cherries are the favored fruit for this dessert, although plums or pears may also be used.

Preparation time 40 minutes
Total cooking time 45 minutes
Serves 4

1 fresh peach or 2 canned peach halves, drained of syrup
8 oz. fresh cherries
2 cups whipping cream
1 vanilla bean, split lengthwise
6 egg yolks
1 egg
1 tablespoon dessert mix for custard-style puddings (see Chef's tip)
3 tablespoons all-purpose flour
2 tablespoons Cointreau
confectioners' sugar, for dusting

One Preheat the oven to 300°F. If you are using a fresh peach, blanch it in boiling water for 10–20 seconds, then transfer to a bowl of iced water. Peel the peach and cut around the fruit towards the pit. Gently twist the halves in opposite directions to expose the pit, then lift out the pit with a knife. If the peach is too slippery, simply cut the flesh from the pit. Process or purée one peach half and measure out 3 tablespoons of purée. Slice the remaining peach half into neat segments and set aside. Pit the cherries and set aside.

Two Place the cream in a heavy-bottomed saucepan with the vanilla bean, then heat until scalding—this is when bubbles form around the edge of the cream surface, yet the cream is not boiling. Remove the vanilla bean.

Three Whisk the egg yolks and the whole egg together in a large bowl. Beat in the dessert mix and flour, then stir in the peach purée. Whisk in the scalded cream. Add the Cointreau and stir.

Four Lightly grease a 2-quart shallow baking dish or casserole dish with softened butter. Place all the fruit in the dish. Pour the custard over the fruit and bake for about 40 minutes, or until a skewer inserted into the center of the dessert comes out clean. Remove from the oven and immediately sift the confectioners' sugar all over the top. Serve warm.

CHEF'S TIP *Dessert mix for custard-style puddings can be bought at supermarkets specializing in import goods.*

Crêpes Suzette

*In this illustrious dessert, very fine crêpes are warmed in a lightly
caramelized orange butter sauce, then doused with Cointreau and ignited
to flaming glory, usually at the table in front of the diners.*

***Preparation time** 30 minutes
+ 30 minutes resting*
***Total cooking time** 45 minutes
Makes 12 crêpes*

CREPE BATTER
*3/4 cup all-purpose flour
1 teaspoon sugar
2 eggs, plus 1 egg yolk, lightly beaten
2/3 cup milk
2 tablespoons clarified butter, melted
(see page 520)*

*clarified butter, for cooking
(see page 520)*

SAUCE
*4 white sugar cubes
5 oranges
3 tablespoons clarified butter, melted
(see page 520)
1/4 cup sugar
3 tablespoons Cointreau
2 tablespoons brandy*

One To make the batter, sift the flour into a bowl with a pinch of salt and the sugar. Make a well in the center, then add the eggs and extra egg yolk. Mix well with a wooden spoon or whisk, gradually incorporating the flour. Combine the milk with 1/4 cup water and gradually add to the batter. Add the clarified butter and beat until smooth. Cover and set aside for 30 minutes.

Two Melt a little clarified butter over medium heat in a heavy-bottomed or nonstick 6-inch crêpe pan or skillet and cook the crêpes in clarified butter, following the method in the Chef's techniques on page 538.

Three To make the sauce, rub all the sugar cube sides over the peel of an orange to soak up the oily zest, then crush the cubes with the back of a wooden spoon. Squeeze the oranges to produce 1 1/4 cups liquid. Over low heat, melt the clarified butter in a wide shallow skillet or sauté pan. Dissolve the crushed sugar in the butter, then add the sugar. Cook, stirring, for 2 minutes.

Slowly add the orange juice, keeping clear of the pan as the mixture may spit. Increase the heat to medium and simmer until reduced by a third.

Four Fold the crêpes in half, then into triangles. Place them in the orange sauce, slightly overlapping, with their points showing. Tilt the pan, scoop up the sauce and pour it over the crêpes to moisten them well.

Five Cook over low heat for 2 minutes. Turn off the heat and have a saucepan lid ready in case you need to put out the flame. Pour the Cointreau and brandy over the sauce without stirring. Immediately light the sauce with a match, standing back from the pan. Serve the crêpes on warmed plates with vanilla ice cream.

CHEF'S TIP *If you have any leftover crêpes, they can be stacked and then wrapped in aluminum foil and frozen in an airtight bag.*
To defrost, simply refrigerate them overnight, then peel off to use as needed.

---

about crêpe pans...

If you make crêpes or omelets on a regular basis, it is a good idea to invest in a special pan which you use only for these two things. A nonstick pan is perfect for both crêpes and omelets, though you can season a cast iron skillet yourself.

Tarte Tatin

*This delicious upside-down tart was invented by the Tatin sisters, who ran
a hotel-restaurant in the Sologne region at the turn of the century. It
was first served in Paris at Maxim's, where it is still a house specialty.*

***Preparation time** 50 minutes
+ 20 minutes chilling*
***Total cooking time** 1 hour 20 minutes
Serves 6–8*

PASTRY
*½ cup unsalted butter, at room
temperature
3 tablespoons sugar
1 egg, beaten
1–2 drops vanilla extract, optional
1⅔ cups all-purpose flour*

*¼ cup sugar
⅓ cup unsalted butter
8–11 x 7 oz. medium cooking apples,
peeled, cored and halved and tossed
in 1 teaspoon lemon juice (see Chef's
tips)*

One To make the pastry, cream the
butter and sugar in a bowl, using a
wooden spoon or an electric mixer. Add
the egg and vanilla in two or three
stages, mixing well before each addition.
Sift the flour with a pinch of salt, add to
the mixture and stir until smooth. Bring
the dough together with your hands to
form a rough ball, flatten with the palm
of your hand to a ½-inch thickness
and wrap in plastic wrap. Chill for
20 minutes.

Two Preheat the oven to 350°F. Roll out
the chilled dough to a round, ⅛ inch
thick, place on a parchment paper-lined
baking sheet and refrigerate.

Three In an 8-inch flameproof skillet
(with sloping sides), place the sugar and
butter together. Cook over medium
heat, stirring constantly, for 10 minutes,
or until it begins to bubble and just
color slightly.

Four Cook the apples and add the pastry
following the method in the Chef's
techniques on page 538. Make small
slits in the top of the pastry to let the
steam escape. Put the skillet on a baking
sheet and bake for about 15–20 minutes,
or until the pastry is nicely colored.

Five Remove from the oven and allow to
sit for 2 minutes. Place a serving platter
over the skillet and tilt to allow any
juices to flow out into a bowl. In one
swift motion, flip the pan over, giving it
a good shake to loosen the apples.
Carefully lift the pan. If there is any
extra liquid, drizzle it over the apples.

CHEF'S TIPS *Choose a tart apple that
will hold its shape when cooked, such as
Cortland, Northern Spy, Winesap, York
Imperial or Granny Smith.*

*It is important to have a pan large
enough to allow you to baste the apples.*

*The apples will give off liquid, so the
caramel must be well reduced before the
pastry goes on.*

Gratin of summer berries

Beneath a luscious froth of sabayon, quickly broiled until golden brown, lies an assortment of fresh sweet berries for a delectable summer dessert.

Preparation time *20 minutes*
Total cooking time *20 minutes*
Serves 4

2³/4 cups mixed berries, such as strawberries, blueberries, raspberries and blackberries
2 eggs
2 egg yolks
5 tablespoons sugar
1 tablespoon Kirsch

One Wash the strawberries, dry well, discard the stems and cut each strawberry in half. Sort the remaining berries to make sure they are all fresh. Arrange the fruit on four flameproof plates or individual shallow dishes.

Two Half-fill a large saucepan with water and heat until simmering. Have ready a heatproof bowl that will fit over the pan without actually touching the water.

Three To make the sabayon, place the eggs, egg yolks, sugar and Kirsch in the bowl, then place the bowl over the pan of simmering water, making sure the bottom of the bowl is not touching the water. Whisk or beat with an electric mixer for 10–15 minutes, or until the mixture is thick and creamy and leaves a trail as it falls from the whisk or beaters.

Four Preheat the broiler to high. Spoon the sabayon over the berries and quickly broil until the sabayon is brown all over. Serve immediately.

CHEF'S TIP *The plates of fruit can be arranged in advance, but cover with plastic wrap so they do not dry out.*

Hot Cointreau and orange soufflés

A beautifully risen, hot soufflé is always a sight to behold. This spectacular dessert, flavored simply with the sweetness of sun-drenched orange, will create a sensation among even the most discerning dinner guests.

***Preparation time** 35 minutes*
***Total cooking time** 20 minutes*
Serves 6

softened butter, for coating
⅓ cup sugar, for coating
2 tablespoons orange juice
2 teaspoons grated orange zest
1 tablespoon Cointreau
1 cup milk
½ vanilla bean, split lengthwise
4 eggs, separated
1 tablespoon all-purpose flour
1 tablespoon cornstarch
sifted confectioners' sugar, for dusting

One Preheat the oven to 350°F. Using a pastry brush, brush the insides of six ½-cup soufflé dishes with softened butter, working the brush from the bottom upwards. Refrigerate to set and repeat.

Two Half-fill a soufflé dish with sugar, and without placing your fingers inside the dish, rotate it so that a layer of sugar adheres to the butter. Tap out the excess sugar and repeat with the remaining soufflé dishes.

Three Place the orange juice and grated zest in a small saucepan over medium-high heat. Simmer for 3–5 minutes to reduce the volume by three-quarters—the mixture should be quite syrupy. Pour in the Cointreau, scraping the bottom of the saucepan with a wooden spoon. Remove from the heat and allow to cool.

Four Bring the milk and vanilla bean slowly to a boil. In a bowl, and using a wooden spoon, mix together ¼ cup of the sugar and two of the egg yolks, then mix in the flour and cornstarch. Remove the vanilla bean from the boiling milk; stir a little of the milk into the egg mixture, then add all the mixture to the milk in the saucepan. Stir rapidly with the wooden spoon over medium heat until the mixture thickens and comes to a boil. Boil gently for 1 minute to cook the flour, stirring to prevent sticking.

Five Pour the mixture into a clean bowl, stir to cool it slightly, then beat in the reduced orange sauce. Stir in the remaining two egg yolks and dab a small piece of butter over the surface to melt and prevent a skin from forming. (If you prefer, place a sheet of parchment paper on the surface instead.)

Six In a clean, dry bowl, whisk the egg whites until they form soft peaks. Add the remaining sugar and whisk for 30 seconds. Add a third of the egg whites to the custard and lightly beat in until just combined. Using a large metal spoon, fold in the remaining egg whites gently but quickly. Do not overmix, as this will cause the mixture to lose volume and become heavy.

Seven Place the soufflé dishes on a baking sheet. Spoon in the mixture to completely fill each dish, smooth the surface of each soufflé and sprinkle with sifted confectioners' sugar. Roll your thumb around the inside of each dish to create a ridge that will enable the soufflé to rise evenly (see page 539). Bake for 12 minutes, or until well risen with a light crust. The soufflés should feel just set when pressed lightly with a fingertip. Serve at once.

CHEF'S TIP *This soufflé—to the end of step 4—can be prepared a few hours in advance.*

Rhubarb crumble

Also called a rhubarb crisp, this simple dessert is a great way to use up excess ripe, in-season fruit. In this version, tangy rhubarb perfectly complements the buttery, crumbly topping.

Preparation time 30 minutes
Total cooking time 40 minutes
Serves 6

2 tablespoons strawberry jam
5 cups trimmed rhubarb, cut into
1-inch pieces
2 tablespoons Demerara or
turbinado sugar
1/3 cup whole wheat flour
1/2 cup all-purpose flour
6 tablespoons unsalted butter, cut into
cubes and chilled
1/2 cup granulated, Demerara or
turbinado sugar
1 tablespoon pumpkin seeds, toasted
1 tablespoon hazelnuts (filberts),
toasted and roughly chopped

One Put the strawberry jam in a wide, shallow frying pan with 2 tablespoons water, then add the rhubarb in a single layer with the 2 tablespoons of Demerara or turbinado sugar. Bring to a boil, then immediately lower the heat to a simmer, cover tightly with a lid or piece of aluminum foil and cook for 5 minutes. The acidity of rhubarb does vary quite a lot, so taste and add more sugar if necessary.

Two Transfer the rhubarb into a 5-cup, 8 x 2½-inch flameproof dish. Spread out evenly, then pour over enough rhubarb juice to come halfway up the rhubarb. Set aside to cool. Preheat the oven to 350°F.

Three Sift the whole wheat and all-purpose flours into a large bowl and put the husks left in the sifter from the whole wheat flour back into the bowl. Rub the butter into the flour using your fingertips until the mixture resembles

fine bread crumbs. Continue to rub in the butter until small lumps begin to form, then add the sugar, pumpkin seeds and the chopped hazelnuts and toss to incorporate thoroughly.

Four Scatter the crumble mixture evenly over the rhubarb in the dish without

pressing it down, then bake for 20–30 minutes, or until the topping is golden brown.

Five Dust with a little extra sugar if you wish, and serve the crumble warm or cold with whipped cream, custard or vanilla ice cream.

Maple pudding

*This family favorite, a steamed pudding, is served
with a delicious cinnamon-flavored syrup that should
be poured over just before serving.*

Preparation time *35 minutes*
Total cooking time *2 hours*
Serves *6*

*1 cup unsalted butter, at room
temperature
1 cup sugar
4 eggs, beaten
1/2 teaspoon vanilla extract
finely grated zest of 2 lemons
2 cups self-rising flour
1/3 cup maple syrup*

SAUCE
*1 cinnamon stick
1/4 vanilla bean
1/2 cup maple syrup
grated zest and juice of 1 lemon*

One Prepare an 8-cup pudding basin or heatproof glass bowl for steaming (see page 539).

Two Put the butter and sugar in a bowl and, using a wooden spoon or electric mixer, beat together until light and creamy. Add the eggs in six additions, beating well between each addition, then mix in the vanilla and lemon zest. Sift the flour onto the mixture and fold the flour in using a large metal spoon or plastic spatula.

Three Place the syrup in the bottom of the basin or bowl and spoon the sponge mixture on top. Cover and steam for 1 hour 40 minutes, following the

steaming method in the Chef's techniques on page 539. To test when the pudding is done, pierce with a skewer. If it comes out clean, the pudding is cooked (though it may still look a bit sticky from the syrup).

Four To make the sauce, put the cinnamon, vanilla, syrup, lemon juice and zest and 1 1/4 cups water in a saucepan and bring to a boil. Simmer for 15 minutes to reduce by a third, then remove the cinnamon and vanilla bean.

Five Leave the pudding for 10 minutes before removing the string, aluminum foil and parchment paper. Unmold and serve with the maple syrup sauce.

Steamed orange pudding

*Hot, light and full of flavor, this pudding will brighten
the gloom of a winter's day like a burst of summer sunshine.
Serve with orange sauce or custard.*

Preparation time 30 minutes
Total cooking time 1 hour 45 minutes
Serves 6

⅓ cup thin-cut marmalade
2 large oranges, peel and
pith removed, and segmented
⅓ cup unsalted butter,
at room temperature
½ cup sugar
finely grated zest of 1 orange
2 large eggs, beaten
1½ cups self-rising flour
milk, for mixing

ORANGE SAUCE
1¼ cups orange juice
2 egg yolks
½ teaspoon cornstarch
3 tablespoons sugar
1 teaspoon Grand Marnier
or Cointreau

One Prepare a 5-cup pudding mold measuring 6 inches across the top, following the method in the Chef's techniques on page 539.

Two Spoon the marmalade into the pudding mold. Thinly slice the oranges, then line the mold with the orange slices, from the marmalade bottom to the top of the bowl.

Three In a bowl, beat the butter with a wooden spoon or electric mixer to soften. Slowly add the sugar, beating until light and fluffy. Mix in the orange zest. Add the eggs in four additions, beating well after each addition. Sift in the flour and quickly fold into the mixture using a large metal spoon or plastic spatula. As the last traces of flour are mixed in, add a little milk to make a soft consistency: the mixture should drop from the spoon with a quick flick of the wrist.

Four Immediately transfer the mixture to the pudding mold and steam, covered, for 1½–1¾ hours, or until the pudding is springy to the light touch of a finger, following the method in the Chef's techniques on page 539.

Five When cooked, carefully remove the pudding from the steamer. Remove the foil and paper, place a warm plate over the pudding mold and carefully turn the pudding over and remove the mold. (If you are not serving the pudding immediately, place the mold back over the pudding to prevent the pudding from drying out.)

Six To make the orange sauce, bring the orange juice to a boil in a small saucepan. In a bowl, beat the egg yolks, cornstarch and sugar until thick and light. Pour the hot orange juice into the bowl, mix until blended, then return to the pan. Cook over medium heat, stirring constantly with a wooden spoon, until the mixture coats the back of the spoon and the sauce does not close over when a line is drawn across the spoon with a finger.

Seven Remove from the heat, strain into a bowl, then stir in the Grand Marnier or Cointreau. If you are not using the sauce right away, dust the surface lightly with sugar to prevent a skin from forming. The sugar can be stirred in just before serving. Serve the sauce warm or cold with the pudding.

Bread pudding with panettone

When the yearning strikes for a homey dessert, bread pudding is hard to beat. For special occasions, this humble and economical dish can be transformed into something really marvelous with candied fruits, a dash of rum, some brioche or, as in this case, Italian panettone.

Preparation time 20 minutes
Total cooking time 50 minutes
Serves 4

1/4 cup golden raisins
2 tablespoons rum, brandy
or amaretto liqueur
8 oz. panettone
3 eggs
1/4 cup sugar
2 cups milk
1 vanilla bean, split lengthwise
1 tablespoon apricot jam, warmed
and strained
confectioners' sugar, for dusting

One Preheat the oven to 325°F. Place the raisins in a 9-inch oval baking dish or casserole. Pour the alcohol over the top.

Two Cut the panettone horizontally to make two or three round slices about 1/2 inch thick, then remove the crust. Cut each slice into quarters (almost triangles). Neatly overlap them in the bottom of the dish.

Three Lightly whisk the eggs and sugar in a heatproof bowl until just combined. Place the milk and vanilla bean in a saucepan, bring to a boil, then slowly pour the scalded milk into the egg and sugar mixture, whisking constantly.

Four Pour the mixture through a fine sieve into the dish, over the panettone. Place the dish in a larger baking dish half-full of hot water. Bake for 40–45 minutes, or until the custard has set and is golden brown. Remove the pudding from the oven and, while still warm, brush the surface with the warm apricot jam. Sprinkle with confectioners' sugar and serve either hot or cold.

CHEF'S TIPS *If the panettone is not sweet, add some sugar to taste.*

Raisin loaf is a perfect alternative to panettone as it already has a loaf shape. Simply cut off the crusts, slice the bread and cut each slice in half to form triangles.

Pears poached in red wine

A light yet satisfying end to a meal, this colorful dessert can be dressed up even further by adding some prunes to poach with the pears in the spiced wine syrup.

Preparation time *45 minutes*
Total cooking time *50 minutes*
Serves 4

*6 cups full-bodied red wine
(such as Cabernet Sauvignon)
1³/4 cups sugar
2 cinnamon sticks
1 vanilla bean
1 whole clove
zest of 1 lemon
zest of 1 orange
4 pears
3 tablespoons red currant jelly
2 oranges
fresh mint leaves, to garnish
fresh raspberries or red currants,
to garnish*

One In a heavy-bottomed saucepan, bring the wine, 1¼ cups of the sugar, the spices, lemon zest and orange zest to a boil.

Two Peel the pears, leaving the stems intact, and remove the blossom end using the tip of a vegetable peeler or a small knife. Place the pears in the hot wine, cover with a round of aluminum foil or parchment paper, and simmer over low heat for 20 minutes, or until tender to the point of a sharp knife, turning or basting the pears if the liquid does not cover them completely. (The actual cooking time will depend on their ripeness.) Remove the pears from the wine and set aside to cool.

Three Bring the wine to a boil, then reduce the heat and simmer for 15 minutes, or until reduced in volume by a third. Add the red currant jelly and allow it to melt completely, then strain and set aside to cool.

Four Thinly peel the oranges using a vegetable peeler, avoiding the bitter white pith. Cut the zest into very thin strips and place in a small saucepan with cold water. Bring to a boil, then drain and rinse well in cold water. Drain the zest and set aside. In the same pan, mix the remaining sugar with 1 cup water and boil until the sugar dissolves. Add the drained orange zest, reduce the heat and simmer for 2–3 minutes, or until the syrup thickens and the zest has absorbed the sugar and appears to be translucent.

Five Carefully arrange the pears in a serving dish and cover with the wine syrup. Sprinkle with the orange zest, garnish with mint and decorate with raspberries or red currants.

CHEF'S TIP *For a rich, dark color in the pears, soak the pears in the poaching liquid overnight.*

Fruit cobbler

The word "cobbler" in this contect originates from the nineteenth century and refers to a fruit pie with a scone topping. This cobbler has a golden hazelnut and apricot topping over summer's late fruit.

Preparation time *1 hour*
+ 20 minutes refrigeration
Total cooking time *40 minutes*
Serves 6

TOPPING
2¼ cups all-purpose flour
2 teaspoons baking powder
5 tablespoons unsalted butter,
cut into cubes and chilled
3 tablespoons sugar
2 eggs, beaten
3 tablespoons milk
¾ cup finely chopped hazelnuts
(filberts)
2½ oz. dried apricots, finely chopped

COMPOTE
¼ cup sugar
1½ tablespoons unsalted butter
2 cloves
1 cinnamon stick
½ vanilla bean, split lengthwise
2 Granny Smith apples, peeled, cored
and cut into eighths
2 ripe pears, peeled, cored and
and cut into eighths
3 fresh apricots, halved and pitted,
or 6 canned apricot halves
2 fresh peaches, halved, pitted and
and cut into eighths, or 4 canned
peach halves, sliced
3 fresh plums, halved and pitted,
or 3 canned pitted dark plums,
halved
finely grated zest of 1 lemon
finely grated zest of ½ orange
pinch of pumpkin pie spice
pinch of ground cinnamon

1 egg yolk
confectioners' sugar, for dusting

One Brush a round 8½ x 1½-inch flameproof dish with melted butter.

Two To make the topping, sift the flour and baking powder into a bowl. Rub the butter into the flour using your fingertips until the mixture resembles fine bread crumbs. Lightly stir in the sugar, make a well in the center and add the eggs and milk. Bring the mixture roughly together using a pastry blender. Add the hazelnuts and apricots and stir the ingredients together to form a dough, then shape into a ball and flatten slightly. Wrap in plastic wrap and place in the refrigerator for 20 minutes.

Three To make the compote, first prepare a caramel using the sugar and 3 tablespoons water, following the method in the Chef's techniques on page 540. After the caramel has stopped cooking, return to the heat and remelt the caramel gently, then mix in the butter, cloves, cinnamon stick, vanilla bean and apples and cook covered for

5 minutes. Add the pears, apricots, peaches and fresh plums, cover and gently cook for 5 minutes, stirring occasionally. (If using canned plums, add at the end of the 5 minutes cooking time or they will break up.) Discard the flavorings, stir in the lemon and orange zest and the ground spices, and pour the compote into the prepared dish.

Four Preheat the oven to 415°F. On a lightly floured surface, roll out the topping dough to ⅝ inch thick, then cut out rounds using a 2½-inch biscuit cutter. Arrange the rounds, slightly overlapping, on top of the hot compote.

Five Beat the egg yolk and 1 teaspoon water together to make an egg wash and brush over the top of the cobbler. Do not brush the cut sides or the egg will set and prevent rising. Bake for 15 minutes, or until well risen and golden brown. Cool for 5–10 minutes before serving, then dust with sifted confectioners' sugar and serve with cream or ice cream.

Sticky toffee puddings

Dates are the secret ingredient that makes these little desserts so wickedly delicious, while the toffee sauce ensures they remain famously sticky.

Preparation time *40 minutes*
+ 1 hour soaking
Total cooking time *40 minutes*
Serves 10

1 cup pitted and chopped dates
1/3 cup raisins
grated zest of 1/2 lemon
1 teaspoon baking soda
2 tablespoons coffee extract
or 1 tablespoon instant coffee mixed
with 2 tablespoons boiling water
3 1/2 tablespoons unsalted butter,
at room temperature
1 cup light brown sugar
4 eggs, beaten
2 cups self-rising flour

SAUCE
1 vanilla bean, split lengthwise
4 tablespoons unsalted butter
2/3 cup Demerara or turbinado sugar
1/2 cup whipping cream

One Brush ten 2/3-cup pudding molds or ramekins with melted butter and chill before brushing with butter again, then dust with flour and tap out the excess. Preheat the oven to 350°F.

Two Put the dates, raisins and lemon zest in a bowl. Sprinkle with the baking soda and coffee extract, pour on 1 cup boiling water, cover and set aside to soak for one hour.

Three Put the butter and sugar in a bowl and, using a wooden spoon or electric mixer, beat until light and creamy. Add the eggs in six additions, beating well between each addition. Sift the flour and a pinch of salt onto the mixture and fold in using a large metal spoon or plastic spatula. Add the date and raisin mixture

with its liquid and stir gently to make a loose batter.

Four Spoon the mixture into the molds to three-quarters full. Make a slight hollow in the center of the mixture and bake for 20–30 minutes, or until springy to the touch.

Five To make the sauce, scrape the vanilla seeds into a saucepan and add the bean, butter, sugar and cream and stir for 3 minutes to dissolve the sugar, then simmer over medium-low heat, without stirring, until smooth and golden. Remove and discard the vanilla bean, set the sauce aside and keep warm.

Six When the puddings are cooked, allow to rest for 10 minutes, then unmold. Serve warm with the toffee sauce and whipped cream.

CHEF'S TIP *If 10 puddings are too many, you could either halve the recipe or freeze the extra puddings. When you are ready to use the frozen puddings, defrost, then wrap in aluminum foil and reheat in a 350°F oven for 20 minutes.*

Traditional rice pudding

This classic favorite, so simple to prepare, cooks slowly and gently in the oven, allowing the rice time to absorb all the liquid. The result is delightfully soft and creamy.

Preparation time *5 minutes*
+ 30 minutes resting
Total cooking time *2 hours*
Serves 4

3 cups milk
1¹/₂ tablespoons sugar
2–3 drops vanilla extract
¹/₃ cup short-grain rice
unsalted butter, for topping
freshly grated nutmeg, to taste

One Combine the milk, sugar, vanilla extract and rice in a 4-cup pie plate or flameproof dish and allow to rest for 30 minutes. Preheat the oven to 350°F.

Two Dot the butter over the mixture, sprinkle some nutmeg over the top and cover with aluminum foil. Place the dish on the middle shelf of the oven and bake for 1 hour, stirring once or twice with a fork.

Three Remove the foil and reduce the oven temperature to 300°F. If serving the pudding cold, bake for another 45 minutes, allow to cool, then refrigerate until ready to serve. If serving hot, cook for 1 hour, or until a brown skin forms and the interior of the pudding is soft and creamy. Serve hot with a teaspoon of strawberry jam or cold with poached red plums.

CHEF'S TIPS *If the rice pudding is too dry, adjust the consistency before serving by lifting the skin to one side and adding a little cold milk.*

To vary the flavor of this pudding, use cinnamon in place of the vanilla and the nutmeg, or sprinkle some golden raisins or chopped candied citrus in with the rice before cooking.

Baked apple and fruit charlotte

As legend has it, this famous molded dessert was named after the wife of George III, England's famous "mad" king. It is traditionally set in a tall, bucket-shaped mold.

Preparation time 30 minutes
+ 1 hour cooling
Total cooking time 1 hour 20 minutes
Serves 6

14 thin slices white bread, crusts removed
³⁄₄ cup unsalted butter
3 medium Granny Smith apples, peeled, cored and finely chopped
3 medium tart cooking apples, peeled, cored and finely chopped
½ cup lightly packed brown sugar
pinch of ground cinnamon
½ teaspoon ground nutmeg
½ cup finely chopped walnuts
⅓ cup golden raisins or mixed dried fruits
2 tablespoons marmalade (optional)
grated lemon zest (optional)
¼ cup smooth jam (see Chef's tips)

One Brush a 5-cup charlotte mold with softened butter. Cut six slices of bread in half to form rectangles; cut five slices in half at a diagonal to form triangles. Reserve the remaining three slices of bread.

Two Turn the mold upside down and place the bread triangles on top, overlapping the edges to completely cover the top of the mold. Hold the triangles in place and, using the mold as a guide, trim the excess edges with scissors so the triangles will fit inside the bottom of the mold exactly.

Three Melt ²⁄₃ cup of the butter, dip the trimmed triangles in, then line the bottom of the mold. Dip the rectangles in butter and arrange around the sides, overlapping the edges until the mold is completely covered, filling any gaps with the bread trimmings. Dip the reserved slices of bread in the butter and set aside.

Four To make the filling, melt the remaining butter in a large skillet. Add the apples, cover the pan with parchment paper and then a lid. Cook the apples over low heat for 15–20 minutes, or until they are soft and of the consistency of applesauce. Add the brown sugar and stir over high heat for 5 minutes, or until the mixture falls from the side of the spoon in wide drops. Stir in the cinnamon, nutmeg, walnuts and raisins. Remove from the heat. Add the marmalade, and perhaps a little grated lemon zest. Set aside to cool.

Five Preheat the oven to 375°F. Ladle the filling into the mold until half-full. Cover the filling with half the reserved bread slices, press down firmly, then add the remaining filling. If the filling is not level with the mold lining, trim the bread with the tip of a small knife or scissors. Cover with the remaining reserved bread, filling any gaps. Press in gently and cover with foil.

Six Place the charlotte on a baking sheet and bake for 45 minutes to 1 hour, or until golden and firm. Allow to cool completely before unmolding onto a serving plate: this should take 1 hour.

Seven Warm the apricot jam and 2 tablespoons water in a small saucepan over low heat until melted. Using a pastry brush, brush the mixture over the surface of the charlotte to give a light glaze.

CHEF'S TIPS *A soufflé dish or a 4-inch-deep cake pan can be used instead of a charlotte mold.*

If the jam is very fruity, it will be easier to brush onto the charlotte if it has been strained after warming.

For extra kick, you can replace the raisins with 1–2 tablespoons chopped candied ginger and the nutmeg with ground ginger.

As an indulgent and luxurious accompaniment, whip ²⁄₃ cup whipping cream with 2 tablespoons sugar, then stir in 2 tablespoons of Calvados.

Eve's pudding

As the name of this English dessert suggests, it should be made with apples, which take on a tempting caramelized sweetness under the light sponge cake and golden almonds.

Preparation time 25 minutes
Total cooking time 45 minutes
Serves 6

COMPOTE
3½ tablespoons unsalted butter, softened
⅓ cup sugar
2 cloves
½ teaspoon ground cinnamon
1 vanilla bean, split lengthwise
4–5 Golden Delicious apples, peeled, cored and cut into eight pieces

ALMOND TOPPING
½ cup unsalted butter, at room temperature
½ cup sugar
finely grated zest of 1 lemon
½ teaspoon vanilla extract
3 eggs, beaten
¼ cup all-purpose flour
⅔ cup ground almonds or almond meal, sifted
¾ cup sliced almonds

2 tablespoons apricot jam
confectioners' sugar, for dusting

One Brush a 6-cup flameproof baking dish, ¾ inch deep, with melted butter.

Two To make the compote, put the butter and sugar in a saucepan and stir over low heat until the butter has melted and the sugar has dissolved. Add the cloves, cinnamon and vanilla bean, then add the apples and mix to coat. Cover and cook very gently for 5 minutes, or until the apples are just starting to soften. Discard the flavorings and spread the apples evenly over the bottom of the dish. Allow to cool. Preheat the oven to 350°F.

Three To make the topping, put the butter, sugar, lemon zest and vanilla in a bowl and, using a wooden spoon or electric mixer, beat until light and creamy. Add the beaten eggs in six additions, beating well between each addition. Sift the flour and a pinch of salt onto the mixture, scatter on the ground almonds and, using a large metal spoon or spatula, fold in gently to combine. Spoon over the apple mixture, smooth the top and sprinkle with the sliced almonds. Bake for

30–35 minutes, or until the topping is firm to the touch.

Four In a small saucepan, heat the apricot jam with 2 teaspoons water. When the mixture has melted and begins to boil, strain it into a small bowl and, while still hot, brush it over the surface of the dessert. Leave for 1 minute, then dust with sifted confectioners' sugar. Serve with whipped cream.

Oeufs à la neige

In English, this amazing dessert is better known as "floating islands,"
or more literally "snow eggs." A rich custard sauce (crème anglaise)
is topped with meltingly soft meringues and drizzled with caramel.

Preparation time *40 minutes*
Total cooking time *40 minutes*
Serves 6–8

SYRUP
³/4 cup sugar

CREME ANGLAISE
2 cups milk
1 vanilla bean
6 egg yolks
¹/2 cup sugar

MERINGUES
6 egg whites
¹/2 cup sugar

CARAMEL
¹/3 cup sugar
3 tablespoons water
lemon juice, to taste

One To make the syrup, dissolve the sugar in 2 quarts water over low heat. Bring to a boil, then reduce the heat and simmer gently to dissolve the sugar.

Two To make the crème anglaise, prepare a large bowl of ice or iced water and place a smaller bowl inside. Put the milk and vanilla bean in a heavy-bottomed saucepan, and just bring to a boil. Make the custard using the method in the Chef's techniques on page 541. Strain into the bowl in the ice. Set aside to allow to cool, stirring occasionally.

Three To make the meringues, beat the egg whites in a clean, dry bowl until stiff peaks form. Add the sugar and beat until smooth and glossy. Shape into "eggs" using two large spoons dipped in water, then poach in the gently simmering syrup for 3 minutes; do not crowd the

saucepan. Turn using a slotted spoon and poach for 3 more minutes. Drain on a dish towel and set aside to cool.

Four Make the caramel following the method in the Chef's techniques on page 540. Stop the cooking immediately by resting the saucepan in a large bowl of iced water for a few seconds. Remove the saucepan from the water and keep the caramel warm or it will harden.

Five To serve, fill a shallow serving bowl with crème anglaise and top with poached meringues. Drizzle the caramel over the top and serve the remaining sauce in a sauce boat.

Traditional Christmas pudding

*This richest of fruit puddings is dense, dark and sweet. We have given
two traditional methods—boiling and steaming. Both are easy to
make in advance and can be reheated easily on Christmas day.*

*Preparation time 45 minutes
+ overnight marinating*
Total cooking time 10–12 hours
Serves 8

MARINATED FRUITS
2 cups golden raisins
2 cups raisins
2 cups currants
1/4 cup candied cherries
1/3 cup candied citrus peel
1/3 cup dates, pitted and chopped
1 1/2 teaspoons pumpkin pie spice
1 teaspoon ground cinnamon
1 teaspoon ground nutmeg
1/4 teaspoon ground ginger
zest of 2 oranges and juice of 1 orange
zest of 1 lemon
1/2 cup stout, such as Guinness
1/2 cup brandy

PUDDING
1 2/3 cups apples, peeled, cored
and grated
1 1/4 cups all-purpose flour
1/2 cup ground almonds
6 1/2 oz. suet, grated
3/4 cup dark brown sugar
2 1/2 oz. cups fresh white bread crumbs
2 eggs, beaten
2 tablespoons molasses

3 tablespoons brandy

One To make the marinated fruits, place all the ingredients in a large bowl and mix together well. Cover with plastic wrap and leave overnight in a cool place.

Two The next day, prepare the pudding by placing all the ingredients in a bowl and making a well in the center. Add the marinated fruits and mix to a soft batter.

Three To boil the pudding, place a 28-inch square of cheesecloth or a kitchen towel in a saucepan of water and bring to a boil. Drain, then, wearing rubber gloves, squeeze out. Lay the cloth out flat and dust generously with flour. Using your hand, smooth the flour evenly onto the cloth. Place the pudding mixture into the center of the cloth. Gather the cloth tightly around the mixture and twist it as tightly as you can to force the mixture into a round ball shape. Tie string around the twisted cloth as tightly and as close to the pudding as possible.

Four Bring a saucepan of water to a boil, large enough for the pudding to move around in and with a saucer or trivet at the bottom. Put the pudding on the saucer or trivet, cover and boil for 10–12 hours.

Five Lift the pudding from the saucepan and carefully remove the string. Leave the pudding for 5 minutes, then loosen the cloth, unmold the pudding onto a plate and gently peel off the cloth.

Six To steam the pudding, prepare a 10-cup pudding basin following the method in the Chef's techniques on page 538. Pour the pudding mixture into the basin, cover and simmer for 10 hours, adding more boiling water as needed. Let rest for 15 minutes, then remove the string, foil and paper and unmold.

Seven In a small saucepan, warm the brandy. At the table, pour it over the pudding and ignite it at arm's length. Serve with whipped cream or brandy butter (see page 370).

CHEF'S TIP *To prepare ahead, steam or boil the pudding for 8 hours, then allow to cool (for the boiled pudding, hang up to dry overnight). Remove the cloth or paper and make sure the surface is completely dry. Cover again with dry cloth or new parchment paper and store in a cool place. To reheat, cook for 2 hours, then leave for 15 minutes.*

Sherry trifle

This famous British dessert is a Christmas tradition—it includes sherry-soaked sponge cake, red fruit and rich custard sauce. If you prefer a nonalcohol version, substitute orange juice for the sherry.

Preparation time *55 minutes*
+ 1 hour 20 minutes chilling
Total cooking time *30 minutes*
Serves 8

SPONGE CAKE
3 eggs
1/3 cup sugar
1/2 cup all-purpose flour
2/3 cup raspberry jam

2–3 tablespoons sweet sherry
1 1/4 cups fresh or frozen raspberries
1 1/4 cups fresh or frozen blackberries
2 cups whipping cream
1/4 cup confectioners' sugar
1/4 teaspoon vanilla extract
2 tablespoons pistachio nuts, chopped
8 strawberries, halved

CUSTARD SAUCE
2 cups milk
1/4–1/3 cup dessert mix for custard-style puddings (see Chef's tip)
1/4–1/3 cup superfine sugar
2/3 cup whipping cream

One Preheat the oven to 425°F. Brush a 10 x 12-inch jelly roll pan with melted butter, line the bottom with parchment paper and brush again with butter.

Two To make the sponge cake, bring a saucepan half full of water to a boil, then remove from the heat. Have ready a heatproof bowl that will fit over the saucepan without actually touching the water. Place the eggs and sugar in the bowl, then place over the saucepan of simmering water. Beat for 4 minutes, or until tripled in volume. When the beaters are lifted, the mixture should fall in a ribbon-like trail. Remove the bowl from the saucepan and continue beating for 2 minutes, or until the mixture is cold. Sift the flour onto the mixture and, using a large metal spoon, fold in until just combined. Pour into the prepared pan, lightly level with a flexible bladed knife and bake for 6 minutes, or until pale golden and springy to the touch of a finger. Slide the sponge cake in its paper onto a rack and allow to cool, then turn over onto a clean piece of parchment paper and remove the paper on which it was baked. Spread the sponge cake thinly with jam and, using the paper, roll up from one long side into a jelly roll shape. Wrap in waxed paper and chill for 20 minutes.

Three Discard the paper and, using a serrated or sharp knife, cut the roll into 1/4-inch slices. Arrange the slices across the bottom and up the side of a large glass bowl with a wide, flat bottom. Fill the center with any remaining slices, drizzle the sherry over the sponge cake and add the raspberries and blackberries, leveling the top. Cover the bowl with plastic wrap and chill until needed.

Four To make the custard sauce, bring the milk almost to a boil in a deep, heavy-bottomed saucepan. Place the dessert mix and sugar in a bowl, add the cream and quickly whisk to blend and prevent lumps. Whisk in about a third of the hot milk, then pour the mixture back into the saucepan. Bring to a boil over low-medium heat, whisking vigorously, then remove from the heat. Continue to gently whisk for 5 minutes while the custard sauce cools to a warm but still flowing mixture, then pour over the fruit. Cover the surface with plastic wrap and chill for at least 1 hour.

Five Whisk the cream, confectioners' sugar and vanilla together until soft peaks form. Decorate the trifle with this cream mixture and top with the nuts and strawberries. Chill until ready to serve.

CHEF'S TIP *Dessert mix for custard-style puddings is available from supermarkets specializing in import goods.*

Pavlovas with fragrant fruit

*These dramatic, feather-light mounds of pillowy meringue
are a treat when combined with champagne-steeped
fruit and kirsch-flavored heavy cream.*

Preparation time *20 minutes*
Total cooking time *2 hours 10 minutes*
Makes 6

PAVLOVAS
*6 egg whites
1 cup superfine sugar
1 teaspoon white wine vinegar
2 teaspoons boiling water*

*1/4 cup superfine sugar
1/2 vanilla bean, split lengthwise
1 cup sparkling wine
or champagne
2 lb. mixed soft fruit,
such as strawberries, raspberries,
pitted black cherries
and blackberries
1 cup whipping cream
1 1/2 tablespoons confectioners' sugar
3/4 cup plain yogurt
1 1/2 tablespoons kirsch*

One Preheat the oven to 250°F. Line two baking sheets with parchment paper.

Two To make the pavlovas, place the egg whites in a clean dry bowl and beat them with a hand whisk or an electric mixer until soft peaks form. Gradually add the sugar, vinegar and boiling water and whisk continuously until the meringue is thick and glossy.

Three Using 2 large wet metal spoons, divide and shape the meringue into 6 ovals and place on the prepared baking sheets. Cook for 1 1/2–2 hours, or until the pavlovas are pale and crisp on the outside with soft, chewy centers.

Four To prepare the fruit, place the sugar in a large saucepan with the vanilla bean and sparkling wine and heat gently until simmering. Simmer for 5 minutes, then remove the saucepan from the heat. Add the fruit to the pan and set aside to cool, during which time the soft fruit will gently poach in the cooling liquid. Remove the vanilla bean from the fruit just before serving.

Five Using a hand whisk, whip the cream until it just forms soft peaks, then sift in the confectioners' sugar and fold in with the yogurt and kirsch.

Six To serve the dessert, place the pavlovas on plates and top with a generous spoon of kirsch-flavored cream. Place 2 tablespoons of the fruit on top of each pavlova, allowing the juice to drizzle down the sides, and serve the remaining fruit around the bottom of the dessert or in a separate bowl.

CHEF'S TIP *If you prefer a neater shape for the pavlovas, pipe into 6 rounds using a pastry bag with a plain 3/4-inch tip.*

Chocolate and Cointreau mousse

Mousse in French literally means froth or foam. This melt-in-the-mouth mousse marries the classic flavors of chocolate and orange, is simple to prepare, and makes a magical finale to any meal.

Preparation time 40 minutes
+ 1 hour refrigeration
Total cooking time 5 minutes
Serves 4–6

4 oz. semi-sweet baking chocolate
3 tablespoons unsalted butter
1/4 cup orange juice
3 tablespoons cocoa powder
2 eggs, separated
2 tablespoons Cointreau
1/3 cup whipping cream
1 egg white
2 tablespoons sugar
orange segments and whipped cream,
to serve

One Place the chocolate, butter and orange juice in the top of a double boiler over a pan of barely simmering water. When the chocolate and butter have melted, stir in the cocoa powder. Remove from the water and whisk in the egg yolks and Cointreau. Allow to cool.

Two In a chilled bowl, beat the cream until soft peaks form. Cover and refrigerate until ready to use.

Three Beat all the egg whites in a clean, dry bowl until soft peaks form. Add the sugar; beat until smooth and glossy.

Four Using a large metal spoon, gently fold the egg whites into the cooled chocolate mixture. Before they are completely incorporated, fold in the whipped cream. Spoon the mixture into individual serving dishes or a large serving bowl and refrigerate for at least 1 hour. Serve with orange segments and whipped cream.

Gooseberry fool

England is the home of this old-fashioned but delicious dessert made of cooked, strained and puréed fruit, chilled and folded into custard and whipped cream. Traditionally, fool is made from gooseberries, although any fruit may be used.

***Preparation time** 40 minutes
+ 2 hours refrigeration*
***Total cooking time** 25 minutes*
Serves 4–6

GOOSEBERRY PUREE
½ cup sugar
*4 cups fresh gooseberries, trimmed
at both ends*
*1 sheet gelatin or ½ teaspoon
gelatin powder*

2 tablespoons cornstarch
¼ cup sugar
½ cup milk
½ cup plain thick yogurt
¼ cup whipping cream
1 egg white
⅓ cup whipping cream, to serve
4–6 macaroons, to serve

One To make the purée, reserve 1 tablespoon of sugar and place the rest in a heavy-bottomed saucepan with 1 cup water. Stir over low heat until the sugar dissolves. Bring to a boil, add the fruit, reduce the heat and simmer for 10 minutes, or until tender. Strain off the liquid. Purée the fruit in a food processor, then stir in the reserved sugar. Soak the gelatin sheet or powder, following the method in the Chef's techniques on page 541.

Two In a separate heatproof bowl, combine the cornstarch and 1 tablespoon of the sugar. Add ¼ cup of the milk and stir until smooth. Bring the remaining milk almost to a boil, then quickly remove from the heat and whisk it into the cornstarch and sugar. Place in a clean pan and whisk over low heat until the mixture boils and thickens. Remove from the heat.

Three Stir the soaked gelatin into the hot custard until dissolved, then cover with parchment paper and allow to cool. Stir in the fruit purée and yogurt, mixing well.

Four Whip the cream until soft peaks form, then fold into the custard. Whisk the egg white in a clean, dry bowl until stiff, then whisk in the remaining sugar and fold into the custard.

Five Pipe or spoon the fool into tall glasses, ensuring there are no air pockets. Chill for 2 hours to set.

Six Serve with some freshly whipped cream and macaroons.

CHEF'S TIP *If the gooseberries are tart, sweeten them with a little sugar. Frozen gooseberries may be used in this recipe if fresh are not available.*

Iced raspberry soufflé

This chilled raspberry soufflé always looks wonderful and is a great conversation piece. It can also be made days—if not weeks—ahead, leaving more time for you to spend with your guests.

Preparation time *45 minutes + 6 hours freezing + 30 minutes resting*
Total cooking time *10 minutes*
Serves 4–6

2¼ cups raspberries
1 cup sugar
5 egg whites
2¼ cups whipping cream
fresh raspberries, to garnish
sprigs of fresh mint, to garnish

One Purée the raspberries in a food processor, then press them through a fine sieve to eliminate the seeds. Measure out 1¼ cups of raspberry purée and set aside.

Two Cut out a piece of parchment paper to measure 10 x 3½ inches. Wrap the paper around the outside of a 1-quart, 7-inch-diameter soufflé dish so that it extends above the rim to make a collar. Secure the overlapping paper in place with tape or kitchen string, trying to keep the paper free of creases.

Three Place the sugar and ¼ cup water in a medium heavy-bottomed saucepan and heat gently to dissolve the sugar. Bring the syrup to a boil, then follow the method in the Chef's techniques for making Italian meringue on page 539.

Four In a separate bowl, whip 1½ cups of cream until it forms soft peaks.

Five Using a metal spoon, gently fold the meringue into the reserved raspberry purée until thoroughly mixed, then fold in the cream until the streaks disappear. Be careful not to overmix, as this will cause the cream to thicken and separate and make the soufflé look grainy.

Six Spoon the mixture into the soufflé dish right up to the edge of the paper collar, then gently smooth the surface of the soufflé. Place in the freezer for a minimum of 6 hours. Just before serving, peel off the paper collar and allow the soufflé to rest for 30 minutes to soften.

Seven Whip the remaining ¾ cup cream and use it to decorate the top of the soufflé. Finally, garnish the soufflé with the fresh raspberries and sprigs of mint.

Cherry brandy snap baskets

You can make the brandy snap baskets and the ice cream for this pretty and unusual dessert in advance, then just fill the baskets when you're ready to serve.

Preparation time *20 minutes*
+ 30 minutes chilling
Total cooking time *15 minutes*
Makes 6

BRANDY SNAP BASKETS
¼ cup unsalted butter
¼ cup light brown sugar
2 tablespoons golden syrup
or dark corn syrup
½ cup all-purpose flour
few drops of vanilla extract

2 cups vanilla ice cream,
preferably homemade
2 cups morello cherries, drained,
pitted and finely chopped
2 tablespoons port
sprigs of fresh mint, to decorate

One To make the brandy snap baskets, place the butter, sugar and golden syrup in a small saucepan and heat gently until the sugar has dissolved. Allow to cool for 1 minute, then stir in the flour and vanilla extract. Transfer to a small bowl and chill for 30 minutes. Preheat the oven to 350°F.

Two Remove the ice cream from the freezer and allow to slightly soften for 10 minutes, without allowing to melt. Mix the cherries and port into the softened ice cream. Cover and return to the freezer to firm up.

Three Line two baking sheets with parchment paper. Divide the brandy snap dough into six even-size pieces and roll into round balls. Place three balls on each baking sheet, leaving plenty of space between them, and flatten into a round with moistened fingertips. Bake for 5–6 minutes.

Four Have ready six teacups upside down on the work surface. Allow the cookies to rest for 1 minute after baking, then use a flexible bladed knife to drape one over each cup, pressing it into a basket shape. Allow the cookies to cool and set into shape.

Five Set a basket in the center of each plate and fill with two scoops of ice cream. Serve immediately, decorated with a sprig of mint.

Coffee granita with panna cotta

*A coffee-flavored granita teamed with a silky
Italian custard makes a refreshing start to the day.*

Preparation time *1 hour*
+ overnight chilling
Total cooking time *20 minutes*
Serves 4

1 cup sugar
1/4 cup instant dark-roast coffee
2 tablespoons coffee liqueur, optional
2 teaspoons gelatin powder
2 vanilla beans, split lengthwise
1 cup milk
1 cup whipping cream

One Simmer 3/4 cup water and 3/4 cup of the sugar in a saucepan for 10 minutes. Mix the coffee with a little water to form a paste, stir in and allow to cool.

Two Add 2 cups water and the coffee liqueur. Pour the granita into a shallow plastic or metal container and allow to freeze overnight.

Three Dissolve the gelatin powder in 2 tablespoons cold water. Scrape the vanilla seeds into a saucepan and add the beans, milk, cream and remaining sugar. Bring to a boil, strain into a bowl and discard the beans.

Four Add the gelatin to the hot milk mixture, then stir to melt. Place the bowl inside a bowl of ice water and stir until the gelatin begins to set (as the spoon is drawn through it, you will see a line across the bottom of the bowl). Pour into four 2/3-cup gelatin molds or ramekins. Chill overnight.

Five Half an hour before serving, refrigerate four plates. Release the panna cotta from the molds by wrapping in a hot cloth and turning over. Scoop out the granita in flakes by drawing a fork or the side of a metal spoon across its surface. Serve on the chilled plates with the panna cotta.

Chocolate profiteroles

The name "profiterole" is derived from the French word profit, *and originally meant a small gift, which is just what these chocolate-smothered cream puffs are.*

Preparation time *30 minutes*
Total cooking time *30 minutes*
Serves 6

2 quantities cream puff pastry (see page 545)
1 egg, lightly beaten and strained, to glaze

FILLING
1½ cups whipping cream
1½ tablespoons sugar
1–2 drops vanilla extract

confectioners' sugar, to dust
chocolate sauce, to serve
(see page 369)

One To make the profiteroles, preheat the oven to 400°F. Brush a baking sheet with melted butter and refrigerate until needed. Put the cream puff pastry into a pastry bag fitted with a ³/₈-inch plain tip.

Two With the tip about ½ inch above the baking sheet, pipe well-spaced balls 1 inch in diameter, then stop the pressure on the bag and quickly pull away. Brush the top of each ball with the strained egg, making sure that it does not run down the sides as it will burn during cooking. Lightly press down the top of each ball with the back of a fork to ensure an even shape when rising. Bake for 15–20 minutes, or until well risen and golden brown. The profiteroles should sound hollow when the bottoms are tapped. Make a small hole in the bottom of each using the point of a small knife. Transfer to a wire rack to cool thoroughly.

Three To make the filling, beat the cream, sugar and vanilla together until stiff peaks form. Spoon the filling into a pastry bag fitted with a small round tip and pipe a little into the bottom of each profiterole.

Four To serve, stack the profiteroles in a pyramid in a glass bowl or on individual plates. Dust lightly with sifted confectioners' sugar and serve with the warm chocolate sauce drizzled over.

Vanilla ice cream

No commercial ice cream can ever compare with the creamy, decadent richness of the homemade variety. This classic favorite is peppered with fine black specks: the tiny seeds of the vanilla bean, which release a fabulous flavor. For a light, smooth result every time, and minimal fuss, an ice-cream machine is highly recommended.

Preparation time 20 minutes
+ churning or beating + freezing
Total cooking time 10 minutes
Serves 4

5 egg yolks
1/3 cup sugar
1 1/2 cups milk
1 vanilla bean, split lengthwise
1/2 cup whipping cream

One Whisk the egg yolks and sugar in the top of a double boiler until thick and creamy and almost white. Bring the milk and vanilla bean slowly to a boil in a heavy-bottomed saucepan. Gradually whisk the boiling milk into the eggs and sugar, then transfer the mixture to a clean pan. Stir constantly with a wooden spoon over low heat for 3–5 minutes, or until the custard thickly coats the back of the spoon. Make sure that the mixture does not boil, as this will cause it to separate.

Two Pour through a fine strainer into a clean bowl. Place the bowl in some iced water to cool. When the custard is very cold, stir in the cream, then pour the mixture into an ice-cream machine and churn for 10–20 minutes, or until the paddle leaves a trail in the ice cream, or the ice cream holds its own shape. Remove from the machine and freeze in an airtight, stainless steel container for 3–4 hours or overnight.

Three Alternatively, freeze the custard and cream mixture in a 1-quart container for 3 hours, or until firm. Scoop the firm mixture into a large bowl and beat with an electric mixer for 1–2 minutes, or until thick and creamy. Return the mixture to the container and freeze for 3 hours. Repeat the beating and freezing process twice, then freeze the ice cream overnight.

CHEF'S TIP *This ice cream can take on a range of flavors. A little coffee extract may be added to the custard at the end of step 1, or 1/3–2/3 cup chopped chocolate may be added to the milk before boiling. Another delicious option is to fold amaretto liqueur or crushed cookies into the frozen ice cream before it is stored.*

Zabaglione with ladyfingers

*This deliciously light Zabaglione must be eaten immediately
after it is made. It takes only a few minutes to whisk
and serve and is perfect for unexpected guests.*

Preparation time 15 minutes
Total cooking time 20 minutes
Serves 4–5

LADYFINGERS
2 eggs, separated
1/4 cup caster sugar
1/2 cup all-purpose flour
confectioners' sugar, to dust

ZABAGLIONE
4 egg yolks
1/2 cup sugar
1/3 cup Marsala

One Preheat the oven to 400°F. Line a baking sheet with parchment paper. Fit a pastry bag with a 1/2-inch plain tip.

Two To make the ladyfingers, whisk the egg yolks and sugar in a bowl until creamy and almost white. In a separate bowl, whisk the egg whites until stiff peaks form when the whisk is lifted. With a large metal spoon or plastic spatula, fold a third of the egg white into the yolk mixture. Sift half the flour into the yolk mixture and carefully fold in, then add another portion of egg white. Repeat with the remaining flour and egg white, taking care not to overmix. Spoon the mixture into the pastry bag and pipe 3-inch pieces slightly apart on the baking sheet. Dust liberally with the sifted confectioners' sugar, then allow to rest at room temperature for 5 minutes to dissolve the sugar and create a pearl effect. Bake for 10 minutes, or until golden brown. Remove the ladyfingers from the baking sheet by lifting the parchment paper with the biscuits, then placing them upside down on the work surface. Sprinkle the back of the paper with water to make it easy to peel off.

Turn the ladyfingers over and cool on a wire rack.

Three To make the Zabaglione, bring a pan half-full of water to a boil, then turn the heat as low as possible. Whisk the egg yolks and sugar in a heatproof bowl until almost white. Mix in the Marsala. Place the bowl over the barely steaming water and whisk until the mixture increases to four times its volume and is firm and frothy. Pour into four large wine glasses and serve immediately with the ladyfingers.

CHEF'S TIP *Zabaglione is an excellent standby dessert for unexpected guests. If you do not have any of the traditional Italian Marsala, you can use some Madeira instead.*

Lemon delicious

Also known as "Lemon surprise," this wonderful dessert separates as it cooks into a light soufflé sponge topping with a tart lemon sauce hidden beneath.

***Preparation time** 25 minutes*
***Total cooking time** 40 minutes*
Serves 4

*¼ cup unsalted butter,
at room temperature
⅓ cup sugar
finely grated zest of 1 lemon
2 large eggs, separated
2 tablespoons all-purpose flour
3 tablespoons lemon juice
1 cup milk
confectioners' sugar,
for dusting*

One Preheat the oven to 350°F. Brush with melted butter an 8¼ x 6 x 1¾-inch flameproof dish.

Two Using a wooden spoon or electric mixer, beat the butter to soften it, then beat in the sugar in small additions. Continue beating until the mixture is light and creamy, then mix in the lemon zest and egg yolks until well blended. Gently fold in the flour, followed by the lemon juice.

Three In a small saucepan, warm the milk until tepid, then fold it into the lemon mixture.

Four Put the egg whites in a large clean dry bowl, add a pinch of salt and beat them with a hand whisk or electric mixer until soft peaks form. Using a plastic spatula or a large metal spoon, mix 1 tablespoon of the egg white into the lemon mixture to soften it, then carefully fold in the remaining egg white, being careful not to lose volume.

Five Pour the mixture into the prepared dish, then set in a baking pan and pour warm water into the baking pan to come about halfway up the side of the dish and make a water bath. Bake for 30–35 minutes, or until the top is a pale golden brown and firm to the light touch of a finger. Serve the dessert hot or chilled. If you are serving cold, dust with a little sifted confectioners' sugar.

CHEF'S TIP *When the lemon juice meets the butter, the mixture may curdle. However, when you add the milk, the mixture should become smooth again (make sure the milk is barely warm—if it is too hot, the flour and yolks may cook and the mixture may then become too heavy).*

Summer puddings

Perfect for entertaining, these pretty English puddings need to be prepared the day before to allow the fruit juices to flavor the bread and turn it that distinctive vivid pink color.

Preparation time *30 minutes
+ overnight refrigeration*
Total cooking time *5 minutes*
Serves 6

*18 thin slices good-quality day-old
white bread
2 lb. mixed soft fruits, such as
blackberries, raspberries,
strawberries and black currants,
fresh or frozen and hulled
up to 1/2 cup sugar, depending on the
sweetness of the fruit*

One Cut the crusts from the bread and discard. Reserving two or three slices for the top, cut rounds and strips out of the remaining slices to fit the bottom and sides of six 1/2-cup ramekins or pudding molds, or a 4-cup pudding basin or heatproof glass bowl. Make sure the bottom and sides are completely lined and that there are no spaces between the slices of bread.

Two Halve or quarter the strawberries if large, then put all the fruit in a large saucepan with 2 tablespoons water and add the sugar, to taste. Cover and cook over low heat for 5 minutes, or until the juices are running from the fruit and they are just tender but still whole.

Three Ladle the fruit and juices into the bread-lined ramekins, molds, basin or bowl until it reaches almost to the top of the bread, reserving any excess. Cover with the reserved slices of bread, trimming to fit snugly onto the surface of the fruit.

Four Place on a baking sheet to catch any excess juices and cover with a plate and a weight of 2 lb. if using the basin or

bowl, or smaller weights if using the ramekins or molds (you can use cans). Chill overnight in the refrigerator.

Five When ready to serve, remove the weights and unmold the puddings. Serve the puddings cold with the extra fruit and juice spooned over and a sorbet, ice cream or cream.

CHEF'S TIP *For the best color and texture, use fewer strawberries than the other softer and darker fruit.*

Chocolate roulade

Whipped cream and fresh raspberries fill this delicate chocolate cake roll. It is also delicious with other fresh fruits, such as strawberries or peaches.

Preparation time *25 minutes*
+ 20 minutes refrigeration
Total cooking time *8–10 minutes*
Serves 6

CHOCOLATE SPONGE CAKE
2 eggs
¼ cup sugar
⅓ cup all-purpose flour
1 tablespoon unsweetened cocoa

FILLING
⅔ cup whipping cream
3 tablespoons confectioners' sugar
1 pint fresh raspberries

unsweetened cocoa and confectioners' sugar, to dust

One To make the sponge cake, preheat the oven to 400°F. Line a 11 x 7 x 1½-inches jelly roll pan with parchment paper. Put the eggs and sugar in the top of a double boiler over barely steaming water, off the heat, making sure the insert is not touching the water. Using an electric mixer, beat for 5–7 minutes, or until the mixture becomes thick and creamy, has doubled in volume and leaves a trail as it falls from the beaters. The temperature of the mixture should never be hot, only warm. Remove the insert from the water and continue to beat until the mixture is cold.

Two Sift the flour and cocoa together and, using a large metal spoon, carefully fold it into the egg mixture. Stop folding as soon as the flour and cocoa are just combined or the mixture will lose its volume. Pour the mixture into the pan and spread it evenly using a flexible bladed knife. Bake for 6–8 minutes, or until springy to the light touch of a finger. Remove the cake from the pan while still hot by sliding it, with the paper on, to a wire rack to cool. Allow to cool, then turn it over onto a large piece of parchment paper or clean cloth and remove the paper that was used for baking.

Three To make the filling, beat the cream with the confectioners' sugar until firm peaks form. Spread the cream onto the cake and sprinkle with the raspberries. Roll up by picking up the paper or cloth at one of the longer sides and pushing it down and away from you while rolling, finishing with the seam underneath. Trim each end and refrigerate for 20 minutes. Sprinkle sifted cocoa and confectioners' sugar onto the roulade.

Molded fruit terrine

*This luscious dessert yields a truly fruit-filled flavor with every tingling mouthful.
The secret is to use two loaf pans instead of one, sitting one on top of the
other to prevent the fruit from floating to the top before the gelatin has set.*

Preparation time *40 minutes
+ 1–2 nights refrigeration*
Total cooking time *5–10 minutes*
Serves 8

*¹/₂ cup black currants
³/₄ cup red currants
³/₄ cup blueberries
1³/₄ cups strawberries
3 cups raspberries
4 gelatin sheets
or 2 teaspoons gelatin powder
1 cup rosé wine
2 tablespoons sugar
1 tablespoon lemon juice
¹/₄ cup strained raspberry purée
(see Chef's tips)*

One Pick through all the fruit and remove any stalks, then gently mix the fruit together in a bowl, taking care not to bruise or damage any of it.

Two Soak the gelatin sheets or powder, following the method in the Chef's techniques on page 541.

Three Carefully arrange the fruit into a loaf pan measuring 9 x 5 x 3 inches, placing the smaller fruits on the bottom.

Four In a small saucepan, heat half the wine until it begins to simmer. Remove the saucepan from the heat and add the sugar, gelatin and lemon juice. Stir to dissolve. Add the remaining wine and the raspberry purée. Reserve ²/₃ cup of the liquid and pour the rest over the fruit. Cover with plastic wrap. Place a lightly weighted 9-inch loaf pan on top, then refrigerate for at least 1 hour, or overnight if possible, until the mold has set. When it is set, remove the top loaf pan and plastic wrap.

Five Gently warm the reserved wine mixture and pour over the surface of the mold. Cover again with plastic wrap and refrigerate overnight to set.

Six Just before serving, unmold the terrine by dipping the bottom of the pan very briefly in hot water and inverting it onto a plate. Slice the terrine, decorate with some extra fresh berries, and serve with crème fraîche.

CHEF'S TIPS *Straining about 1¹/₄ cups of raspberries will produce the required quantity of raspberry purée.*

Do not rinse the raspberries, and only rinse the other fruit if it is sandy.

Small strawberries give the best results in this fruit terrine, but if they are not available, you could use larger strawberries cut in half.

Bavarian vanilla cream

A bavarois is an egg-based custard folded through with whipped cream, and flavored with chocolate, coffee, praline or even fruit. This bavarois is simply laced with real vanilla.

Preparation time *1 hour*
+ 1 hour refrigeration
Total cooking time *10 minutes*
Serves 4

*3 gelatin sheets or 1¹/₂ teaspoons
gelatin powder
2 eggs, separated
¹/₄ cup sugar
1 cup milk
1 vanilla bean, split lengthwise
¹/₂ cup whipping cream,
lightly whipped*

One Lightly grease four 1-cup gelatin molds of any shape (or use a 1-quart mold). Soak the gelatin sheets or powder, following the method in the Chef's techniques on page 541.

Two Beat the egg yolks and sugar in a bowl until thick, creamy and almost white. Slowly bring the milk and vanilla bean to a boil.

Three Follow the method for making custard in the Chef's techniques on page 541. Stir the soaked gelatin into the hot custard, ensuring the gelatin dissolves completely. Strain into a clean bowl, then leave over a bowl of ice until almost at the point of setting, stirring occasionally, and checking often.

Four Whisk the egg whites until stiff—they should stand in shiny peaks when the whisk is lifted. Using a metal spoon, fold the lightly whipped cream into the cold custard, then carefully fold in the whites.

Five Spoon the mixture into the molds and refrigerate for at least 1 hour, or until set. Unmold the cream by gently shaking at an angle of 45°, or dipping the bottom of the mold briefly in boiling water and tapping out onto a serving dish.

CHEF'S TIPS *The egg whites should not be whisked too far in advance: resting will make the volume drop, and also result in a dry, grainy texture. Adding a pinch of sugar while the egg whites are still frothy will stabilize them and help them whisk stiff more easily.*

Ensure that the custard is cold before adding the cream: if the cream melts, the dessert will lose its volume.

Lemon tart with Italian meringue

*This delicious short pastry shell is smothered
in a creamy lemon filling and a layer of satiny meringue.
It should be baked and served on the same day.*

*Preparation time 45 minutes
+ 40 minutes refrigeration*
Total cooking time 45 minutes
Serves 6

*1 quantity short pastry (see
page 544 and Chef's tip)*

LEMON FILLING
3 egg yolks
2/3 cup sugar
2 teaspoons finely grated lemon zest
juice of 3 lemons
2 tablespoons unsalted butter

3/4 cup sugar
4 egg whites
*1 tablespoon confectioners' sugar,
for dusting*

One Preheat the oven to 350°F. Gently roll the pastry between two sheets of parchment paper to 1/8 inch thick, then ease into a lightly greased, shallow 9-inch fluted tart pan with removable bottom. Bake blind for 10 minutes, following the method in the Chef's techniques on page 547. Remove the pie weights or rice and the paper. Bake for 10 more minutes, or until the center begins to color. Remove from the oven and cool on a wire rack.

Two To prepare the filling, whisk or beat the egg yolks and sugar in the top of a double boiler until light and creamy. Add the lemon zest, juice and then the butter. Place over a saucepan of barely simmering water and whisk constantly for 15–20 minutes, or until thickened. When ready, the mixture will leave a "ribbon" when drizzled from the whisk. While the filling is still hot, pour it into the cooled tart shell.

Three Place the 3/4 cup sugar and 3 tablespoons water in a medium heavy-bottomed saucepan and heat gently to dissolve the sugar. Bring to a boil, then follow the Chef's techniques for making Italian meringue on page 539.

Four Place the meringue in a pastry bag fitted with a 1/2-inch star tip. Starting in the center, pipe the meringue in continuous concentric circles covering the entire tart, keeping the meringue inside the pastry edge. Dust the surface with confectioners' sugar. Bake for 5 minutes, or until the meringue is lightly colored. Allow to cool and then refrigerate for 20 minutes, or until the filling is set.

CHEF'S TIP *If possible, refrigerate the dough overnight; it helps to prevent the pastry from shrinking during baking.*

about lemons...

Lemons vary in acidity and sweetness acording to their variety. Taste the lemon juice and adjust the sugar accordingly if you need to. Lemons give up their juice much more easily when they are warm and you can heat them for a couple of seconds in the microwave to make them produce more.

Chocolate and chestnut terrine

This rich, chilled terrine is a terrific dessert for unexpected guests. It freezes well for up to three months. Serve thinly sliced.

Preparation time *20 minutes*
+ 12 hours refrigeration
Total cooking time *10 minutes*
Serves 10–12

6 oz. good-quality semi-sweet chocolate, chopped
¹/₃ cup unsalted butter, at room temperature
¹/₃ cup sugar
12 oz. canned unsweetened chestnut purée
¹/₄ teaspoon vanilla extract
¹/₄ teaspoon instant coffee, dissolved in 1 teaspoon hot water
2 tablespoons rum
good-quality semi-sweet chocolate, for shaving
fresh berries or orange segements, to garnish

One Grease an 8¹/₂ x 4¹/₂ x 2¹/₂-inch loaf pan or ceramic terrine. Line the bottom with parchment paper. Grease the paper.

Two Place the chocolate in the top of a double boiler over hot water and stir until melted. Remove the insert from the water and allow to cool for 5 minutes.

Three In a mixing bowl, beat the butter to soften, then add the sugar and beat until pale and light. Beat in the chestnut purée until softened, then the melted chocolate until thoroughly blended. Mix in the vanilla, coffee and rum. Transfer to the loaf pan, smooth the top, cover with plastic wrap or aluminum foil, and refrigerate for 12 hours.

Four To serve, loosen the sides of the terrine using a small flexible bladed knife, then unmold and remove the paper. Using a vegetable peeler, shave off curls from the edge of the chocolate bar and use these to garnish the terrine. Serve in slices with fresh berries or segments of orange.

Touraine crémets with raspberry coulis

A specialty of Angers and Saumur, these simple yet delicious crémets may be served with a raspberry coulis or fresh berries. Traditionally they are made without the confectioners' sugar and served with fresh cream and plenty of white sugar.

***Preparation time** 20 minutes
+ 1 hour setting time*
Serves 4

*³/4 cup whipping cream
1³/4 cups cream cheese (see Chef's tip)
¹/2 cup confectioners' sugar
sprigs of fresh mint, to garnish
red berries, to garnish*

RASPBERRY COULIS
*3¹/3 cups fresh raspberries
²/3 cup confectioners' sugar
few drops of lemon juice*

One Line four 3¹/2-inch wide ramekins with pieces of cheesecloth large enough to hang over the top of the molds. Pour the cream into a bowl, place the bowl into a bowl filled with ice cubes and a little water and lightly whip the cream until it leaves a trail, but just runs if the bowl is tipped. Add the cream cheese and whip until creamy. Stir in the confectioners' sugar and pour the mixture into the ramekin dishes. Fold the excess cheesecloth over to cover the mixture and place in the refrigerator for at least 1 hour.

Two To make the raspberry coulis, blend the raspberries in a food processor, add the sugar and lemon juice to taste and then pass the purée through a fine strainer. To obtain a deep red coulis, do not blend the purée for too long—doing this incorporates air and will cause it start to become pink.

Three Turn the cheesecloth back over the top edge of the molds, then turn the molds over carefully onto individual plates and remove the molds then the muslin. Pour some of the raspberry coulis around each crémet and decorate with the mint and red berries.

CHEF'S TIP *For a lighter dessert you can use fromage blanc.*

Orange blossom crème caramel

*A refreshing and elegant dessert that can
be prepared a day before if you wish, making
it an ideal sweet finish to a dinner party.*

***Preparation time** 25 minutes
+ 4 hours chilling*
***Total cooking time** 55 minutes*
Makes 6

1 cup superfine sugar
2 cups milk
1/2 vanilla bean, split lengthwise
grated zest of 1 orange
3 eggs, beaten
2 egg yolks
1 teaspoon orange blossom water

One Preheat the oven to 300°F.

Two Prepare a caramel using 1/3 cup of the sugar and a tablespoon of water, following the method in the Chef's techniques on page 540. When the caramel has stopped cooking, reheat over a low heat if set, then pour into six 1/2-cup ramekins. Swirl a little to coat the sides and bottom of the ramekins, holding the ramekins in a cloth to protect your hands.

Three Bring the milk, vanilla bean and orange zest to a boil slowly in a small saucepan. In a bowl, whisk together the eggs, egg yolks, remaining sugar and the orange blossom water until creamy, then whisk in the boiling milk and pour the mixture through a strainer into a pitcher, discarding the vanilla bean and orange zest.

Four Pour the mixture onto the caramel in the ramekins and place the ramekins in a roasting pan. Fill the roasting pan with hot water a third of the way up the ramekins and bake for 30–35 minutes, or until just set. Remove the ramekins from the roasting pan and allow to cool slightly before refrigerating for at least 4 hours or overnight.

Five To serve, run the blade of a flexible bladed knife around the edge of each crème caramel, then place the center of a dessert plate over the ramekin and unmold onto the plate, carefully lifting off the ramekin and allowing the liquid caramel to run over the dessert.

Petits pots au chocolat

*These dainty little chocolate custards are prepared and cooked
in a very similar way to crème caramel, except that they are much
richer, with a fine, smooth texture that melts in the mouth.*

*Preparation time 10 minutes
+ refrigeration
Total cooking time 45 minutes
Serves 6*

1 1/2 cups milk
1/3 cup whipping cream
2 oz. semi-sweet chocolate, chopped
1/2 vanilla bean, split lengthwise
1 egg
3 egg yolks
1/3 cup sugar
whipped cream and grated chocolate,
to serve

One Preheat the oven to 325°F. Place the milk, cream, chocolate and vanilla bean in a heavy-bottomed saucepan and bring to a boil. Using a wooden spoon, cream the egg, egg yolks and sugar together until thick and light. Pour in the melted chocolate mixture and stir to blend. Strain into a large liquid measuring cup and discard the vanilla bean. Remove any froth by skimming across the top with a metal spoon.

Two Pour the mixture into six 1/3-cup ceramic pots or espresso cups, filling them up to the top. Set the pots in a baking dish and pour in enough hot water to come up to about 1/2 inch below their rims. Bake for 30 minutes, or until the surface of the custard feels elastic when you touch it with your finger, and your finger comes away clean. If this is not the case, continue to cook for a little while longer.

Three Remove the pots from the water and allow to cool. When cold, place the whipped cream in a pastry bag fitted with a star-shaped tip. Pipe rosettes onto the pots and sprinkle with chocolate.

Tiramisù

Layers of ladyfingers soaked in coffee and Kahlua, rich mascarpone cream and a generous dusting of cocoa powder make this Italian classic a favorite everywhere.

Preparation time *35 minutes + chilling*
Total cooking time *None*
Serves 4–6

3 egg yolks
1/2 cup sugar
3/4 cup mascarpone cheese
1 1/4 cups whipping cream
1/4 cup Kahlúa
2 cups strong coffee, cooled
36 ladyfingers
cocoa powder, for dusting

One Beat the egg yolks with the sugar until the sugar has dissolved and the mixture is light. Add the mascarpone and mix well. Beat the cream into stiff peaks and gently fold into the mascarpone mixture, then spread a thin layer of the mascarpone cream over the bottom of a deep 14-inch oval dish.

Two Add the Kahlúa to the coffee. Dip the ladyfingers into the coffee, soaking them well. Depending on the freshness of the ladyfingers, they may require more or less soaking, but be careful not to oversoak. Arrange a layer of ladyfingers close together in the dish—you may need to break them to fit the shape of your dish. Cover with another layer of the mascarpone cream, then another layer of ladyfingers, arranging them in the opposite direction to the first layer. Repeat the layers, finishing with mascarpone cream. Smooth the top and keep chilled until ready to serve. Generously dust with cocoa powder just before serving. Tiramisù is best made several hours in advance so that the flavors have time to blend before serving.

Individual lemon cheesecakes

*Refreshingly lemony with a ginger base, the
ever-popular cheesecake is here served in
individual portions with a red grape jelly top.*

*Preparation time 20 minutes + 1 hour
chilling + overnight chilling
Total cooking time 5 minutes
Makes 6*

5 oz. gingersnaps
1/4 cup unsalted butter, melted
1 1/4 cups regular cream cheese
grated zest and juice of 3 lemons
1 1/4 cups condensed milk
2/3 cup plain yogurt
2 level teaspoons unflavored gelatin
3/4 cup red grape juice

One Place the cookies in a plastic bag and crush them using a rolling pin, then stir in the melted butter. Alternatively, place in a food processor and use the pulse button to produce fine crumbs. Drizzle the melted butter over and pulse again until it has been thoroughly mixed into the crumbs.

Two Set six 3 x 2 3/4 inch baking rings (see Chef's tips) onto a small baking sheet lined with waxed paper and divide the crumb mixture between them. Press the crumbs into the bottom of the rings using a flat-bottomed glass. Chill while you make the filling.

Three In a medium bowl using an electric mixer, or in the clean food processor, combine the cream cheese, lemon zest and juice and condensed milk until completely smooth. Add the yogurt and blend for a few seconds only to combine. Divide the cheese mixture between the rings, leaving a small gap at the top for the jelly, then place in the refrigerator overnight to set.

Four In a small saucepan, sprinkle the gelatin over half the grape juice and allow to rest until it swells. Place over a low heat and whisk until the gelatin has completely dissolved. Remove from the heat, stir in the remaining grape juice and cool to room temperature. Carefully spoon a layer of grape jelly over each cheesecake, then chill in the refrigerator for 1 hour.

Five To serve, hold a hot cloth momentarily around the cheesecakes to help the rings slide off, then transfer carefully to serving plates using a flexible bladed knife.

CHEF'S TIPS *Small cans with the tops and bottoms removed make a good substitute for the ring molds. Wash thoroughly and line each with a strip of waxed paper before use.*

If your baking rings are not tall enough, line them with a collar of waxed paper to give added height.

Stewed rhubarb with ginger

*This tangy rhubarb compote (shown bottom right)
is enhanced by the color and flavor of the
red currant jelly and enlivened by the ginger.*

Preparation time 10 minutes
Total cooking time 20 minutes
Serves 4

3 tablespoons red currant jelly
2 lb. rhubarb
1 oz. crystallized or glacé ginger, finely chopped
a little granulated, Demerara or turbinado sugar

One In a small bowl, beat the red currant jelly with a spoon until smooth, pour into a wide saucepan and add 4 tablespoons water.

Two Trim and discard the leaves and the bottom of the stems from the rhubarb. Cut the rhubarb into 1-inch slices and add to the saucepan in a single layer.

Three Bring to a boil and immediately turn the heat down to a bare simmer. Cover tightly with a lid or aluminum foil and cook for 10–15 minutes, or until the rhubarb is tender. The rhubarb should still hold its shape. Be careful to cook the rhubarb very gently or you will end up with a purée.

Four Transfer to a bowl, add the ginger and taste. You may require a little sugar sprinkled over at this stage, depending on the acidity of the rhubarb. Allow to cool slightly and serve warm or, if you prefer, prepare the day before and leave to chill overnight.

CHEF'S TIP *The acidity of the rhubarb will vary considerably so the recipe is only a guide as to sweetness. Add as much sugar as you require. Serve the rhubarb by itself or with thick yogurt.*

Eastern rice pudding

*The cardamom adds a distinctly Eastern flavor
to this creamy rice pudding (shown top right).*

Preparation time 5 minutes
Total cooking time 25 minutes
Serves 4

seeds of 4 cardamom pods, crushed
1³/4 cups whipping cream
1³/4 cups milk
¹/3 cup superfine sugar
¹/3 cup short-grain rice

One Combine the crushed cardamom pods, the cream and the milk in a medium saucepan. Bring to a boil, remove from the heat, allow to cool slightly and stir in the sugar and rice. At this stage, the rice mixture can be refrigerated overnight or it can be cooked immediately.

Two Bring the mixture to a boil, lower the heat and cook, stirring constantly as it begins to thicken, for 20–25 minutes, or until the rice is just soft and the liquid has become creamy. The pudding should have a soft, flowing consistency and when a spoon is drawn through, the bottom of the saucepan should be seen and the pudding should flow quickly to fill the parting behind it. (Remember that the rice will continue to thicken slightly when removed from the heat.) Serve with dried fruit or a fruit conserve.

patisserie

Croissants

Croissants require time and effort to produce, but the rich buttery results will astound friends and family. For step-by-step guidance on how to make croissants, see page 548.

Preparation time 3 hours + resting
+ chilling overnight
Total cooking time 20 minutes
Makes 12–16

1 lb. all-purpose flour
1 teaspoon salt
1/4 cup superfine sugar
1 1/4 cups milk
1/2 oz. fresh yeast or 1/4 oz. package
dried yeast
1 1/3 cups unsalted butter,
at room temperature
2 egg yolks, lightly beaten
whole almonds, to decorate

ALMOND CREAM
1/4 cup unsalted butter, softened
1/4 cup superfine sugar
1 egg, beaten
1/3 cup ground almonds
2 tablespoons all-purpose flour
zest of 1/2 lemon

One Sift the flour, salt and sugar into a large bowl and make a well in the center. Heat the milk to warm, stir in the yeast and 1 tablespoon of the flour until dissolved, then allow to rest until bubbles form. Add to the dry ingredients and bring together to form a soft dough, then turn out onto a floured work surface and knead for 5 minutes, or until smooth and elastic. Transfer the dough to a floured bowl and cover. Set aside in a warm area for 1 hour, or until doubled in volume.

Two Meanwhile, put the butter between 2 sheets of plastic wrap and roll it out into a rectangle measuring 8 x 4 inches.

Three Once the dough has risen, punch it down and transfer to a floured work surface. Roll into a rectangle 16 x 5 inches. The dough should be just over twice as long as the butter and a little bit wider. Place the butter on the lower half of the dough and fold the dough over to completely enclose the butter. Seal the edges with your fingertips. Turn the dough so that the fold is on the right-hand side and lightly roll the dough into a large rectangle twice as long as it is wide. Brush off excess flour and fold the dough into even thirds like a letter, with the bottom third up towards the middle and the top third down. Chill in plastic wrap for 20 minutes.

Four To make the almond cream, beat the butter and sugar together using a wooden spoon or an electric mixer, until light and creamy. Gradually add the egg, a third at a time, beating well between each addition. Stir in the ground almonds, flour and lemon zest.

Five Remove the dough from the refrigerator and cut it in half. On a well-floured surface, roll each piece of dough into a large rectangle, and trim it to 8 3/4 x 4 1/2 inches. Using a triangular template with a base measuring 7 inches and sides measuring 5 1/2 inches, cut the rectangles into 6 triangles (you should be left with 2 end triangles). Along the wide end of the triangle, pull down to form a longer triangle and spoon a little almond cream onto the wide base. Roll the dough up, starting from the wide end, to form crescents, tucking the triangular point underneath the dough. Place the croissants on baking sheets and lightly brush with the egg yolk. Cover the croissants with plastic wrap and refrigerate overnight.

Six Remove the croissants from the refrigerator and set aside to rise for 30–45 minutes, or until doubled in size. Do not hurry this process by putting the croissants anywhere too warm, or the butter in the dough will melt. Preheat the oven to 400°F. Toast the almonds under a broiler until golden.

Seven Once the croissants have doubled in size, gently brush all over with a second layer of egg and decorate with the almonds. Bake for 15–20 minutes, or until golden.

Brioche

Brioche, a light yeast dough enriched with butter and eggs, is wonderful served with butter and jam for breakfast or brunch, or as an accompaniment to stewed fruit. There are many ways to mold brioche dough—here it has been molded into the traditional brioche à tête, where the small ball on top represents the "head" of the brioche.

Preparation time 30 minutes
+ 4 hours rising
Total cooking time 25 minutes
Makes 1 large loaf or 4 small loaves

3 tablespoons warm milk
1/4 oz. package dried yeast
3 cups bread or all-purpose flour
1/4 cup sugar
1 teaspoon salt
6 eggs, lightly beaten
3/4 cup unsalted butter, at room temperature
1 egg, beaten and mixed with 2 tablespoons of water, to glaze

One Pour the milk into a bowl and dissolve the yeast in it. Add 1 tablespoon of the flour, cover and set aside until bubbles start to appear. Sift the remaining flour, sugar and salt into a large bowl, make a well in the center and add the beaten eggs and yeast mixture. Gradually mix the flour into the wet ingredients to make a sticky dough, then transfer to a floured surface.

Two Lift and throw the dough down on the work surface with floured hands for 20 minutes, or until the dough forms a smooth ball. Place in an oiled bowl and turn the dough over to coat with the oil. Cover and let rise at room temperature for 2–2 1/2 hours, or until the dough has doubled in volume.

Three Turn out the dough, punch down, cover and allow to rest for 5 minutes, then transfer to the work surface again. Place the soft butter on top of the dough and pinch and squeeze both together until they are well combined. Knead for 5 more minutes, or until the dough is

smooth again. Cover and allow to rest for 5 minutes.

Four Brush a 5-cup brioche mold or four small 2-cup brioche molds liberally with melted butter. If using the small molds, divide the dough into four pieces. Set aside a quarter of each piece of dough. Shape the large pieces into balls and drop them into the molds seam side down. Make a hole in the top of each ball using your finger and shape the reserved pieces into tear-drop shapes to fit into the holes. Press down to seal. Cover and allow to rise for 1–1 1/2 hours,

or until the molds are half to three-quarters full. Preheat the oven to 400°F. Lightly brush with the egg glaze and bake for 20–25 minutes, or until a nice golden brown. Turn out and allow to cool on a wire rack.

CHEF'S TIP *To make raisin brioche, simply soak 2 tablespoons chopped raisins in some rum to plump them up. Drain and add to the dough after the butter has been incorporated.*

Fruit tartlets

These traditional pastries are at their best when there is a summer bounty of red fruit and berries. You can also make one large tart, which would be the perfect end to a summer picnic.

***Preparation time** 45 minutes
+ 30 minutes chilling*
***Total cooking time** 30 minutes*
Makes 6

PASTRY CREAM
1¼ cups milk
⅓ cup lemon juice
grated zest of 2 lemons
4 egg yolks
⅓ cup superfine sugar
2 tablespoons all-purpose flour
2 tablespoons cornstarch

1 quantity sweet pastry (see page 546)
1¾ cups mixed berries
⅓ cup apricot jam

One Brush six 3 x ¾-inch tartlet pans with removable bottoms with melted butter. Preheat the oven to 400°F.

Two To make the pastry cream, place the milk, lemon juice and zest in a saucepan and bring slowly to a boil. In a bowl, whisk the egg yolks with the sugar until light in color. Sift in the flour and cornstarch and whisk until well blended. Pour half the boiling milk into the yolk mixture, whisk well and return to the saucepan with the remaining milk. Bring to a boil, stirring constantly, and boil for 1 minute to completely cook the flour. Remove from the heat and spread the pastry cream onto a baking sheet to cool quickly. Cover the surface with waxed paper to prevent a skin from forming and allow to cool. When cool, whisk until smooth.

Three Roll out the pastry on a floured surface to ⅛-inch thickness. Cut six 5-inch circles of pastry to fit the pans, then ease into the pans, prick the bottom of each pastry shell with a fork and refrigerate for 20 minutes. Blind bake the pastry shells for 10 minutes, following the method in the Chef's techniques on page 547. Remove the pie weights or rice and paper from the pastry shells and return to the oven for another 5 minutes, or until they are golden. Remove the fruit tartlets from the oven, allow to rest for 2 minutes, then remove from their pans and place on a wire rack to cool.

Four Pipe or spoon the pastry cream into the pastry shells to three-quarters full, leveling the surface, then pile the berries on top so that the tarts all look generously filled.

Five In a small saucepan, heat the apricot jam with 3 tablespoons water. When the mixture begins to boil, strain into a bowl and, while still hot, brush a thin layer of glaze over the cooled tartlets. Serve warm or at room temperature.

Melting moments

*As their name suggests, these melt-in-the-mouth cookies with
their soft buttercream and jam filling are simply irresistible.*

Preparation time *45 minutes*
Total cooking time *20 minutes per
baking sheet*
Makes about 30

*1 cup unsalted butter,
at room temperature
3/4 confectioners' sugar, sifted
1 teaspoon finely grated lemon zest
2 egg yolks
2¹/3 cups all-purpose flour
2¹/2 tablespoons raspberry jam, beaten
confectioners' sugar, to dust*

BUTTERCREAM
*¹/3 cup sugar
1 egg white
¹/3 cup unsalted butter,
at room temperature*

One Preheat the oven to 350°F. Brush
two baking sheets with melted butter.
Using a wooden spoon or an electric
mixer, cream together the butter,
confectioners' sugar and lemon zest until
light and fluffy.

Two Add the egg yolks and mix
thoroughly. Sift in the flour and stir with
a wooden spoon until the mixture comes
together to make a smooth soft paste.
Spoon into a pastry bag with a ¹/3-inch
star tip.

Three Pipe enough ⁵/8–³/4-inch rosettes to
fill the prepared baking sheets, spacing
well apart. Bake for 10–12 minutes, or
until the edges are golden. Cool on a
wire rack. Repeat with the remaining
mixture, preparing the baking sheets as
in step 1.

Four To make the buttercream, in a small
saucepan, over low heat, dissolve ¹/4 cup

of the sugar in 1 tablespoon water,
stirring occasionally. Increase the heat
and bring to a boil. Simmer without
stirring for 3–5 minutes. To prevent
crystals of sugar from forming, wipe
down the sides of the saucepan with a
brush dipped in water.

Five Meanwhile, beat the egg white until
stiff. Add the remaining sugar and beat
until stiff and shiny and peaks form
when the beaters are lifted. While

beating the mixture, pour in the
bubbling syrup in a thin steady stream,
aiming between the bowl and the beaters.
Continue to beat until the mixture is
cold. Gradually add the soft butter.

Six Divide the cookies into pairs and
spread jam on the flat side of one of each
pair. Using a plain ¹/4-inch tip, pipe a
little buttercream onto the other cookie,
sandwich the pair together and dust
lightly with sifted confectioners' sugar.

LE CORDON BLEU ✶ COMPLETE COOK

Florentines

Accredited to Austrian bakers, this wonderful mixture of sugar, butter, cream, nuts and fruit has its origins in Italy. Crisp to eat, they have the added allure of a chocolate base, which is optional though traditional.

Preparation time *20 minutes +*
10 minutes resting
Total cooking time *15 minutes per sheet*
Makes 25–30

1/2 cup unsalted butter
1/2 cup sugar
3 1/4 oz. candied orange peel, finely chopped or mixed peel
1 oz. glacé cherries, cut into 8 pieces
2/3 cup blanched sliced almonds
3/4 cup blanched almonds, chopped
2 tablespoons whipping cream
8 oz. good-quality dark chocolate, chopped

One Preheat the oven to 350°F. Brush two baking sheets with melted butter.

Two Melt the butter in a small saucepan, stir in the sugar, slowly bring to a boil and remove from the heat. Add the candied peel, cherries, the sliced and chopped almonds and mix well. Whisk the cream until it is thick and gently stir it into the warm mixture. Set aside for 10 minutes, or until cool and thick.

Three Using a heaping teaspoon of mixture for each Florentine, spoon on enough mounds of the mixture to fill both baking sheets (see Chef's techniques, page 555). Space well apart as the cookies will spread. Bake for 5 minutes, or until lightly set. Using a large biscuit cutter or a cup, shape the spread mixture into neat rounds by pulling in the edges. Return to the oven for 4 minutes. Reshape with the cutter and allow to cool for 3 minutes, or until firm enough to remove from the tray. Carefully lift them with a flexible bladed knife and cool on a wire rack. Repeat

with the remaining mixture, preparing the sheets as instructed in step 1. Warm the mixture a little if it has cooled too much to spoon easily.

Four Bring a saucepan half-full of water to a boil, then remove from the heat. Put the chocolate in a heatproof bowl and place over the pan of steaming water, without touching the water. Stir occasionally until the chocolate has melted and then cool to room temperature. Using a flexible bladed knife, spread on to the smooth underside

of the florentines. Return to the rack until the chocolate is just setting. Run a fork through the chocolate to make wavy lines and set at room temperature.

CHEF'S TIP *Florentines make excellent petits fours if made with 1/2 teaspoon of mixture. They will store in an airtight container for up to 1 week. Any extra raw mixture can be stored in the refrigerator for 1 week.*

Almond and hazelnut macaroons

*These nutty macaroons are crisp on the outside
with a meltingly soft inside (pictured far right).*

Preparation time 20 minutes
Total cooking time 25 minutes
Makes 36

1/4 cup hazelnuts
2 tablespoons ground almonds
1 cup confectioners' sugar
2 egg whites
pinch of superfine sugar

One Preheat the oven to 350°F.

Two Place two baking sheets together and line the top sheet with parchment paper (this prevents the bottom of the macaroons from overbrowning).

Three Toast the hazelnuts by placing on a baking sheet and toasting for 3–5 minutes, taking care not to let the hazelnuts burn. Allow to cool, then place in a food processor and pulse until finely ground.

Four Reduce the oven temperature to 315°F. Sift the almonds, hazelnuts and confectioners' sugar into a bowl, then sift again to make sure that they are thoroughly mixed. In a separate bowl, whisk the egg whites with the pinch of sugar until stiff and shiny and the mixture forms stiff peaks when the whisk is lifted.

Five Using a metal spoon, carefully fold the dry ingredients into the egg whites, trying not to lose any air. The mixture should be shiny and soft, not liquid.

Six Spoon into a pastry bag with a 1/3-inch tip. Pipe 3/4-inch-wide rounds onto the prepared baking sheets, allowing room for expansion. Bake, in 2 batches if necessary, for 15–20 minutes, or until golden and crisp, checking the macaroons frequently.

Seven Cool on the baking sheets for a few minutes, then remove onto a wire rack.

Palmiers

*These supremely simple cookies show off perfect
homemade puff pastry to its best effect (pictured right).*

Preparation time 20 minutes
Total cooking time 20 minutes
Makes 15

1/4 cup sugar
2 level teaspoons ground cinnamon

1/2 quantity puff pastry
(see page 542)

One Preheat the oven to 425°F and brush a baking sheet with melted butter.

Two Mix the sugar and cinnamon together in a bowl and use instead of flour to dust the work surface. Quickly roll the dough out to a 1/4-inch-thick rectangle and sprinkle generously with the sugar and cinnamon. Fold the short sides in three times to meet in the center, sprinkle with more sugar and cinnamon, then fold in half as if you were closing a book. Cut horizontally across the pastry into 1/2-inch slices and place onto the prepared sheet with a cut side uppermost. Flatten gently with a rolling pin and sprinkle with more sugar. Bake for 10 minutes, then turn the palmiers over and bake for another 10 minutes, or until richly caramelized. Cool on a wire rack.

CHEF'S TIP *For an easy, quick dessert, sandwich together the palmiers with a small amount of brandy cream made by whipping together 1 cup whipping cream and 1 tablespoon each of confectioners' sugar and brandy.*

Madeleines

These well-known individual, shell-shaped miniature cakes are traditionally served plain, with coffee or tea. They are also a perfect accompaniment to desserts such as pears poached in red wine.

Preparation time 15 minutes
+ 10 minutes resting
Total cooking time 10 minutes
Makes 12

2 eggs
3 tablespoons sugar
2 teaspoons Demerara or turbinado
sugar
1¹/2 teaspoons honey
³/4 cup all-purpose flour
1 teaspoon baking powder
pinch of salt
¹/4 cup unsalted butter, melted,
but cool
confectioners' sugar, to dust

One Preheat the oven to 350°F. Butter a 12-cup madeleine pan, chill in the refrigerator until set, butter lightly a second time and chill. Dust with flour and tap out the excess to leave a fine coating.

Two Separate the eggs. Put the whites in a bowl. Combine the yolks in another bowl with half the sugar, the Demerara sugar and honey and, using an electric mixer, beat until tripled in volume and pale in color. With well-cleaned beaters, beat the whites until stiff, then add the remaining sugar and beat until stiff and shiny. Fold a third of the mixture into the yolk mixture.

Three Sift the flour, baking powder and a small pinch of salt together into a bowl. Fold half the dry ingredients into the yolk mixture, using a rubber spatula, followed by a third of the meringue, then add the remaining dry ingredients. Fold in the final third of meringue and, just as it disappears, pour in the butter and very carefully fold in until just combined. Do not overfold at any stage. Pipe, using a pastry bag fitted with a ¹/4-inch plain tip, or spoon carefully into the pan cups until they are two-thirds full. Set aside to rest for 10 minutes.

Four Bake in the upper half of the oven for 8–10 minutes, or until pale golden brown and springy when lightly touched, or until a fine skewer comes out clean when inserted into the center. Turn the madeleines out of the pan and set aside to cool on a wire rack. Dust the madeleines generously with the sifted confectioners' sugar and serve with the shell sides up.

CHEF'S TIP *You can vary the flavor by adding the finely grated zest of half a lemon to the egg mixture.*

Saint-Honoré

*During the Middle Ages, most pastries were produced by the clergy,
hence the religious names or connotations they still have today.
Saint Honoré is the patron saint of pastry-makers.*

Preparation time 1 hour
+ 30 minutes chilling
Total cooking time 1 hour 30 minutes
Serves 6–8

*1/2 quantity sweet pastry
(see page 546)
1 quantity cream puff pastry
(see page 545)
1 egg, beaten, to glaze
1 cup sugar*

CHANTILLY CREAM
*3/4 cup whipping cream, chilled
1/3 cup confectioners' sugar
1 teaspoon vanilla extract*

One Preheat the oven to 350°F. Grease two baking sheets with melted butter and chill. Lightly flour the work surface and roll the pastry out to 1/8-inch thick. Cut out a round 8 inches in diameter for the bottom of the Saint-Honoré. Place on one of the chilled baking sheets, pierce with a fork and brush lightly with beaten egg.

Two Spoon the cream puff pastry into a pastry bag fitted with a large 1/2-inch pastry tip and pipe a ring of cream puff pastry around the edge of the sweet pastry, about the same thickness as the sweet pastry. Pipe another ring inside the first one, touching the outer ring, and brush with the egg. Bake for 40 minutes, or until the pastry is well browned and the cream-puff pastry well puffed. Do not open the oven door for the first 15 minutes or the cream puff pastry will collapse. Cool on a wire rack.

Three On the other chilled baking sheet, pipe small balls of cream puff pastry, the size of walnuts, leaving a space of at least 2 inches between them. Glaze with the beaten egg and smooth the tops so they are uniform. Bake for 40 minutes, or until the balls are well browned and puffed. Remove from the oven and cool on a wire rack.

Four To make the caramel, put the sugar and 1/4 cup water in a small, heavy-bottomed saucepan and then follow the method in the Chef's techniques on page 540. Working quickly, carefully dip one side of each pastry ball into the caramel and allow to cool on a buttered baking sheet for 2 minutes. Then dip the pastry

balls in again on the other side and quickly lay at regular intervals around the edge of the Saint-Honoré bottom.

Five To make the Chantilly cream, pour the cream into a bowl and add the sugar and vanilla. Using a whisk or electric mixer, beat the cream until it forms soft peaks.

Six Place the cream in a pastry bag fitted with a large star tip, then fill the center of the bottom with cream. Refrigerate the Saint-Honoré for at least 30 minutes before serving.

Thin apple tart

*This spectacular tart—Tarte fine aux pommes—has a very fine crisp sweet short pastry base
spread with almond cream and topped with glazed apples. This recipe calls for
Golden Delicious apples, but you can use any apple that holds its shape when cooked.*

Preparation time *1 hour*
+ 40 minutes refrigeration
Total cooking time *1 hour*
Serves 6–8

PASTRY
1 cup all-purpose flour
1/3 cup confectioners' sugar
3 tablespoons unsalted butter
1 egg yolk
few drops of vanilla extract

ALMOND CREAM
1/4 cup confectioners' sugar
2 tablespoons unsalted butter, softened
1 teaspoon vanilla extract
1 egg yolk
1/4 cup ground almonds

2–3 Golden Delicious apples,
or similar variety
juice of 1 lemon
apricot jam, to glaze

One To make the pastry, sift the flour and confectioners' sugar into a bowl, then cut in the butter until the mixture resembles bread crumbs. Make a well in the center and add the egg yolk, a few drops of vanilla, a pinch of salt and enough cold water to help form a dough. Turn out onto a lightly floured surface and gather the dough together to make a smooth ball. Cover with plastic wrap and refrigerate for 30 minutes, or until just firm.

Two Preheat the oven to 350°F. Remove the plastic wrap from the chilled pastry, then very gently roll out the pastry between two sheets of parchment paper to a thickness of 1/8 inch. Carefully ease the pastry into a greased, 9-inch fluted tart pan with removable bottom.

Three Bake the unfilled shell blind for 20 minutes, following the method in the Chef's techniques on page 547. Remove the pie weights or rice and paper, then bake for another 10 minutes, covering the pastry with aluminum foil if it looks as though it might burn. Remove from the oven and allow to cool.

Four To make the almond cream, beat together the confectioners' sugar, butter

and vanilla until light and creamy. Add the egg yolk and beat well, then add the ground almonds. Spread the mixture in an even layer over the cooled pastry shell.

Five Peel, quarter and core the apples, then sprinkle them with lemon juice. Thinly slice the apples and arrange in overlapping circles over the layer of almond cream. Bake for 20–25 minutes, or until the apples are cooked. Place on a wire rack to cool.

Six When the tart has cooled, place some apricot jam in a small saucepan and bring to a boil. (Add a spoonful of water if the jam becomes too thick for spreading.) Strain the jam and, using a pastry brush, lightly dab the surface of the tart with the jam—this will give the apples a nice shine and prevent them from drying out.

CHEF'S TIPS *Work quickly and lightly, handling the pastry as little as possible.*

Cool the tart before brushing it with the apricot jam. If the tart is still hot, the fruit will simply soak up the jam and the tart will lose its shine when it cools.

about apples...

Golden Delicious apples are used for this recipe (as for Tarte Tatin) because they hold their shape when cooked, without breaking up. Other suitable varieties for this type of dish are Cox and Fuji.

Chocolate éclairs

In French, éclair means literally "lightning." The name of these filled cream-puff pastries is possibly due to the fact that they rarely last long on the plate!

Preparation time 1 hour
Total cooking time 1 hour 15 minutes
Makes 12

1 quantity cream puff pastry
(see page 545)
1 egg, beaten, to glaze

PASTRY CREAM
1 cup milk
1 teaspoon vanilla extract
2 egg yolks
1/4 cup sugar
2 tablespoons all-purpose flour
2 tablespoons cornstarch

CHOCOLATE GANACHE
3 oz. semi-sweet chocolate, chopped
into small pieces
1/3 cup whipping cream

One Preheat the oven to 350°F. Grease a baking sheet with softened butter and chill until set.

Two Fill a pastry bag fitted with a medium plain tip with the cream puff pastry. Pipe 3–4-inch logs on the baking sheet. Lightly brush with the beaten egg. Take care not to let any of the egg drip down the sides as this may prevent the dough from rising evenly. Press gently with a fork. Bake for 30–35 minutes, or until crisp and golden. Immediately remove from the baking sheet and cool on a wire rack.

Three To make the pastry cream, place the milk and vanilla in a saucepan and bring slowly to a boil. In a bowl, whisk the egg yolks with the sugar until light in color. Sift in the flour and cornstarch and whisk until blended. Pour half the boiling milk into the yolk mixture,

whisk well, then return the mixture to the saucepan of milk. Bring to a boil, stirring constantly, then boil for 1 minute to completely cook the flour. Remove from the heat and spread the pastry cream on a baking sheet to cool quickly. Cover the surface with waxed paper to prevent a skin from forming. Allow to cool completely.

Four To make the chocolate ganache, place the chocolate in a small bowl. Bring the cream to a boil in a small saucepan and pour it over the chocolate. Wait a few seconds, then gently stir until the chocolate is completely melted and smooth.

Five Using the tip of a small sharp knife, make a small hole at one end on the

underside of each éclair. Place the cooled pastry cream in a bowl and whisk until smooth, then spoon the cream into a pastry bag fitted with a small tip. Push the tip into one of the holes and fill the entire cavity with the pastry cream. Hold the éclair in the palm of your hand and stop adding the filling just at the moment you can feel it expanding. A little of the cream will ooze out once the tip is removed; wipe this off.

Six Using a small knife or metal spatula, carefully spread the chocolate ganache over the tops of the éclairs. Allow the éclairs to rest in a cool place until the ganache has set.

LE CORDON BLEU ✠ COMPLETE COOK

Millefeuille

Millefeuille, meaning "a thousand leaves," refers to the layers of puff pastry used in this recipe. Filled with a delicious vanilla cream, a millefeuille may be served as one large pastry or cut into individual portions.

*Preparation time 1 hour
+ 15 minutes resting
Total cooking time 40 minutes
Serves 6*

*1 quantity puff pastry
(see page 542)
strawberries, to garnish
confectioners' sugar, to dust*

PASTRY CREAM
*3 cups milk
1 vanilla bean, split lengthwise
9 egg yolks
³/4 cup sugar
²/3 cup all-purpose flour
¹/3 cup cornstarch*

One Preheat the oven to 425°F. Divide the dough in half and roll each piece into a square, ¹/8-inch thick. Place a square on a buttered baking sheet lined with parchment paper, and pierce all over with a fork to prevent the dough from rising too much. Let the pastry rest in the refrigerator for 15 minutes. Before baking, cover the pastry with a second sheet of parchment paper and another baking sheet. Bake for 10–15 minutes. Flip the pastry over and bake for 10 minutes more, or until light golden all over. Remove the top baking sheet and paper and allow to cool on a wire rack. Repeat with the other square.

Two To make the pastry cream, place the milk and vanilla bean in a saucepan and bring to a boil. In a bowl, whisk the egg yolks with the sugar until light in color. Sift in the flour and cornstarch and whisk until blended. Remove and discard the vanilla bean. Pour half the boiling milk into the yolk mixture, whisk well, then return the mixture to the saucepan of milk. Bring to a boil, stirring constantly, and boil for 1 minute to completely cook the flour. Remove from the heat and spread the pastry cream on a baking sheet to cool quickly. Cover the surface with waxed paper to prevent a skin from forming.

Three Trim the edges of the cooked pastry with a serrated knife and reserve the trimmings, then cut each square in half. Save the neatest piece for the top. Whisk the cooled pastry cream until smooth. Pipe or spoon a third of the cream onto a piece of puff pastry, cover with a second piece of pastry and pipe another third of the cream on top. Repeat with the third piece of pastry and remaining cream. Place the last piece of pastry on top and press lightly. Smooth any cream that comes out of the sides with a flexible bladed knife, and fill any holes. Crush the pastry trimmings and press onto the sides. Decorate with the strawberries and dust with sifted confectioners' sugar.

Brioche plum tart

This delicious tart is made from a soft brioche dough and filled with a vanilla cream and fresh ripe plums. Perfect for serving at brunch or the end of a summer party.

***Preparation time** 45 minutes*
+ overnight refrigeration
***Total cooking time** 45 minutes*
Serves 6

BRIOCHE DOUGH
1¼ cups bread or all-purpose flour
½ teaspoon salt
1 tablespoon sugar
2 teaspoons milk
1½ teaspoons fresh yeast
or 1 teaspoon dried yeast
2 eggs, lightly beaten
¼ cup unsalted butter, at room
temperature

PASTRY CREAM
2 cups milk
½ vanilla bean, split lengthwise
5 egg yolks
½ cup sugar
2½ tablespoons all-purpose flour
2½ tablespoons cornstarch

3–5 plums, halved and pitted
¼ cup apricot jam

One To make the brioche dough, sift the flour and salt into a large bowl, stir in the sugar and make a well in the center. Heat the milk in a saucepan until lukewarm; remove from the heat. Add the yeast, stir until dissolved and pour into the dry ingredients. Add the eggs and beat to make an elastic dough (do this using your hand, with fingers slightly apart and a slapping motion from the wrist or with the dough hook attachment on an electric mixer). Place the butter in a bowl, soften it with a wooden spoon and add to the dough in three or four batches. Continue to beat until the dough is smooth and has a silky shine. Place the dough in a large bowl that has been sprinkled with flour to prevent sticking. Cover loosely with greased plastic wrap and refrigerate for at least 8 hours or overnight. Grease a 1-inch-deep, 8-inch fluted tart pan with removable bottom with softened butter and set aside.

Two Punch the dough down, folding the sides toward the center. Remove from the bowl and knead for 1 minute on a lightly floured surface. Roll out into a ⅛–¼-inch-thick round. Line the tart pan with the dough (see Chef's techniques, page 547) and then chill for 20 minutes. Preheat the oven to 325°F.

Three To make the pastry cream, place the milk and vanilla bean in a saucepan and bring slowly to a boil. In a bowl, whisk the egg yolks with the sugar until light in color. Sift in the flour and cornstarch and whisk until blended. Remove and discard the vanilla bean. Pour half the boiling milk into the yolk mixture, whisk well, then return the mixture to the saucepan of milk. Bring to a boil, stirring constantly, and boil for 1 minute to completely cook the flour. Remove from the heat and spread the pastry cream on a baking sheet to cool quickly. Cover the surface with waxed paper to prevent a skin from forming and allow to cool. Whisk the pastry cream until smooth before using.

Four Spread the pastry cream over the brioche and arrange the plums, cut side down, on top. Bake for 40 minutes, or until the brioche is crisp and golden. Cool on a wire rack before removing from the pan. Heat the apricot jam with 1 tablespoon water until melted. Bring to a boil, then strain and brush over the plums to glaze.

---

about plums...

You can vary the look of this recipe according to the color of the plums you use. Some have a yellow flesh whereas others have a deep, dark red flesh. Skin colors also vary. You could also use greengages (sweet green European plums) if you like.

Lemon tart

This lemon tart is the perfect end to any meal, with just the right balance of tangy lemon and sweetness. Try substituting other citrus fruits such as orange or lime, or a combination of two fruits.

Preparation time *30 minutes + refrigeration*
Total cooking time *50 minutes*
Serves 8

*1 quantity sweet pastry (see page 546)
confectioners' sugar, to dust*

FILLING
*2/3 cup whipping cream
4 eggs
2/3 cup sugar
juice of 4 lemons, about 3/4 cup
finely grated zest of 1 lemon*

One Brush a 1 1/2-inch-deep, 8-inch fluted tart pan with removable bottom with melted butter.

Two On a floured surface, roll out the pastry into a round about 1/4 inch thick and line the tart pan (see Chef's techniques, page 547). Chill the pastry for 30 minutes. Preheat the oven to 375°F. Bake blind (see Chef's techniques, page 547) for 10 minutes until the pastry is firm. Remove the pie weights and paper and if the bottom of the pastry looks wet, bake for 3–4 minutes longer. Reduce the heat to 275°F.

Three To make the filling, warm the cream in a small saucepan over low heat. In a large bowl, whisk together the eggs, sugar and lemon juice. Stir in the warmed cream. Pass the mixture through a fine strainer, then stir in the grated lemon zest and pour into the pastry shell. Bake for 35 minutes, or until the filling is just firm to the touch. When the tart comes out of the oven it will appear quite soft in the middle. Allow to cool completely, then remove from the pan and chill for several hours or overnight, until the filling is firm enough to cut. Dust with sifted confectioners' sugar just before serving.

CHEF'S TIP *Keep the tart refrigerated and use within 3 days.*

Pithiviers

*This pastry originated in the town of Pithiviers in central France. It is the traditional cake served on Epiphany,
January 6th, when a bean is added to it. The guest who gets the bean becomes king or queen for the day.
During the winter holidays, these cakes can be seen adorned with gold crowns in French bakeries.*

Preparation time 45 minutes
+ refrigeration
Total cooking time 40 minutes
Serves 4–6

1 quantity puff pastry
(see page 542)
1 egg, beaten, to glaze
2 tablespoons sugar

ALMOND CREAM
3 tablespoons unsalted butter, softened
3 tablespoons sugar
¼ cup ground almonds
1 egg
2 teaspoons all-purpose flour
2 teaspoons rum

One Preheat the oven to 425°F. Cut the puff pastry in half and roll into two 8-inch squares. Place on parchment paper-lined baking sheets and chill.

Two To make the almond cream, beat the butter and sugar together, add the almonds and egg and mix well. Stir in the flour, then the rum. Chill.

Three Remove one of the baking sheets of pastry from the refrigerator. Using a plate or large round pastry ring, make a light imprint on the pastry 5½ inches in diameter. Brush around the imprint with the beaten egg. Place the almond cream in the center and spread it into a dome, taking care not to touch the glazed dough. Place the second piece of pastry over the first and press the edges to seal.

Four Using the tip of a teaspoon, gently press around the edge of the pastry to make small, uniform semicircles—creating a scalloped effect. Chill for 10 minutes, then use a small sharp knife

to cut away the pattern marked by the spoon. Preheat the oven to 400°F.

Five Make a syrup by mixing the sugar with 2 tablespoons water in a small saucepan. Stir over medium heat until the sugar dissolves, then bring to a boil. Remove from the heat and cool.

Six Brush the pastry with the egg glaze, without letting any drip down the sides, as this will prevent the pastry from rising properly. Using the tip of a small knife,

score the top of the pastry in a spiral pattern. Bake for 10 minutes, then reduce the heat to 350°F and bake for 25 minutes more, or until golden brown. Remove from the oven and immediately brush the top with the syrup to give it a shine. Serve the pithiviers warm.

LE CORDON BLEU COMPLETE COOK

Praline dacquoise

*Dramatically striped and flavored with light praline buttercream,
this dessert can be made up to a day ahead of time and chilled,
leaving you precious time when entertaining.*

Preparation time 1 hour 30 minutes
+ 20 minutes chilling
Total cooking time 20 minutes
Serves 8

ALMOND SPONGE CAKE
3/4 cup ground almonds
1/2 cup all-purpose flour
1 cup superfine sugar
1/3 cup milk
9 egg whites

HAZELNUT BUTTERCREAM
1/2 cup superfine sugar
2 egg whites
2/3 cup unsalted butter, softened
*2 tablespoons chocolate hazelnut
spread, such as Nutella*
2/3 cup sliced almonds
confectioners' sugar, to decorate
cocoa powder, to decorate

One Preheat the oven to 375°F. Line an 8 1/2 x 13-inch jelly roll pan with parchment paper and brush with melted butter.

Two To make the almond sponge cake, sift the ground almonds, flour and two-thirds of the superfine sugar together into a bowl. Add the milk and 1 egg white and beat with a wooden spoon until smoothly blended. Add a little more milk if the mixture is too stiff. In a separate clean, dry bowl, whisk the remaining egg whites until stiff peaks form, then gradually whisk in the remaining third of the superfine sugar to form a stiff and shiny meringue. Using a large metal spoon or rubber spatula, carefully fold a third of the meringue into the almond sponge cake mixture until well incorporated, then gently fold in the remaining meringue in three or four additions. Do not fold too much or the mixture will lose volume.

Three Spread gently over the prepared baking sheet and bake for 7–10 minutes, or until golden and springy. Loosen the edges with the point of a knife and turn out onto a wire rack covered with waxed paper. Do not remove the paper used in baking.

Four To make the hazelnut buttercream, put three-quarters of the sugar and 4 tablespoons water in a small heavy-bottomed saucepan. Stir over low heat until the sugar dissolves completely. Using a wet pastry brush, brush any sugar crystals from the side of the saucepan. Increase the heat and boil without stirring until the syrup reaches soft-ball stage, which is around 250°F. If you don't have a candy thermometer, drop 1/4 teaspoon of the syrup into iced water. The ball of syrup should hold its shape but be soft when pressed.

Five Meanwhile, whisk the egg whites until very soft peaks form, then add the remaining sugar and whisk until stiff and glossy. Continue whisking and carefully pour in the hot syrup, pouring between the beaters and the side of the bowl. Whisk until cold. Gradually whisk in the butter and chocolate spread until well blended.

Six Using a serrated knife, trim the edges of the sponge cake to neaten and cut into three 8 x 4-inch pieces, discarding the paper. Use one third of the butter-cream to cover the first layer of sponge cake, cover with the second piece and repeat with another third of buttercream. Top with the remaining sponge cake. Coat the top and sides with the remaining buttercream and smooth with a flexible bladed knife. Chill for 20 minutes, or until set.

Seven Toast the sliced almonds under a broiler until golden. Dust the cake with confectioners' sugar. Cut 1/2-inch strips of paper and lay on top of the cake at 5/8-inch intervals. Dust with sifted cocoa and remove the paper carefully to show brown and white lines. Press the toasted almonds onto the sides.

Pecan tart

This French version of the classic Southern pecan pie uses a rich, sweet pastry baked in the distinctive tart pan. The filling, however, remains the same—simply superb—especially when served with whipped cream.

Preparation time 20 minutes
+ 30 minutes resting
***Total cooking time** 50 minutes*
Serves 6–8

3/4 *quantity sweet pastry (see page 546)*

FILLING
2 eggs
pinch of salt
2 tablespoons unsalted butter, melted
2/3 cup light corn syrup
2/3 cup lightly packed dark brown sugar
1 teaspoon vanilla extract
1 cup pecans, coarsely chopped

One Preheat the oven to 325°F. Roll the dough out to 1/8 inch thick and line a 1-inch-deep, 9-inch fluted tart pan with removable bottom (see page 547).

Two To make the filling, beat the eggs in a bowl. Add the salt, butter, corn syrup, brown sugar and vanilla and mix until well combined.

Three Sprinkle the pecans over the bottom of the pastry shell, then pour in the filling. Bake for 45–50 minutes, or until the filling has just set. If the filling puffs up too much, reduce the oven temperature to 300°F.

Four Leave in the pan for 5 minutes, or until cool enough to handle. Remove to a wire rack and cool completely.

CHEF'S TIP *The pecans can be left whole or use almost any nut, such as walnuts, hazelnuts or macadamias.*

Tartelettes amandines

These small almond cakes are a well-loved patisserie classic and are perfect for serving with coffee. Amandine is the name given to various almond-flavored French pastries and cakes.

Preparation time *45 minutes*
Total cooking time *20 minutes*
Makes 18

ALMOND CREAM
1/2 cup unsalted butter, softened
1/2 cup superfine sugar
grated zest of 1 lemon
2 eggs, beaten
2/3 cup ground almonds
1/4 cup all-purpose flour
few drops of vanilla extract

1 quantity sweet pastry (see page 546)
1/3 cup seedless raspberry jam
2/3 cup sliced almonds
4 tablespoons apricot jam
1/3 cup confectioners' sugar, sifted
few drops of pink food coloring

One To make the almond cream, beat the butter, sugar and lemon zest together using a wooden spoon or an electric mixer until light and creamy. Gradually add the eggs, a sixth at a time, beating well between each addition. Stir in the ground almonds, flour and the vanilla extract. Transfer to a pastry bag fitted with a 3/4-inch tip and refrigerate.

Two Brush eighteen 2 1/2 x 3/4-inch tartlet pans with removable bottoms with melted butter. Roll out the pastry on a floured surface to 1/8-inch thickness. Cut out eighteen 4-inch rounds of pastry to fit the tartlet pans, then ease them into the pans and prick the bottoms of each pastry round with a fork. Preheat the oven to 350°F.

Three Beat the raspberry jam with a spoon until soft and fluid, then place a little on the bottom of each tartlet. Pipe in the almond cream until the tartlets

are three-quarters full and bake for 12–15 minutes, or until golden. Cool the tartlets in the pans on a wire rack. Toast the sliced almonds under a broiler until golden, taking care not to burn them.

Four In a small saucepan, heat the apricot jam with 2 tablespoons water. When the mixture begins to boil, strain it and, while still hot, brush it over the tartlets. Arrange the toasted almonds over one-half of each tartlet.

Five In a small bowl, mix the confectioners' sugar, 2 teaspoons of water and a tiny amount of the pink food coloring until the mixture is smooth and just delicately pink. Spoon the icing thinly over the half of the tartlets without the toasted almonds.

Opéra

Adapted from a complex French recipe, this dessert is a true work of art. It consists of layers of sponge cake, chocolate ganache, buttercream and coffee syrup, finished with a rich chocolate frosting.

***Preparation time** 1 hour 45 minutes + refrigeration*
***Total cooking time** 1 hour*
Serves 4–6

ALMOND SPONGE CAKE
2/3 cup confectioners' sugar
3 tablespoons all-purpose flour
2 1/2 oz. ground almonds
3 eggs
1 tablespoon unsalted butter, melted and cooled
3 egg whites
1 tablespoon sugar

CHOCOLATE GANACHE
6 oz. semi-sweet chocolate, finely chopped
1/2 cup milk
1/2 cup whipping cream
3 tablespoons unsalted butter, softened

COFFEE SYRUP
2 tablespoons sugar
2 tablespoons instant coffee

BUTTERCREAM
1/3 cup sugar
1 egg white
1 tablespoon instant coffee
1/3 cup unsalted butter, softened

One To make the sponge cake, preheat the oven to 425°F. Line an 11 x 7 x 1 1/2-inch jelly roll pan with parchment paper. Sift the confectioners' sugar and flour into a large bowl. Stir in the almonds. Add the eggs and beat until pale. Fold in the butter. Beat the egg whites until stiff, add the sugar and beat until stiff peaks form. Beat a third of the egg whites into the almond mixture, then fold in the remainder until just combined. Pour onto the pan and gently spread. Bake for 6–7 minutes, or until golden and springy. Loosen the edges with the point of a knife. Turn out onto a wire rack covered with waxed paper. Do not remove the paper used in baking.

Two To make the ganache, put the chocolate in a bowl. Heat the milk and 2 tablespoons of the cream until just at boiling point. Pour into the chocolate, add the butter and whisk until smooth. Allow to set until spreadable.

Three To make the coffee syrup, put the sugar and 1/3 cup water in a small saucepan and stir until dissolved. Bring to a boil and add the coffee.

Four To make the buttercream, put the sugar and 1 tablespoon water in a small heavy-bottomed saucepan. Make a sugar syrup by following the method in the Chef's techniques on page 546. Meanwhile, beat the egg white until very soft peaks form. Continue beating and carefully pour in the hot syrup, pouring between the beaters and the side of the bowl. Beat until cold. Dissolve the coffee in 1 teaspoon of boiling water, cool to room temperature and add to the butter. Beat in half the egg white, then carefully fold in the other half until well combined.

Five Cut the cake crosswise into three pieces. Soak one piece with a third of the coffee syrup, then spread with half the buttercream. Cover with the second piece of cake, soak with syrup and spread with half the ganache. Cover with the last piece of cake, soak with the remaining syrup and top with the remaining buttercream. Smooth the top and refrigerate until the buttercream is firmly set.

Six Melt the remaining ganache in the top of a double boiler. Heat the remaining cream until just at boiling point and stir into the ganache. Cool until spreadable and spread over the top of the cake.

LE CORDON BLEU 🏵 COMPLETE COOK

Fraisier

*This is a wonderful cake for an elegant picnic, or to end a light
summer meal. If pink marzipan is not available, knead a few drops
of red food coloring through the marzipan until the color is uniform.*

***Preparation time** 1 hour 50 minutes
+ cooling*
***Total cooking time** 40 minutes*
***Serves** 6–8*

GENOESE SPONGE
*3 eggs
1 egg yolk
1/2 cup sugar
1 cup all-purpose flour
1 tablespoon unsalted butter,
melted and cooled*

SYRUP
*1/3 cup sugar
2 tablespoons Kirsch*

CREME MOUSSELINE
*1 cup milk
1 vanilla bean
1/4 cup sugar
2 egg yolks
3 tablespoons all-purpose flour
3 tablespoons cornstarch
1 tablespoon Kirsch
1/2 cup unsalted butter, softened*

*3 1/3 cups strawberries, hulled
2 1/2 tablespoons strawberry jam,
strained
3 oz. pink marzipan*

One Preheat the oven to 350°F. To make the Genoese sponge, whisk or beat the eggs, egg yolk and sugar in a heatproof bowl over a saucepan of hot steaming water until it leaves a trail. Remove from the heat and whisk until cold. Sift the flour, fold it into the mixture, then fold in the melted butter. Pour into a lightly greased 8-inch springform pan and bake for 20–25 minutes, or until the cake shrinks from the side of the pan. Run a knife inside the ring to release the cake, then cool on a wire rack. Cut the cold cake horizontally in half.

Two To make the syrup, dissolve the sugar in 1/4 cup water in a small saucepan over low heat. Bring to a boil and boil for 1 minute, then stir in the Kirsch.

Three To make the crème mousseline, bring the milk and vanilla bean to a boil. In a bowl, whisk the sugar and egg yolks until pale, then stir in the flour and cornstarch. Strain the milk into the yolk mixture, whisking constantly. Return the mixture to the saucepan and stir rapidly over medium heat until thickened, then boil for 1 minute, stirring constantly. Remove from the heat to cool completely. Add the Kirsch and gradually beat in the butter, whisking well between each addition.

Four Set aside a strawberry for decoration. Halve a third of the strawberries and quarter the rest. To assemble, place a cake layer in the clean, dry springform ring (placed on a flat plate), baked side down. Brush with some syrup, spread with a little jam and some of the mousseline. Place the halved strawberries around the outer edge of the cake, the cut sides facing out.

Five Spoon the mousseline into a pastry bag fitted with a 1/2-inch tip. Pipe into the gaps between the strawberries. Arrange the remaining strawberries over the cake, then cover with the remaining mousseline. Smooth the surface and gently press the other cake layer on top.

Six Remove the springform ring. Brush on more syrup and thinly spread with jam. Dust a work area with confectioners' sugar, roll out the marzipan to a 1/8-inch-thick round, and cut a round with the springform ring. Lift the marzipan onto the cake and smooth the top. Heat the remaining jam, dip in the whole strawberry and place it on top of the cake.

Chocolate-dipped fruits

*These are a clever idea for serving as petit fours with coffee
after a meal. You can use many different kinds of fruit
as long as the surface remains dry.*

Preparation time *20 minutes*
+ 15 minutes refrigeration
Total cooking time *10–15 minutes*
Serves 4–6

1 lb. strawberries
2 clementines or mandarin oranges
6 oz. bittersweet chocolate, chopped
*1 tablespoon vegetable shortening or
cooking oil*

One Line a baking sheet with waxed or parchment paper. Clean the strawberries by brushing with a dry pastry brush, or rinsing them very quickly in cold water and drying well on a thick layer of paper towels. Discard any berries with soft spots. Peel the clementines or mandarin oranges and remove as much of the white pith as possible, then break the fruit into individual segments.

Two Put the chocolate in a bowl. Half-fill a saucepan with water and bring to the boil. Remove from the heat and place the bowl over the saucepan, making sure it is not touching the water. Allow the chocolate to melt slowly. Stir in the shortening or oil, and mix until melted and completely incorporated. Remove the bowl from the saucepan and place on a folded towel to keep it warm.

Three Holding the berries by their stems or hulls, dip each berry about three-quarters of the way into the chocolate, so that some of the color of the fruit still shows. Gently wipe off any excess chocolate on the edge of the bowl and place the coated strawberries on their sides on the baking sheet. Repeat with the clementines or mandarins, drying each segment on paper towels before dipping. If the chocolate becomes too thick, reheat the water, remove from the heat and place the bowl over the saucepan until the chocolate returns to the required consistency.

Four Once all the fruit has been dipped in the chocolate, place in the refrigerator for 15 minutes, or until the chocolate has just set. Remove from the refrigerator and keep in a cool place until ready to serve. Do not serve directly from the refrigerator—the cold temperature will inhibit the full flavor and sweetness of the fruit, and the chocolate will be too hard.

CHEF'S TIPS *Any fruit can be used, but the best results are with ones that can be left whole or have a dry surface.*

If the strawberry stems are too short, use a toothpick to dip them.

Use a small pair of tongs for the clementine or mandarin slices—do not use a toothpick as it will pierce the fruit, and the juices will prevent the chocolate from coating evenly.

White chocolate fudge

*Made with creamy white chocolate, this fudge is
extra sweet, so eat it in small quantities, if you can.*

Preparation time *15 minutes*
+ 2 hours refrigeration
Total cooking time *7 minutes*
Makes about 50 pieces

*1 ¹/₃ cups sugar
2 tablespoons unsalted butter
pinch of salt
¹/₂ cup evaporated milk
1 vanilla bean
10 oz. good-quality white chocolate,
chopped
¹/₂ cup pistachio nuts*

One Grease a 7-inch square cake pan.
Put the sugar, butter, salt and evaporated
milk in a large saucepan. Split the vanilla
bean in half lengthwise and scrape the
small black seeds into the saucepan with
the point of a knife. Add the bean to the
saucepan. Bring to a boil over medium
heat, stirring constantly with a wooden
spoon. Lower the heat and simmer for
5 minutes, stirring constantly.

Two Remove the saucepan from the heat
and lift out the vanilla bean with a fork
or slotted spoon. Stir in the chopped
chocolate until it has melted completely
and the mixture is smooth. Stir in the

pistachios and pour into the pan.
Refrigerate for 2 hours, or until firm.

Three Cut into small squares and serve in
paper petit four cups. Store in the
refrigerator for up to a week.

CHEF'S TIPS *Chopped hazelnuts may
be substituted for the pistachios.*

*Using a vanilla bean will give a
delicious flavor to the fudge, but if
you don't want to see the black seeds,
use ¹/₂ teaspoon vanilla extract instead.*

Amaretti

*Traditionally made with bitter almonds, this recipe uses
the more readily available blanched almonds.*

***Preparation time** 10 minutes*
***Total cooking time** 15 minutes per sheet*
Makes about 40

*1/2 cup blanched almonds, halved or
chopped*
1/3 cup sugar
1 egg white
3 teaspoons Amaretto liqueur
2 drops almond extract
confectioners' sugar, to dust

One Preheat the oven to 350°F. Line two baking sheets with parchment paper.

Two Place the almonds and the sugar in a food processor and process to a fine powder. Add the egg white, Amaretto and almond extract and process to form a soft dough.

Three Spoon the mixture into a pastry bag fitted with a 5/8-inch plain tip. Pipe enough 1-inch rounds to fill the two baking sheets, spacing the cookies well apart. Hold the tip 1/2 inch away from the sheet to form well-rounded shapes. Bake for 12–15 minutes, or until golden. Cool on a wire rack. Repeat with the remaining mixture, preparing the baking sheets as instructed in step 1. Dust with confectioners' sugar while still warm.

CHEF'S TIPS *For a good result, make sure the almonds and sugar are finely ground before adding the egg white.*

To be traditionally Italian, place two cookies flatside together and wrap in colored tissue paper, twisting the ends. They look wonderful piled on a serving plate or given as gifts.

For a variation, top each cookie with half an almond before baking.

Chocolate rum truffles

In the true style of truffles, these petits fours are highly decadent and very rich. They are delicious served with coffee as a special after-dinner treat.

Preparation time 40 minutes
+ refrigeration
Total cooking time 10 minutes
Makes 24

10 oz. good-quality bittersweet chocolate, finely chopped
1/3 cup whipping cream
1 teaspoon vanilla extract
1 1/2 tablespoons dark rum
cocoa powder, to dust

One Put the chopped chocolate in a bowl. Place the cream and vanilla in a small saucepan and heat until it is just at boiling point. Pour the cream directly over the chopped chocolate. Gently mix with a whisk until the mixture is smooth. If there are any lumps, place the bowl over a saucepan of barely steaming water, off the heat, and lightly stir for a moment to melt any remaining chocolate. Mix in the rum and refrigerate the ganache until it is set.

Two Form the ganache into small balls using a melon baller, or pipe it into small balls using a pastry bag fitted with a plain tip. Return to the refrigerator to set. Roll the balls between your palms to form a perfect ball, then roll in the cocoa powder, using a fork to roll them around until evenly coated.

CHEF'S TIP *Since these truffles are not dipped in chocolate before they are rolled in the cocoa powder, they should be eaten within 2–3 days. Store in an airtight container in the refrigerator. Roll the truffles in the cocoa powder a second time before serving.*

White bread

Baking fresh bread is one of the most pleasurable ways to feed family and friends and is also a relaxing way to spend an afternoon. Start with this classic white loaf.

***Preparation time** 20 minutes + rising
(4 hours 30 minutes)*
***Total cooking time** 40 minutes*
Makes a 1½-lb. loaf

*1 oz. fresh yeast or 1 tablespoon
dried yeast*
1 tablespoon sugar
4 cups bread flour
1 teaspoon salt
2 tablespoons butter, softened
milk to glaze

One Prepare the yeast with 1¼ cups water and the sugar following the method in the Chef's techniques on page 550.

Two Sift the flour and salt into a large mixing bowl and make a well in the center. Add the yeast mixture and butter to the well and gradually bring the mixture together with your hands, or use an electric mixer fitted with a dough hook on slow speed, until a rough dough is formed. Turn out the dough onto a lightly floured work surface and knead for 10 minutes, or until it is smooth and elastic (see Chef's techniques, page 550). Alternatively, knead in an electric mixer on medium speed for 5 minutes.

Three Return the dough to a clean, lightly oiled bowl and turn once to coat the surface in oil. Cover with a clean, damp kitchen towel and let the dough rise at room temperature until doubled in size (the rising time will depend on the temperature of your kitchen).

Four Turn out the dough onto a lightly floured work surface and knead gently for 2–3 minutes until smooth. Roll into a 10 x 18-inch rectangle and shape the loaf by rolling up tightly into a sausage shape (see Chef's techniques, page 551).

Five Butter a baking sheet and lift the bread onto it, seam side down. Use a very sharp knife to cut diagonal slashes in a crisscross pattern on the top of the loaf (see Chef's techniques, page 552). Cover the dough with a damp kitchen towel and let it rise again until nearly doubled in size. Towards the end of this time, preheat the oven to 415°F.

Six Brush the risen loaf with the milk and bake for 35–40 minutes, or until golden brown and hollow sounding when tapped on the bottom. Remove from the baking sheet and cool on a wire rack.

CHEF'S TIP *To make bread rolls, divide the dough into 16 even-size pieces and roll each piece on a lightly floured work surface in the hollow of your hand until it forms a round and smooth ball. Bake for 15–20 minutes.*

Baguette

Professional bakers use a special flour for baguettes that is not readily available to the home cook, but using a mixture of bread and all-purpose flours produces an excellent version of this classic French bread.

Preparation time *45 minutes + rising*
(3 hours 30 minutes)
Total cooking time *25 minutes*
Makes four *³/4-lb. loaves*

1 oz. fresh yeast or 1 tablespoon
dried yeast
5 cups bread flour
3 cups all-purpose flour
1 tablespoon salt

One Prepare the yeast with 2½ cups water following the method in the Chef's techniques on page 550.

Two Sift the flours and salt into a large mixing bowl and make a well in the center. Add the yeast mixture to the well and gradually bring the mixture together with your hands, or use an electric mixer fitted with a dough hook on slow speed, until a rough dough is formed. Turn out the dough onto a lightly floured work surface and knead for 10 minutes, or until it is smooth and elastic (see Chef's techniques, page 550). Alternatively, knead the dough in an electric mixer on medium speed for 5 minutes.

Three Return the dough to a clean, lightly oiled bowl and turn once to coat the surface in oil. Cover with a clean, damp kitchen towel and let the dough rise at room temperature until doubled in size (the rising time will depend on the temperature of your kitchen).

Four Turn out the dough onto a lightly floured work surface and knead gently for 2–3 minutes until smooth. Divide the dough into 4 pieces, shape each piece into a rough rectangle about 12 inches long and roll tightly into long baguette shapes.

Five Sprinkle flour over a baking sheet and lift the bread onto the baking sheet, allowing plenty of space between each loaf. Spray the loaves with a fine mist of water and sprinkle with flour. Use a very sharp knife to cut 5 diagonal slashes on the top of each loaf, to a depth of ¼ inch (see Chef's techniques, page 552). Cover with a damp kitchen towel and let the dough rise again until nearly doubled in size. Towards the end of this time, preheat the oven to 425°F.

Six Bake the risen baguettes for 20–25 minutes, or until golden brown, crisp and hollow sounding when tapped on the bottom. Remove from the baking sheet and cool on a wire rack.

Petits pains au lait

These small rolls are made with an enriched bread dough and milk for a soft texture and golden crust. They are great as dinner rolls to accompany a French meal.

Preparation time 40 minutes
+ rising (3–4 hours)
Total cooking time 15 minutes
Makes 16 dinner rolls

*1 oz. fresh yeast or 1 tablespoon
dried yeast
1 tablespoon sugar
4 cups bread flour
1 teaspoon salt
¼ cup powdered milk
2 tablespoons butter, softened
milk, to glaze
3 tablespoons sugar, to decorate
(optional)*

One Prepare the yeast with 1¼ cups water and the sugar following the method in the Chef's techniques on page 550.

Two Sift the flour, salt and powdered milk into a large mixing bowl and make a well in the center. Add the yeast mixture and butter to the well and gradually bring the mixture together with your hands, or use an electric mixer fitted with a dough hook on slow speed, until a rough dough is formed. Turn out the dough onto a lightly floured work surface and knead for 10 minutes, or until the doughh is smooth and elastic (see Chef's techniques, page 551). Alternatively, you can knead the dough in an electric mixer on medium speed for 5 minutes.

Three Return the dough to a clean, lightly oiled bowl and turn once to coat the surface in oil. Cover with a clean, damp kitchen towel and let the dough rise at room temperature until doubled in size (the rising time will depend on the temperature of your kitchen).

Four Turn out the dough onto a lightly floured work surface and knead gently for 2–3 minutes until smooth. Divide the dough into 16 even-size pieces. Roll each piece on a lightly floured work surface in the hollow of your hand until it forms a round and smooth ball, then flatten slightly and roll into miniature loaves with elongated ends.

Five Butter two large baking sheets and place the rolls on them, allowing plenty of space between each one. Cover with a damp kitchen towel and let the dough rise again until nearly doubled in size. Towards the end of this time, preheat the oven to 415°F.

Six Brush the risen rolls with the milk and, using scissors, snip into the tops of the rolls along their length to a depth of ½ inch (see Chef's techniques, page 552). Sprinkle with the sugar, if using, and then bake for 10–12 minutes, or until golden brown and hollow sounding when tapped on the bottom. Remove from the baking sheets and cool on a wire rack.

Whole wheat bread

*Whole wheat flour is added here to thick,
honey-like malt to make a superb loaf.*

Preparation time 25 minutes + rising
(2 hours 30 minutes)
Total cooking time 35 minutes
Makes a 2-lb. loaf

1¼ oz. fresh yeast or 1¼ tablespoons
dried yeast
4 cups whole wheat flour
1 teaspoon salt
1 teaspoon sugar
2 tablespoons butter
2 teaspoons barley malt
1 egg, beaten, to glaze

One Prepare the yeast with 1¼ cups water following the method in the Chef's techniques on page 550.

Two Place the flour, salt and sugar into a large mixing bowl, stir to mix and make a well in the center. Melt the butter in a small saucepan over low heat, then add the barley malt and stir until smooth. Add this to the well with the yeast mixture. Using your hand, with your fingers slightly apart, gradually draw the flour into the liquid. Continue until all the flour has been incorporated and a soft dough is formed. Turn out the dough onto a lightly floured work surface and knead for 10 minutes, or until smooth and elastic (see Chef's techniques, page 551).

Three Return the dough to a clean, lightly oiled bowl and turn once to coat the surface in oil. Cover with a clean, damp kitchen towel and let the dough rise at room temperature until doubled in size (the rising time will depend on the temperature of your kitchen).

Four Butter and flour a 9 x 5 x 3-inch loaf pan, tapping out any excess flour.

Turn out the dough onto a lightly floured work surface and knead for 1 minute. Using your hands, pat out to a square slightly longer than the pan and spray with a fine mist of water. Shape the loaf by rolling up tightly into a sausage shape (see Chef's techniques, page 551), then lift the bread into the prepared pan, seam side down. Cover with a damp kitchen towel and let the dough rise again until nearly doubled in size. Towards the end of this time, preheat the oven to 450°F.

Five Brush the risen loaf with egg. Use a very sharp knife to make a slash down the length of the loaf (see Chef's techniques, page 552). Bake for 30–35 minutes, or until golden brown and hollow sounding when tapped on the bottom. Remove from the pan and cool on a wire rack.

CHEF'S TIP *Barley malt is available from health food stores and has a similar consistency to honey.*

Country sourdough

Prolonged yeast fermentation gives the characteristic taste to this sourdough loaf. The starter needs to begin fermenting about two days before the loaf is made.

Preparation time *30 minutes + rising (2 days in advance for starter and 3 hours 30 minutes for rising)*
Total cooking time *55 minutes*
**Makes two 1-lb. loaves*

STARTER
1 cup bread flour
1 teaspoon fresh yeast or ¹/₂ teaspoon dried yeast
1 cup buttermilk or beer

SPONGE
1 teaspoon fresh yeast or ¹/₂ teaspoon dried yeast
1 cup bread flour

2 teaspoons fresh yeast or 1 teaspoon dried yeast
1 teaspoon salt
2 teaspoons sugar
4 tablespoons butter, softened
5 cups white bread flour
1 egg, beaten, to glaze

One To make the starter, begin two days before you want to make the bread. Sift the flour into a large bowl and crumble the yeast over the surface. Heat the buttermilk or beer until lukewarm and mix into the flour using a wooden spoon until a smooth batter is formed. Cover and leave for 8–12 hours at room temperature, or until the starter begins bubbling a little.

Two Prepare the sponge. Add the yeast and 1 cup lukewarm water to the starter and beat with a wooden spoon until the yeast has dissolved. Stir in the flour until smooth, scrape down the sides of the bowl, cover and leave at room temperature for 8–12 hours.

Three On the day you want to bake the bread, place the fermenting starter into a large mixing bowl or the bowl of an electric mixer fitted with a dough hook. Add the last amount of yeast, the salt, sugar, butter and a quarter of the flour, and beat until a smooth paste is formed. Add the remaining flour in three stages, beating well between them. You should have a soft dough. Turn out the dough onto a lightly floured work surface and knead for 10 minutes,

or until smooth and elastic (see Chef's techniques, page 551).

Four Return the dough to a clean, lightly oiled bowl and turn once to coat the surface in oil. Cover with a clean, damp kitchen towel and allow the dough to rise at room temperature until it has doubled in size (the rising time will depend on the temperature of your kitchen).

Five Turn out the dough onto a lightly floured work surface and then divide in half and knead gently for 5 minutes until smooth. Shape the two pieces of dough into round loaves. Dust a baking sheet with flour, lift the loaves onto the sheet and brush them with the beaten egg. Use a very sharp knife to cut a pattern like spokes on a wheel on the top of the loaves (see Chef's techniques, page 552). Cover the dough with a damp kitchen towel and let it rise again until nearly doubled in size. Towards the end of this time, preheat the oven to 375°F.

Six Bake the risen loaves for 45–50 minutes, or until deep golden with a good crust. Remove from the baking sheet and cool on a wire rack.

about bread starters...

Sourdough bread was traditionally made using a starter fermented with wild yeasts. However, these days, as in this recipe, a little baker's yeast is used to get the starter going. The flour in the mixture gives the yeast food to live on and the buttermilk or beer helps the fermentation.

Rye bread

Rye is grown in the cool areas of northern and eastern Europe and Scandinavia and makes a distinctively dense, slightly bitter-tasting bread.

Preparation time *30 minutes*
+ rising (4 hours)
Total cooking time *20 minutes*
Makes *2 x ³/4-lb. loaves*

1 oz. fresh yeast or 1 tablespoon dried yeast
1 teaspoon superfine sugar
2¹/2 cups bread flour
2 cups rye flour
1 teaspoon salt
1 tablespoon powdered milk
1 tablespoon butter, softened

One Prepare the yeast with 1¹/4 cups water and the sugar following the method in the Chef's techniques on page 550.

Two Sift the flours and salt into a large mixing bowl, stir in the powdered milk and make a well in the center. Add the yeast mixture and butter to the well and gradually bring the mixture together with your hands, or use an electric mixer fitted with a dough hook on slow speed, until a rough dough is formed. Turn out the dough onto a lightly floured work surface and knead for 10 minutes, or until smooth and elastic (see Chef's techniques, page 551). Alternatively, knead in an electric mixer on medium speed for 5 minutes.

Three Return the dough to a clean, lightly oiled bowl and turn once to coat the surface in oil. Cover the dough with a clean, damp kitchen towel and let it rise at room temperature until doubled in size (the rising time will depend on the temperature of your kitchen).

Four Turn out the dough onto a lightly floured work surface, divide in half and knead gently for 2–3 minutes until smooth. Dust 2 baking sheets with flour. Shape the 2 pieces of dough into round loaves and place onto the sheets. Use a very sharp knife to cut diagonal slashes in a crisscross pattern on top of the loaves (see Chef's techniques, page 552). Spray the loaves with a fine mist of water and lightly dust the tops with flour. Cover with a damp kitchen towel and let the dough rise again until nearly doubled in size. Towards the end of this time, preheat the oven to 400°F and place a flameproof dish of hot water in the bottom of the oven to produce steam that will help form a crust on the bread.

Five Bake the risen loaves for 20 minutes, or until browned and hollow sounding when tapped on the bottom. Remove from the baking sheets and cool on a wire rack.

Pretzels

If you like store-bought pretzels, then you will really enjoy these—they're shaped into loose knots, sprinkled with kosher salt and baked to produce a soft, chewy texture. Serve as a snack to go with beer or wine.

Preparation time *30 minutes + rising
(3 hours 30 minutes)*
Total cooking time *25 minutes*
Makes 16 pretzels

*3/4 oz. fresh yeast or 3 1/2 teaspoons
dried yeast
1 cup milk
5 cups bread flour
2 tablespoons salt
3 eggs
1 1/2 tablespoons kosher salt*

One Prepare the yeast with the milk following the method in the Chef's techniques on page 550.

Two Sift the flour and 1 teaspoon of the salt into a large mixing bowl and make a well in the center. Add the yeast mixture and 2 of the eggs to the well and whisk with a fork for a few seconds to break up the eggs. Gradually bring the mixture together with your hands, or use an electric mixer fitted with a dough hook on slow speed, until a rough dough is formed. Turn out the dough onto a lightly floured work surface and knead for 10 minutes, or until smooth and elastic (see Chef's techniques, page 551). Or knead in an electric mixer on medium speed for 5 minutes.

Three Return the dough to a clean, lightly oiled bowl and turn once to coat the surface in oil. Cover with a clean, damp kitchen towel and let the dough rise at room temperature until doubled in size (the rising time will depend on the temperature of your kitchen).

Four Turn out the dough onto a lightly floured work surface and knead gently for 2–3 minutes until smooth. Divide the dough into 16 even-size pieces and roll each piece on a lightly floured work surface into a 14-inch long sausage shape, covering the dough with a damp cloth while you work to prevent it from drying out. Tie each sausage into a loose knot, leaving a large hole in the center. Butter two baking sheets. Then, cut out sixteen 6-inch square pieces of parchment paper, place one under each pretzel and place the pretzels onto the baking sheets, leaving plenty of space between them. Cover the dough with a damp kitchen towel and allow to rise again until nearly doubled in size.

Five Preheat the oven to 400°F. Bring a large saucepan of water to a boil with the remaining salt (not the kosher salt), then reduce the heat to a simmer. Using a slotted spoon, lower the pretzels a few at a time, still on their squares of paper, into the water, being careful not to knock air out of the delicate dough. Poach for 1 minute per batch (the paper will automatically peel off in the water, after which you can discard it). Drain on paper towels and return to the baking sheets.

Six Beat the remaining egg and brush over the surface of the pretzels. Gently press the kosher salt onto the surface of the pretzels and bake for 10–15 minutes, or until pale golden. Remove from the baking sheets and cool on a wire rack.

Pumpkin and cardamom rolls

*These rolls are a golden orange in color and their texture
is crunchy with pumpkin seeds. Great with butter and honey
or as an accompaniment to a bowl of winter vegetable soup.*

Preparation time *25 minutes
+ rising (2 hours)*
Total cooking time *15 minutes*
Makes 12 rolls

*1 oz. fresh yeast or 1 tablespoon
dried yeast*
4 cups bread flour
1 tablespoon powdered milk
1 teaspoon salt
2 teaspoons ground cardamom
1 tablespoon molasses
2 tablespoons butter, softened
*3/4 cup fresh or canned pumpkin purée
(see Chef's tip)*
3 tablespoons pumpkin seeds
1 egg yolk, beaten, to glaze

One Prepare the yeast with 1 cup water following the method in the Chef's techniques on page 550.

Two Sift the flour, powdered milk, salt and ground cardamom into a large mixing bowl and make a well in the center. Stir the molasses into the yeast mixture and add the mixture to the well along with the butter and pumpkin purée. Gradually bring the mixture together with your hands, or use an electric mixer fitted with a dough hook on slow speed, until a fairly soft dough is formed (depending on the moisture content of the pumpkin purée used, you may need to add a little additional flour). Turn out the dough onto a lightly floured work surface and knead for 10 minutes, or until smooth and elastic (see Chef's techniques, page 551). Alternatively, knead in an electric mixer on medium speed for 5 minutes.

Three Return the dough to a clean, lightly oiled bowl and turn once to coat the surface in oil. Cover with a clean, damp kitchen towel and let the dough rise at room temperature until doubled in size (the rising time will depend on the temperature of your kitchen).

Four Turn out the dough onto a lightly floured work surface, then add the pumpkin seeds and knead for 3–4 minutes until the dough is smooth and the pumpkin seeds have been distributed evenly without breaking them up. Divide the dough into 12 even-size pieces. With your palms flat, roll each piece on a lightly floured work surface into an 8-inch piece and tie in a loose knot, tucking the ends underneath. Butter a baking sheet and lift the rolls onto it. Cover with a damp kitchen towel and let the dough rise again until nearly doubled in size. Towards the end of this time, preheat the oven to 425°F.

Five Mix the beaten yolk with a tablespoon of water and a pinch of sugar and salt, then gently brush over the risen rolls. Bake for 10–15 minutes, or until golden brown and hollow sounding when tapped on the bottom. Remove from the baking sheet and then cool on a wire rack.

CHEF'S TIP *To make pumpkin purée, cook 1 1/3 cups peeled and cubed pumpkin until tender. Purée with a potato masher or in a food processor.*

---

about pumpkins...

Depending on which country you live in, pumpkin is a changeable term. In some countries, it applies only to the traditional round vegetable, and in others it refers to all other kinds of squash as well. Almost any winter pumpkin or squash variety can be used for this recipe as long as it has a hard flesh and a sweet flavor.

Bagels

Whether plain or sprinkled with sesame or poppy seeds, these yeasted bread rolls, characteristic of Jewish baking, are delicious served warm with butter. The traditional shiny, hard crust is achieved by boiling the bagels before baking them. See page 548 for step-by-step instructions to accompany this recipe.

Preparation time 50 minutes
+ 1 hour rising
Total cooking time 25 minutes
Makes 12 large or 24 small bagels

2 tablespoons dried yeast
2 tablespoons oil
2 teaspoons salt
3 tablespoons sugar
4 cups bread or all-purpose flour
1 egg, beaten, to glaze

One Dissolve the yeast in 1 cup lukewarm water, then add the oil.

Two Combine the salt, sugar and flour in a bowl, then make a well in the center. Add the yeast mixture and gradually incorporate the flour until a dough forms. Continue working the dough until the sides of the bowl come clean. Knead the dough for 10 minutes, then shape it into a ball and place in the bottom of the bowl. Cover with a moist towel and set aside in a warm place to rise for 30–45 minutes, or until double in size. Line two baking trays with parchment paper.

Three Once the dough has doubled in size, punch it down and knead for 8–10 minutes, then divide into 12 or 24 pieces. Roll them into tight balls. Push a finger through the center of each ball and gently enlarge the hole until the dough resembles a doughnut. Place on a floured baking sheet, cover with a moist towel and allow to rise again for 15 minutes. Preheat the oven to 400°F.

Four In the meantime, bring a large saucepan of water to a simmer. Cook the bagels in the water for 1–2 minutes on each side, then remove and place on the lined baking sheets. Allow to cool for 5 minutes. Brush each bagel with beaten egg and bake for 20–25 minutes, or until golden brown.

CHEF'S TIP *Once the bagels have been brushed with the egg, they can be sprinkled with poppy seeds or sesame seeds before baking.*

Fougasse

Traditionally eaten in Provence on Christmas Eve as one of thirteen desserts symbolizing Christ and his disciples, each region in France now has its own version of this oldest of French breads.

***Preparation time** 40 minutes*
+ rising (4 hours)
***Total cooking time** 10 minutes*
Makes 6 rolls

1/2 oz. fresh yeast or 2 teaspoons
dried yeast
5 1/2 cups bread flour
1 1/2 teaspoons salt
1/2 cup sugar
3 eggs, beaten
grated zest and juice of 1 large orange
2 tablespoons brandy
6 tablespoons butter, softened
1/2 cup high-quality candied citrus
peel, chopped
2 tablespoons butter, melted
2 tablespoons orange blossom water

One Prepare the yeast with 1/3 cup water following the method in the Chef's techniques on page 550.

Two Begin preparing the dough by sifting the flour into a large mixing bowl, adding the salt and sugar and following the sponging method in the Chef's techniques on page 550. In a small bowl, mix together the eggs, orange zest and juice and brandy, pour into the well after the yeast has risen and stir to form a soft dough. Add the butter, squeezing and folding it until fully incorporated. Turn out the dough onto a lightly floured work surface and knead for 10 minutes, or until smooth and elastic (see Chef's techniques, page 551). Or knead in an electric mixer on medium speed for 5 minutes.

Three Return the dough to a clean, lightly oiled bowl and turn once to coat the surface in oil. Cover with a clean, damp kitchen towel and let the dough rise at room temperature until doubled in size (the rising time will depend on the temperature of your kitchen).

Four Turn out the dough onto a lightly floured work surface and gently knead in the citrus peel for 5 minutes, or until the dough is smooth and the peel is evenly distributed. Divide into 6 even-size pieces and, on a lightly floured work surface, roll each into a 6 x 8-inch oval, 1/2 inch thick.

Five Place the fougasse on a board and use a very sharp knife to cut slashes through to the board, beginning in the center of one side and working outwards to give shell-like grooves. Butter two baking sheets and place the fougasse on them, allowing plenty of space between each one. Cover the dough with a damp kitchen towel and let it rise again until nearly doubled in size. Towards the end of this time, preheat the oven to 400°F.

Six Brush the risen fougasse with half the melted butter and bake for 7–10 minutes, or until golden brown. Remove the bread from the oven and, while the bread is still warm, brush with the remaining butter and the orange blossom water. Remove the bread from the sheet and set aside to cool on a wire rack.

Challah

An impressive four-strand braided loaf with a light,
creamy inside and a rich flavor, challah is traditionally
made as a Jewish Sabbath offering.

Preparation time *20 minutes + rising*
(2 hours 45 minutes)
Total cooking time *40 minutes*
Makes a 2³⁄4-lb. loaf

1 oz. fresh yeast or 1 tablespoon
dried yeast
1 tablespoon sugar
6 cups bread flour
1 teaspoon salt
6 tablespoons butter, softened
3 eggs, beaten
2 egg yolks, beaten, to glaze
1–2 tablespoons poppy seeds

One Prepare the yeast with ¹⁄3 cup water and 1 teaspoon of the sugar following the method in the Chef's techniques on page 550.

Two Sift the flour and salt into a large mixing bowl and make a well in the center. Add the yeast mixture, the remaining sugar, butter, eggs and 1 cup lukewarm water to the well. Using your hand, with fingers slightly apart, gradually draw the flour into the liquid. Continue until all the flour has been incorporated and the dough comes together to form a soft ball. The dough should be soft and hold its shape without sticking (you may need to add a little more flour or water). Turn out onto a lightly floured work surface and knead for 10 minutes, or until smooth and elastic (see Chef's techniques, page 551). Or knead in an electric mixer on medium speed for 5 minutes.

Three Return the dough to a clean, lightly oiled bowl and turn once to coat the surface in oil. Cover with a clean, damp kitchen towel and allow to rise at room temperature until doubled in size (the rising time will depend on the temperature of your kitchen).

Four Turn out the dough onto a lightly floured work surface and knead for 1 minute. Cover with a clean, damp kitchen towel and set aside for 5 minutes, then divide the dough into four pieces. Roll each piece on a lightly floured work surface into a 20-inch-long sausage shape. Pinch the four strands together firmly at one end and place on the work surface in front of you with the join at the top. Starting with the left outside strand, take it under the two middle strands and then back over the top of the nearest one. Repeat with the outside right strand. Continue this sequence until the loaf has been braided all the way to the bottom, then seal the ends firmly and neatly.

Five Butter a baking sheet and place the braid onto it. Cover the dough with a damp kitchen towel and let it rise again until nearly doubled in size. Towards the end of this time, preheat the oven to 425°F.

Six Mix a tablespoon of water with the egg yolks and brush the risen loaf with half the mixture. Bake for 10 minutes, then brush again with the egg yolk mixture and sprinkle liberally with the poppy seeds. Return to the oven and bake, covering the top with aluminum foil if the loaf starts to brown too much, for another 25–30 minutes, or until hollow sounding when tapped on the bottom. Remove from the baking sheet and cool on a wire rack.

Hot cross buns

The irresistible aroma of these spiced buns, especially once they are toasted and buttered, means that they will be baked all year round, not just on Good Friday.

Preparation time 25 minutes + rising
(2 hours 30 minutes or overnight)
Total cooking time 20 minutes
Makes 16

1 oz. fresh yeast or 1 tablespoon
dried yeast
²/₃ cup milk
4 cups bread flour
2 teaspoons pumpkin pie spice
¹/₄ cup sugar
2 teaspoons salt
2 eggs, beaten
8 tablespoons butter, softened
1 cup golden raisins

TOPPING AND GLAZE
4 tablespoons all-purpose flour
6 tablespoons sugar
4 tablespoons milk
¹/₂ teaspoon pumpkin pie spice

One Prepare the yeast with the milk following the method in the Chef's techniques on page 550.

Two Sift the flour, pumpkin pie spice, sugar and salt into a large mixing bowl and make a well in the center. Add the yeast mixture and the egg to the well and gradually bring the mixture together with your hands, or use an electric mixer fitted with a dough hook on slow speed, until a soft dough is formed. Turn out the dough onto a lightly floured work surface and knead for 10 minutes, or until smooth and elastic (see Chef's techniques, page 551). Knead the softened butter into the dough until it is fully incorporated and the dough is silky and soft.

Three Return the dough to a clean, lightly oiled bowl and turn once to coat the surface in oil. Cover with a clean, damp kitchen towel and let it rise at room temperature until doubled in size (the rising time will depend on the temperature of your kitchen) or leave it overnight in the refrigerator.

Four Turn out the dough onto a lightly floured work surface and knead in the golden raisins until they are just evenly distributed. Divide into 16 even-size

pieces and, on a lightly floured work surface, roll each piece in the hollow of your hand until it forms a round and smooth ball. Butter a baking sheet and place the buns slightly apart on the sheet. Cover with a damp kitchen towel and let the dough rise again until nearly doubled in size (the buns will be touching when they are ready). Towards the end of this time, preheat the oven to 400°F.

Five To make the topping and glaze, mix together the flour, 4 tablespoons of the sugar and 2–3 tablespoons of water to form a smooth, thick paste. Place in a pastry bag fitted with a small plain tip and pipe the paste across the risen buns in continuous straight lines so that each bun has a cross on top.

Six Bake the buns for 10–15 minutes, or until golden and hollow sounding when tapped on the bottom. Meanwhile, heat the milk, remaining sugar and pumpkin pie spice in a small saucepan until the sugar has dissolved. Brush this glaze over the buns as they come out of the oven. Remove the buns from the baking sheet, set aside to cool on a wire rack, then brush again with some of the glaze. Serve plain or split and toasted with some butter.

Stollen

This sweet, yeasty German Christmas bread is usually made several weeks in advance to allow the flavor of the spices to mature. When baked, it is liberally brushed with butter for a delicious crust.

Preparation time 1 hour + 4 hours rising + overnight marinating
Total cooking time 45 minutes
Makes 2 stollen (16 servings each)

1 teaspoon ground pumpkin pie spice
1 cup chopped mixed candied citrus peel
1/4 cup glacé cherries, quartered
2/3 cup sliced almonds
2 tablespoons rum
zest of 2 small lemons
1 1/4 cups raisins
1/3 cup milk
1 oz. fresh yeast
or 1 tablespoon dried yeast
3 cups all-purpose flour
1/4 cup superfine sugar
3/4 cup unsalted butter
1 egg, beaten
8 oz. marzipan
1 egg and 1 egg yolk, beaten, to glaze
2 tablespoons unsalted butter, melted
confectioners' sugar, to dust

One Mix together the spice, candied citrus peel, cherries, almonds, rum, lemon zest and raisins. Cover and allow to marinate overnight.

Two Put the milk in a small saucepan and heat until tepid. Pour in a bowl and dissolve the yeast in it. Sift 1 cup of the flour and 1 1/2 teaspoons of the sugar into a bowl. Make a well in the center and pour in the yeast mixture. Mix to a smooth paste and cover with plastic wrap. Leave in a warm place for 40 minutes, or until doubled in size.

Three Using your fingertips, rub the butter into the remaining flour until the mixture resembles fine bread crumbs, then stir in the remaining sugar and 1/2 teaspoon salt. Pour in the beaten egg and mix well.

Four Add the risen yeast mixture to the dough and mix until smooth. Add the marinated ingredients and stir in, then turn the mixture out onto a lightly floured work surface and knead to a smooth elastic dough. Place the dough in a large lightly floured bowl, cover with a damp cloth and let it rise in a warm place for 2–2 1/2 hours, or until doubled in size.

Five Brush two large baking sheets with melted butter and set aside. Cut the marzipan in half and then roll out both halves on a surface that is lightly dusted with confectioners' sugar to form two 8 x 1-inch cylinders.

Six Turn out the dough onto a lightly floured surface and knead gently for 2 minutes, or until smooth once more, then divide in two. Roll each piece into a rectangle about 9 x 10 inches, and place a cylinder of marzipan down the center of each. Sprinkle with a few drops of water and close the dough around the marzipan, sealing the edges by pressing them together. Place on the prepared baking sheets seam side down, cover with a damp cloth and let it rise for 50 minutes, or until doubled in volume. Preheat the oven to 350°F. Lightly brush the stollen with the beaten egg and bake for 35–45 minutes, or until well risen and golden.

Seven Remove from the oven and, while the stollen is still warm, brush with the melted butter and dust liberally with confectioners' sugar. Transfer to a wire rack to cool completely, then slice to serve.

CHEF'S TIPS *This recipe makes two stollen, which is perfect if you are baking for a large Christmas gathering. Otherwise, wrap one in plastic wrap, then aluminum foil, and freeze for up to 3 months.*

A stollen makes a lovely Christmas gift, wrapped in cellophane and tied with ribbon.

Panettone

Individually made and wrapped in cellophane and ribbons, this Milanese Christmas specialty is a wonderful gift. High-quality crystallized fruit will taste much better than store-bought chopped candied peel.

Preparation time 25 minutes + rising
(4 hours or overnight) + 1 hour
or overnight soaking
Total cooking time 45 minutes
Makes six 1/4-lb. loaves

1/2 cup golden raisins
1/3 cup mixed candied fruits,
finely chopped
1/2 cup Cointreau
1 tablespoon orange blossom water
1 oz. fresh yeast or 1 tablespoon
dried yeast
1/3 cup sugar
4 cups bread flour
1 teaspoon pumpkin pie spice
1 teaspoon salt
1/2 cup milk, lukewarm
8 tablespoons butter, softened
2 eggs, beaten
1/2 cup macadamia nuts, chopped

One Prepare 6 cans, about 4 inches high and 2 3/4 inches in diameter (washed soup cans are ideal), by brushing with melted butter and lining the bottoms and sides with parchment paper. Allow a 1 1/2-inch collar to extend above the rims of the cans. Brush a second time with butter to smooth down the edges of the paper.

Two Place the raisins, candied fruits, Cointreau and orange blossom water in a small bowl and allow to soak for at least 1 hour, or overnight if possible.

Three Prepare the yeast with 2 tablespoons warm water and a pinch of the sugar following the method in the Chef's techniques on page 550.

Four Sift the flour, pumpkin pie spice, salt and all but 2 tablespoons of the remaining sugar into a large mixing bowl and make a well in the center. Drain the soaked fruits, reserving the Cointreau soaking liquid, and add to the well. Add the warm milk, butter, eggs, nuts and yeast mixture. Gradually bring the mixture together with your hands, or use an electric mixer fitted with a dough hook on slow speed, until a soft dough is formed. Turn out the dough onto a lightly floured work surface and knead for 10 minutes, or until smooth and elastic (see Chef's techniques, page 551).

Five Return the dough to a clean, lightly oiled bowl and turn once to coat the surface in oil. Cover with a clean, damp kitchen towel and let the dough rise at

room temperature until doubled in size (the rising time will depend on the temperature of your kitchen) or leave overnight in the refrigerator.

Six Turn out the dough onto a lightly floured work surface and knead gently for 2–3 minutes. Divide the dough into six even-size pieces and then roll each piece of dough into a tight ball on a lightly floured work surface. If any fruit or nuts break through the surface of the dough, remove these and press into the bottom of the balls to prevent them from burning. Place in the prepared cans, put on a baking sheet and cover with a damp kitchen towel. Let the dough rise again until it has risen nearly to the top of the cans. Towards the end of this time, preheat the oven to 350°F.

Seven Bake the risen panettone for 30–40 minutes, or until golden brown and hollow sounding when tapped on the bottom, covering with a piece of aluminum foil after the first 15 minutes.

Eight Meanwhile, prepare a glaze by adding water, if necessary, to the reserved soaking liquid from the fruit so you have 1/4 cup liquid. Heat in a saucepan with the last 2 tablespoons of sugar until the sugar has dissolved completely. Brush the top of the baked panettone twice with the glaze while still warm, then remove from their cans and cool on a wire rack. The panettone can be stored in an airtight container for up to 1 month.

English muffins

*English muffins were originally lightly split around
the edges using a fork, then toasted on both sides,
pulled open and spread thickly with butter.*

*Preparation time 30 minutes
+ 1 hour 20 minutes rising
Total cooking time 15 minutes
Makes 12 muffins*

*2 teaspoons dried yeast
3¼ cups bread or all-purpose flour
1½ teaspoons salt
1 teaspoon sugar
1 teaspoon unsalted butter, softened*

One Gently heat 1 cup water in a small
saucepan until it feels warm, not hot, to
the touch. Remove from the heat and
stir in the yeast until it is dissolved.

Two Sift the flour, salt and sugar into a
large bowl, make a well in the center
and pour in the yeast mixture. Melt the
butter (again, it should not be too hot)
and pour it into the well. Using your
hand with fingers slightly spread apart,
gradually bring the flour into the liquid
and blend well. Turn the dough out onto
a floured work surface and knead for
2–3 minutes, or until smooth.

Three Place the dough in a clean bowl
that has been sprinkled with a little
flour. Cover with plastic wrap and allow
to rest in a warm place for about 1 hour,
or until doubled in size.

Four Sprinkle a baking sheet with flour.
Preheat the oven to 425°F. Turn out the
dough onto a lightly floured work
surface and knead until smooth. Roll the
dough to about ½ inch thick and, using
a 2¾-inch plain biscuit cutter dipped in
flour, cut out rounds and place them on
the baking sheet. Re-roll any leftover
dough and repeat. Cover the baking
sheet with plastic wrap and rest in a
warm place for 15–20 minutes, or until

the muffins have risen slightly. Bake for
15 minutes, turning halfway through the
cooking time. Remove from the baking
sheet and cool on a wire rack.

CHEF'S TIPS *These muffins can also be
cooked on top of the stove in a griddle*
*or dry heavy-bottomed skillet over low
heat. Turn over when lightly browned
and cooked through.*

*English muffins are halved before
toasting. They are delicious spread with
butter and jam.*

Crumpets

Light and airy crumpets toasted on a fork in front of an open fire have always been a British tea-time delight, but they also make a special treat for brunch and may be toasted under the broiler or in a toaster.

Preparation time 10 minutes
+ 1 hour 50 minutes resting
Total cooking time 45 minutes
Makes 8 crumpets

1½ cups milk
1 tablespoon dried yeast
3 cups all-purpose flour
½ teaspoon salt
½ teaspoon baking soda
oil or clarified butter, for cooking

One Pour the milk into a saucepan and heat until warm, remove from the heat and stir in the yeast.

Two Sift the flour and the salt into a bowl and make a well in the center. Pour in a little of the milk mixture and beat with a whisk, electric mixer or your hand to mix in a little of the flour to make a smooth paste. Repeat this process until all the liquid has been added and all the flour incorporated, then beat until completely smooth. Cover with a plate or plastic wrap and leave in a warm place for approximately 1–1½ hours, or until doubled in size and full of bubbles. Dissolve the baking soda in ¾ cup water. Add it to the batter and mix well. Cover and set aside for 15–20 minutes.

Three On the top of the stove, heat a griddle or a wide heavy-bottomed skillet to medium heat and brush with a little oil or clarified butter. Lightly butter or oil the inside of two or more 3½–4-inch biscuit cutters or crumpet rings, and put them in the pan.

Four Pour in the crumpet batter to a thickness of ½ inch, lower the heat to very low and cook for 7–8 minutes. The bubbles will rise as the crumpets cook. The crumpets are ready to turn over when the top has dried out enough to form a skin (see Chef's techniques, page 549). Loosen the rings, turn the crumpets over and brown the second side for 1–2 minutes. Remove and cool on a wire rack, covered with a clean towel to prevent them from drying out. Repeat with the remaining batter as the rings become free. If the batter thickens while resting, add a little water to thin it.

Five To serve, preheat a broiler and toast the crumpets well on the first cooked side, then brown more lightly on the second side. Spread the lightly broiled side with butter and serve immediately.

CHEF'S TIP *If you don't have crumpet rings, you can use egg rings instead.*

Scotch pancakes

These small, thick, sweet pancakes (pictured top right) are also known as drop scones in England and are served hot and buttered with a fruity or a sweet accompaniment.

Preparation time 8 minutes
+ 1 hour refrigeration
Total cooking time 15 minutes
Makes 12

1 egg, beaten
3 tablespoons sugar
2 tablespoons unsalted butter
1¼ cups milk
1 cup all-purpose flour
½ teaspoon baking soda
½ teaspoon baking powder
½ teaspoon cream of tartar

One In a small bowl, beat the egg with half the sugar. In a small saucepan, melt the butter with the rest of the sugar. Remove from the heat and add the milk and 1 teaspoon cold water to the pan.

Two Sift together the flour, baking soda, baking powder, cream of tartar and a pinch of salt into a large bowl. Make a well in the center. Pour the egg mixture and butter mixture into the well and beat with a wooden spoon or hand whisk until the dry ingredients have disappeared and a smooth batter is formed. Cover and refrigerate for 1 hour or overnight.

Three Brush a large nonstick skillet or griddle with melted butter and place over high heat. Using 2–3 tablespoons batter for each, drop the batter into the pan and cook for 1 minute, or until bubbles rise to the surface. Turn the pancakes over and cook for 1 minute, or until light golden. Serve immediately, or keep warm, wrapped in aluminum foil, in a 300°F oven.

CHEF'S TIP *Serve with butter, lemon juice and sugar, maple syrup or fresh fruit conserves.*

Waffles

Waffles (pictured bottom right), made from a light sweetened batter, have a honeycombed surface ideal for holding large quantities of sweet syrup or honey for those with a particularly sweet tooth.

Preparation time 5 minutes
Total cooking time 40–50 minutes
Makes about 8–10 waffles

2 cups all-purpose flour
1 tablespoon sugar
1½ teaspoons baking powder
½ teaspoon salt
1½ cups milk or buttermilk
2 tablespoons unsalted butter, melted
2 eggs

One Sift together the flour, sugar, baking powder and salt into a large bowl.

Two In a separate bowl, combine the milk, melted butter and eggs. Gradually add to the flour mixture and mix together until blended.

Three Preheat a waffle iron according to the manufacturer's instructions. Once hot, lightly brush with oil. Pour in the recommended amount of batter and cook until golden brown in color and crispy. Serve with whipped butter and honey or maple syrup.

LE CORDON BLEU ✠ COMPLETE COOK

Danish pastries

Although this recipe may be time-consuming, nothing quite matches the taste of this freshly made, rich and flaky yeast dough.

Preparation time 3 hours + refrigeration
Total cooking time 30 minutes
Makes 28

8 cups bread or all-purpose flour
1/3 cup sugar
4 teaspoons salt
2 tablespoons dried yeast
3 cups warm milk
1 3/4 cups unsalted butter, chilled
1 egg, beaten
1/2 cup sliced almonds
confectioners' sugar, to dust

PASSIONFRUIT CREAM FILLING
2 tablespoons sugar
2 large egg yolks
2 teaspoons all-purpose flour
2 teaspoons cornstarch
1/2 cup passionfruit juice or pulp

OR

ORANGE CREAM FILLING
2 tablespoons sugar
2 large egg yolks
2 teaspoons all-purpose flour
2 teaspoons cornstarch
1/2 cup orange juice

One Grease and flour a baking sheet. Sift the flour, sugar and salt into a large bowl and make a well in the center. Cream the yeast with 3 tablespoons of the milk. Stir in the remaining milk and pour into the well in the dry ingredients. Gradually mix in the flour with your fingers until the mixture makes a soft dough. Knead the dough on a floured surface until it is smooth and elastic. Cover with plastic wrap in a bowl and chill for 10 minutes.

Two To make the passionfruit cream filling, mix together the sugar, egg yolks, flour and cornstarch. Bring the juice to a boil in a medium saucepan. Add a little to the sugar mixture, stir to blend, then add the sugar mixture to the saucepan. Bring the mixture to a boil, stirring constantly, and cook for 1 minute. Cover and allow to cool.

Three To make the orange cream filling, proceed exactly as for the passionfruit filling above, using the orange juice instead of the passionfruit juice or pulp.

Four On a floured surface, roll out the dough into a rectangle three times as long as it is wide and 1/8 inch thick. Tap and roll out the butter within two long sheets of plastic wrap into a rectangle,

the same width as, but two-thirds the length of, the dough. Unwrap and lay the butter on the top two-thirds of the dough. Fold the exposed third of the dough up over the butter and fold the top third down.

Five Turn the dough to look like a book, with the binding on the left, and roll again into a rectangle and fold into three layers. Repeat twice, wrapping in plastic wrap and chilling for 20 minutes between each roll.

Six On a floured surface, roll the dough into a 1/8-inch-thick square or rectangle. Cut into 5 x 4-inch rectangles and place on the baking sheet.

Seven To make the Danish pastries, preheat the oven to 400°F. Spoon the filling into a pastry bag and pipe into the center of each pastry. Bring up the corners and press together firmly. Set aside in a warm place to rise for 30 minutes. Brush with the egg, avoiding the sides of the pastry because this will prevent the dough from rising as it cooks. Sprinkle with a few sliced almonds and bake for 15–20 minutes, or until golden. Cool on wire racks and dust with sifted confectioners' sugar, if desired.

Orange and poppy seed muffins

Poppy seeds are scattered liberally throughout these muffins, filling them with a delightful flavor and delicate crunch.

Preparation time 20 minutes
Total cooking time 20 minutes
Makes 10 muffins

2¹/₂ cups self-rising flour
¹/₄ teaspoon baking powder
¹/₄ cup sugar
2¹/₂ tablespoons poppy seeds
2 tablespoons finely grated orange zest
¹/₃ cup unsalted butter
¹/₃ cup apricot jam
2 eggs
¹/₃ cup buttermilk
confectioners' sugar, to dust

One Preheat the oven to 400°F. Grease 10 cups of a 12-cup muffin pan with a little melted butter or oil and fill the remaining 2 cups with water. Sift the flour, baking powder and sugar into a large bowl. Stir in the poppy seeds and grated orange zest, and make a well in the center.

Two Melt the butter and jam in a small saucepan over low heat, stirring until smooth. Remove from the heat. Whisk the eggs and buttermilk together. Add the butter and egg mixtures to the well in the dry ingredients. Stir with a metal spoon until the mixture is just combined. Do not overmix—the mixture should be lumpy.

Three Spoon the mixture into 10 cups of the muffin pan, filling each cup three-quarters full. Bake for 12–15 minutes, or until a skewer comes out clean when inserted into the center of a muffin. Cool the muffins in the pan for 5 minutes before lifting out onto a wire rack. Dust with sifted confectioners' sugar before serving. These are delicious with butter.

Banana and ginger muffins

A subtle combination of banana and ginger,
enhanced with the golden nectar of honey,
giving a lovely rich muffin.

Preparation time 20 minutes
Total cooking time 25 minutes
Makes 12 muffins

2½ cups self-rising flour
1 teaspoon ground ginger
½ cup firmly packed brown sugar
⅓ cup finely chopped preserved
or crystallized ginger (see Chef's tip)
¼ cup unsalted butter
3 tablespoons honey
½ cup milk
2 eggs
2 ripe bananas, mashed

TOPPING
½ cup cream cheese, softened
3 tablespoons confectioners' sugar
2 teaspoons finely grated lemon zest

preserved or crystallized ginger,
to decorate

One Preheat the oven to 425°F. Brush a 12-cup muffin pan with melted butter or oil. Sift the flour and ground ginger together into a large mixing bowl. Stir in the brown sugar and chopped ginger, and make a well in the center of the mixture.

Two Place the butter and honey in a small saucepan and stir over low heat until melted. Remove from the heat. Whisk the milk and eggs together.

Three Add the butter mixture, egg mixture and the bananas to the well in the dry ingredients. Stir with a metal spoon until just combined. Do not overmix—the mixture should be lumpy. Spoon the mixture into the muffin pan, filling each cup about three-quarters full. Bake for 20 minutes, or until a skewer comes out clean when inserted into the center of a muffin. Cool the muffins in the pan for 5 minutes, then lift out onto a wire rack to cool completely before spreading with the topping.

Four To make the topping, beat the cream cheese, confectioners' sugar and grated lemon zest until light and creamy. Spread onto the muffins and decorate with thin slices of preserved or crystallized ginger.

CHEF'S TIP *Whether you use preserved or crystallized ginger, it's best to rinse the pieces briefly in cool water to remove the syrup or sugar coating before chopping or slicing.*

Blueberry muffins

These classic muffins may be made with either fresh or frozen blueberries and are particularly good served warm for breakfast or brunch. Try substituting raspberries or blackberries or a combination of these, gently folding them in to keep them whole.

Preparation time 15 minutes
Total cooking time 30 minutes
Makes 6 jumbo muffins

3 cups self-rising flour
2/3 cup all-purpose flour
1/2 cup firmly packed brown sugar
1 cup fresh or frozen blueberries
(see Chef's tip)
2 eggs
1 cup milk
1 teaspoon vanilla extract
1/2 cup unsalted butter, melted
confectioners' sugar, to dust

One Preheat the oven to 425°F. Brush a 6-cup jumbo muffin pan with melted butter or oil. Sift the flours into a large mixing bowl, stir in the sugar and blueberries, and make a well in the center.

Two Whisk the eggs, milk and vanilla together, and add to the well in the dry ingredients. Add the butter, and stir with a metal spoon until just combined. Do not overmix—the mixture should be lumpy.

Three Spoon the mixture into the muffin pan, filling each cup about three-quarters full. Bake for 30 minutes, or until a skewer comes out clean when inserted into the center of a muffin. Cool the muffins in the pan for 5 minutes before lifting out onto a wire rack. Dust the muffins generously with sifted confectioners' sugar before serving. These are delicious sliced in half and spread with butter.

CHEF'S TIP *If using frozen blueberries, use them straight from the freezer. Do not allow them to thaw, or they will discolor the muffin mixture.*

Chocolate chip cookies

These cookies, originally created at the Toll House Inn in Massachusetts in the 1920s, became so popular that small round chocolate pieces, known as "chips," were marketed especially for them.

***Preparation time** 20 minutes*
***Total cooking time** 20 minutes per baking sheet*
Makes 24

1/2 cup unsalted butter, softened
1/2 cup light brown sugar
1/3 cup sugar
1 egg, lightly beaten
1/4 teaspoon vanilla extract
1 1/4 cups all-purpose flour
pinch of baking powder
1/2 cup ground almonds
1 cup semi-sweet chocolate chips

One Preheat the oven to 350°F. Brush two baking sheets with melted butter and refrigerate until set.

Two Using a wooden spoon or an electric mixer, cream the butter and sugars until light and fluffy. Gradually add the egg and vanilla, beating well after each addition.

Three Sift the flour, baking powder and ground almonds together. Fold half into the creamed mixture. When almost incorporated, add the rest of the sifted mixture, then add the chocolate chips as you fold.

Four Divide into 24 portions and roll into balls. Place the balls, spaced well apart, on the two prepared baking sheets and flatten slightly. Bake for 15–20 minutes, or until golden brown. Remove from the baking sheets while still hot and transfer to a cooling rack. Repeat with the remaining mixture, preparing the baking sheets as instructed in step 1. When completely cold, store the cookies in an airtight container.

Rum babas

These spongy cakes soaked in a rum syrup are said to have been named by a Polish king after his storybook hero, Ali Baba. Here they are served with a vanilla-flavored Chantilly cream and fresh fruit.

Preparation time *1 hour + 1 hour rising*
Total cooking time *30 minutes*
Serves 8

DOUGH
2 cups all-purpose or bread flour
1 teaspoon salt
1 teaspoon sugar
1/2 oz. fresh yeast or 1/4 oz. dried yeast
1/3 cup milk
3 eggs, beaten
1/2 cup raisins, soaked
in 1 tablespoon rum
3 tablespoons melted butter, just warm

SYRUP
2 cups water
1/3 cup sugar
zest of 1 lemon
1 cardamom pod
2 bay leaves
1/2 orange, roughly chopped
2 tablespoons dark rum

CHANTILLY CREAM
1 1/4 cups whipping cream
1 tablespoon confectioners' sugar
1/2 teaspoon vanilla extract

3 tablespoons apricot jam
fresh fruit, such as strawberries and raspberries, to decorate

One Brush eight individual pudding molds or a 4-cup ring mold with melted butter, then dust with some flour and tap out the excess.

Two To make the dough, sift the flour, salt and sugar into a large bowl and make a well in the center. Put the yeast in a small bowl. In a small saucepan, warm the milk until tepid, then add to the yeast. Stir to dissolve, then mix in 1 tablespoon flour and set aside until foamy. When foamy, add to the beaten eggs and pour into the well in the flour. Prepare the dough, following the method in the Chef's techniques on page 549. Preheat the oven to 415°F.

Three Bake the babas for 12 minutes (25 minutes for a large one), or until golden. Loosen the babas and unmold onto a wire rack to cool. Prick all over with a fine skewer.

Four To make the syrup, gently heat all the ingredients except the rum together in a medium saucepan, stirring to dissolve the sugar, then bring to a boil and boil for 15 minutes to reduce the

syrup and thicken slightly. Remove the saucepan from the heat and leave for 5 minutes to infuse the flavors. Strain, discard the flavorings, return the syrup to the saucepan and reheat. Remove from the stove and stir in the rum. Pour the syrup into a shallow dish and roll the cold babas in the hot syrup. Place the babas on a wire rack over a plate to drip off excess syrup and to cool completely.

Five To make the Chantilly cream, pour the cream into a bowl and add the confectioners' sugar and vanilla. Using a hand whisk or electric mixer, whip the cream until it just forms soft peaks that hold as the whisk is lifted from the bowl.

Six In a small saucepan, heat the apricot jam with 1 tablespoon water. When the mixture has melted and begins to boil, strain it into a small bowl and, while still hot, brush it over the babas, then allow to cool.

Seven Serve the babas with the Chantilly cream and fruit. If you have made a large rum baba, fill the center of the ring with the cream and fruit.

about rum...

Light and dark rum have different flavors when used in cooking. Dark rum still contains natural flavors from the sugarcane molasses and so has a stronger taste. Light rum has had all the pigmentation and impurities filtered out.

Shortbread

Shortbread can be made with all-purpose flour alone, however the texture is greatly enhanced by using a combination of flours. Adding rice flour produces a light result, while semolina will give a crunchy texture.

Preparation time *10 minutes*
+ 10 minutes refrigeration
Total cooking time *25 minutes*
Makes 8

1/2 cup unsalted butter, at room temperature
1/4 cup sugar
1 cup all-purpose flour
1/3 cup rice flour or fine semolina, sifted twice
2 tablespoons sugar, to dust

One Preheat the oven to 350°F.

Two Beat the butter in a wide bowl until smooth. Gradually beat in the sugar. Add the all-purpose flour and rice flour or semolina and stir with a fork until well blended.

Three Press the mixture into a 7–8-inch springform or round cake pan with a removable bottom. Make sure that the mixture is level and pierce the surface evenly with a fork. Place in the refrigerator to chill for 10 minutes.

Four Sprinkle the surface of the shortbread with the extra sugar and bake for 25 minutes, or until golden.

Five While the shortbread is still hot, carefully remove from the pan and cut into eight wedges, using a large sharp knife. (Don't separate the pieces of shortbread, however, or they will dry out.) After 5 minutes, the shortbread will be firmer—transfer it to a wire rack and sprinkle with a little more sugar.

CHEF'S TIPS *The shortbread may rise or wrinkle slightly during baking—this is quite normal.*

The shortbread will keep for up to a week if stored in an airtight container or wrapped in foil.

Viennese fingers

These wonderful chocolate-dipped cookies simply melt in the mouth.

Preparation time 25 minutes
Total cooking time 10 minutes per baking sheet
Makes 16

½ cup unsalted butter, at room temperature
2–3 drops vanilla extract
1 teaspoon finely grated lemon zest
⅓ cup confectioners' sugar
1 egg, lightly beaten
1¼ cups all-purpose flour
6 oz. semi-sweet chocolate, chopped

One Brush two baking sheets with melted butter and refrigerate. Preheat the oven to 400°F.

Two Using a wooden spoon or electric mixer, cream the butter, vanilla, lemon rind and sugar until light and fluffy. Gradually add the egg, a little at a time, beating well after each addition. Sift in the flour and stir to mix.

Three Spoon the mixture into a pastry bag with a ½-inch star tip. Pipe enough 2½–3-inch pieces to fill the prepared baking sheets, spacing them slightly apart. Bake for 7–10 minutes, or until golden brown. Cool on a wire rack. Repeat with the remaining mixture,

preparing the cooled baking sheets as instructed in step 1.

Four Place the chocolate in the top of a double boiler over steaming water, off the stove. Make sure that the bottom of the insert doesn't touch the water. Stir until the chocolate melts. Dip one end of each cookie in the chocolate and cool on a baking sheet lined with waxed paper.

CHEF'S TIP *For a variation, pipe the dough into rosettes 1½ inches wide (see Chef's techniques, page 555). When cooked, divide the cookies into pairs. Spread the bottom of one with jam, then stick together. Dust with confectioners' sugar and place in paper petit fours cups.*

Gingersnaps

*The tantalizing spicy aroma of these cookies as they come out
of the oven is bound to test your willpower. It will be difficult to wait
for them to cool and become hard and crunchy as they should do.*

Preparation time 15 minutes
+ 1 hour 30 minutes refrigeration
Total cooking time 15 minutes per
baking sheet
Makes about 40

1/4 *cup unsalted butter, at*
room temperature
3/4 *cup sugar*
1 egg
1/4 *cup molasses*
2 teaspoons white wine vinegar
2 cups bread or all-purpose flour
1 1/2 *teaspoons baking soda*
1/2 *teaspoon ground ginger*
pinch of ground cinnamon
pinch of ground cloves
pinch of ground cardamom
sugar, to coat

One Preheat the oven to 375°F. Line two baking sheets with parchment paper.

Two Using a wooden spoon or an electric mixer, cream together the butter and sugar until light and fluffy. Add the egg, a little at a time, beating well after each addition. Add the molasses and vinegar and mix well.

Three Sift together the flour, baking soda, ground ginger, cinnamon, cloves and cardamom and stir into the butter mixture. Bring a ball of dough together with your hands, wrap in plastic wrap and chill for 1 1/2 hours or until firm.

Four Divide the dough into four and, using the palms of your hands, roll each piece into a rope. Cut each rope into 10 pieces and roll the pieces into balls. Spread the sugar on a flat plate. Roll each ball through the sugar, place on the prepared sheets spaced well apart and

press down slightly to flatten. Refrigerate the remaining dough until needed. Bake for 10–15 minutes, or until golden brown. Repeat with the remaining mixture, preparing the baking sheets as instructed in step 1.

CHEF'S TIPS *This cookie dough can be prepared in advance, rolled in the sugar and slightly flattened. Wrap in plastic wrap and freeze as individual pieces. To bake, place the frozen balls on a lined baking sheet and bake at 375°F for 20 minutes.*

If you are baking more than one sheet of cookies in a nonconvection oven, swap them around halfway through, to make sure they cook evenly.

Chocolate brownies

*The smell of brownies baking may be irresistible, but it
doesn't compare with the sensation of sinking your teeth into the finished
product. The thick chocolate frosting makes these twice as delectable.*

Preparation time *20 minutes
+ refrigeration*
Total cooking time *50 minutes*
Makes about 16

*³/4 cup unsalted butter, softened
1 tablespoon vanilla extract
³/4 cup sugar
¹/3 cup chopped semi-sweet chocolate
2 eggs, lightly beaten
³/4 cup all-purpose flour
pinch of salt
1 teaspoon baking powder
1³/4 cups walnuts, coarsely chopped*

FROSTING
*¹/3 cup whipping cream
²/3 cup chopped semi-sweet chocolate
3 tablespoons unsalted butter, softened*

One Grease an 8-inch square baking pan, and sprinkle with flour or line the bottom with parchment paper. Cream the butter, vanilla extract and sugar together in a large bowl with a wooden spoon or an electric mixer until light and fluffy. Preheat the oven to 325°F.

Two Put the chocolate in the top of a double boiler over hot water, off the heat, making sure the insert is not touching the water. Allow the chocolate to melt slowly, stirring until smooth, then remove the insert from the water.

Three Gradually add the eggs to the creamed butter in about six additions, beating well after each addition, then stir in the melted chocolate.

Four Sift together the flour, salt and baking powder into a bowl, and add the chopped walnuts. Add to the chocolate mixture, and stir until just combined.

Pour into the pan and bake for 45 minutes, or until firm and springy to the touch of a finger. Cool in the pan.

Five To make the frosting, pour the cream into a small saucepan and heat until just at boiling point. Remove from the heat and add the chocolate. Stir to melt, then whisk in the butter. Transfer to a bowl and refrigerate until cooled and slightly thickened before spreading on top of the brownies. Refrigerate until

the frosting is just set. Cut the brownies into squares to serve.

CHEF'S TIPS *If you want you can use pecans instead of walnuts.*

These chocolate brownies are superbly moist and will keep in an airtight container for up to a week.

Rhubarb and almond tart

This tart has a rich, moist filling and can be enjoyed on its own, or with crème anglaise (custard sauce) or ice cream. It keeps well and can be made a few days in advance. Fresh plums, apricots or pears can be used instead of rhubarb.

Preparation time 1 hour
+ 40 minutes refrigeration
Total cooking time 40 minutes
Serves 6–8

PASTRY
1/2 cup unsalted butter, softened
1/4 cup sugar
1 egg, beaten
1 2/3 cups all-purpose flour

ALMOND CREAM
1/3 cup unsalted butter, softened
1/3 cup sugar
2 teaspoons finely grated lemon zest
2 eggs
1/2 cup ground almonds
1 tablespoon all-purpose flour

2 tablespoons raspberry jam
1 stalk rhubarb, thinly sliced
2 tablespoons sliced almonds
2 tablespoons apricot jam
confectioners' sugar, to dust

One To make the pastry, beat the butter and sugar in a bowl until well blended using a wooden spoon or an electric mixer. Add the egg gradually, beating well after each addition. Sift in the flour and a pinch of salt and mix lightly using a flexible bladed knife until the mixture just comes together—do not overmix. Gather together to form a rough ball and place on a large piece of plastic wrap. Gently flatten to 1/2-inch thickness, then wrap and refrigerate for 20 minutes.

Two To make the almond cream, beat the butter, sugar and lemon zest in a small bowl using a wooden spoon, whisk or electric beaters. Gradually beat in the eggs. Stir in the almonds and flour and set aside.

Three To assemble, roll out the pastry on a floured surface (or between two sheets of parchment paper) 1/8 inch thick. Ease into a greased, shallow 8-inch fluted tart pan with removable bottom. Trim the edges, pierce the bottom lightly with a fork and spread with raspberry jam. Spread the almond cream over the top, just level with the pastry edge. Decorate with rhubarb, slightly pushing into the almond cream. Sprinkle with sliced almonds and chill for 20 minutes.

Four Preheat the oven to 350°F. Place the tart on a baking sheet and bake for 10 minutes to help set the pastry. Reduce the oven temperature to 325°F and bake for another 30–35 minutes, or until the almond filling is golden brown and springs back when lightly touched.

Five In a small saucepan, heat the apricot jam with 1 tablespoon water. When the mixture has melted and begins to boil, strain it into a small bowl, and while still hot, brush it over the tart. Allow the jam to cool, then sift a light dusting of confectioners' sugar over the top.

CHEF'S TIPS *Handle the pastry as little as possible: work quickly and lightly. Always chill pastry before rolling as this makes it easier to manage. Allowing the pastry to rest just before baking helps prevent shrinkage and loss of shape.*

To make the pastry in a food processor, process the flour, butter and sugar into fine crumbs, add the egg and process in short bursts until the pastry just comes together. Turn out onto a lightly floured surface and work the pastry together by hand.

---

about rhubarb...

Spring or forced rhubarb grown in hothouses has a tender stem and bright, reddish pink color. Older field-grown rhubarb is a darker red with a tougher stem that may need to be peeled. Some rhubarb gives off more liquid than others and this may affect the appearance of the dish but it does not alter the flavor.

Madeira cake

This English favorite is a rich but simple cake sprinkled with candied lemon zest just before baking. It is usually served with a glass of Madeira, hence the name. Some chefs also sprinkle the baked cake with Madeira before it cools.

Preparation time 30 minutes
Total cooking time 1 hour 25 minutes
Serves 6

1 lemon
1 cup sugar
1 cup unsalted butter, at room
temperature
4 eggs, beaten
2 cups all-purpose flour

One Preheat the oven to 300°F. Line a 6-cup loaf pan, about 8½ x 4½ x 2 inches (see Chef's techniques, page 553). Grease the paper and dust with flour.

Two To candy the lemon zest, peel the zest from the lemon using a vegetable peeler, then with a small knife, scrape away any white pith from the inside of the strips. Place the strips flat on a cutting board and cut into fine needle-like shreds using a large sharp knife. Place the shreds in a small saucepan, cover with water, and bring to a boil. Boil for 1 minute, strain and rinse with cold water, then repeat. In a separate small saucepan, combine 3 tablespoons of the sugar with 2 tablespoons water and, stirring to dissolve the sugar, bring slowly to a boil. Add the fine shreds of lemon zest and simmer for 5 minutes, or until the zest is translucent. Remove from the syrup, using a fork, and spread out on waxed paper to cool.

Three Following the creaming method in the Chef's techniques on page 554, cream the butter and remaining sugar and gradually beat in the eggs.

Four Sift the flour into the bowl and fold into the mixture carefully, using a plastic spatula. Spoon the mixture into the prepared loaf pan and smooth the top (see Chef's techniques, page 555). Sprinkle the candied zest evenly over the top of the cake and bake for 1 hour 15 minutes, or until a skewer comes out clean when inserted into the center (see Chef's techniques, page 556).

Five Allow the cake to cool for 5 minutes in the pan, then turn out onto a wire rack and peel off the paper. When completely cooled, wrap the cake in plastic wrap until ready to serve to keep it moist.

Angel food cake

*Easy to make and exceptional to eat, this light, airy "down home" specialty
is best cut with a serrated knife or separated into pieces with two forks.
It's wonderful served simply with the season's fresh fruit.*

Preparation time 10 minutes
Total cooking time 50 minutes
Serves 6

1¹/2 cups sugar
1 cup all-purpose flour
12 egg whites, at room temperature
pinch of salt
1 teaspoon cream of tartar
4 drops vanilla extract
2 drops almond extract
confectioners' sugar, to dust
strawberries, halved, to garnish

One Preheat the oven to 350°F. Have ready an angel food cake pan, measuring 9¹/2–10 inches across the top and 4 inches in depth. The pan needs no preparation.

Two Sift 1 cup of the sugar together with the flour. Repeat the sifting process six times, then set aside. Beat the egg whites in a large bowl, using an electric mixer, until they are foamy with soft peaks. Add the salt, cream of tartar, vanilla and almond extract and 1 tablespoon water, and when bubbles form, add the remaining sugar, a few tablespoons at a time. Beat in well until all the sugar has dissolved and the mixture stands in very stiff peaks.

Three Add the sifted flour and sugar and, using a rubber spatula, carefully fold in to blend thoroughly. Spoon into the pan and pull a flexible bladed knife, upright in the pan and touching the bottom, through the mixture in a circle. This will remove pockets of air and help to blend.

Four Bake for 50 minutes, or until the cake springs back when lightly touched with your finger (see Chef's techniques, page 556). Turn the pan upside down onto a wire rack and allow the cake to cool completely in the pan so that it will not collapse as it cools. To remove, the cake may require loosening around the edge with a flexible bladed knife. Transfer to a serving plate, dust with the sifted confectioners' sugar and garnish with strawberries.

CHEF'S TIP *This cake can either be served plain with whipped cream and strawberries, or drizzled with melted chocolate. Alternatively, coat with whipped cream flavored with strong coffee or melted chocolate.*

Black Forest torte

This Kirsch-flavored chocolate cake, traditionally filled with whipped cream and sour morello cherries bottled in alcohol, comes from the Black Forest region of Germany. This version uses readily available sweet black cherries.

Preparation time 1 hour + refrigeration
Total cooking time 30 minutes
Serves 8

3 egg yolks
3 eggs
1/2 cup sugar
3/4 cup all-purpose flour
1/4 cup cocoa powder
3 oz. good-quality semi-sweet
chocolate
3 cups whipping cream
1–2 drops vanilla extract
confectioners' sugar, to dust

CHERRY FILLING
2 teaspoons cornstarch
16 oz.-can pitted black sweet cherries,
drained, reserving 1/3 cup of
the syrup

KIRSCH SYRUP
1/4 cup sugar
3 tablespoons Kirsch

One Preheat the oven to 350°F. Line an 8-inch-diameter, 2 1/2-inch-deep spring-form or round cake pan (see Chef's techniques, page 552).

Two Bring a saucepan of water to a boil, then remove from the heat. Following the beating method in the Chef's techniques on page 554, combine the yolks, eggs and sugar in a heatproof bowl or the top insert of a double boiler. Place over the pan without touching the water and beat briskly until the mixture leaves a trail on its surface when the whisk is lifted. Remove the bowl or insert from the water and whisk the mixture until cold. Sift the flour and cocoa together and, using a plastic spatula, gently fold into the cold mixture until just combined. Do not overfold. Pour into the pan and bake for about 20 minutes, or until the cake springs back when lightly touched (see Chef's techniques, page 556). Turn out onto a wire rack to cool.

Three To make the cherry filling, mix the cornstarch with a little syrup from the cherries to make a runny paste. Put the remaining syrup in a small saucepan and bring to a boil. Remove from the heat, stir in the cornstarch paste, return to the heat and stir until boiling. Remove from the heat, add all but eight cherries, reserving them for decoration, and allow to cool.

Four To make the Kirsch syrup, gently warm the sugar with 1/4 cup water in a small saucepan, stirring to dissolve the sugar. Bring to a boil, remove from heat, add the Kirsch and allow to cool.

Five Using a vegetable peeler, peel off small curls from the chocolate. In a large bowl, beat the cream with an electric mixer until thick and just pourable, add the vanilla and a pinch of sugar, then beat to soft peaks. Reserve a quarter of the cream for decoration.

Six To assemble the cake, use a serrated knife to cut the cake into three horizontal layers. Spoon the Kirsch syrup over each. Place the top cake on a plate or board with the crust side down and spread or pipe some cream onto it. Cover with the middle cake layer. Spread a thin layer of cream on top, leaving a thicker border of cream around the edge. Spread the cherry filling within the border. Cover with the last piece of cake. Spread the top and sides thinly with cream and chill for 10 minutes. Repeat covering with the cream until an even coat is achieved. Press the chocolate curls around the sides and pipe rosettes with the reserved cream on top. Decorate with the reserved cherries, sprinkle the rosettes with chocolate and dust with confectioners' sugar.

Dundee cake

This classic Scottish fruitcake is made with raisins, candied citrus peel and almonds and flavored with rum. With its traditional almond-covered top, Dundee cake is popular at tea time both in Scotland and throughout Britain.

Preparation time *30 minutes + 5 days storing*
Total cooking time *2 hours*
Serves 10

4¹/2 cups raisins, chopped
¹/2 cup chopped mixed candied citrus peel
2 tablespoons dark rum
1 cup unsalted butter, at room temperature
1 cup dark brown sugar
6 eggs, lightly beaten
1 tablespoon marmalade
2³/4 cups all-purpose flour
2 teaspoons baking powder
¹/2 teaspoon salt
¹/2 cup ground almonds
1 cup blanched whole almonds
2 tablespoons apricot jam, strained

One Preheat the oven to 325°F. Double line an 8–9-inch-diameter, 2¹/2-inch-deep springform or round cake pan (see Chef's techniques, page 552). Grease the paper and dust with flour.

Two Combine the raisins, mixed citrus peel and rum in a glass bowl and set aside to soak. Using the creaming method (see Chef's techniques, page 554), cream the butter and sugar and gradually beat in the lightly beaten eggs. Once all the eggs have been added, beat in the marmalade.

Three Sift the flour, baking powder and salt into a large bowl and stir in the ground almonds. Add the soaked fruit and rum and fold into the flour with a rubber spatula. Fold this into the creamed mixture in three batches, until well combined. Spoon into the pan and gently smooth the top using the back of a wet spoon (see Chef's techniques, page 555). Decorate the top with the blanched almonds and bake on the middle shelf of the oven for 2 hours. Cover the cake with aluminum foil after 1 hour to prevent it from browning too much. Cool in the pan for 5 minutes, then remove from the pan and allow to cool on a wire rack, leaving the paper liner on. Store the cake wrapped in cheesecloth moistened with rum in an airtight container in a cool place for at least 5 days to develop the full flavor.

Four To serve, remove the wrapping and paper, melt the jam with 1 tablespoon water in a small saucepan and brush the top of the cake to make it shine.

Ginger and carrot cake

The finely chopped ginger, lemon zest and combination of spices give this moist cake its delicious flavor. Enhanced by the soft creamy frosting, this cake is bound to disappear quickly.

Preparation time 25 minutes
Total cooking time 45 minutes
Serves 8

6 egg yolks
3/4 cup sugar
1 2/3 cups shredded carrots
1/2 cup all-purpose flour
1 teaspoon baking powder
large pinch of ground cinnamon
large pinch of ground ginger
small pinch of ground cloves
pinch of salt
2/3 cup ground almonds
1 cup finely ground hazelnuts
1 cup cake crumbs
zest of 1 lemon, finely grated
6 large egg whites
1 oz. preserved or crystallized ginger,
rinsed and finely chopped

CREAM CHEESE FROSTING
1/3 cup unsalted butter, at room
temperature
1/3 cup cream cheese
1 1/2–2 cups confectioners' sugar
1/2 teaspoon vanilla extract

One Preheat the oven to 375°F. Line an 8–9-inch-diameter springform or round cake pan (see Chef's techniques, page 552). Grease the parchment paper and dust with flour.

Two Bring a saucepan of water to a boil and remove from the stove. Using the beating method (see Chef's techniques, page 554), combine the egg yolks and half the sugar in a heatproof bowl or the top insert of a double boiler. Place over the pan, without touching the water. Beat until the mixture is thick and pale. Remove the bowl or insert from the water and stir in the carrots.

Three Sift together the flour, baking powder, ground spices and salt. Stir in the almonds, hazelnuts, cake crumbs and lemon zest.

Four In a separate bowl, beat the egg whites until they form soft peaks. Add the remaining sugar and beat until stiff shiny peaks form.

Five Using a rubber spatula, fold one third of the egg whites into the carrot mixture, then fold in one-third of the dry ingredients. Repeat, alternating, until the mixture is almost combined. Add the chopped ginger and fold in to fully combine. This must be done gently to retain as much air in the mixture as possible. Pour into the cake pan and bake for 35–45 minutes, or until a skewer comes out clean when inserted into the center (see Chef's techniques, page 556). Cool in the pan for 10 minutes before removing from the pan and transferring to a wire rack to cool.

Six To make the cream cheese frosting, beat all the ingredients together until creamy. When the cake has cooled completely, spread with the topping.

Apple pie

*When pilgrims first arrived, they brought with them
apple seeds and a love of pies, sowing a national love affair with this
cherished homey dessert. Cooking apples yield the best results.*

Preparation time 1 hour
Total cooking time 1 hour
Serves 4–6

PASTRY
2 cups all-purpose flour
2/3 cup unsalted butter, cubed
2 tablespoons sugar

FILLING
1 1/2 lb. large tart green apples
1/2 cup sugar, plus extra for sprinkling
1 teaspoon ground cinnamon
1/4 teaspoon ground nutmeg
3 tablespoons all-purpose flour
1 tablespoon lemon juice
3 tablespoons unsalted butter, cubed

One Preheat the oven to 350°F. To make the pastry, work together the flour, butter, sugar and a pinch of salt in a food processor until the mixture resembles fine bread crumbs. With the motor running, add 2 tablespoons iced water and process until the mixture just comes together. Remove the dough, divide in half and flatten each portion into a thick round. Cover with plastic wrap and chill in the refrigerator for 15–20 minutes.

Two To make the filling, peel, quarter and core the apples, then slice thinly and place in a large bowl. Combine the sugar, cinnamon, nutmeg, flour and a good pinch of salt, and sprinkle the mixture over the apple. Add the lemon juice and toss well.

Three On a lightly floured surface, roll out a pastry round 1/8 inch thick, and 2 inches wider than a greased, shallow 9-inch pie plate. Carefully roll the dough onto a rolling pin, or fold into quarters, then ease into the pie plate. With your fingertips, press the dough into the plate to remove any air bubbles. Using a sharp, floured knife, trim the excess pastry, leaving a 1-inch border of dough overhanging the rim.

Four Add the filling, then with a pastry brush, brush the pastry edges with water. Roll the remaining dough to the same thickness as before. Dot the apple with butter, place the dough on top and cut four steam vents. Trim away the excess pastry, leaving a 1/2-inch overhang, then press the edges together to seal them. Flute the edges by pinching the pastry between thumb and index finger into a zigzag design. Brush the top with water and sprinkle with extra sugar, then bake for 55–60 minutes. Cool the pie on a rack, and serve warm or cold.

Flourless chocolate cake

*Served with Chantilly cream and a sprinkling of sliced almonds,
this dense chocolate cake makes a lovely dessert, but is perfect
for a little chocolate indulgence on any occasion.*

Preparation time *30 minutes*
Total cooking time *50 minutes*
Serves 8

*³/4 cup lightly packed light
brown sugar
1 cup unsalted butter, softened
4 eggs, separated
6 oz. semi-sweet chocolate, grated
1¹/4 cups ground almonds
3 tablespoons sugar
2 tablespoons sliced almonds*

CHANTILLY CREAM
*1¹/4 cups whipping cream
few drops of vanilla extract
2 tablespoons confectioners' sugar*

One Lightly grease a 9-inch round cake pan and line the bottom with parchment paper. Preheat the oven to 300°F.

Two Cream the brown sugar and butter in a large bowl until light and pale. Beat in the egg yolks one at a time, beating well after each addition. Stir in the chocolate and ground almonds. In a separate bowl, beat the egg whites until stiff, beat in the sugar, then fold into the chocolate mixture in four additions. Do not overfold, or the mixture will lose its volume. When there are no more streaks of white in the chocolate mixture, pour into the pan and bake for 50 minutes, or until the cake springs back when lightly touched in the center. Allow the cake to cool completely before removing from the pan.

Three To make the Chantilly cream, beat the cream with the vanilla and sugar until stiff peaks form. Keep chilled until ready to serve with the cake and a sprinkling of sliced almonds.

Simnel cake

This rich English fruitcake, bursting with spices and coated with almond paste, is now associated with Easter. The name of the cake comes from the Latin word simila, *meaning "the very best wheat flour."*

Preparation time 50 minutes
Total cooking time 2 hours
Serves 8–12

¾ cup unsalted butter, at room temperature
¾ cup sugar
3 eggs, lightly beaten
1½ cups all-purpose flour
1 teaspoon baking powder
1 teaspoon ground allspice
1 teaspoon ground ginger
small pinch of ground cloves
1 teaspoon ground cinnamon
¼ cup ground almonds
pinch of salt
2 cups dried currants
¾ cup raisins
zest of 1 orange and 1 lemon, finely grated
3 tablespoons Grand Marnier
1¼ lb. marzipan
¼ cup apricot jam, strained
¼ cup confectioners' sugar
few drops of lemon juice

One Preheat the oven to 300°F. Double line an 8-inch-diameter, 4-inch-deep, straight-sided cake pan (see Chef's techniques, page 553). Grease the paper and dust with flour.

Two Using the creaming method in the Chef's techniques on page 554, cream the butter and sugar together and gradually add the eggs.

Three Into a separate bowl, sift together the flour, baking powder, allspice, ginger, cloves, cinnamon, ground almonds and a large pinch of salt. Add the currants, raisins, and orange and lemon zest, and mix to combine (see Chef's techniques, page 554). Stir the dry ingredients, then the Grand Marnier into the butter mixture, until incorporated. Spoon half the mixture into the pan and smooth the surface using the back of a spoon.

Four Lightly sprinkle a work surface with confectioners' sugar and place a third of the marzipan on it. Roll out into a round 7¾ inches in diameter. Place the marzipan onto the cake mixture in the pan and cover with the remaining cake mixture. Level the surface and make a hollow in the center of the cake using the back of a wet spoon (see Chef's techniques, page 555). Bake for 1¾–2 hours, or until a skewer comes out clean when inserted into the center

of the cake. Transfer to a wire rack to cool for 5–10 minutes. Turn out the cake and carefully peel off the paper, then cool completely.

Five Lightly sprinkle the work surface with confectioners' sugar again and roll out another a third of marzipan into a round 8 inches in diameter. Score the marzipan with the back of a knife in a crisscross pattern. Heat the apricot jam, with 2 teaspoons of water in a small saucepan until melted. Lightly brush the top and sides of the cake with the warm jam and place the marzipan round onto the cake. Divide the remaining marzipan into 11 even-size pieces. Using your hands, roll each piece into a ball. Place these balls around the top edge of the cake, using a little jam to make them stick, and flatten them slightly, using a metal spatula.

Six Place the cake under the broiler for 1–2 minutes, until the marzipan is lightly browned, then remove and place the cake onto a cardboard round covered in foil. Sift the confectioners' sugar into a small bowl and mix with enough lemon juice to make a stiff paste. Spoon into a pastry bag fitted with a small writing tube and pipe "Simnel" in the center of the cake. It is traditional, though not obligatory, to pipe the name "Simnel" on the cake.

Iced Christmas cake

This classic Christmas cake can be started in November or early December and iced later. If you are short on time, you can keep the decorations much simpler with just holly leaves and berries.

Preparation time *3 hours + 1 week and resting over 2 nights*
Total cooking time *3 hours*
Serves 10

²/₃ *cup currants*
2 cups golden raisins
³/₄ *cup raisins*
¹/₃ *cup chopped mixed candied citrus peel*
¹/₄ *cup glacé cherries*
1¹/₄ *cups all-purpose flour*
¹/₄ *cup unsalted butter, at room temperature*
¹/₄ *cup light brown sugar*
3 eggs, beaten
zest and juice of 1 lemon and 1 orange
¹/₄ *teaspoon vanilla extract*
1 tablespoon molasses
1 teaspoon pumpkin pie spice
³/₄ *cup rum or brandy*
¹/₃ *cup apricot jam*
1 lb. marzipan
clear alcohol, such as gin or vodka, for brushing
3 lb. fondant

ROYAL ICING
1 egg white
1³/₄ *cups confectioners' sugar, sifted*
juice of ¹/₂ *lemon*
red, green and yellow food coloring

One Double line an 8-inch round cake pan following the method in the Chef's techniques on page 553. Preheat the oven to 315°F.

Two Place the fruit in a bowl and mix in half the flour. Beat the butter and brown sugar until light and creamy. Add the eggs a little at a time, beating well after each addition. Beat in the lemon and orange zest and juice, the vanilla and the molasses. Sift the remaining flour and spice onto the butter mixture and beat well. Stir in the fruit.

Three Place the mixture in the prepared pan and press on the center with the back of a wet spoon. Bake for 3 hours, or until a skewer inserted into the center comes out clean. Cover with aluminum foil if it is browning too quickly. Cool in the pan on a wire rack, then make several holes in the cake with a skewer.

Four Without removing the paper, wrap the cake tightly in plastic wrap and store in a cool place for at least 1 week, soaking regularly with a little of the rum or brandy.

Five Level the surface of the cake with a sharp knife, then turn bottom side up. In a small saucepan, melt the jam and brush over the cake, then place on a thin 8-inch board. Add marzipan and ice the cake following the method for making and using royal icing in the Chef's techniques on page 557.

Six To decorate the cake, pull a walnut-size piece of icing from the remaining soft icing and color it yellow. Make a small star and present shape. Divide the remaining icing into two-thirds and a third. Color the larger amount green and the smaller red. Cover and set aside the red. Roll out the green icing to a ¹/₈-inch thickness on a surface dusted with confectioners' sugar. Cut out a ¹/₂ x 30-inch ribbon, cover and set aside. Cut out 8 holly leaves. Gather the remaining icing, color a darker green and form a Christmas tree by making a cone shape and randomly snipping the sides with scissors. Use the red icing to make a red ribbon, 12 holly berries and a small present to go under the tree.

Seven Twist together the two pieces of ribbon and wrap around the cake, fixing with some of the reserved icing at four intervals for a drape effect. At each fixed point, stick on two holly leaves and three berries. Allow to dry overnight.

Eight The next day, arrange the tree and presents on top of the cake. Mix the remaining royal icing with the food colorings and then pipe "Merry Christmas" onto the center of the cake and add extra decorations on the tree and presents.

Mincemeat pies

Homemade mincemeat pies are a delicious treat to enjoy with drinks when guests visit over Christmas. These ones are made with tender short pastry and a brandy-laced mincemeat.

Preparation time *1 hour + 40 minutes chilling (make the mincemeat 1 week in advance)*
Total cooking time *20 minutes*
Makes 12

MINCEMEAT (SEE CHEF'S TIP)
8 oz. ground or finely chopped suet, grated
2 Granny Smith apples, peeled, cored and roughly chopped
2/3 cup chopped mixed candied citrus peel
2 cups raisins
2 cups golden raisins
1 2/3 cups currants
1/4 cup slivered almonds
3/4 cup Demerara or turbinado sugar
1/2 teaspoon ground pumpkin pie spice
large pinch ground nutmeg
large pinch ground cinnamon
finely grated zest and juice of 1/2 lemon
1/3 cup brandy

PIE PASTRY
1 1/2 cups all-purpose flour
1/2 cup unsalted butter, chilled and cut into cubes
1 1/2 tablespoons lard, chilled and cut into cubes
1 egg yolk
2 drops vanilla extract

superfine sugar, to dust

One To make the mincemeat, place the suet, apples, citrus peel and raisins in a food processor and, using the pulse button, break down roughly. Place in a large bowl, add the remaining ingredients and stir to combine well.

Two Spoon the mincemeat into four 2-cup sterilized canning jars, pressing down to force out any air. Screw on the tops tightly and store in the refrigerator for at least 1 week.

Three To make the pastry, sift the flour and some salt into a large bowl and add the butter and lard. Rub the butter and lard into the flour between your thumbs and fingertips until it resembles fine bread crumbs. Make a well in the center. In a bowl, mix together the egg yolk, vanilla and 1 1/2 tablespoons water and pour into the well. Mix with a round-bladed knife until large lumps form. Pull together and turn out onto a lightly floured surface. Knead very gently for no more than 20 seconds until just smooth, then wrap in plastic wrap and refrigerate for at least 20 minutes.

Four Brush a 12-cup shallow muffin pan or tart pan with melted butter. Preheat the oven to 400°F. On a lightly floured surface, roll out two-thirds of the pastry to a thickness of 1/8-inch. Using a 3-inch biscuit cutter, cut out rounds and press lightly into the cups. Chill while rolling out the remaining pastry as above. Using a 2 3/4-inch biscuit cutter, cut rounds for the top of each pie. Place on a baking sheet lined with plastic wrap and chill for 20 minutes.

Five Fill each pastry-lined cup with 1 tablespoon of mincemeat. Take the pastry rounds, brush the outer edges with water, then place damp side down on the mincemeat. Gently press the top and bottom pastry edges together to seal. Brush the tops with cold water and lightly dust with the sugar. Using the point of a sharp knife, make a small hole in the center of each.

Six Bake for 20 minutes, or until golden. Serve hot with whipped cream or brandy butter (see page 371).

CHEF'S TIP *The mincemeat is best left to mature over a few weeks or months. Any unopened jars should be stored in cool, dark and dry conditions or in the refrigerator.*

Treacle tart

*This English dessert can be served hot
or cold and is delicious accompanied by either
a warm stirred custard or vanilla ice cream.*

*Preparation time 40 minutes
+ 30 minutes refrigeration*
Total cooking time 1 hour
Serves 8

1 quantity short pastry (see page 544)
1 egg and 1 egg yolk, beaten, to glaze

FILLING
1¼ cups golden syrup (see Chef's tip)
or dark corn syrup
⅔ cup whipping cream
1 egg
zest of 1 lemon, finely grated
¼ cup ground almonds
1 cup fresh bread crumbs

One Grease a 1-inch-deep, 8-inch fluted tart pan with removable bottom with butter.

Two Roll out two-thirds of the pastry on a floured surface to a round about ⅛ inch thick. Line the pan (see Chef's techniques, page 547) and chill for about 30 minutes. Preheat the oven to 400°F. Bake blind (see Chef's techniques, page 547) for 10–15 minutes until firm. Remove the pie weights or rice and paper and cool. Reduce the oven temperature to 350°F.

Three To prepare the lattice top, roll out the remaining pastry to ⅛ inch thick. Cut strips of pastry ⅝ inch wide and long enough to reach across the tart. Refrigerate while preparing the filling.

Four To make the filling, place the syrup in a saucepan and heat gently until warm. In a bowl, mix together the cream and egg. Add the lemon zest and warm syrup and stir to blend. In a separate bowl, mix together the ground almonds and bread crumbs, make a well in the center and pour in the liquid. Slowly incorporate the dry ingredients until the mixture is smooth. Pour into the prepared pastry shell, filling to just below the rim.

Five Brush the rim of the pastry shell with the egg glaze. Wipe off any splashes on the tart pan because they will stick and make the tart difficult to remove. Beginning in the center and working outwards, lay half the pastry strips on the surface of the tart ⅝ inch apart. Cut off at the edges by pressing down with your thumbs. Place the second layer of strips on the diagonal, again starting in the center, to create a lattice pattern. Brush with the remaining glaze. Bake for 25–35 minutes, or until golden brown. Cool slightly before removing from the pan.

CHEF'S TIP *Look for golden syrup in supermarkets specializing in import foods, or gourmet food stores.*

Pumpkin tart

*While pumpkin pie is the traditional favorite served with Thanksgiving dinner,
this version is also a treat after any cold weather meal. It has a warm,
spicy aroma and is delicious served with sweetened whipped cream.*

*Preparation time 20 minutes
+ refrigeration
Total cooking time 45 minutes
Serves 6–8*

*½ quantity sweet pastry
(see page 546)*

FILLING
*¾ cup pumpkin purée (see Chef's tips)
2 eggs
3 tablespoons sugar
large pinch salt
small pinch of ground cloves
small pinch of ground cinnamon
small pinch of ground nutmeg
small pinch of ground ginger
2 tablespoons whipping cream*

One Brush a shallow, 8-inch fluted tart pan with removable bottom with melted butter.

Two Roll out the pastry on a floured surface to a circle about ⅛-inch thick and line the tart pan (see Chef's techniques, page 547). Refrigerate for 30 minutes.

Three Preheat the oven to 375°F. Bake blind (see Chef's techniques, page 547) for 10 minutes. Remove the pie weights or rice and paper and then bake for 5–10 minutes more, or until the center begins to color. Allow to cool. Reduce the oven temperature to 325°F.

Four To make the filling, place the pumpkin purée, eggs, sugar, salt, spices and cream in a bowl and whisk until smooth and blended. Pour into the pastry shell. Bake for 25–30 minutes, or until the filling is firm to the touch. Allow to cool slightly, then remove from

the pan and transfer to a serving plate. Serve warm, cut into wedges, or allow the tart to cool, then chill for at least 30 minutes to serve cold.

CHEF'S TIPS *Pumpkin purée is available canned, but to prepare a delicious alternative, take 10 oz. butternut or hubbard squash, peel and cut it into pieces, remove the seeds, and place in a saucepan. Barely cover with cold water and add ¼ cup sugar. Bring to a simmer, cover and simmer until the squash is tender. Drain well and purée*

the squash in a blender, food processor or by pressing it through a strainer.

If serving the tart cold, add shine to the surface with an apricot glaze: Melt ¼ cup apricot jam with 1 tablespoon water until liquid. Strain, then brush the glaze across the surface, avoiding going over the same area twice to prevent streaks.

To give the pastry added crunch, try stirring ¼ cup chopped walnuts into the dry ingredients before mixing.

Langues-de-chat

Langue-de-chat, *the French term for cat's tongue, is the name given to these cookies due to their shape. Delicately flavored, light and crisp, these cookies can be served with a sweet soufflé or as an elegant accompaniment to coffee.*

Preparation time 15 minutes
Total cooking time 10 minutes per sheet
Makes about 50

3/4 cup confectioners' sugar
1/3 cup unsalted butter, at
    room temperature
3–4 drops vanilla extract
3 egg whites, lightly beaten
3/4 cup all-purpose flour

One Preheat the oven to 400°F. Brush two baking sheets with melted butter and refrigerate.

Two Using a wooden spoon or electric mixer, cream the confectioners' sugar and butter together. When the mixture is pale and light, beat in the vanilla.

Three Add the egg whites slowly, beating constantly and being careful not to allow the mixture to curdle. If it does, add a large pinch of the measured flour.

Four Sift the flour into the bowl, then using a large metal spoon or rubber spatula, gently fold the flour into the butter mixture, mixing lightly until combined. Spoon into a pastry bag fitted with a 1/3-inch plain tip and pipe enough 3-inch pieces to fill the baking sheets.

Leave at least 2 inches between the cookies as they will spread during baking. Bake for 7–10 minutes, or until the edges are golden brown, but the centers yellow.

Five Use a flexible bladed knife or fish lifter to remove the cookies from the sheet while they are still warm. If they cool and become too brittle to move, return them to the oven to warm just until they can be moved. Repeat with the remaining mixture, preparing the sheets as instructed in step 1.

CHEF'S TIP *Langues-de-chat can be used to line molds that are then filled with light creamy mixtures such as mousses, chilled to set and unmolded. Store the cookies in an airtight container for up to 2 weeks.*

Lunettes

Lunettes is the French word for spectacles. Made to represent spectacles, these cookies are elegant for tea time, but also fun for children.

***Preparation time** 30 minutes
+ 30 minutes refrigeration*
***Total cooking time** 10 minutes per sheet*
Makes 10

*¹/₄ cup ground almonds
1 cup all-purpose flour
¹/₄ cup unsalted butter
1 teaspoon finely grated lemon zest
¹/₄ cup sugar
¹/₂ egg, beaten
3 tablespoons apricot jam
confectioners' sugar, to dust
4 tablespoons raspberry jam*

One Preheat the oven to 350°F. Brush two baking trays with melted butter and dust lightly with flour. Sift together the almonds and flour.

Two Using a wooden spoon or electric mixer, cream together the butter, lemon zest and sugar until light and fluffy. Add the egg, a little at a time, beating well after each addition. Add the flour and almonds and stir together to form a rough dough. Draw together by hand to form a ball, wrap in plastic wrap, flatten slightly and refrigerate for about 30 minutes. Roll out the dough between two sheets of parchment paper to about a ¹/₈-inch thickness.

Three Using a 3-inch oval cookie cutter, cut out 20 cookies and transfer as many as will fit comfortably to the baking sheets. Using a ¹/₂-inch cutter, or the end of a ¹/₂-inch pastry tip, cut out two holes from half the cookies. These will become the tops of the lunettes. Refrigerate the rest of the dough until needed.

Four Bake for 10 minutes, or until light golden. While still warm, remove from the baking sheets to a wire rack. Repeat with the remaining mixture, preparing the baking sheets as instructed in step 1.

Five Warm the apricot jam, brush over the base of the whole cookies and sandwich together with a cookie with holes in the top.

Six Dust with sifted confectioners' sugar. Beat the raspberry jam in a bowl until it becomes liquified. Fill a pastry bag fitted with a ¹/₄-inch plain tip and fill in each of the holes on the sandwiched biscuits with the jam. If you don't have a pastry bag, drop the jam from the tip of a teaspoon.

· LE CORDON BLEU ·

chef's techniques

Stock techniques

MAKING BROWN STOCK

Roasting the bones gives a good color to the stock and helps to remove the excess fat. In a 450°F oven, roast 3 lb. beef or veal bones for 40 minutes, adding 1 quartered onion, 2 chopped carrots, 1 chopped leek and 1 chopped celery stalk halfway through.

Transfer to a clean stockpot. Add 4 quarts water, 2 tablespoons tomato paste, 1 bouquet garni and 6 peppercorns. Simmer for 3–4 hours, regularly skimming off any impurities that rise to the surface with a flat strainer.

Ladle the stock in batches into a fine strainer over a bowl. Gently press the solids with the ladle to extract all the liquid. Refrigerate for several hours and then remove the solidified fat from the surface. Makes 6–8 cups.

MAKING LAMB STOCK

Put 3 lb. of lamb bones in a large stockpot. (You may need to ask your butcher to chop the lamb bones so they will fit in your stockpot.) Cover with water and bring to a boil. Drain and rinse the bones.

Transfer the bones to a clean stockpot and add 1 quartered onion, 2 chopped carrots, 1 chopped leek, 1 chopped celery stalk, 3 quarts of water, 1 bouquet garni and 6 peppercorns.

Simmer for 2–3 hours, regularly skimming off any impurities that rise to the surface with a flat strainer.

Ladle the stock in batches into a fine strainer over a bowl. Gently press the solids with the ladle to extract all the liquid. Refrigerate for several hours and then remove the solidified fat from the surface. Makes 6 cups.

Stock techniques

MAKING CHICKEN STOCK

Cut up 1½ lb. chicken bones and carcass and put in a stockpot with 1 chopped onion, 1 chopped carrot, 1 chopped celery stalk, 4 quarts of water, 1 bouquet garni and 6 peppercorns.

Simmer for 2–3 hours, regularly skimming off any impurities that rise to the surface with a flat strainer. Ladle the stock in batches through a strainer into a clean bowl, then allow to cool.

Refrigerate the stock overnight and then remove the solidified fat. If you can't leave overnight, skim, then drag the surface of the hot strained stock with paper towels to remove the fat. Makes 6–8 cups.

MAKING FISH STOCK

Remove the eyes and gills. Soak 4 lb. chopped fish bones and trimmings in salted water for 10 minutes; drain. Transfer to a clean stockpot with 2½ quarts water, 12 peppercorns, 2 bay leaves, 1 chopped celery stalk, 1 chopped onion and the juice of 1 lemon.

Simmer for 20 minutes, regularly skimming off any impurities that rise to the surface with a flat strainer.

Ladle the stock in batches through a fine strainer into a clean bowl. Gently press the solids with the ladle to extract all the liquid. Refrigerate to cool. Makes 6 cups.

Sauce techniques

TO FREEZE STOCK

To freeze, boil the stock down to reduce to 2 cups. Allow to cool and freeze until solid. Transfer to a plastic freezer bag and seal. To make 2 quarts stock, add 6 cups water to 2 cups concentrated stock.

CLARIFYING BUTTER

Clarifying is removing the water and solids from butter, which makes it less likely to burn. To make about 1/3 cup clarified butter, cut 6 oz. butter into small cubes. Place in a small saucepan set into a larger saucepan of water over low heat. Melt the butter, without stirring.

Remove the saucepan from the heat and allow to cool slightly. Skim the foam from the surface, being careful not to stir the butter.

MAKING A BOUQUET GARNI

Wrap the green part of a leek loosely around a bay leaf, a sprig of thyme, some celery leaves and a few stems of parsley, then tie with string. Leave a long tail to the string for easy removal.

Pour off the clear yellow liquid, being very careful to leave the milky sediment behind in the pan. Discard the sediment and store the clarified butter in an airtight container in the refrigerator.

LE CORDON BLEU ✠ COMPLETE COOK

Sauce techniques

MAYONNAISE

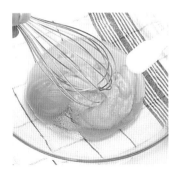

Bring all the ingredients to room temperature. Place a large, deep bowl on a damp kitchen towel to prevent it from moving. Put the egg yolks and a pinch of salt in the bowl and mix with a hand whisk or electric mixer.

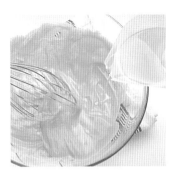

Put the oil in a pitcher that is easy to pour from. While whisking constantly, pour a steady thin stream of oil into the mixture. Begin with a small amount and stop pouring periodically to allow each addition to emulsify to a thick cream mixture.

Continue until a third of the oil has been added and the mayonnaise has begun to thicken. Add the vinegar to make the texture slightly thinner. Continue adding the oil, then stir in the mustard. Adjust the flavor by adding more vinegar, salt or pepper. Add 1–2 tablespoons boiling water if it curdles or separates.

HOLLANDAISE SAUCE

Whisk the egg yolks and water together in a heatproof bowl until foamy. Place the bowl over a saucepan half-filled with simmering water and whisk until thick. The bowl should not touch the water. Gradually whisk in the butter.

Continue adding the melted butter, over very low heat, whisking constantly. The sauce must not be allowed to get too hot, otherwise it may curdle. The sauce should be thick enough to leave a trail on the surface when the whisk is lifted.

Once all the butter is incorporated, strain the sauce into a clean bowl, stir in the lemon juice and then season with salt and pepper.

Seafood techniques

SHUCKING OYSTERS

Scrub the oysters in cold water. Place an oyster, rounded side down, on a thick, doubled cloth in the palm of your hand. Use a shucker with a protection shield, and always protect the hand holding the oyster with the thick cloth.

Insert an oyster knife through the pointed end of the oyster at the hinge where the top and bottom shells meet. Work the knife in until at least 1¹/₄ inches inside. Twist the knife to separate the shells.

Slide the knife between the oyster and the top shell, cut through the hinge muscle and remove the top shell.

Slide the knife between the oyster and the bottom shell to release it. Remove the oyster and pour any liquor through a cheesecloth-lined strainer into a bowl to get rid of any sand. Reserve the liquor.

PREPARING SHRIMP

Remove the shell, being careful to keep the flesh intact. Leave the tail end intact if specified in the recipe.

Make a shallow cut along the back of the shrimp with a small knife to expose the dark intestinal vein.

Remove the vein with the tip of the knife and discard. Rinse the shrimp and pat dry with a paper towel.

Seafood techniques

PREPARING CRAB

This method can be used on most crabs. Mud crab, shown here, needs extra care as the shell is very hard. Twist the claws to remove them. Use your thumb as a lever to pry off the hard top shell. Scoop out any creamy brown meat and reserve. Wash and dry the shell well.

Discard the soft stomach sac from the main body of the crab and remove the grey spongy fingers (gills). Scrape out and reserve any more creamy brown meat.

Cut the main body of the crab in half lengthwise, then remove the white meat from the body using the end of a teaspoon or fork.

CLEANING MUSSELS

Clean the mussels by scrubbing the shells with a brush to remove any sand. Scrape any barnacles off with a knife.

Pull off any beards from the mussels.

Discard any mussels that are broken, are not tightly closed or do not close when lightly tapped on a work surface.

Seafood techniques

KILLING LOBSTER

Place the lobster in the freezer for about 2 hours to desensitize it. Hold the lobster, tail down, under a heavy cloth. Using a large, sharp knife, place the point in the center of the head and quickly pierce through to the cutting board, cutting down and forward between the eyes.

REMOVING LOBSTER TAIL MEAT

This simple technique makes it easy to present the lobster tail meat in neat, elegant portions. Turn the lobster on its tail. Using a pair of kitchen scissors, cut lengthwise down each side of the belly.

Pull the soft undershell back, exposing the meat of the lobster tail.

CLEANING SCALLOPS

If the scallops are in their shells, remove them by sliding a knife under the white muscle and orange roe. Wash the scallops to remove any grit or sand, then pull away the small, tough, shiny white muscle and the black vein. If the orange roe is attached, leave intact.

Pull the tail meat from the shell, keeping it in a single piece.

Seafood techniques

PREPARING LOBSTER BISQUE

Cut the lobsters in half lengthwise. Remove and discard the sac in the head and the vein down the center of the tail.

Twist off the claws and hit them with a rolling pin or the bottom of a small, heavy saucepan to crack them.

Using a large, sharp knife, cut across the tail into three or four pieces.

PREPARING LOBSTER AMERICAINE

Twist and remove the two main claws, if applicable, from where they meet the body. Separate the head from the tail. Cook the claws and tail according to the method in the recipe.

Remove the flesh from the tail by snipping with scissors around the edge of the flat undershell and pulling it away.

Using your fingers, gently ease the flesh out of the tail in one piece. Reserve the shell.

With a large, sharp knife, split the head in two lengthwise. Remove and reserve any coral (roe) and green-grey tomalley (liver). Discard the stomach sac found behind the mouth. Chop the head shell into large pieces.

Seafood techniques

FILLETING ROUND FISH

Using a filleting knife, cut off the fins and cut out the gills behind the head and discard.

Make a small cut at the bottom of the stomach, then cut along the underside, stopping just below the gills. Pull the innards out and discard. Wash the fish.

Make a cut around the back of the head, then working from head to tail, cut along the backbone. Holding the knife flat, use long strokes to cut away the flesh, then pull the flesh away from the bones.

FILLETING FLAT FISH

Lay the fish dark side up. Cut around the outside of the fish with a filleting knife where the flesh meets the fins.

Cut down the center of the fish from head to tail with a sharp knife. Make sure you cut all the way through to the bone.

Working from the center of the fillet to the edge, cut away one fillet with long, broad strokes of the knife, without leaving too much flesh. Remove the other fillet in the same way, then turn the fish over and repeat.

Seafood techniques

Lay the fish skin side down and cut across the flesh at the tail. Dip your fingers in salt so that you can get a good grip, grasp the tail and, starting at the cut, work the knife away from you at a shallow angle using a sawing action.

SERVING SALMON

Place the cooked salmon on a piece of parchment paper before you begin. Using a sharp knife, cut the skin just above the tail, then cut through the skin along the back and in front of the gills. Using the knife to help you, work from head to tail to peel off and discard the skin.

Place a serving plate under one side of the parchment paper and flip the fish over onto the plate, using the paper to help you. Remove the rest of the skin. Remove the head if preferred.

PIN-BONING FISH

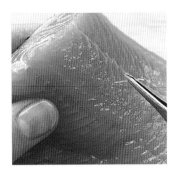

To remove the small bones left in fish such as salmon or red mullet, run your fingers along the flesh, pressing lightly to find the bones. Remove any fine pin bones with a pair of tweezers or your fingers.

Scrape away any dark flesh with a knife. Split down the center of the top fillet, then carefully remove and lay the two quarter fillets on each side of the salmon.

Remove the backbone by peeling it back from the head end. Snip it with scissors just before the tail. Remove any other stray bones and replace the two fillets.

Poultry techniques

JOINTING A CHICKEN

Use a pair of poultry shears to cut through the length of the breastbone.

Cut through the top third of the breast, leaving two equal portions. You can also remove the wing tips at this stage, if you wish.

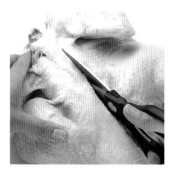

Turn the chicken over and cut down either side of the backbone to completely remove it. The backbone should come away in one piece.

Separate the leg from the thigh by cutting through the leg joint.

Following the natural contours of the thigh, cut through to separate the breast and wing piece from the thigh and leg.

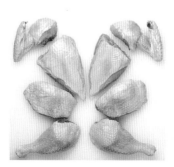

You now have eight chicken portions of equal size.

Repeat with the other half to produce four pieces.

Poultry techniques

REMOVING THE WISHBONE

Pull the skin back from the neck cavity. Use your fingers to feel for the wishbone just inside—you may need to slit the skin a little. Cut around the wishbone with a sharp knife, then scrape the meat away.

Cut the wishbone away at the joint and lift it out.

TRUSSING FOR ROASTING A CHICKEN

Rinse the bird inside and out, then dry with paper towels. Use ordinary household string to truss. Tie the legs together, wrapping the string under the tail first.

After tying the legs, take the string towards the neck of the bird, passing it down between the legs and the body.

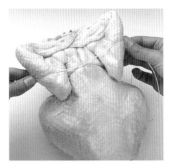

Turn the bird over and cross the string over in the center, underneath the wings. Wrap the string around the wings to keep them flat.

Tie the string into a knot or bow to secure the chicken wings in place. Trim off the ends of the string and the chicken is ready for roasting.

Poultry techniques

SCRAPING A DRUMSTICK

Removing the meat from the bone can be tricky. Pull the skin off the legs, from the fat end of the drumstick.

Hold the knuckle end of the drumstick and use a sharp knife to cut around the bone, then scrape away the flesh.

PREPARING QUAIL

Pull off any feathers. Pull the skin back from the neck cavity and cut around the wishbone. Scrape away any meat and cut away at the base. Pull out the wishbone.

Place the quail breast side down and cut through the skin down the center of the back. Using a knife, scrape the flesh away from the carcass, holding the skin as you do so.

When you reach the thigh joints, break the joints so the legs stay attached to the skin and flesh. Continue scraping around the carcass all the way round.

Scrape carefully around the breast bone, and the skin and flesh should pull away in one piece. Reserve the carcass.

Carving techniques

CARVING TURKEY

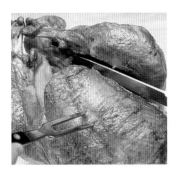

Place the turkey breast side up on a board. Cut off the wings, then the legs, cutting through the thigh bones that connect the legs to the body.

Hold the turkey steady with a carving fork and slice down diagonally through the breast meat, holding the knife parallel to the rib cage. Repeat on the other side.

Cut through each thigh and drumstick joint. Hold the thigh steady with a fork and carve the thigh meat, keeping the knife parallel to the bone.

PREPARING HAM

With a sharp knife, cut a circle in the skin at the top of the ham near the knuckle. Push your thumbs or fingers under the skin and gently pull it from the cut circle and remove.

With a sharp knife, trim the fat to leave a 1/2-inch thickness of fat. Score the fat with cuts crosswise and then diagonally to form a diamond pattern. Be careful not to cut the flesh.

To carve the ham, cut a small wedge from the top of the ham and remove. Hold the leg steady with a carving fork and slice evenly towards the knuckle. The slices will increase in size as you carve.

Pasta techniques

MAKING AND ROLLING PASTA WITH A MACHINE

Place the flour, salt, olive oil and eggs or egg yolks in a food processor and mix in short bursts until the mixture forms large crumbs.

Fold the sheet into three and pass through the machine again at the thickest setting. Repeat this rolling and folding ten times, lightly flouring the pasta dough and machine to prevent sticking.

Gently press the mixture between your finger and thumb to check if it will come together smoothly. If not, continue to process for a few bursts.

Without folding, continue to pass the dough through progressively thinner settings, until it has passed through the finest setting. Repeat with the remaining pieces of dough.

Turn out onto a lightly floured surface and knead for 2 minutes into a smooth dough. Wrap in plastic wrap and refrigerate for 20 minutes. Secure a pasta machine to the edge of a table.

MAKING TAGLIATELLE

Divide the dough into pieces as specified in the recipe. Cover with plastic wrap and work with one piece at a time. Flatten into a rectangle and roll through the lightly floured pasta machine on the thickest setting.

Pass the sheet of pasta through a floured pasta machine fitted with the tagliatelle attachment. Or roll up the sheet of pasta and cut into ribbons with a knife. Cook immediately or allow to dry in a single layer. The tagliatelle may be dried on a floured towel hanging over the back of a chair for 1–2 hours.

Pasta techniques

MAKING AND ROLLING PASTA BY HAND

This is the traditional method for making pasta without a food processor. Sift the flour and salt onto a work surface. Make a large well in the center with your hand and add the eggs or egg yolks, and olive oil.

Using your fingertips, gradually incorporate the flour into the wet ingredients.

With a pastry scraper or by hand, keep bringing the flour into the center, making a dough. Knead for 10 minutes, or until smooth and elastic. Divide the dough into pieces as specified in the recipe. Cover with plastic wrap.

To roll out the pasta by hand, use a large, lightly floured work surface and roll out the dough as thinly as possible, fold in half and roll again, bringing the furthest end over the rolling pin and gently stretching it. Roll and fold the dough ten times. Roll out to the thickness required.

MAKING RAVIOLI

Lightly brush a little water or egg around each mound of filling.

Place the second sheet of pasta on top and press firmly around each mound to expel any air and to seal. Using a rolling cutter or plain biscuit cutter, cut out each ravioli.

Alternatively, use the ravioli cutter on a pasta machine. Place two pasta sheets into the floured machine and two mounds of filling in the grooves. Turn the handle of the machine to cut. Any uncooked ravioli may be refrigerated or frozen in single layers between sheets of waxed paper.

Vegetable techniques

PEELING TOMATOES

Bring a large saucepan of water to a boil. Using a very sharp knife, score a small cross in the bottom of each tomato. Cut around and remove any stems on the tomatoes.

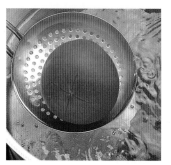

Blanch the tomatoes in the saucepan of boiling water for 10 seconds. Remove and plunge into a bowl of ice cold water to stop the cooking and keep the flesh firm.

Pull away the skin from the cross, and discard the skins.

If a recipe calls for the removal of the tomato seeds, cut the tomato in half and use a teaspoon to gently scoop out the seeds.

PREPARING WHOLE ARTICHOKES

Break off the artichoke stem at the bottom, pulling out the fibers that attach it to the bottom.

Pull off the outer leaves and place the artichoke in a saucepan of boiling salted water with the juice of 1 lemon. Weigh down with a plate and simmer for 20–35 minutes.

Test for doneness by pulling at one of the leaves. If it comes away easily, the artichoke is done. Cut off the top half of the artichoke and discard.

Remove the hairy choke in the middle of the artichoke with a spoon. The artichoke bottom is now ready to use.

534

Vegetable techniques

ROASTING BELL PEPPERS

Roasting bell peppers allows you to remove their skins and produces a delicious sweet flavor. Preheat a broiler. Cut the peppers in half and remove the seeds and membrane.

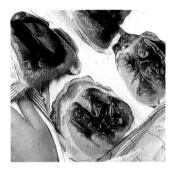

Roast the peppers until the skin blisters and blackens. Place in a plastic food bag and allow to cool. When cool, peel off the skin.

PREPARING ASPARAGUS

Tying a bunch of asparagus makes it easier to handle during cooking. Grasp the asparagus bunch in the center. Holding the end of a string with thumb and finger, wrap the string around the upper part three times, cross over and wrap the lower part three times. Secure with a knot.

Cook the asparagus in boiling water until tender.

Drain, then plunge into a bowl of iced water to stop the cooking process and refresh the asparagus. This process helps retain the vibrant color of blanched vegetables. Drain and then untie.

Vegetable techniques

PUREEING POTATOES

Potatoes may be puréed in several ways—but do not use a food processor or the result will be gluey.
You can hold a strainer securely over a bowl and press the cooked potatoes through using a wooden spoon.

Or place the cooked potatoes in a mouli grater or food mill set over a bowl. Turn the handle to force the potato through.

Or push the cooked potatoes a little at a time through a ricer into a large bowl.

SLICING POTATOES WITH A MANDOLINE

Attach the potato to the mandoline guard. This will make it easier and safer to work with.

For thin slices, work the potato against the straight blade, set to the thickness specified in the recipe.

For long thin strips of potato, work the potato against the shredding blade.

Vegetable techniques

ROLLING UP SPRING ROLLS

Cut each spring roll wrapper in half. Divide the filling among all the wrappers and roll up tightly. (Spring roll wrappers are very delicate and should be covered with a damp cloth while you work.) Seal the edges using cornstarch paste.

DEEP-FRYING

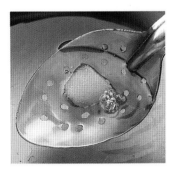

When deep-frying, fill the fryer one-third full of oil; do not leave it unattended. Pat food dry with paper towels before deep-frying. Preheat the oil in a deep-fat fryer or deep saucepan to 350°F. Place a bread cube in the oil: if it sizzles and turns golden brown in 15 seconds, the oil is hot enough.

CHINESE PANCAKES

Using a fork or chopsticks, slowly incorporate the flour into the water until a soft dough forms. Turn out onto a floured surface and knead for 5 minutes, or until smooth. Cover and allow to rest for 15 minutes.

Divide the dough into six and roll into balls. Flatten one ball, brush lightly with some sesame oil and place another flattened round of dough on top. Roll out into 8½-inch rounds, about 1/16-inch thick.

Heat a dry skillet over medium-high heat. Place a pancake in the hot pan and cook for 50–60 seconds, or until blistered and colored. Flip over and cook for another 30–40 seconds.

Transfer the pancake to a plate and, while it is still hot, carefully peel it apart, being careful of any hot steam. Repeat with the remaining pancakes.

Dessert techniques

MAKING CREPES

Melt some clarified butter or oil over medium heat in a 6–7 inch heavy-bottomed or nonstick pan. When the pan starts to smoke, pour out any excess butter.

Stir the batter well and pour into the pan from a pitcher, starting in the centre and swirling the pan to create a thin coating. Tip out any excess.

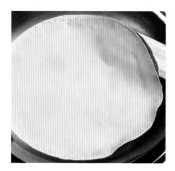

Cook for 1 minute until bubbles appear, the batter sets and the edges are brown. Carefully loosen and lift the edges with a flexible bladed knife. Turn and cook for 30 seconds until golden. Remove from the pan and cook the remainder.

MAKING TARTE TATIN

Add the apples to the pan of bubbling sugar and butter and arrange upright in a circular pattern.

Make sure the apples are tightly packed as they will reduce in size as they cook. Cook and baste the apples for 45 minutes over medium heat, or until the apples are soft and the syrup has reduced and is dark brown.

Remove the apples from the heat. Working quickly, place the round of pastry on top of the apples. Use the handle of a spoon to tuck the edges into the pan.

Dessert techniques

STEAMING PUDDINGS

Thickly brush a pudding basin or heatproof glass bowl with melted butter. Line the bottom of the basin or bowl with a round of parchment paper.

Lay a sheet of aluminum foil on the work surface and cover with a sheet of parchment paper. Make a large pleat in the middle and brush the paper with some melted butter.

Place the mixture in the basin or bowl and hollow the surface slightly with the back of a wet spoon. Place the aluminum foil, paper side down, across the top and tie string around the rim and over the top to make a handle.

Place a saucer or trivet in a large saucepan and rest the basin or bowl on it. Half-fill the saucepan with boiling water and bring to a boil. Cover and simmer until cooked, adding more boiling water if needed.

MAKING ITALIAN MERINGUE

Boil without stirring until the syrup reaches the soft-ball stage, 234–240°F on a candy thermometer. If you do not have a candy thermometer, drop ¼ teaspoon of the syrup into iced water: it should hold its shape but be soft when pressed.

In a large heatproof bowl, beat the egg whites into soft peaks, using a hand whisk or electric mixer. Avoiding the whisk, add the hot syrup in a thin steady stream, beating constantly until thick and glossy. Beat until cold.

MAKING A SOUFFLE RIDGE

Spoon the mixture into the soufflé dish and then run your thumb around the inside of the dish. The ridge this creates will help the soufflé rise evenly.

Dessert techniques

MAKING SUGAR SYRUP

Stir the sugar and water over low heat until the sugar dissolves completely.

To prevent sugar crystals from forming, brush down the side of the saucepan with a brush dipped in water.

Boil without stirring until the syrup reaches the soft-ball stage, 234–240°F on a candy thermometer.

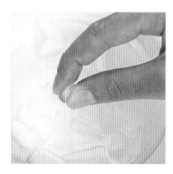

If you do not have a candy thermometer, drop 1/4 teaspoon of the syrup into iced water: it should hold its shape but be soft when pressed.

MAKING CARAMEL

Place the granulated sugar and water in a heavy-bottomed saucepan. Fill a shallow pan with cold water and set it next to the stove.

Stir over low heat until the sugar dissolves completely. To prevent sugar crystals from forming, brush down the side of the saucepan with a brush dipped in water.

Bring to a boil and simmer until the caramel takes on a deep golden color. Swirl the saucepan to prevent the caramel from coloring unevenly.

Stop the cooking by plunging the bottom of the saucepan into the cold water for a few seconds.

Dessert techniques

MAKING CUSTARD

Whisk the hot, infused milk or cream into the beaten eggs and sugar. Pour into a clean saucepan.

Stir gently over low heat with a wooden spoon for 10–15 minutes, or until the custard coats the back of the spoon and leaves a clear parting when a finger is drawn across. Do not boil, or the eggs will scramble.

Strain the warm custard through a fine strainer into a clean pitcher to remove any lumps.

USING GELATIN

Gelatin sheets have no flavor or color, give a softer set than gelatin powder, and are easier to use. Lower the sheets of gelatin into a bowl of cold water, adding each sheet separately to prevent sticking. Allow to soak for a few minutes, or until softened.

When the sheet is soft and pliable, carefully remove it and squeeze out any excess liquid. If you are using gelatin powder, dissolve each teaspoon of gelatin in 1 tablespoon of water, following the manufacturer's instructions.

Baking techniques

PUFF PASTRY

Preparation time *1 day*
Total cooking time *None*
Makes 1 lb.

DOUGH BASE
2 cups bread or all-purpose flour
1 teaspoon salt
2–3 drops of lemon juice
1/2 cup water
3 tablespoons unsalted butter, melted

1/3 cup unsalted butter, chilled

Sift the flour and salt onto a work surface and make a well in the center. Add the lemon juice, water and butter and blend together with your fingertips.

One To make the dough base, sift the flour and salt onto a cool work surface and make a well in the center. Add the lemon juice to the water, then place in the well with the butter and mix together with your fingertips. With the side of a flexible bladed knife or a pastry scraper, use a cutting action to gradually mix in the flour and work it into the butter mixture until the dry flour disappears and the mixture resembles loose crumbs. Bring together with your hands and knead lightly, adding a few drops of water if necessary, to make a smooth soft ball of dough.

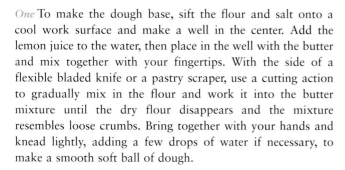

Cut an "X" on top of the pastry with a sharp knife.

Two Cut an "X" on top of the dough to prevent shrinkage, then wrap in lightly floured parchment paper or plastic wrap. Chill for 1 hour in the refrigerator—this will make the dough more pliable for rolling. Place the chilled butter between two pieces of parchment paper or plastic wrap. Tap it with the side of a rolling pin and shape into a 3/4-inch-thick square. This action will make the butter pliable to roll, without melting it.

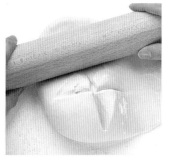

Unwrap the chilled dough and place it on a lightly floured surface. Roll from just off center to form a cross shape with a mound in the center.

Three Unwrap the dough and place it on a lightly floured cool surface. Roll the dough from just off center to form a cross shape with a mound in the center.

Four Place the butter on the central mound and fold over the four sides of the dough to enclose it completely.

Place the butter on the central mound and fold over the four sides of the dough to enclose it.

Five Roll over the top and bottom of the dough to seal the edges. On a lightly floured surface, roll the dough into a 5 x 14-inch rectangle.

Six Fold in three by folding the bottom third up towards the middle and the top third down. Brush off the excess flour and make sure that the edges all meet neatly. Make an indentation with your finger to record the first roll and fold. Wrap in plastic wrap and chill for 30 minutes.

Seven Give the dough a quarter turn with the folded side on your left as if it was a book. With a rolling pin, gently press down to seal the edges.

Eight Repeat steps 5–7 three more times, remembering to record each roll with an indentation and chilling for 30 minutes after each roll. After two rolls and folds, you should have two indentations. The finished pastry should have four indentations and will start to look smoother as you continue to roll and fold. Allow the dough to rest in the refrigerator for a final 30 minutes. The puff pastry is now ready to use. It can be frozen whole, or cut into smaller portions, then used as needed.

CHEF'S TIPS *This pastry requires more effort and time than other pastries, but the result is a lovely buttery and flaky base for any tart or pastry. If you are short of time, purchased sheets of frozen puff pastry can be used.*

When making puff pastry, work on a cool surface to prevent the butter from melting and making a heavy dough. In hot weather, it may be necessary to refrigerate the dough for an extra 15 minutes during the final resting.

Making puff pastry is not difficult, but it is time consuming, so make two or three quantities at the same time and freeze the extra. Thaw the pastry by keeping it overnight in the refrigerator. Puff pastry will keep in the refrigerator for 4 days and in the freezer for 3 months.

Seal the edges of the dough by pressing down with a rolling pin. Roll the pastry into a rectangle.

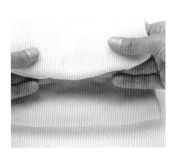

Fold the dough in three by folding the bottom third up towards the middle and the top third down.

After chilling the dough, put it on the surface in front of you as before and turn it a quarter turn so that it looks like a book with the binding on the left. Press down to seal the edges, then roll, fold and chill again.

Continue rolling, folding and chilling, trying to maintain an even finish and neat corners.

Baking techniques

SHORT PASTRY

***Preparation time** 10 minutes + 20 minutes chilling*
***Total cooking time** None*
Makes 1 lb. (2 tart shells)

1²/₃ cups all-purpose flour
large pinch of salt
¹/₃ cup unsalted butter, chilled
1 egg, lightly beaten
2–3 teaspoons water

One In a large bowl, sift together the flour and salt. Cut the butter into ½-inch cubes and add to the flour.

Two Rub the butter into the flour using your fingertips until the mixture resembles fine bread crumbs.

Three Make a well in the center and pour in the combined egg and water.

Four Slowly work the mixture together with a flexible bladed knife or pastry scraper until it makes a rough ball. If it is slightly sticky, add a little more flour. Turn out onto a lightly floured cool surface and knead very gently until just smooth (no more than 20 seconds). Wrap the pastry in plastic wrap and chill for at least 20 minutes before using.

CHEF'S TIP *This quantity of pastry is enough to line two shallow 7–8-inch tart pans. If only making one tart, divide the pastry into two pieces and wrap separately in plastic wrap. Use one piece and put the second one in a plastic bag and seal airtight, to freeze and use another time.*

Put the cubes of butter in the flour and salt, and rub into the dry ingredients.

Continue rubbing the butter into the flour until the mixture resembles fine bread crumbs.

Pour the combined egg and water into the well.

Slowly work the mixture together with a flexible bladed knife until it makes a rough ball.

Baking techniques

CREAM PUFF PASTRY

Preparation time 5 minutes
Total cooking time 10–15 minutes
Makes 8 oz.

½ cup all-purpose flour
½ cup water
3 tablespoons unsalted butter, cubed
pinch of salt
pinch of sugar
2 eggs

One Sift the flour onto a sheet of parchment paper. Place the water, butter, salt and sugar in a saucepan. Heat until the butter and water come to a boil. Remove from the heat and add the flour all at once.

Two Mix well using a wooden spoon. Return to the heat and mix until a smooth ball forms and the paste leaves the sides of the pan.

Three Remove from the heat and place the paste in a bowl. Lightly beat the eggs in a small bowl. Using a wooden spoon or an electric mixer, add the eggs to the paste a little at a time, beating well after each addition.

Four The mixture is ready to use when it is smooth, thick and glossy.

CHEF'S TIPS *It is essential when making cream puff pastry to measure the ingredients carefully, because too much moisture can cause the cream puff pastry to collapse. Traditionally, bakers weigh the eggs in order to determine the weight of the dry ingredients.*

Don't be fooled by golden colored cream puff pastry. If the cracks of the cream puff pastry are still light yellow or much lighter than the rest of the cream puff pastry, this indicates that the interior is not quite done. Reduce the temperature to 325°F and continue baking.

Once boiling, remove from the heat and immediately stir in the sifted flour.

Return the saucepan to the heat and cook until the mixture makes a smooth ball that comes away from the side of the saucepan.

Remove from the heat and transfer the mixture to a bowl. Gradually beat in the eggs with a wooden spoon.

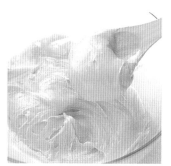

The mixture is ready to use when it is smooth, thick and glossy.

Baking techniques

SWEET PASTRY

Preparation time 10 minutes + 20 minutes chilling
Total cooking time None
Makes 1 lb. (2 tart shells)

1²/₃ cups all-purpose flour
large pinch of salt
¼ cup unsalted butter
⅓ cup sugar
1 egg, lightly beaten
1–2 drops vanilla extract

One In a large bowl, sift together the flour and salt. Cut the butter into ½-inch cubes and add to the flour. Rub the butter into the flour using your fingertips until the mixture resembles fine bread crumbs.

Two Stir in the sugar and make a well in the center. Pour in the combined egg and vanilla and slowly work the mixture together using a fork or flexible metal spatula. If the dough is too dry, sprinkle it with a little water until it just holds together.

Three Turn the dough out on to a lightly floured surface. Using the palm of your hand, smear the dough away from you until it is smooth.

Four Gather the dough into a ball and flatten it slightly. Wrap in plastic wrap and place in the refrigerator to chill for 20 minutes before using.

CHEF'S TIPS *This quantity of pastry is enough to line two shallow 8–9 inch tart pans. If only making one tart, divide the pastry in half and wrap separately in plastic wrap. Use one piece and put the second one in a plastic bag and seal airtight to freeze and use another time.*

Sift the flour and salt into a large bowl. Cut the butter into small cubes and rub into the flour.

Stir in the sugar. Make a well in the center of the dry ingredients and add the combined egg and vanilla.

Using the palm of your hand, smear the dough away from you on a lightly floured surface several times until smooth.

Shape the dough into a ball and flatten slightly.

Baking techniques

LINING A TART PAN

Place the dough over a rolling pin and unroll loosely over the pan. Be very careful when handling the dough to avoid stretching it.

Press the sides of the pastry into the flutes or sides of the pan by using a small ball of excess pastry.

Use a rolling pin to trim the pastry edges. Gently but firmly roll across the top of the pan. Refrigerate for 10 minutes.

Pierce the pastry shell with a fork to allow steam to escape during baking.

BAKING BLIND

Baking the pastry before adding the filling prevents the bottom from becoming soggy during cooking. Cut a sheet of parchment paper 2 inches larger than the tart pan and crush the paper lightly into a ball. Open out the paper, then lay it inside the pastry shell.

Spread a layer of pie weights or rice over the paper, then press down gently so that the weights or rice and the paper rest firmly against the sides of the shell.

Bake according to the time specified in the recipe, or until firm. Remove the weights or rice and paper.

If indicated in the recipe, rebake until the pastry looks dry and is evenly colored.

Baking techniques

CROISSANTS

When the dough has risen, punch it down, then roll it out to a rectangle just over twice as long as the butter and a little wider. Put the butter on the lower half of the dough and bring the dough over to enclose it.

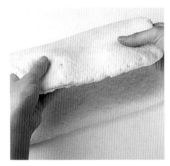

Turn the dough so the fold is on the right, then roll out into a rectangle. Fold the dough into three even layers, like a letter, with the bottom third up and the top third down. Chill, then repeat twice.

Cut the dough in half and roll out into two large rectangles. Using a triangular template, cut the rectangles into six triangles (you will be left with the two end pieces).

Roll the triangles from the wide end to shape crescents.

BAGELS

Roll the dough into tight balls, push your finger through the center of each ball and gently enlarge the hole until the dough resembles a doughnut.

Cook the bagels in simmering water for 1 minute on each side.

Brush the bagels with beaten egg before baking for 20–25 minutes. They can be sprinkled with poppy or sesame seeds before baking.

Baking techniques

MAKING BABA DOUGH

Using the fingers of one hand, held lightly apart, bring the ingredients together to form a soft elastic dough. Mix with your hand for about 5 minutes, or until smooth.

Add the raisins and rum and mix with your hand to combine. Scrape down the sides of the bowl and pour the warm butter over the surface of the dough.

Cover and allow to rise for 30 minutes, or until doubled in volume. Mix the baba mixture to incorporate the butter.

Spoon the mixture into a pastry bag fitted with a 3/4-inch plain tip and pipe into the molds. Cover with a damp cloth and allow to rise until the mixture reaches the tops of the molds.

LAYERING PHYLLO PASTRY

Place the sheets of phyllo pastry on a work surface and cover with a damp dish towel. Work with one sheet at a time, keeping the rest covered to prevent them from drying out.

Brush the first sheet with melted butter, then place another sheet on top and brush again with melted butter. Repeat until you have the number of layers specified in the recipe.

CRUMPETS

Cook the crumpets until bubbles appear. They are ready to turn over when the top has dried out enough to form a skin.

Baking techniques

If using active dry yeast, place the water in a small glass bowl and sprinkle the yeast and sugar, if specified in the recipe, over it. Let dissolve for 5 minutes, then stir with a wooden spoon.

Sift the flour into a large mixing bowl, add the salt and sugar, if specified in the recipe, and make a well in the center. Add the yeast mixture.

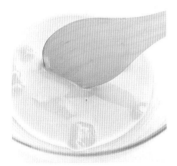

If using quick-rise yeast, crumble the yeast into a small glass bowl and add the water and sugar, if specified in the recipe. Cream together, then stir in a pinch of flour. Let sit until bubbles form on the surface.

Draw in some of the flour from the sides of the bowl to form a soft paste in the well. Cover the bowl with a clean, damp kitchen towel and let it sit for about 30 minutes to expand slightly.

If using quick-rise yeast, sift the yeast into a bowl with all the dry ingredients. The yeast will be activated when the liquid is added.

Add the remaining liquid ingredients, as specified in the recipe, to the well and stir in the rest of the flour to form a soft dough.

Baking techniques

KNEADING

Kneading is very important to distribute the yeast and allow gluten to develop. Place the dough on a lightly floured work surface and begin to knead it.

Flatten the dough away from you, then fold it over towards you and continue this kneading.

As the dough becomes more stretchy, use the heel of your hand to push half of the dough away from you as you pull the other half towards you. Rotate the dough as you knead.

The dough is well kneaded when it is smooth, shiny and elastic. A finger mark pressed into the dough should spring back immediately.

SHAPING A LOAF

Roll out the dough into a large rectangle, then roll it up tightly into a sausage shape and press gently to seal the seam.

Fold the dough in on itself, using your thumbs to ensure the center is tucked in tightly (this will help create a good texture in the center of the loaf).

Before placing in a pan or on a baking sheet, simply tuck the ends under to give a neat finish to the bread.

Baking techniques

SLASHING AND SNIPPING CRUST

Slashing or snipping the crust of the bread helps it bake without tearing and creates a larger area of crust. Use a very sharp knife or scalpel to make slashes in the surface of the bread before or after it has risen.

Use a pair of scissors to make snips in the surface of the bread just before baking. This gives a chevron effect.

LINING A CAKE PAN

This method of lining can be used for cake pans of any shape to prevent the cake from sticking. Put the pan on a sheet of parchment paper. Trace around the bottom with a pencil, then cut out a circle just inside the pencil marking.

Brush the inside of the pan evenly with melted butter.

Position the piece of paper in the bottom of the greased pan. If applicable to the recipe, line the side of the pan.

Grease the paper inside the pan, then sprinkle with all-purpose flour and rotate to coat the bottom and side evenly. Tap out any excess flour.

Baking techniques

DOUBLE LINING A PAN

Fold a piece of parchment paper in two and wrap around the pan. Mark and cut the end 3/4 inch longer than the circumference.

Cut two rounds of paper to fit the bottom of the pan and place one on the bottom of the pan. Snip cuts along the folded edge of the paper.

Secure the snipped paper, cut edge down, inside the pan. Cover with the other round. Grease and flour the pan if directed to in the recipe.

Fold a sheet of parchment paper, craft paper or newspaper in half lengthwise and wrap it around the outside of the pan. Secure with string or tape.

LINING A RECTANGULAR PAN

Put the pan in the center of a piece of parchment paper. Make a diagonal cut from each corner of the paper to the corners of the pan.

Fold the paper between the cut edges to make it easier to put in position in the pan.

Overlap the corners of the paper and press to secure. Grease and flour the pan if directed to in the recipe.

Baking techniques

CREAMING METHOD

(All the ingredients, including the eggs, should be brought to room temperature before use.) Cream the butter first to soften in the large bowl of an electric mixer or a large glass bowl. Add the sugar.

Beat the butter and sugar together until light and creamy. Use an electric mixer or a wooden spoon.

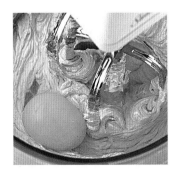

Add any flavorings and gradually beat in the eggs one at a time. Beat well after each egg to prevent curdling. If the mixture does curdle, add a little of the measured flour.

BEATING METHOD

Put the eggs and sugar together in a heatproof bowl. Or use the top insert of a large double boiler.

Place the bowl or insert over a saucepan of hot water, without allowing the bottom of the bowl to touch the water, and beat using a hand whisk or electric portable mixer until the mixture is thick enough to leave a trail when the hand whisk is lifted.

Remove the bowl or insert from the saucepan and continue to beat until cold. Gently fold in the sifted ingredients until just combined. Do not overfold or you will lose the air that has been beaten into the mixture.

Baking techniques

SMOOTHING CAKE MIX

Follow the recipe instructions when preparing a cake for the oven. To prevent the cake from peaking and cracking, some recipes will instruct you to make a dip in the center of the mixture with the back of a wet spoon or a rubber spatula.

Alternatively, simply smooth the top of the mixture with the back of a wet spoon.

DROP COOKIES

The dough for drop cookies needs to be soft enough to fall from the spoon. Scoop up balls of dough with a tablespoon and drop them onto the prepared baking sheet.

PIPED COOKIES

Piping cookies, rather than dropping or spooning the dough, gives a more even size and neat appearance. Pipe onto the prepared baking sheet with a shaped tip, spacing them well apart. Alternatively, use a cookie press.

Baking techniques

MAKING FRUIT CAKES

Dried fruits tend to sink to the bottom of cakes. Use this method to help distribute it more evenly. Fruit for cakes should be chopped into small pieces of uniform size.

Stir the fruit through the flour mixture to help prevent it sinking during cooking.

When all the ingredients have been added, spoon the mixture into the prepared pan.

TESTING SPONGE CAKES FOR DONENESS

As ovens vary in their performance, cakes should be tested before removing from the pan in case they require longer cooking. Lightly press the center of the cake with your fingertips; if ready it should spring back and the edge of the cake will have slightly shrunk away from the side of the pan.

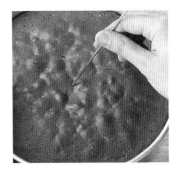

Insert a metal skewer into the center of the cake. It is done when the skewer comes out clean.

Baking techniques

ICING A CAKE

Decorating a cake is easy with store-bought marzipan and fondant. To start, use small pieces of marzipan to fill in any holes in the cake.

On a surface dusted with confectioners' sugar, roll out the remaining marzipan into a round large enough to cover the cake. Using a rolling pin, lift it over the cake.

Ease the marzipan onto the cake, smoothing out any creases. Trim any excess marzipan from around the edge of the cake, then allow to harden overnight.

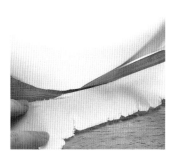

Brush the marzipan with clear alcohol such as gin or vodka, then cover with a ¼-inch layer of fondant, using the same method as for the marzipan. Trim any excess fondant from around the bottom of the cake.

Brush a 10-inch cake board with gin or vodka. Roll out the remaining fondant and cover the board with a ¼-inch layer, then trim any excess fondant from around the edge. Reserve the remaining fondant.

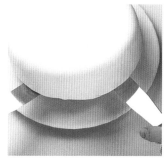

Using two large flat spatulas, transfer the cake to the center of the board.

To make the royal icing, beat together the egg white and half the confectioners' sugar to form a smooth paste. Continue adding sugar until thick, then add the lemon juice to soften to a fairly stiff piping consistency.

Set aside one-third of the royal icing, covering the surface with plastic wrap. Place the remaining royal icing in a pastry bag with a small plain tip and pipe a decorative edge around the seam between the cake and board.

Glossary of terms

À LA Means "in the style of" in French.

AL', ALL', ALLA Means "in the style of" in Italian.

AL DENTE Means "to the tooth" in Italian. Pasta and risotto rice are cooked until they are al dente, meaning the outside is tender but the center still has a little resistance or "bite." Pasta cooked beyond this becomes soggy.

AMARETTI Small cookies like macaroons, made from sweet and bitter almonds. These vary in size, but are usually about 1 inch wide.

AMUSE GUEULE Meaning "mouth pleaser" in French, this tiny appetizer is served before a meal, often as a complimentary taster in a restaurant.

ARTICHOKE The edible flower of a member of the thistle family. Some varieties have thorns and the types vary greatly in size. The largest artichokes are usually boiled before serving, but the smallest and most tender can be eaten raw as antipasto. Most common varieties include Romanesco (large and purple), Precoce di Chioggia (large and green), Violetto Toscano (small and tender enough to eat raw) and Spinoso di Palermo (a purple variety originating in Sicily).

BAIN-MARIE Literally a "water bath" for gentle oven-baking of delicate terrines and desserts. Usually the dish is placed in a roasting pan or other large ovenproof container and then boiling water is poured into the pan to come halfway up the side of the dish.

BAKE To cook in an oven in dry heat, usually until browned on the outside.

BAKE BLIND To bake a pastry case while it is unfilled to set the pastry. The pastry is usually lined with crumpled parchment paper or aluminum foil, which is then spread with a layer of pie weights or uncooked rice or beans. This stops the sides collapsing or the base from bubbling up. The pastry is sometimes baked again without the paper and pie weights to dry it out.

BASTE, TO To spoon melted fat or liquor over food as it cooks to stop it drying out and to add flavor.

BATON A stick of vegetable about 2 x ³/4 x ³/4 inch. Vegetables are cut into batons so they cook evenly.

BATTER A mixture of flour, milk and eggs used for pancakes and waffles and to coat food before frying. Also refers to soft cake, cookie and scone mixtures.

BEARD Also called a byssus, this is the mass of silky threads found at the opening of the shell that mussels use to attach themselves to rocks.

BEAT, TO To incorporate air into a mixture with a spoon, fork or whisk.

BLANCH, TO To cook in boiling water for a few minutes and then refresh in cold water. This keeps color in vegetables and loosens tomato and fruit skins. Also refers to potato chips that are precooked in hot fat before being fully cooked—this improves their texture and color.

BLANQUETTE A white stew (most usually of veal) made with white stock thickened with egg and cream.

BLEND, TO To mix together well.

BOCCONCINI Means literally "small mouthful" and is used to describe various foods, but generally refers to small balls of mozzarella cheese, about the size of walnuts.

BONE, TO To remove the bones from a bird or piece of meat leaving the flesh in its original shape.

BOUQUET GARNI A bundle of herbs used to flavor dishes. Made by tying sprigs of parsley, thyme, celery leaves and a bay leaf in either a piece of cheesecloth or portion of leek.

BRAISE, TO To cook slowly on a bed of chopped vegetables and with a little liquor in a covered pan.

BROWN, TO To cook food until the outer surface caramelizes or a maillard reaction occurs (the reaction between a sugar and an amino acid, which causes food to brown). Browning does not mean cooking through.

BROWN STOCK Stock made from browned beef or veal bones. Beef and veal stock are usually interchangeable, so the term "brown stock" is used. You can make your own using the recipe on page 518, though stock sold in cartons and catering-style powdered stock can also be good if you're short on time.

BRÛLÉ(E), BRÛLER, TO To brown or caramelize under heat. The term is usually applied to sugar, as in the dessert crème brulée. This is usually done under a very hot broiler but a blowtorch can also be used.

BUTTER Butter is flavored both by the lactic fermentation of cream and the diet of the cows from whose milk it is made. Use either salted or unsalted for savory dishes, but always use unsalted butter in sweet recipes.

BUTTERMILK Originally the by-product of the butter-making process—the residue left after cream is churned into butter. Today it is made from pasteurized skim milk to which an acid-producing bacteria is added, thickening it and giving it is characteristic tang.

CALVADOS A spirit made by distilling cider, it is often used in French cooking.

CAPERS The pickled flowers of the caper bush. They are available preserved in brine, vinegar or salt and should be rinsed well and squeezed dry before use.

CARAMELIZE, TO To heat food until the sugars on the surface break down and form a brown coating, which may be sweet or savory.

CASSEROLE A dish consisting of meat and/or vegetables cooked on the stove or in the oven, tightly covered with a lid so that all the flavor is contained. Also the name of the cooking dish.

CEPES The French name for a porcini or boletus mushroom. Usually dried and reconstituted in boiling water, but available fresh in the spring and autumn.

CHASSEUR, À LA A French term for "hunter style", usually meaning with onions and tomatoes. Often described simply as chasseur.

CLARIFIED BUTTER Made by melting butter so that the fat separates out from the impurities and water. The fat is then either removed with a spoon or the water poured off and the butter reset.

Clarified butter keeps for longer than ordinary butter because all the water has been removed and it can be used for cooking at higher temperatures because it has a higher burning point. It is often used in Indian cooking.

COATING CONSISTENCY A liquid that is thick enough to coat a food evenly without running off. Test by pouring over the back of a spoon—a line drawn down the center of the spoon should hold its shape.

CONCASSÉE Meaning finely chopped, this term is usually reserved for peeled, seeded and chopped tomatoes.

CONFIT From the French word for "preserve," confit is usually made from goose or duck meat, cooked in its own fat and then preserved in a jar or pot. It is eaten on its own or added to dishes such as cassoulet for extra flavor.

CORAL The eggs of the female lobster, which turn red when cooked and are used for flavoring sauces. Scallop roes are also sometimes called corals.

CORNICHON The French term for a small gherkin. It you can't find cornichons, you can use cocktail gherkins instead.

COULIS A thick, strained purée, usually of berries, fruit or tomatoes.

COURT BOUILLON A flavored poaching liquid, most often used for cooking fish.

CRÈME DE CASSIS Originating near Dijon in France, crème de cassis is a blackcurrant liqueur used in desserts and also in the drink kir.

CRÈME FRAÎCHE Lightly fermented, this is slightly tart and can often be used instead of cream in cooking.

CRIMP, TO To mark the edge of pastry or cookies or to seal two layers of pastry together in a scalloped pattern.

CROQUETTE Mashed potato, ground meat, fish or vegetables, or any other similar mixture, made into a paste, then formed into log shapes, which are breaded and deep-fried.

CROÛTE, EN Enclosed in pastry before baking (for example, chicken en croûte).

CRUSTACEAN An aquatic animal, such as a crab or lobster with a hard external, segmented shell and soft body.

CUTLET A piece of meat cut through the ribcage with the vertebrae and rib bone still attached.

DARIOLE A small (individual-sized) castle-shaped mold.

DEEP-FRY To fry something in oil. The food is completely immersed in the oil.

DEGLAZE, TO To loosen meat juices and flavors that may have stuck to the bottom of the pan when frying or roasting meat. A liquid is added to the hot pan and the pan is scraped and stirred. The liquid is then added to the dish or used to make gravy.

DEGORGE, TO To salt something like eggplant to make it give up any bitter liquid, or to soak meat or fish in water to get rid of any impurities.

DICE Cut into small cubes. Dice are smaller than cubes.

DIJON MUSTARD A pale yellow mustard, made from verjuice or white wine and mustard seeds that have been ground to a flour. Originating in Dijon, this style of mustard is now made all over France.

DONENESS The point at which something is cooked through.

DRIZZLE, TO To sprinkle liquid in a continuous stream.

DROPPING CONSISTENCY When a mixture such as cake dough falls slowly off a spoon, that is, it won't run off or stay put.

DRY FRY, TO To cook food in a frying pan without any fat.

DUST, TO To sprinkle with a powder such as confectioners' sugar or cocoa.

DUXELLES Chopped shallots or onions and chopped mushrooms sautéed in butter.

EGG GLAZE A glaze used in baking made from eggs and water or milk.

EMULSION A stable suspension of fat in a liquid. This can be uncooked (as in mayonnaise) or cooked (hollandaise).

FEUILLETÉ(E) Meaning flaky and many layered. Used to describe pastries such as puff pastry.

FILLET Boneless piece of fish or meat.

FILLET, TO To take the flesh off the bones of poultry, meat or a fish.

FIVE-SPICE POWDER This Chinese spice mix is generally made with star anise, cassia, Sichuan pepper, fennel seeds and cloves, which gives a balance of sweet, hot and aromatic flavors. Five-spice may also include cardamom, coriander, dried orange rind and ginger.

FLAMBÉ (FLAMBER), TO Meaning "to flame," this involves setting fire to alcohol in order to burn it off, leaving just the flavour behind.

FLAT-LEAF PARSLEY Also known as Italian or continental parsley. Used as an ingredient rather than a garnish, unlike curly parsley.

FLUTE Indentations made in the edges of pastry either to help seal it together or for decoration.

FOLD IN, TO To mix two things together using a gentle lifting and turning motion rather than stirring, to avoid losing trapped air bubbles. Used for cake mixtures and meringues. Usually done with a spatula.

FRENCH, TO To trim the meat away from the bones of chops or ribs leaving the bone exposed.

FROMAGE FRAIS A fresh white cheese with a smooth creamy consistency. There are a number of varieties, with their differences lying mainly in their fat content, which may affect the cooking qualities. Generally fromage frais makes a good low-fat alternative to cream.

FRY, TO To seal the surface of food quickly by cooking it in hot fat.

FUMÉ French for smoked.

GIBLETS The neck, gizzard, liver and heart of chicken, turkeys and other poultry. Traditionally used for adding flavor to gravy

GLAZE A coating that is applied to a surface to make it shine or to help it color when cooked, such as an egg wash for uncooked pastry and an apricot glaze for fruit tarts.

GOOSE FAT This is a soft fat that melts at low temperature and is used a lot in the cooking of southwest France to give a rich texture to dishes. It is available in cans from butchers. Duck fat can be substituted, although it needs to be heated to a higher temperature.

GORGONZOLA A blue cheese, originally made in Gorgonzola in Italy but now produced in other regions as well. It melts well and is often used in sauces. If not available, use another strong-flavored full-fat blue cheese, such as Stilton or Roquefort.

GOUJON A small piece of fried fish. The term is now also used for a piece of chicken breast meat.

GRUYÈRE This is a pressed hard cheese with a nutty flavor, commonly made in Switzerland and the French Alps from unpasteurized cow's milk. Although French Gruyère does have a slightly different flavor to the Swiss variety, the two are interchangeable in recipes. Gruyère is pale yellow and very firm and close-textured with a sprinkling of small holes. The best Gruyère has a slight glistening of moisture around the holes.

HAND-HOT 37°C—the temperature at which a liquid feels neither hot nor cold. Also known as blood temperature and lukewarm.

HARICOT BEANS The general French name for beans, though the term is also used to mean just a kind of small, dried bean. Dried haricot beans come in many different varieties, including cannellini (kidney-shaped beans), flageolet (white or pale green beans) and navy beans (used to make baked beans). When slow-cooked in stews such as cassoulet they become tender. They also break down very well to give a smooth purée.

HOCK The lower half of an animal's leg between the foot and lower limb.

HORS D'OEUVRES Small dishes, both hot and cold, served at the start of a meal. Soup is not an hors d'oeuvre but a separate course on its own.

HULL, TO To remove the stalks from berry fruit.

JULIENNE To cut a vegetable or citrus rind into short, thin strips (julienne strips), the size and shape of matchsticks. Vegetables used as a garnish or to be served in soups are often julienned for decorative purposes or to ensure quick even cooking.

JUNIPER BERRIES Blackish-purple berries with a resinous flavor. Used in stews and robust game dishes. Crush the berries lightly before use to release their flavor.

KNEAD, TO To mix a stiff dough by manipulating it by hand or with a mechanical dough hook in order to make it smooth. In bread-making, this also helps develop the gluten.

KNOCK BACK *OR* PUNCH DOWN, TO To knead gas bubbles out of a yeast-risen dough.

KNOCK UP, TO To separate the layers of puff pastry by running the back of the knife up the sides of the cut surface.

LARDONS Short strips of pork fat or slab bacon.

LIAISON A thickening agent for a sauce, soup or stew made from eggs and cream, beurre manié or starches such as arrowroot. A liaison is added at the end of cooking.

LOIN Butchery term for the back portion of an animal comprising the last four vertebrae attached to the ribs and the ribless vertebrae along with all the attached meat. Can also be used to describe the same piece without bones.

MACERATE, TO To soak food in a liquid so it absorbs the flavor of the liquid. Often used to describe soaking fruit in alcohol and sugar syrup.

MÂCHE Also known as corn salad or lambs lettuce. Small salad leaves which grow in rosette-like bunches.

MADEIRA A type of fortified wine from the Portuguese island of Madeira. There are a number of different varieties of Madeira, from sweet (Malmsey or Malvasia and Bual), to medium (Verdelho) and dry (Sercial).

MARINADE A collection of wet ingredients in which foods are soaked so they take on flavor and, sometimes, to tenderize. Many marinades include an acid such as fruit juice (to tenderize meat) and an oil.

MARROWBONE Leg bone, usually veal or beef which contains marrow. Buy pieces already cut into sections.

MARSALA A fortified wine from Marsala in Sicily that comes in varying degrees of dryness and sweetness. Dry Marsalas are used in savory dishes, and sweet ones in desserts such as zabaglione. Do not try to use sweet Marsala in savory dishes.

MARYLAND An Australian term for the leg and thigh portion of chicken.

MASCARPONE A cream cheese originally from Lombardia in Italy. Made with cream rather than milk, it is very high in fat. Mascarpone is generally used in desserts such as tiramisu and is also a good substitute for cream in sauces.

MEDALLION A small round piece of lean meat.

MEUNIÈRE, À LA A lightly floured food, usually fish, cooked in butter and garnished with lemon juice and parsley.

MIREPOIX Chopped vegetables on which pieces of meat are braised. They add flavor to the finished dish.

MISE EN PLACE To collect together, weigh and prepare the ingredients of a recipe before the actual assembling or cooking takes place.

MONTER, TO To add volume to an ingredient such as cream or egg white by whipping in air, or to add butter to a sauce at the end of cooking to make it shiny.

MUSSELS Bivalve molluscs that grow in clusters around sandbanks, rocks and other objects in the sea. They hold onto rocks with a mass of long silky threads found at the opening of the shell. There are many varieties worldwide, including green-lipped mussels from New Zealand, the common mussel and the European. Smaller mussels are often more tender than large.

OLIVE The fruit of the olive tree, which was first cultivated some 3000 years ago for fruit and oil. Today, olives are grown around the Mediterranean, where they originated, but also in North and South America and Australia. Fresh green olives are available from the summer and are picked before they start to turn black, while fresh black olives are available from the autumn through to winter. Though green and black olives have a different flavor, they can be used interchangeably in recipes unless the final color is a factor.

OLIVE OIL Extra-virgin and virgin olive oils are pressed without any heat or chemicals and are best used in simple uncooked dishes and for salads. Pure olive oil can be used for cooking or deep-frying. The color of olive oil is governed by the type of olive used and does not indicate quality. Olive oil is best stored in dark-colored glass bottles or cans.

ORANGE BLOSSOM WATER This is produced when the flower of the bitter orange is distilled. Orange flower water is a delicate flavoring used in some dessert recipes.

OYSTERS Bivalve molluscs that grow, wild or farmed, on coastlines around the world. There are many varieties, including the European (known as "native" in Britain), which has a round flat shell; the Portuguese, an oyster with a concave whitish-brown shell, now though to be the same as the Pacific

oyster; the greyish shelled American oyster; and the Sydney rock oyster. Oysters should be bought live, with the shells closed. If buying open oysters, prick the little hairs around the edge of the flesh—these will retract if the oyster is alive. Unopened oysters will keep in the fridge for a week. If open, store in their liquid and eat within 24 hours.

PANCETTA Cured belly of pork, somewhat like bacon. Available in flat pieces or rolled up (*arrotolata*), and both smoked and unsmoked. Generally used, either sliced or cut into cubes, as an ingredient in dishes like spaghetti carbonara.

PAPILLOTE, EN To cook food (often fish) wrapped in a paper package, which puffs up. Dishes cooked like this are served at the table. Papillote also describes the white paper frill used to decorate tips of bones.

PARBOIL, TO To half-cook something in boiling water. Most commonly used for potatoes before roasting.

PARMA HAM This prosciutto comes from traditionally reared pigs fed on the whey from making Parmigiano Reggiano. It has a sweet taste and is only flavored with salt. Parma hams can be identified by the stamp on the skin showing the five-pointed star of the Dukes of Parma. Other prosciutto can be used if Parma ham is unavailable.

PASS, TO To push food through a fine strainer.

PASSATA Meaning "puréed," this most commonly refers to a smooth uncooked tomato pulp bought in cans or jars. The best ones have no added flavorings.

PÂTÉ A cooked paste of meat, poultry or fish, either set in a terrine or cooked in pastry "en croute."

PAUPIETTE A stuffed, rolled piece of meat or fish.

PECORINO One of Italy's most popular cheeses, with virtually every region producing a version. Made from sheep's milk and always by the same method, although the result varies according to the milk and aging process used.

POACH, TO To cook gently in a barely simmering liquid.

POUSSIN A baby chicken weighing about 14 oz–1 lb. Poussins are often spatchcocked and broiled or stuffed. Usually one poussin is served per person, though slightly bigger ones are adequate for two people.

PROSCIUTTO Italian name for ham. Prosciutto crudo is cured ham and includes Parma ham and San Daniele. Prosciutto cotto is cooked ham.

PROVE, TO To allow a yeasted dough to rise; also to heat a frying pan or wok with oil or salt and then rub the surface, thus filling in any minute marks with the mixture and making it nonstick.

PURÉE A fine, soft, almost pourable paste of processed or pounded food.

PUY LENTILS Tiny green lentils from Puy in central France that are thought to be of a high quality. Puy lentils do not need to be presoaked and do not break down when cooked. They have a firm texture and go very well with both meat and fish. Traditionally they are served with a mustard vinaigrette.

REDUCE, TO To boil a liquid in order to evaporate off water. This thickens the liquid and intensifies the flavor.

REFRESH, TO To put just-cooked items into cold water to prevent them from cooking further.

REST/RELAX, TO To leave pastry in the fridge to allow the gluten, which will have been stretched during rolling, to contract again. Also means to leave batters until the starch cells in the flour have swelled through contact with the liquid; or to leave meat to let the juices settle back into the flesh before carving.

RISOTTO RICE Round-grained, very absorbent rice, cultivated in northern Italy. Risotto rice comes in four categories, classified not by quality but by the size of each grain. The smallest, Riso Comune (common rice) is very quick to cook (12–13 minutes) and is ideal for rice pudding. Semifino rice includes varieties like vialone nano and cooks in about 15 minutes. Fino takes a minute longer and has more bite. The largest, Superfino, includes arborio and carnaroli and takes 20 minutes to cook until al dente.

ROAST, TO To cook in an oven at a high temperature without any covering to give a crisp, well-browned exterior and a just-cooked moist interior. Usually applied to meat or vegetables, though anything can be roasted.

ROUX A mixture of flour and fat cooked together and then used as a thickening agent, for example, in sauces and soups. A white roux is cooked until just a pale yellow, a blonde roux until it is a gold color and a brown roux until it is a darker golden brown.

RUB IN OR CUT IN, TO To integrate hard fat into flour by cutting the fat in with a pastry blender or fingertips until the mixture resembles bread crumbs.

SAFFRON The dried dark orange stigmas of a type of crocus flower, which are used to add aroma and flavor to food. Only a few threads are needed for each recipe as they are very pungent (and expensive).

SALT COD Cod that has been gutted, salted and dried. Different from stockfish, which is just dried but not salted. Popular in northern Europe. A center-cut fillet of salt cod tends to be meatier than the thinner tail end, and some varieties are drier than others so the soaking time does vary. Also sold as morue, bacalao, bacalhau and baccala.

SAUTER (SAUTÉ), TO To shallow-fry food in hot fat while shaking the pan and tossing the food.

SCALLOP, TO To form a decorative fluted rim in a pastry edge by pushing in the edge with one finger while pushing the pastry on both sides of that piece in the opposite direction with the other thumb and finger.

SCORE, TO To make a shallow cut with a knife without cutting all the way through.

SEASON, TO To add flavor to something, usually with salt and pepper, or to smooth out the surface of a pan using hot oil or salt.

SEIZE When melted chocolate turns into a lumpy mass because a tiny amount of liquid, usually condensed steam, drips into it.

SHANK Part of the leg of beef, veal, lamb or pork.

SHUCK, TO To open bivalves such as oysters or to remove the husks, shells or pods from seeds.

SIMMER, TO To maintain a cooking liquid at a temperature just below boiling point.

SKIM, TO To remove fat or impurities from the surface of a liquid with a large spoon, ladle or skimmer.

SPONGE A bubbly, batter-like mixture made by mixing flour, yeast and a liquid and allowing it to rest for several hours. The first step in some bread-making recipes. A type of fatless cake.

STEAM, TO To cook in the steam given off by boiling or simmering water.

STIR-FRY, TO To cook pieces of food quickly in a wok using only a little oil and moving them around constantly.

SUET Hard fat from around the kidneys which is particularly good for cooking. Buy pre-grated or grate your own from a block or piece.

TOMALLEY The green-colored liver of a lobster.

TOULOUSE SAUSAGE A general term for meaty pork broiling sausages, often sold in a coil.

TRUFFLES Considered an expensive delicacy, truffles are the most valuable of all fungi due to their increasing rarity and the labor-intensive methods of harvest (they are sniffed out by specially trained dogs or pigs). The black truffles found in France, specifically around Périgord, are often considered the best black truffles in the world. Truffles are best eaten fresh, but can also be bought preserved in jars and only need to be used in small amounts to flavor dishes.

TRUSS, TO To hold something, usually meat or poultry, in shape with string or skewers while it cooks.

VANILLA EXTRACT Made by using alcohol to extract the vanilla flavor from pods and not to be confused with artificial vanilla essence, which is made with synthetic vanillin. The pods are picked when green, at which stage they have no flavor, and left to sweat and dry in the sun, causing them to turn deep brown. Vanilla extract is strong and should be used sparingly.

WHIP, TO To incorporate air into something by beating it (for example, cream or egg white) with a whisk or to form an emulsion by the same means (as with mayonnaise).

YEAST Available both fresh and dried. Fresh yeast is sold as a compressed solid and should be moist and creamy grey in colour and smell pleasantly yeasty. Dried yeast, available as "active dry" and "quick rise," is sold in granules and has twice the potency of fresh yeast. For every 15 g of fresh yeast specified, you could use 7 g dried yeast instead.

ZEST The colored outer layer of citrus fruit that contains the essential oils.

Index

LE CORDON BLEU ✦ COMPLETE COOK

Thunder Bay Press,
an imprint of the Advantage Publishers Group,
5880 Oberlin Drive, San Diego, CA 92121-4794
www.advantagebooksonline.com

First published in 2002 by Murdoch Books, a division of Murdoch Magazines, GPO Box 1203, Sydney NSW 2001, Australia
© Design and photography Murdoch Books® 2002
© Text Le Cordon Bleu 2002
All rights reserved. Published 2002

Editors: Kim Rowney, Jane Price
Food Editor: Lulu Grimes
Design Concept: Vivien Valk
Designer: Alex Frampton
US Editor: Kerry MacKenzie

Publisher: Kay Scarlett
Group General Manager: Mark Smith

PRINTED IN CHINA by Toppan Printing Hong Kong Ltd.

ACKNOWLEDGMENTS

Murdoch Books and Le Cordon Bleu would like to express their gratitude to the Master Chefs of Le Cordon Bleu schools, whose
knowledge and expertise have made this book possible especially: Chef Terrien, Chef Boucheret, Chef Deguignet, Chef Pinaud,
Chef Bernardé, Chef Chalopin, Chef Lebouc, Chef Chantefort, Chef Thivet, Paris; Chef Lewis, Chef Males, Chef Walsh, Chef Power,
Chef Carr, Chef Paton, Chef Poole-Gleed, Chef Wavrin, Chef Barraud, Chef Bidault, London; Chef Filliodeau, Chef Guiet, Chef Beyer,
Chef Guiriec, Chef Price, Chef Baisas, Chef Pagés, Chef Lavest, Chef Irazouqui, Chef Chabert, Chef Petibon, Ottawa; Chef Summers,
Chef Beech, Chef Watkins, Chef Lowe, Adelaide; Chef Boutin, Chef Harris, Chef Rego, Chef Belcher, Chef Findlay, Chef Hood,
Chef Masse, Sydney;. Chef Benoit, Peru; Chef Yamashita, Chef Oddos, Chef Kato, Chef Poilvet, Chef Gros, Chef Hori, Chef Peguero,
Chef Honda, Chef Lederf, Chef Guilhaudin, Tokyo; Chef Martin, Chef Carmago, Brazil.

A very special acknowledgment to Denise Spencer-Walker, Kaye Baudinette, James McIntosh and Laurence Giaume who have been
responsible for the co-ordination of the Le Cordon Bleu team under the Presidency of André J.Cointreau.